THE DIE-HARDS IN THE GREAT WAR

a 2

MILITARY HISTORIES BY EVERARD WYRALL

THE HISTORY OF THE SECOND DIVISION, 1914-1918

THE WEST YORKSHIRE REGT. IN THE WAR, 1914-1918

THE HISTORY OF THE 62nd (W.R.) DIVISION, 1914-1919

THE HISTORY OF THE KING'S REGT. (LIVERPOOL) 1914-1919

THE HISTORY OF THE SOMERSET LIGHT INFANTRY, 1914-1919

THE EAST YORKSHIRE REGT. IN THE GREAT WAR, 1914-1918

THE LINCOLNSHIRE REGT. 1914-1918
(*shortly*)

THE DUKE OF CORNWALL'S LIGHT INFANTRY, 1914-1918
(*shortly*)

THE GLOUCESTERSHIRE REGT, 1914-1918
(*shortly*)

THE 19th DIVISION, 1914-1918
(*shortly*)

THE 17th ROYAL FUSILIERS, 1914-1919
(*shortly*)

THE DIE-HARDS IN THE GREAT WAR

A HISTORY OF THE DUKE OF CAMBRIDGE'S OWN (MIDDLESEX REGIMENT), 1914-1919, COMPILED FROM THE RECORDS OF THE LINE, SPECIAL RESERVE, SERVICE, AND TERRITORIAL BATTALIONS.

BY

EVERARD WYRALL

AUTHOR OF "THE HISTORY OF THE SECOND DIVISION, 1914-1918"; "THE WEST YORKSHIRE REGIMENT IN THE WAR, 1914-1918"; "THE HISTORY OF THE 62nd (W.R.) DIVISION, 1914-1919," Etc., Etc., Etc.

VOL. II. 1916-1919

LONDON:
HARRISON & SONS, LTD., 45, ST. MARTIN'S LANE, W.C.2.

Printed and bound by Antony Rowe Ltd, Eastbourne

"Mons," "Le Cateau," "Retreat from Mons," **Marne, 1914,** "Aisne, 1914, '18," "La Bassée, 1914," "Messines, 1914, '17, '18," "Armentières, 1914," "Neuve Chapelle," "**Ypres, 1915, '17, '18,**" "Gravenstafel," "St. Julien," "Frezenberg," "Bellewaarde," "Aubers," "Hooge, 1915," "Loos," "Somme, 1916, '18," "**Albert, 1916, '18,**" "**Bazentin,**" "Delville Wood," "Pozières," "Ginchy," "Flers-Courcelette," "Morval," "Thiepval," "Le Transloy," "Ancre Heights," "Ancre, 1916, '18," "Bapaume, 1917, '18," "Arras, 1917, '18," "Vimy, 1917," "Scarpe, 1917, '18," "Arleux," "Pilckem," "Langemarck, 1917," "Menin Road," "Polygon Wood," "Broodseinde," "Poelcappelle," "Passchendaele," "**Cambrai, 1917, '18,**" "St. Quentin," "Rosieres," "Avre," "Villers-Bretonneux," "Lys," "Estaires," "Hazebrouck," "Bailleul," "Kemmel," "Scherpenberg," "**Hindenburg Line,**" "Canal du Nord," "St. Quentin Canal," "Courtrai," "Selle," "Valenciennes," "Sambre," "France and Flanders, 1914–18." "Italy, 1917–18." "Struma," "Doiran, 1918," "Macedonia, 1915–18," "**Suvla,**" "Landing at Suvla," "Scimitar Hill," "Gallipoli, 1915." "Rumani," "Egypt, 1915–17." "Gaza," "El Mughar," "**Jerusalem,**" "Jericho," "Jordan," "Tell 'Asur," "Palestine, 1917–18." "**Mesopotamia, 1917–18,**" "Murman, 1919." "Dukhovskaya," "Siberia, 1918–19."

CONTENTS

CHAPTER	PAGE
XXVII.—The British Advance and the German Retreat to the Hindenburg Line, 1917	1
XXVIII.—The Battles of Arras, 1917	27
XXIX.—The Flanders Offensive: I. The Battle of Messines, 1917 . . .	79
XXX.— ,, ,, II. The Battles of Ypres, 1917 . . .	91
XXXI.—The Battle of Cambrai, 1917	145
XXXII.—The Last Winter in the Trenches . . .	171
XXXIII.—The German Offensives of 1918: I. In Picardy .	189
XXXIV.— ,, ,, ,, II. In Flanders .	223
XXXV.— ,, ,, ,, III. In Champagne	233
XXXVI.—The Advance in Picardy	237
XXXVII.— ,, ,, Flanders	243
XXXVIII.—The Breaking of the Hindenburg Line . .	245
XXXIX.—The Final Advance: I. In Flanders . .	265
XL.— ,, ,, ,, II. In Artois . . .	275
XLI.— ,, ,, ,, III. In Picardy . . .	281
XLII.—The Eastern Theatre of the War: I. Italy and Salonika .	293
XLIII.— ,, ,, ,, ,, II. Palestine .	309
XLIV.—India and Mesopotamia	331
XLV.—Siberia and the Murmansk Adventure . .	363
Conclusion	377

LIST OF MAPS

I.—The Battles of Arras, 1917	. .	*Facing page*	76
II.—The Battles of Ypres, 1917	. .	,, ,,	142
III.—The Battle of Cambrai, 1917	. .	,, ,,	170
IV.—The German Offensive, 1918	. .	,, ,,	220
V.—The Advance to Victory, 1918	. .	,, ,,	290
VI.—Third Battle of Gaza, 1917	. .	,, ,,	328
VII.—Mesopotamia	. . . .	,, ,,	360

" Die hard, 57th. Die hard."

> Colonel Inglis, Commanding 57th Foot, at Albuhera, 16th May, 1811. (Page 3, Vol. I.)

" Men, we can only die once: if we have to die, let us die like men—like Die-Hards." (Page 169, Vol. I.)

> 2/Lieut. R. P. Hallowes, V.C., 4th Bn. Middlesex Regt., killed at Bellewaarde Ridge, 30th September, 1915.

CHAPTER XXVII.

The British Advance and the German Retreat to the Hindenburg Line, 1917.*

INTRODUCTION.

TO the student of the Great War and also to the young soldier wishing to know why his Regiment was engaged in certain operations therein, the general situation in France and Flanders at the beginning of 1917 is of profound interest, for the Germans expected to be beaten before the end of that year.

The exhausting and costly Battles of the Somme, 1916, had, nevertheless, achieved their object. The German pressure on Verdun had been relieved, the enemy's main forces had been held to the Western Front, and his strength considerably weakened—a weakness which was soon to show itself. Although the Allies were in a similar condition, the enemy could not be allowed to recuperate and strengthen his defences, which had been badly battered and, in many places, broken. The Allied offensive therefore continued.

At Chantilly (French General Headquarters) on 15th November, 1916, there was held a conference of the Entente military representatives to decide upon a plan of campaign during the coming year. Marshal Joffre and Sir Douglas Haig represented the French and British Armies respectively.

It was decided at this conference to launch a series of offensives on all fronts which were to be " so timed as to assist each other by depriving the enemy of the power of weakening any one of his fronts in order to reinforce another " : the word " fronts " means not only France and Flanders, but Italy and Russia and the minor theatres of war.

* The official period for the British Advance is from 11th January to 13th March, 1917; of the German Retreat from 14th March to 4th April, 1917.

A

The Allied Armies were to be ready to begin operations by the middle of February, 1917. But two events interfered with these plans. The Joffre-Haig plan of campaign was altered to such an extent that serious delay occurred. Marshal Joffre was superseded by General Nivelle, who put forward a plan of his own, and the Russian revolution made an offensive on that front impossible. Nivelle's plan was a sharp and decisive offensive from along the French front, the British Armies taking only a subsidiary part in the operations, whilst in the Joffre-Haig plan they were jointly to undertake the main attack.

The change necessitated a readjustment of Sir Douglas Haig's plans. His offensive, originally designed for February, was postponed until April, when the Arras Battle was due to open. The French were to follow soon after with their great offensive, and if this did not succeed within a reasonable period the British offensive was to be transferred to Flanders. Thus the Battles of Arras, 1917, and the Battles of Ypres, 1917.

Before, however, the Arras offensive opened the enemy, weakened by his losses during 1916 and forced to shorten his front, beat a retreat to the Hindenburg Line, and the Fifth British Army, instead of attacking from the line of the Ancre simultaneously with the advance of the Third British Army on its left, had now to follow up the retiring enemy and establish itself in front of his new line of defence—a very powerful system of trenches.

The British front line south of Arras had been extended in order to meet the wishes of the French Commander-in-Chief, who desired to concentrate all his available troops for his offensive, which formed a part of the Spring operations. By the end of February Sir Douglas Haig had taken over the French line from just south of Les Bœufs to west of the town of Roye.* This addition entailed the maintenance of an exceptionally active front (including the whole of the Somme Battle front) of 110 miles, and threw a further heavy burden upon the British forces. Nevertheless the operations on the Ancre as well as certain minor enterprises and raids were carried out as intended.

It will be remembered that the last operations of 1916 in which Battalions of the Middlesex Regiment were engaged

---

* The official despatches state that this extension was decided on in January, 1917, but as early as December, 1916, British Divisions (4th and 8th Divisions, for instance) had begun to take over portions of the line south of Les Bœufs.

took place on 18th November, when an attack was delivered against the German defences overlooking the villages of Pys and Grandcourt, during which valuable positions were gained on a front of about five thousand yards. A simultaneous attack north of the Ancre by the 4th Canadian, 18th, 19th, 37th and 32nd Divisions considerably improved the British positions in the Beaucourt Valley. But now winter had set in and had put an end to offensive operations, and throughout the remainder of November and December the maintenance and improvement of trenches and communications behind them claimed the energies of the troops.

The 1st January, 1917, saw no less than 15 Battalions of the Middlesex Regiment in France and Flanders. The 1st Battalion and 18th (Pioneers) Battalion of the 33rd Division were out of the line occupying an area 5 or 6 miles east of Abbeville: the 2nd Battalion (8th Division) held front-line trenches about 2 miles east of Combles: the 4th Battalion (37th Division) was in the Festubert sector: the 1/7th and 1/8th Middlesex of the 56th Division were in the Neuve Chapelle trenches: about 12 miles due west of Arras the 11th Battalion of the 12th Division was resting and training: the 12th Battalion (18th Division) was also out of the line training in an area about Abbeville: the 13th Battalion (24th Division) was still in the Loos sector: the 16th Middlesex of the 29th Division were 7 miles west of Amiens: the 17th Battalion (2nd Division) occupied an area 10 miles north-east of Abbeville: the two Battalions with the 41st Division, *i.e.*, 19th and 23rd Middlesex, were in the line in the Kemmel sector, and, finally, the extreme right of the British line, 5 miles north of Peronne, was held by the 40th Division, in which were the 20th and 21st Middlesex. Thus, when the New Year dawned, only the 2nd, 16th, 20th and 21st Battalions were on the Somme. The 3rd (28th Division) and 26th (27th Division) Battalions were at Salonika. The 2/10th Battalion (53rd Division) was in Egypt. The 1/9th and 1/10th were in India. Two Battalions—2/7th and 2/8th—having seen service, had been disbanded. Other Battalions (amongst which was the 3/10th, soon to come to France) were in training in England.

1ST JANUARY. 1ST, 2ND, 3RD, 4TH, 1/7TH, 1/8TH, 2/7TH, 2/8TH, 1/9TH, 1/10TH, 2/10TH, 3/10TH, 11TH, 12TH, 13TH, 16TH, 17TH, 18TH, 19TH, 20TH, 21ST, 23RD, 26TH BATTALIONS.

Both in France and Flanders at all hours of the day and night troops were on the move, so that it is not surprising to find early in the year the 12th (18th Division) and 17th (2nd Division) back again on the Somme, floundering amidst the mud and filth about

Miraumont and Pys, fighting hard and giving a good account of themselves in the old Die-Hard spirit. Truly, the Somme battlefields were freely sprinked with the blood of Middlesex men.

I.

The Actions of Miraumont,
17th and 18th February, 1917.

In January the 3rd, 7th and 11th Divisions carried out several small operations against the German lines on the Beaumont Hamel Spur, which finally ended in the capture of that important position. The whole of the Beaucourt Valley was now exposed to the fire of the British guns—an uncomfortable position for the Germans, who fought hard to retain their hold upon the ground. Early in February the attacks were continued, and on the 6th the enemy was compelled to evacuate the last portion of his second-line trenches south of the Ancre between Grandcourt and the Stuff Redoubt. Grandcourt was then swept clear of the Germans, and on the night of 7th Baillescourt Farm, about half-way between Beaucourt and Miraumont, was carried. The clearing of the Beaucourt Valley was resumed on the night of 10th/11th February, when again good progress was made.

At this point the official despatches state that : " An operation on a somewhat larger scale than anything hitherto attempted since the New Year was now undertaken. The object was to carry our line forward along the spur which runs northwards from the main Morval–Thiepval Ridge about Courcelette, and so gain possession of the high ground at its northern extremity." If this advance was successful, Serre, which at this period formed a very pronounced salient, would be almost impossible to hold, and again the enemy would be forced to relax his hold upon the village and system of trenches about that place.

These operations are now known as " The Actions of Miraumont," in which simultaneous assaults were delivered on both banks of the Ancre at 5.45 a.m. on 17th February by the 2nd and 18th Divisions, south of the river, and 63rd Division along the northern banks.* On the 12th and 13th January the 2nd Division relieved the 51st Division in the Courcelette sector,

* From a divisional point of view these operations may be studied further in " The History of the Second Division " (Everard Wyrall), " The 18th Division in the Great War " (G. H. F. Nichols), and " The Royal Naval (63rd) Division "(Douglas Jerrold).

the 6th Brigade (containing the 17th Battalion) being in reserve billets in Aveluy. On the 20th the 17th Middlesex (Lieut.-Colonel H. T. Fenwick) relieved the 17th Royal Fusiliers in the left sub-sector, two companies taking over 11 posts which then formed the front line, the remaining companies in support at Chalk Mound. [17TH BATTALION. 20TH JANUARY.]

The conditions in the front line almost baffle description. Some idea of them may be gathered from the following extract from the private diary of Major-General C. E. Pereira, G.O.C., 2nd Division: "The frontage is 2,500 yards and the right of our line is about 1,000 yards west of Le Sars: the left, a mile south of the eastern edge of Miraumont, Pys being about 1,200 yards north of the centre of our line. The front line consists of 18 disconnected posts and platoons in close support—total, 10 platoons. Behind this there is nothing until one reaches the dug-outs in the West Miraumont road just north of Courcelette, where there are three platoons. There are three platoons in Courcelette, two companies west and two companies south of it—total, two battalions. Ironside Avenue runs forward 800 yards from the West Miraumont road. That is the sole communication trench forward. There are brushwood tracks to near the front line, but they can only be used at night." So difficult were the communications and the surroundings that when the Middlesex took over from the Fusiliers the latter had been unable to locate the right post of the Battalion on their left, viz., the 11th Fusiliers of the 18th Division. Patrols sent out immediately by the Middlesex came back with the report that they were still unable to find this post; indeed, one of the patrols, consisting of 2/Lieut. E. King and two other ranks, failed to return. They had presumably wandered about, eventually falling into the enemy's hands. It was not until the 22nd that the post was located.

The weather was cold and it was freezing hard when towards the end of the month relief came and a period of about three weeks was spent in reserve and support before, on the 16th February, the Battalion moved to Wolfe Huts, Ovillers, to take part in the operations of 17th. "C" and "D" Companies were to be attached to the 99th Brigade as supporting companies, "A" Company to the same Brigade as a carrying party while "B" Company and Battalion Headquarters were to remain at the Huts. [16TH FEBRUARY.]

In bitterly cold weather the 18th Division had relieved the

12TH BATTALION.
15TH JANUARY.

61st in the line south of Grandcourt (and on the left of the 2nd Division) on 15th January, the 54th Brigade going into the sub-sector previously held by the 183rd Brigade. The 12th Middlesex (Lieut.-Colonel W. H. H. Johnston) were, however, in support in Warwick Huts, Aveluy, but spent one tour in the front line before the end of the month. On the 9th February the Battalion again went into the line, taking over Grandcourt village (so blasted by shell fire as to be practically non-existent) and part of Grandcourt Trench: the other part being held by the enemy.

10/11TH FEBRUARY.

The 12th Battalion was now amidst conditions such as their comrades of the 17th Battalion were experiencing. The left Company ("D") was practically all in shell holes, and to find one's way about the line was almost impossible. On the night of 10th/11th February an attempt was made by two platoons to capture that part of Grandcourt Trench lying immediately east of the part held by the Middlesex, up to Sixteen road. But in the bright moonlight the Germans discerned the attack and met it with a perfect hurricane of machine-gun and rifle bullets. The result was a failure which cost the attackers two other ranks killed, and 2/Lieut. Bridgland and two other ranks wounded. In the early hours of 11th a sergeant of "D" Company and a private wandered by mistake into the enemy's lines. Both were captured, though later the private escaped. The Battalion was relieved on 12th and went back to Warwick Huts.

During the next three or four days the weather conditions were perfectly damnable. First a thaw set in, then a hard frost froze everything hard again. Thaw and frost, frost and thaw followed each other with exasperating regularity. One moment the "floor" of the trench would be a filthy mud patch, the next (almost) like an ice-bound pond. The day before the operations were due to take place, *i.e.*, 16th, a heavy thaw set in, which lasted. The prospects were far from pleasing, for it meant that the attackers would have to go forward through thick, clinging mud, splash through shell holes full of dirty, stinking water before ever they reached the enemy's trenches.

The trench maps at this period, in this particular part of the line, give some idea of what the going would be like. There is hardly a yard of the many roads not indicated by dotted lines, the familiar sign of an obliterated road: the guns of both sides had pounded and blasted the countryside to such an awful extent that not only villages, but the communications to and from them, were practically non-existent. No human pen could ever give a true picture of the Somme battlefields—they were indescribable. Man fought not only the enemy but the vilest weather conditions imaginable. 12TH AND 17TH BATTALIONS.

"Zero Hour" for the operations on 17th February was 5.45 a.m. 17TH FEBRUARY.

The night of 16th/17th was pitch black, and in forming up the troops almost had to feel their way forward, so difficult was the going. The attacking battalions were ordered to be in position an hour before "Zero," but even at that hour an inky blackness covered the battlefield. Moreover, the troops had hardly begun to assemble when the sky above the German trenches was illuminated by green and yellow lights—the enemy's barrage call. A furious artillery barrage then fell upon the area in which the assaulting troops were assembling, causing serious casualties. Yet, in spite of heavy losses, the attackers went forward at "Zero Hour" under cover of their own barrage, which by this time was sweeping the enemy's trenches with a tornado of shell.

The 17th Middlesex, however, saw little of the actual fighting. At "Zero Hour" "C" Company moved to the dug-outs in West Miraumont Road, "D" Company to just west of Courcelette, "A" Company to Artillery Lane. "B" Company was with Battalion Headquarters back at Wolfe Huts. After the attack had been made—an attack carried out with great gallantry by the 6th and 99th Infantry Brigades of the 2nd Division, but resulting only in the gain of the first objective, Grandcourt Trench, along the front of the 99th Infantry Brigade—"A" Company carried up munitions to all the posts in the new line. Throughout the day "C" Company held the old British front line and at night returned to West Miraumont dug-outs. There are no records of casualties in the 17th Middlesex on this date.

On the left of the 2nd Division the 18th Division had turned the Germans out of Boom Ravine along the Divisional front, and at the end of the day was consolidating a line some three hundred yards from South Miraumont Trench. In this successful attack the 12th Middlesex of the 54th Brigade had taken an active part.

The objective of the 18th Division was South Miraumont Trench and the high ground south of it. This involved the taking and crossing of the Boom Ravine and (particularly on the

12TH BATTALION.
17TH FEBRUARY.

left of the attack) several small lengths of hostile trench. The 54th Brigade was on the right and the 53rd on the left.

Of the 54th Brigade the 6th Northants (right) and 11th Royal Fusiliers (left) were the assaulting Battalions, with " D " and " B " Companies of the 12th Middlesex as dug-out clearing parties to follow closely in the wake of the two Battalions : " C " Company was detailed as a carrying party, while " A " remained with Battalion Headquarters in reserve.

The weather conditions were wretched in the extreme. A fog lay over the battlefield and a heavy thaw was in progress. The forming-up operations had been accompanied by heavy casualties, for (as the Battalion Diary of the 12th Middlesex records) : " The enemy, partly by reason of spies and partly for other reasons,* succeeded in barraging the troops when forming up in the open, between 4.30 and 5.30 a.m., some 200 yards north of The Gully." It was entirely due to the assembly arrangements and to the skilful and gallant manner in which officers and N.C.Os. handled their men in pitch darkness, over exceedingly slippery ground, with no trenches to guide them, that the Battalions were able to form up at all.

The barrage opened at 5.45 a.m. and was followed closely by the attacking infantry up to Grandcourt Trench. On arrival at the wire in front of this trench the entanglements were found in many places uncut. Only a few narrow passages existed, and the delay in finding these gave the enemy an opportunity to get into position again (he had taken cover during our barrage) both in Grandcourt Trench and Boom Ravine. Both the Northants and Fusiliers cleared the enemy out of the former trench, and by 6.30 a.m. Boom Ravine had also been taken and the troops were forming up just north of it (on the line of the first objective) in order to attack the second objective—South Miraumont Trench.

At this stage casualties had been very heavy, and here it is hardly possible to refrain from mentioning a very gallant N.C.O. —C.S.M. Fitterer—of the 11th Fusiliers, who practically commanded the Battalion, which had lost all its officers. This brave man formed up the remains of his Battalion on the northern side of the Boom Ravine prior to the advance on South Miraumont Trench.

* Extract from Diary of 54th Infantry Brigade : " It has since been discovered from German officers captured during these operations that the enemy had learned from four different sources full details regarding our attack and that he was acquainted with the approximate hour at which the attack was to be launched."

Whilst the assaulting troops were pushing on to the spur south of Petit Miraumont and the second objective, the dug-out clearing Companies of the 12th Middlesex were at work in Boom Ravine. They also had lost heavily during the advance to that place, particularly in officers. The actual fighting of the Middlesex is difficult to follow, for the narratives all deal with the situation generally. Apparently the Northants succeeded in getting into South Miraumont Trench, but were counter-attacked and had to retire to the high ground north of Boom Ravine. Here about two hundred Northants with one hundred Middlesex dug in. On both flanks the situation was reported as uncertain, and at 10.15 a.m. " A " Company of the Middlesex, which had come up at 7.30 a.m. to reinforce, received orders to advance on a wide front astride the Ravine* to a line two hundred yards north of it and dig in, gaining touch with the Suffolks (the right assaulting Battalion of the 53rd Brigade) on the left. This Company (" A ") was in position just as the remnants of the gallant Northants and Fusiliers were retiring from South Miraumont Trench, followed by an enemy counter-attack from a north-easterly direction. The right platoon of " A " Company dealt with this counter-attack in a workmanlike fashion, driving the enemy back over the crest of the ridge and capturing 15 Germans.

On the left the situation was clear, the attack had gone well. But on the right of the 18th Division, the left of the 2nd Division (the K.R.Rifles) had had to give ground during the counter-attack. " A " Company, 12th Middlesex, was therefore ordered to move from their present position and form a defensive flank facing E.N.E. with their left on the right post formed by the Northants.

Meanwhile, " B " and " D " Companies, under the orders of Lieut. Charlesworth (all other officers having become casualties), had completed the dug-out clearing in the Ravine and had reinforced the Fusiliers and Northants along a line of posts 100 yards north of Boom Ravine.

The report of the situation on the right was, however, still conflicting, and " A " Company at the eastern end of the Boom Ravine was ordered to begin a strong post at the junction of the Ravine and the West Miraumont Road—one platoon with four

---

* The Ravine ran north to south, the northern end joining up with the Boom Ravine, which ran east to west and then north-west.

12TH BATTALION.
17TH FEBRUARY.

Lewis guns forming the garrison. The remaining platoons of this Company began to dig in on the line of the first objective, being close at hand if needed. "B" and "D" Companies, facing north, were rather in advance of the platoons of "A." At 3.30 p.m. the Northants advanced their line to the crest of the ridge, but during the night moved their posts back somewhat, bringing the line at dawn on 18th approximately to 200 yards north of Boom Ravine on the right, and about 100 yards north of it on the left. The Brigadier, however, ordered a further short advance to be made and snipers pushed out along the crest of the ridge. This was done without interference, and this position was handed over to the East Surreys of the 55th Brigade, who relieved the Northants and 12th Middlesex during the late afternoon. The latter Battalion then marched back to Marlboro' Huts.

Of "D" and "B" Companies of the Middlesex detailed for "mopping-up" Boom Ravine the Narrative of the 54th Brigade states: "The work of clearing dug-outs in Grandcourt Trench and Boom Ravine was carried out with great thoroughness." But nothing is said in any official diary of the conduct of Sergeant G. Rowe, 12th Middlesex. This gallant N.C.O. led his Company for two days after all the officers had fallen. Neither does it mention Private A. Humphries, who, finding that his platoon had not even a sergeant left, took command, carried on and dug in successfully on the ridge. This ridge was always under heavy shell and rifle fire.

The 12th Middlesex lost in this attack 10 officers, 4 of whom (Lieut. C. A. Haylor and 2/Lieuts. W. B. Godwin, H. B. Kelsey and G. E. Vincent) were killed, the remainder wounded. In other ranks the losses were 28 killed, 104 wounded and 3 missing.

But the Boom Ravine had been captured and a line established within a few hundred yards of Petit Miraumont, and this in face of an enemy who had received full warning of the attack and was well prepared for it. North of the Ancre the attack was also successful.

* * * * *

The ground gained in the Actions of Miraumont, *i.e.*, north and south of the Ancre, gave Sir Douglas Haig complete command over the enemy's artillery positions in the Ancre Valley and over his defences in and around Pys and Miraumont. Serre, still in German possession, was now threatened, and if lost would render Puisieux-au-Mont and Gommecourt equally difficult to hold. **12TH AND 17TH BATTALIONS.**

On 24th February, patrols, pushed out towards the enemy's positions before Pys, Miraumont and Serre, found the ruins of these once pretty villages deserted : the enemy had retired. The three places were occupied immediately. Other patrols, supported by strong infantry detachments, were then pushed forward, and by the evening of 25th the enemy's first system of defence, stretching from north of Gueudecourt to west of Serre, including Luisenhof Farm, Warlencourt-Eaucourt, Pys, Miraumont, Beauregarde Dovecot and Serre had fallen into the hands of the British.

The Thilloys (Ligny-Thilloy and Thilloy) were attacked and captured by the Australians between 25th February and 2nd March. Before the end of February, however, Puisieux-au-Mont and Gommecourt Village and Park had fallen, and the enemy had been driven back to the Le Transloy-Loupart line, but he still held Irles, which formed a salient to his position and was linked up to it at Loupart Wood and Achiet-le-Petit by well-constructed and heavily wired trenches. The capture of Irles was therefore the next step forward.

The assault on this village and its defences was carried out at 5.15 a.m. on the 10th March by the 2nd and 18th Divisions **10TH MARCH.** and was entirely successful. But neither the 17th Middlesex of the former Division nor the 12th Middlesex of the latter Division were engaged with the enemy, and from a regimental point of view the chief interest in the operations lies in the conditions amidst which both Battalions were " carrying on." The 17th were in camp near La Boisselle on the main Albert-Bapaume road, the furnishing of working parties being then their job. The 12th were engaged on similar work on the communications forward, passing terribly uncomfortable nights in dug-outs in Thiepval and Thiepval Wood, or else in tents, some thirty of which had been put up on the Autheuille Road to relieve the congestion in the dug-outs. Battalion Headquarters of the 12th were in The Wunderwerk—a rat-ridden place, pestilential in the extreme.

The capture of Irles* opened the way for the main operations against the centre of the Le Transloy-Loupart line, which was

* Known to the 2nd Division as the " Capture of Grevillers Trench," that being the objective of the Division, which was successfully occupied.

so heavily shelled and the preparatory bombardment so effective that the enemy once more abandoned his positions and, during the night of 12th/13th March, fell back to his third defences, which ran from just west of Barastre–Villers au Flos–Bapaume–Biefvillers–Bihucourt–Ablainzevelle–Ayette, thence north-east to and across, the Scarpe. Loupart Wood and Grevillers were thereupon occupied by the 2nd Division with the 18th Division on the left.

By this time, however, the enemy were everywhere on the move and, in places, " standing not upon the order of his going," was hurrying back with all speed, closely pursued, to his newly prepared defences—the Hindenburg Line.

II.

The Enemy retires to the Hindenburg Line.

" The decision to retire was not reached without a painful struggle. It implied a confession of weakness bound to raise the *morale* of the enemy and lower our own. But, as it was necessary for military reasons, we had no choice—it had to be carried out."
—GENERAL LUDENDORFF.

It will be remembered that, in his official despatches, Sir Douglas Haig stated that one of the threefold objects of the Somme Battles of 1916 was " to wear down the strength of the forces opposed to us," and the above quotation is nothing more nor less than a recognition of the success of the Allied offensive, for General Ludendorff also said in another part of his " Memories " : " It was necessary to shorten our front in order to secure a more favourable grouping of our forces and create larger reserves." Here then lies one of the justifications for the Somme Battles of 1916. Herein also, from a regimental point of view, lies something perhaps even greater—the certain proof that the blood of those gallant Middlesex men, who had given their lives or had suffered grievous wounds, had not been shed in vain.

The Hindenburg (or, as it is called by General Ludendorff, the Siegfried) Line was to be ready by the beginning of March. During its preparation the dastardly work of demolition was carried out over an area of 15 kilometres in breadth in front of (*i.e.*, west of) the new defences, which ran from south-east to north-west, from the Aisne River between Vailly and Soissons roughly along the line La Fere-St. Quentin-Bellenglise-Banteaux-Havrincourt-Bullecourt-Neuville Vitasse, and thence northwards, crossing the Scarpe west of Feuchy to Vimy. The work of blowing up the roads, demolishing cottages, houses and even whole villages, the felling or cutting down of trees, poisoning of wells, deporting the civil population, and turning to utter desolation so that it became known as the " Devastated Area," thousands of acres of France, was to occupy five weeks. The work of desolation, much of which was quite indefensible from a military standpoint, was known as the "Alberich" scheme, and the Chief of the German General Staff stated that : " On February 4th the order was given to carry out 'Alberich' according to plan. The first 'Alberich' day was February 9th. The retreat was to begin on March 16th, but under enemy pressure might start at any earlier date." That the German retreat *did* begin earlier has already partly been shown.

Whilst the Actions of Miraumont were in progress, and the 12th and 17th Battalions of the Middlesex were floundering through the mud and gaping shell holes towards Miraumont, Irles and Grevillers, other battalions of the Regiment in the Somme area and under similar conditions were holding the line and keeping a watchful eye on the enemy. *12TH AND 17TH BATTALIONS.*

In the area between Cléry, on the Somme, and Les Bœufs, no less than six battalions of the Regiment held sub-sectors of the front line at various dates between the 1st January and 14th March (the official date of the beginning of the German Retreat to the Hindenburg Line). These battalions were 1st and 18th (33rd Division), 2nd (8th Division), 16th (29th Division), and 20th and 21st (40th Division). Cléry, Bouchavesnes, Marrières Wood, Rancourt and Pierre Vaast Wood, Sailly-Saillisel, Morval, Combles, Maurepas and Curlu are all well-known names in the Middlesex Regiment. *1ST, 18TH, 2ND, 16TH, 20TH, 21ST BATTALIONS.*

From the 18th July, 1916, when they moved back into the line in Bazentin-le-Petit Wood, to the end of the year, the 1st Middlesex were not engaged in any major operations with the enemy. The activities of the Battalion are therefore given in the form of a summary. On the 19th July 2/Lieut. Calder was killed and 2/Lieut. S. Burrell badly wounded whilst talking to the Brigadier at the entrance to Battalion Headquarters dug-out : Lieut. S. Burrell died of wounds on 20th. The next day, after a *1ST BATTALION.*

perfect inferno in the line, the Battalion (in Brigade) marched to Dernancourt. The Battalion had lost heavily: 6 officers had been killed and 15 wounded; in other ranks the losses were 58 killed, 270 wounded, 63 missing—total, 391. But on 26th a draft of 1 N.C.O. and 534 other ranks arrived. On 13th August the Battalion again moved back to the line, first in reserve in Mametz Wood and then to the front line on 14th in High Wood. Two Companies—" B " and " C "—supported an attack by the 2nd Argylls on 18th and heavy fighting took place. The Battalion moved back to Mametz Wood on 19th, after a terrible time forward. The tour from 14th to 19th had cost the Die-Hards 1 officer wounded, 25 other ranks killed, 96 wounded, and 9 missing. On the 25th the Battalion was back again in the front line just north of Delville Wood. There is no other word in which to describe this part of the line than that of " damnable." It had just been captured and was in a horrible condition and shelled continuously. On 26th 2/Lieut. T. G. Carless was wounded and many other rank casualties were suffered. On 28th Lieut. H. R. Waterman and 2/Lieut. E. Scott-Waring Green were both killed by shell fire. When relief came on 30th the Battalion had lost during the tour 2 officers killed and 3 wounded, 34 other ranks killed, 77 wounded, and 7 missing. From 1st to 20th September, the Battalion was out of the line resting and training, but on the latter date moved into the Hebuterne trenches—an uneventful tour. The first three weeks of October were similarly uneventful until, on 23rd, the Middlesex moved to Trones Wood *via* Mametz and Montauban. The wood was a mass of broken trees and shell holes and still full of the remains of dead Germans—a ghastly place in which to bivouac. On the 24th, during a reconnaissance of the line east of Les Bœufs, Captain J. E. Coughlan was killed and Captain G. N. A. Cursons wounded by a shell. On that day the Battalion went into the line east of Les Bœufs.

The enemy was attacked on 28th October, the objective of the Brigade being the German positions in front of Le Transloy, known as Rainy Trench and Dewdrop Trench, and the dug-outs and points north-east of the latter. Zero hour was 5.30 a.m. " A " and " C " Companies led the attack of the 1st Middlesex, an attack splendidly successful, for by 9.30 a.m. the whole objective was in their hands and handed over to a relieving battalion (4th Suffolk Regt.) that night. That success was dearly bought, for

one officer (2/Lieut. C. A. T. Benson) was killed and seven officers 1ST BATTALION.
(Capt. E. W. Shaw, Lieuts. C. R. Smith and H. C. O. Buchanan,
and 2/Lieuts. R. B. Holman, E. Auckland, R. A. Buckingham,
and A. W. C. Hodges) were wounded ; 35 other ranks were killed,
136 wounded, and 29 were missing—total all ranks, 208. On
relief the Battalion moved back to the Flers line. Back again
into the line at Les Bœufs on 1st November until 3rd (2/Lieut.
Billman was wounded on 2nd), thence to Carnoy and Meaulte
(where they were told they were going " right back for a long
rest "), followed by a move to Huppy, where they stayed until the
morning of 5th December, continues the story of the 1st Battalion.
On the 5th December, however, the Battalion entrained at Pont
Remis and began to move south to the new portion of the line
the British were just taking over from the French. On the 14th
the 1st Middlesex went into the line just north-east of Bouchavesnes—they were then on the extreme right of the whole British
line in France and Flanders. The tour was, however, uneventful,
and when the Battalion was relieved they had lost only 5 other
ranks killed and 18 wounded. On the last day of the year the
1st Middlesex were in camp at Brucamps.

The 1st Battalion* (Lieut.-Colonel J. Elgee) and the 18th
(Pioneers—Lieut.-Colonel H. Storr, commanding), of the 33rd
Division, were east of Abbeville when the New Year dawned,
but by 11th February had moved down to the Somme again and 11TH FEBRUARY.
were in the Cléry sector.

The front-line trenches were about 1,200 yards east of Cléry,
and here the 1st Battalion had, between 11th and 16th February,
a very uncomfortable time. The enemy, very much on the
alert, kept the Die-Hards under periodical, but violent, bursts
of rifle-grenade and trench-mortar fire, whilst the guns of both
sides indulged in artillery duels. A trench-mortar bomb killed
2/Lieut. R. P. Dickason on 14th. The next day " D " Company,
then in reserve on Marne Crest, had a bad time, as the German
guns plastered their position with H.E. shells. Dug-outs were
blown in. Another shell wounded 2/Lieut. A. H. Maisey very
badly ; he died on 16th of his wounds. The tour ended on 16th, 16TH FEBRUARY.

* The Battalion Diary for 15th contains the following entry : " 26 suits of armour
arrived for use of bombers," but details of the armour are not given. The French used
armour comprising stomach, thigh, chest and shoulder pieces. Two types of shields
were tried by us in France, the Chemico and the Dayfield. The use of armour was,
however, abandoned, being considered too heavy and cumbersome, and after trial it was
withdrawn.

1ST BATTALION.
25TH FEBRUARY.

the next beginning on 25th near Road Wood, to reach which the men had to move along communication trenches knee-deep in parts in mud and water. In the midst of purgatory, however, the Battalion Diary still reports "men very cheerful." On the 2nd March Lieut.-Colonel Elgee left the Battalion for England on account of continued ill-health, and Major H. A. O. Hanley assumed command. On this date the Battalion moved back into the Bethune Road sector: on the 3rd 2/Lieuts. Pain and Rowntree were wounded: on the 4th the 8th Division, on the left of the 33rd, attacked the enemy, taking many prisoners and a few machine guns, but the 1st Middlesex were not involved.

14TH MARCH. On the 14th March the Battalion was in Camp 124 (near Sailly Laurette) training.

18TH BATTALION.

Hard at work as usual, the Pioneers (18th Middlesex) of the 33rd Division saw little change. They made dug-outs in Marrières Wood, and worked on Maud and Madame Trenches. Casualties were few. They suffered from sickness, no doubt, for who could read the following without a shiver: "'D' Company continued work on dug-outs through the 24 hours—60 men worked by night (in mud and water to the waist) on clearing Macaroni Lane." Gallant fellows! there was no one to sing their praises, but God knows they deserved the best. On the

14TH MARCH.
2ND BATTALION.

14th the Battalion was located in the Aubigny area, training.

We left the 2nd Battalion (Lieut.-Colonel H. W. E. Finch) on 31st October, 1916, resting and cleaning up in Meaulte after having (on 23rd) collared 200 yards of the enemy's trenches just west of Le Transloy. But on 7th November they were back again in the line between Les Bœufs and Le Transloy. This particular part of the line was a very bad patch, for the enemy was doing his utmost to cling to the Le Transloy Ridge, and in consequence his guns were seldom inactive.

The tour lasted only until the night of 10th, but it was quite long enough. On 8th Captain H. W. M. Potter and 2/Lieuts. McCoy, Hill and A. W. Boulter were wounded, 5 other ranks were killed and 7 wounded: on 9th 2/Lieut. T. T. Townsend was wounded, 2 other ranks were killed, 15 wounded and 1 missing: on 10th 3 other ranks were wounded and 4 were missing—total, 41 all ranks for the tour. The remainder of November and almost the whole of December were spent out of the front line, mostly at St. Maulvis, where the Battalion spent Christmas Day with the usual festivities.

On the 27th, however, the Battalion paraded at 6 a.m. and marched to Oisemont *en route* for the front line. From Suzanne the Die-Hards, in 'buses, moved off at 1 p.m. for Maurepas, proceeding by platoons to the trenches, and relieved the 1st Hampshire Regiment. On 30th Lieut.-Colonel B. A. Thompson rejoined and took over command of the Battalion. {2ND BATTALION.}

The front now held by the 8th Division was known as the Priez sector, divided into two sub-sectors, " Castor " on the right and " Pollux " on the left.

The ridge running from Rancourt to Sailly-Saillisel was the main feature, the possession of which, on account of the observation it conferred, was of great importance to each side. St. Pierre Vaast Wood and the valley running up through it from Moislains provided covered lines of approach and places of assembly to shield the Germans in massing for an attack which was confidently expected. This front was held by the 23rd Infantry Brigade, of which the 2nd Middlesex formed part. Unfortunately, the Battalion Diary is exceptionally dry reading for several weeks, and it is not until 26th February (the Battalion being then in the Bouchavesnes North Sector) that casualties are recorded, *i.e.*, 8 other ranks killed, 10 wounded and 2 shellshock. On the 21st February Lieut.-Colonel B. A. Thompson left the Battalion to command the 16th Battalion Middlesex Regiment, and Lieut.-Colonel J. Hamilton Hall assumed command of the 2nd Battalion. On the 27th an unsuccessful raid was attempted. Early March is bare of interest, though it is necessary to note that when the German Retreat officially began on 14th the Battalion was in support trenches in Hospital Wood. {21ST FEBRUARY. 14TH MARCH.}

Reduced to a mere handful (they had lost 24 officers and about 500 other ranks in the great attack on 1st July, 1916) the 16th Middlesex (Lieut.-Colonel J. Hamilton Hall) had moved back to billets in Englebelmer on 4th of that month. On 23rd the 86th Brigade was relieved from duty in the front-line trenches and gradually moved north to the Ypres area, the 16th Middlesex on the 30th proceeding to Camp " C " in a wood three miles east of Poperinghe. August and September were passed in the Salient, in front-line trenches or in support or in reserve, but beyond the ordinary round of trench warfare there is nothing to record during this period. On the 8th October the 16th Battalion (in Brigade) entrained once again for the Somme area, and, on arriving at Amiens, marched to Neuville, other units of the {16TH BATTALION.}

18 The German Retreat 1917

16TH BATTALION.

Brigade moving to Daours. From these two villages the 86th Brigade moved on 13th to the neighbourhood of Mametz Wood: Battalions were on the ridge immediately east. On 19th the Brigade took over front-line trenches, the 16th Middlesex relieving a battalion of the Berkshire Regiment in the Flers sector.

No records exist of what happened during the next four days, the Battalion Diary containing only the casualties for those days, *i.e.*, 20th—5 other ranks killed, 9 wounded; 21st—1 officer and 5 other ranks wounded; 22nd—4 other ranks killed, 14 wounded; 23rd—1 officer missing, 8 other ranks killed, 22 wounded. On the latter date the Battalion was relieved and moved back to Switch Trench, south-east of Flers. The next tour in the line lasted for three days, 25th, 26th and 27th October, but again only the casualties are recorded: 26th—1 officer and 3 other ranks wounded; 27th—3 other ranks killed and 6 wounded. November and December are similarly bare of interest, and on 14th of the latter month the 16th Middlesex were located at Breilly, north-west of Amiens. Here, until 9th January, the Battalion trained, but on the latter date marched to St. Pierre-a-Gouy *en route* for the forward area.

9TH JANUARY.

The 16th January saw the Battalion in the Morval sector. Generally, however, January and almost the whole of February appear to have been uneventful, and it is not until the last day (28th) of the latter month that a somewhat cryptic entry arouses interest. The entry is as follows: " 3 officers, 120 other ranks in action as ' mopping-up ' party, Sailly-Saillisel. Casualties—officers: killed, 1, wounded, 1; other ranks: killed, 3, wounded, 43; missing, 2. Remainder of Battalion, Bronfay to Hardecourt."

28TH FEBRUARY.

Further investigation in the Brigade Diary (for the above quotation is the only entry in the Battalion Diary on 28th February), however, reveals records of an attack on the German trenches east of Sailly-Saillisel on 28th February. The attack was carried out by the 2nd Royal Fusiliers on the right, and the 1st Royal Dublin Fusiliers (with two platoons 1st Lancashire Fusiliers) on the left. The 86th Brigade Operation Orders stated that: " Mopping-up parties will be detailed by the 16th Middlesex as follows: 12 parties, of 10 rank and file each, to be at the disposal of the 1st Royal Dublin Fusiliers." Apparently the attack was a success, but there are no further details of the part played by the "mopping-up" parties; nor are the names of the officer casualties given. On the 3rd March, after a short tour in the front line, the 16th Middlesex were relieved by the 7th Somerset Light Infantry, and by the 5th were located at Mericourt l'Abbe, where training was carried out until 20th.

[margin: 16TH BATTALION. 20TH MARCH.]

It has already been stated that at the beginning of 1917 the extreme right of the British line on the Somme was held by the 40th Division, in which the 20th and 21st Battalions of the Middlesex Regiment were contained.

[margin: 20TH AND 21ST BATTALIONS.]

These two Battalions had arrived in France on 6th June, 1916. The 40th Division was mobilized on 27th May, and on the 5th June both the 20th Middlesex (31 officers and 954 other ranks, under the command of Lieut.-Colonel F. P. Dunlop) and 21st Middlesex (33 officers and 990 other ranks, commanded by Lieut.-Colonel W. H. Samuel) embarked at Southampton for France, arriving at Havre on 6th; with the 12th R. Suffolk Regt. and the 13th Yorkshire Regt. they formed the 121st Brigade.

On 7th all units of the Brigade arrived at Lillers and billeted in Ham-en-Artois, their first billets in France. A period of training followed, during which first instructions in trench warfare were given to the Middlesex in the trenches of the 1st Division at Bully Grenay. The 20th Battalion went into the front-line trenches, on the right of the Double Crassier, for the first time on 25th June, and the next day had one man killed and two wounded: the 21st went in on 28th, having three other ranks killed and eight wounded the first day. On the 3rd July the 121st Brigade relieved the 2nd Brigade (1st Division) in the Maroc sector of the line, the first sub-sector held by the Brigade. The Double Crassier, held by both British and Germans, and part of the German lines known as The Triangle, were the important positions in this sub-sector.

There now followed a period of several months of trench warfare and constant training in bomb-throwing, machine-gun, trench-mortar and patrol work, and although there is little of outstanding general interest in the Diaries for the remainder of 1916, there are several items of interest both to the 20th and 21st Battalions.

On the 20th July the 20th Middlesex made their first raid on the enemy for the purpose of obtaining an identification. No prisoners were taken during the raid, but one German was shot, and from his body valuable identifications were obtained. The

20TH AND 21ST BATTALIONS. raiding parties suffered one officer killed (Lieut. J. F. Ladell), the first officer casualty reported since the arrival of the Battalion in France, and 10 other ranks wounded. Captain J. Baines was killed on 29th. The first officer of the 21st reported wounded was Lieut. Green (10th July). Two other officers (2/Lieut. E. N. Evers on 27th July and 2/Lieut. G. French on 29th July) were also wounded. Casualties in other ranks were of daily occurrence, and the first month in France seems to have been unusually costly for newly arrived Battalions. But the Loos sector was the scene of considerable activity in trench warfare at this period, mine-blowing, bombing, sniping, trench-mortaring and artillery duels taking place at all hours of the day and night.

August was a comparatively quiet month for the 20th Battalion, and, excepting a raid (which was abortive), carried out by the 21st Middlesex on 4th August, the latter Battalion similarly had few excitements. Four officer casualties are recorded in the diary of the 21st—2/Lieut. Jones wounded on 4th, Captain Allingham wounded on 17th, and Lieuts. J. V. Reynolds and W. L. Hudspith wounded on 18th and 19th respectively. Similarly, the month of September was uneventful, one officer of the 21st Battalion—2/Lieut. Macan—being wounded (on 15th). The Somme Battles were claiming the attention of both sides, and little more was done in the quiet sectors but the maintenance of positions and the improvement of the defences.

On 2nd October "A" Company of the 21st Middlesex raided the enemy's trenches, but found them very strongly held, and, after inflicting many casualties, though incurring none, the raiders retired to their own lines.

Another raid—termed a "Minor Enterprise"—with the object of taking prisoners, war material and gathering information concerning the enemy's defences, was carried out on the night of 8th/9th October by 6 officers and 130 other ranks, with two Lewis guns, of the 20th Middlesex. The raiders went over in two parties, "X" and "Y." No prisoners were captured in this raid, though a helmet was found which gave an identification. Several casualties were suffered by the raiders, who returned to their own lines with much information. Another attempt to enter the enemy's trenches, between 3.45 and 5 a.m. on 11th October by the 20th Battalion, resulted in three officers (2/Lieuts. Mallett, Greenhaigh and Wilson) and two other ranks being wounded. The enemy raided the 20th Battalion on the night

23rd/24th October, and 17 men were afterwards missing, whilst four had been killed and 10 wounded during the bombardment which preceded the raid. On the 27th Major F. S. B. Johnson assumed command of the 20th Battalion vice Colonel Dunlop. "B" Company of the 21st raided the enemy on 18th. The only other item to record is that of one officer casualty, 2/Lieut. German, wounded on 20th October. 20TH AND 21ST BATTALIONS.

On 27th October the 121st Brigade was relieved by the 17th Brigade, the former moving back to Les Brebis and Petit Sains. On 29th the Brigade marched to Bruay, where training was carried out until 2nd November, when in stages, alternated by periods of training, the 40th Division began to move southwards to the Somme area. On the 31st December the 121st Brigade took over the front line, Bouchavesnes North Sector, from the 120th Brigade, the 20th Middlesex going into the left sub-sector, the 21st reamining in support.

But from New Year's Day until the third week in March there is little to record. The weather was at its worst, snow and ice, sleet and mud, and, seemingly, every discomfort known to mankind fell upon the troops, not only in the front-line trenches, but behind the lines in billets or encampments. Maurepas, Bancourt, Camps 21 and 12, and Asquith Flats were cheerless places behind the front line. One Camp is described as very cold and desolate, the huts having no doors, though the ground was covered with snow and ice. On the 25th January the 20th Battalion Diary records that only one company had blankets owing to the scarcity of lorries. In the front-line patrol work and the improvement of the defences kept the troops busy night and day. A careful watch was maintained on the enemy's lines, for already rumours, accompanied by various signs, pointed to a possible early retirement. 1ST JANUARY.

On the 4th March the diaries of the 20th and 21st Battalions mention a demonstration in the form of a discharge of red and green rockets in order to assist a small attack made by the 8th Division. The Germans were in the habit of using red and green rockets as their S.O.S. signals, and the discharge of these coloured lights by the Middlesex had the desired effect of diverting the enemy's bombardment from the 8th Divisional front, where the real attack was taking place, to the 40th Divisional front. On 6th March Lieut.-Colonel Dunlop, commanding the 20th Middlesex, was wounded by a sniper. 4TH MARCH.

20TH AND 21ST BATTALIONS.
13TH MARCH.

The location of both Battalions on 13th March was as follows: The 20th Middlesex were in Camp 17 undergoing training and doing fatigue work; the 21st were similarly out of the front line in Linger Camp, *i.e.*, just north-west of Curlu.

* * * * *

Before the German retreat began certain signs were noticed along the enemy's front which announced the coming retirement. Chief of these was his neglect to repair wire entanglements and defences which had been broken and battered by our guns. True, his machine guns covered the gaps in the wire, but his carelessness about his front-line defences disclosed his intentions. Other things were the sight of columns of smoke behind his lines ascending to the skies; the disappearance of dumps, explosions in his back areas, which could not have been caused by our artillery, seeing the guns were not firing at the time, betokening the destroying of dug-outs, buildings and roads. All these things, added to information gained by our intelligence officers, clearly pointed to the coming retreat.

Along the northern portion of the Somme battlefield, *i.e.*, on both sides of the Ancre, the enemy had not only been forced to retire, but had begun his voluntary retirement before the 14th March. Only along the southern portion of their front opposite the British lines, on both banks of the Somme, did the Germans hold on to their trenches until the last possible moment—the night of 16th/17th March.

Darkness had fallen on the 16th March when suddenly the German trenches were illuminated by red lights. They were not the usual red flares which burned for a few moments and then went out, but steady red lights which threw a lurid glare over the lines of trenches. And they were visible all along the German front from Soissons to just south-east of Arras. They were signals to the German troops to begin their retreat to the Hindenburg Line.

21ST BATTALION.

15TH MARCH.

Of the five Battalions of the Middlesex Regiment* which followed the enemy back to his new defences, the diary of the 21st Battalion is the first to mention the voluntary withdrawal of the enemy. On the 15th March this Battalion had moved back into the front-line trenches in the Clèry sector, the relief being

---

* For the sake of clarity it is more convenient to describe the advance of the five Battalions—20th, 21st, 2nd, 17th and 12th—from right to left, as they were in the line.

completed by 1.30 a.m. on 16th. During the day orders were received from Brigade Headquarters stating the line to be taken up " in the event of voluntary withdrawal by the enemy." At dawn on 16th patrols still found the enemy holding his front line, and his machine gunners and snipers were active. Early on the 17th patrols again went out, but were heavily fired on, for though the bulk of the Germans had already begun their retirement, they left behind machine-gun posts and snipers to cover the retreating troops. At 3 p.m., however, a patrol of the Yorkshire Regiment, near the 21st Middlesex, went out and seized a point in the German lines without opposition. This patrol was immediately followed by others of greater strength, and the German front line was found empty. At 4.45 a patrol from the left Company (" B ") entered the enemy's line unopposed and was immediately followed by two platoons, which established strong posts in these places, reconnoitred the old German support and reserve lines, and blocked all communication trenches. First " A " Company and then " C " crossed the old No Man's Land and established themselves in the enemy's vacated front-line system, which by 7.30 p.m. had been completely occupied. No casualties were suffered during the advance, and only a wild, erratic fire of shrapnel shells from the enemy's artillery disturbed the quietude of the late afternoon. But when darkness had fallen Mt. St. Quentin and Peronne were seen to be in flames, and the horizon was red with the glare from burning villages and what had been the homes of the French peasantry. On 18th patrols of 21st Middlesex reconnoitred the roads through Feuillaucourt, and, pushing on to Mt. St. Quentin, found that place deserted, nor from the eastern exits of the village were there any signs of the enemy. So again the whole Battalion advanced and occupied trenches west of Mt. St. Quentin, from which at dawn on 19th patrols again went forward, penetrating to Bussu with similar results, *i.e.*, no sign of the enemy.

On 19th the 20th Middlesex passed through the 21st Battalion and took over Mt. St. Quentin, with companies pushed out to Bussu and Driencourt—the Bois de Buire. On 27th the 21st Battalion relieved the 20th, the latter again advancing. On the 25th, however, the 40th Division began to move back into Corps Reserve, the 20th and 21st Middlesex moving to Feuillaucourt, where work on the damaged roads was begun. In this position both Battalions remained until 5th April, by which date

2ND BATTALION.

16TH MARCH.

the enemy was settled in his new defences—the Hindenburg Line.

From Hospital Wood the 2nd Middlesex moved up and relieved the 2nd West Yorkshires in the line in front of Rancourt during the evening of 16th March. At what time the Germans withdrew along the front of the 2nd Battalion it is impossible to say, but by the night of 17th the Middlesex had pushed on through St. Pierre Vaast Wood to Wood Lane Trench. On the 18th the enemy again retired, and by night the Battalion was established on the western edge of Vaux Wood, in Vaux Wood Trench, where an outpost line was taken up. Patrols then went forward to the Canal du Nord. On the 19th the West Yorkshires passed through the Middlesex and pushed on to Nurlu, where another outpost line was established. Until the 29th the Battalion alternately relieved, or was relieved by, the West Yorkshires, but on that date in the evening took over Nurlu again. During the night 29/30th the Battalion surrounded Heudecourt, killing two Germans and taking eight others prisoner. At 4.45

30TH MARCH.

p.m. on 30th an attack, in conjunction with the 2nd Devons, was launched against the village and two machine guns and five more prisoners were taken. The Middlesex then dug in on a line running through Revelon and No. 2 Copse. The next day the West Yorkshires again took over the front line, after which the 2nd Battalion marched back to Moislains, where several days were spent in Divisional Reserve. The Die-Hards had, however, won forward within sight of the new Hindenburg Line, which ran just east of Villers-Guislain.

The advance had been made at trifling cost, for between

5TH APRIL.

17th March and the 5th April only two officers are reported wounded—2/Lieut. D. F. Woodhams (22nd March) and Capt. C. K. Smithett (30th March)—while in other ranks the losses are given as 5 killed, 14 wounded and 2 missing.

17TH BATTALION.

13TH MARCH.

The 17th Middlesex (6th Brigade, 2nd Division) on 13th March were on the Aqueduct Road, Le Sars. The King's and Essex Regiments of the same Brigade having pushed on through Loupart Wood and Loupart Trench, evacuated by the enemy, the 17th Battalion was ordered up in support to Grevillers Trench and Gallwitz Switch. But here again the pushing forward of patrols, who found the Germans had retired, was followed by the occupation of the enemy's positions. On the 17th the Middlesex (now in the front line) occupied the villages of Biefvillers and Sapignies. On the 19th the advanced guard of the 6th Infantry Brigade reached Mory, but on relief that night by a brigade of the 18th Division, returned to camp at Courcelette. Working parties were supplied for several days, their tasks being to repair the roads and communications to the front line. On the 22nd March, however, the 2nd Division began to move to a new sector of the line; thus the 17th Middlesex were only in the first stage of the German Retreat. <small>17TH BATTALION. 19TH MARCH. 22ND MARCH.</small>

Side by side with the 2nd Division the 18th Division, on the immediate left, had similarly pushed forward close on the heels of the retreating enemy, and early on the 13th two companies of the 12th Middlesex moved forward into part of the Loupart Line. Another small advance was made on 14th, but it was not until the 17th that " A " and " C " Companies moved on and occupied Bihucourt Trench and village, which had been abandoned by the enemy during the night 16th/17th. On the 18th the Northamptons moved through the Middlesex as the advanced guard, cavalry screens being already out and well forward in the country beyond. In the Battalion Diary on this day the first evidence that the " Alberich " order had been carried out occurs : " The enemy has destroyed most of the houses and cut down all fruit trees. They have also poisoned the wells." On the 19th the 12th Middlesex occupied Behagnies, but on the 20th the 18th Division began also to withdraw from the front line, the IInd Corps having been squeezed out of the line by the Vth Corps, and the 12th Middlesex marched back to Miraumont for the night. On the following day the Battalion moved to Contay, thence to Croisy, Dory and Vers, finally arriving at Guarbecque, their destined training area, on 28th March. The Middlesex men were still in this area when the German Retreat ended. <small>12TH BATTALION. 13TH MARCH. 28TH MARCH.</small>

All four Battalions had suffered very few casualties in following up the retreating enemy. Climatic conditions and heavy going were their worst foes, for they had to flounder through mud, over country devastated and as bare of shelter and cover as a merciless enemy could make it, their only comfort the sure knowledge that the Germans had been *forced* to beat a retreat—an acknowledgment of (at least a temporary) tactical defeat.

A German order issued during the Retreat to the Hindenburg Line contained the following: " Regimental historians will tell us in the future how delighted our officers and men were to return once again to open warfare."

Strange mentality which could see in an enforced retreat a cause for jubilation. No soldier worthy the name relinquished with " delight " ground soaked with the blood of gallant comrades, spent in maintaining it.

Safe in their Hindenburg Line the Germans considered it would be many months before the British could attack them, but ere a few days passed Sir Douglas Haig was hammering at the northern end of the powerful wire entanglements which protected the enemy's new defences.

The Retreat had scarcely ended (5th April) when the Arras offensive opened (9th April), and east of the town the enemy's front line again began to crumble.

CHAPTER XXVIII.

THE BATTLES OF ARRAS: 1917.

9th April—4th May.

IF preparations for the Battles of the Somme, 1916, were extensive, those which preceded the Battles of Arras, 1917, were even more so. The experience gained in the former battles had not been lost. Standard and narrow-gauge railways and roads had to be made, vast stocks of munitions and stores of all kinds collected, hutting and other accommodation for the troops provided, an adequate water supply installed and reservoirs constructed, mining and tunnelling operations carried out, and numerous other preparations made in order to begin, and carry on, the coming offensive.

For three weeks prior to the attack the guns were hardly silent. Night firing, wire-cutting, the bombardment of hostile trenches, strong points and billets continued steadily and with increasing intensity along the whole of the battle front-to-be.

Finally, a few days before the attack was launched the general bombardment began—a bombardment described by General Ludendorff as "short but extraordinarily intense"—during which gas discharges were carried out.

All along the whole front to be attacked day and night raids were undertaken and were mostly successful, the enemy's troops being badly shaken by the terrific and relentless shell fire to which they were subjected.

In the air also there was a struggle of the utmost severity for local supremacy, the British bombing machines causing great damage to the enemy's dumps, railways, aerodromes and billets.

Amidst all these preparations and the awful din of the guns the troops had to be trained for the coming offensive.

Prior to the attack on 9th April the German lines of defence on the British front ran in a general north-westerly direction from St. Quentin to the village of Thilloy-lez-Moffeaines, immediately south-east of Arras: this was the new Hindenburg

Line. From Thilloy the original German trench system ran northwards across the valley of the Scarpe to the Vimy Ridge, which, rising to a height of 475 feet, commanded a wide view to the south-east, east and north. But almost the whole of this Ridge before the attack was in the hands of the enemy.

The enemy's positions to be attacked covered a front of about 15 miles from just north of Croisilles (south-east of Arras) to just south of Givenchy-en-Gohelle, at the northern foot of the Vimy Ridge. It therefore included between 4 and 5 miles of the northern end of the new Hindenburg Line. North of the latter three separate trench systems, connected by a powerful switch line running from the Scarpe at Fampoux to Lievin, formed a highly organised defensive belt from 2 to 5 miles in depth. From 3 to 6 miles further east the Drocourt-Queant line, another new powerful system of defences, forming a northern extension of the Hindenburg Line, was just approaching completion. In truth, Sir Douglas Haig's gallant troops had a stiff task before them!

During the night of 8th/9th April the assaulting troops moved up into their battle positions, and when Zero hour (5.30 a.m.) arrived on the morning of 9th the order of battle, from right to left of the divisions in line, was as follows: The 21st was on the right flank of the Third Army, just south of Henin; the 30th held the line just east of Mercatel, having on the left the 56th (London) Division, who were west of Neuville Vitasse; the 14th Division was east of Beaurains; next came the 3rd and 12th Divisions, south and north of the Arras-Cambrai road respectively; on the left of the 12th was the 15th, between the Arras-Douai Railway and the Scarpe River; north of the Scarpe the Divisions in line were 9th, 34th and 51st (whose left flank was east of the Lens-Arras road); north-west of the latter road, and all along the western slopes of the Vimy Ridge, were five divisions forming the Canadian Corps; the 24th Division was on the left flank of the Canadians. The 37th Division was at Arras, with orders to " go through " between the inner flanks of the 12th and 15th Divisions towards Orange Hill; the 4th Division was in support of the 9th, with orders to " go through " towards Fampoux.

Interesting, however, as the whole battle is, it is not possible to deal with the operations in any sectors other than those in which battalions of the Middlesex Regiment fought the enemy.

Eleven Battalions Engaged

At least 11 battalions took part in the Battles of Arras, 1917, but of these only five were engaged on the first day of the operations. They were the 4th (37th Division), 1/7th and 1/8th (56th Division), 11th (12th Division), and 13th (24th Division), and of these the first-named (4th Battalion) did not " go in " until night.

4TH, 1/7TH, 1/8TH, 11TH AND 13TH BATTALIONS.

Covered from head to foot with the mud of the Ancre, the 4th Middlesex had moved back to Mailly Maillet on 26th November, 1916, but for several weeks (weeks spent out of the line in training and in moving north with the Division) until the Battalion arrived in the Vielle Chapelle area (west of Neuve Chapelle), there is little to record. It was in Vielle Chapelle in October, 1914, that the original 4th Battalion saw heavy fighting. It was here also, on Christmas Day, 1916, that Major-General C. P. A. Hull (who had commanded the Battalion at Mons) visited the Battalion. On 2nd January, 1917, the Middlesex went into the front-line trenches, and, as showing the quiet state of this part of the line, the Battalion during a tour of six days suffered not a single casualty. Billets in Croix Barbee and Locon, and tours in the front line in the Ferme du Bois sector, were similarly uneventful, and about the middle of February the Division moved down to the Loos area, the 4th Middlesex taking over trenches in the 14 bis Right Sector. In March another move was made to Houvin Houvigneul, where, on 12th, Lieut.-Colonel F. Bicknell, who for 18 months had commanded the 4th Battalion, left for England, where he had been appointed an instructor at the Senior Officers' School, Aldershot. Major A. C. Dawson then assumed temporary command of the Battalion until Lieut.-Colonel W. I. Webb-Bowen, the new C.O., arrived on 18th. Training continued at Houvin until 5th April, when the Die-Hards marched to Beaufort, and on the 7th to Noyellette.

4TH BATTALION.

The 37th Division had already received its orders for the attack on 9th April, and the day before operations began the 4th Middlesex marched to Duisans, where bombs, tools and iron rations were drawn. Orders were received from Brigade Headquarters that Zero on the following morning was to be 5.30 a.m., at which hour the Battalion would move forward to their place of assembly.

8TH APRIL.

The 1/7th and 1/8th Middlesex had been withdrawn with other troops of the 56th Division from the Battle of Le Transloy on 9th October, 1916, and had then moved to Flesselles, 8 miles from Amiens.

1/7TH AND 1/8TH BATTALIONS.

1/7TH AND 1/8TH BATTALIONS.

The 1/7th had come out of the line terribly weak. Of the 41 officers who had taken part in the actual fighting only 3 remained—the number was brought up to 7 by the addition of the Quartermaster and officers who had been serving with Brigade and Divisional Headquarters. In other ranks the Battalion numbered about 300. The strength of the 1/8th on reaching Flesselles is not given.

At Flesselles the two Territorial Battalions remained a week, and then (in Division) began to move northwards. On 19th October the 1/7th Battalion marched to Longpre and the 1/8th to Airaines. On 24th the Middlesex entrained for Merville, and on arrival the 1/7th billeted in the town and the 1/8th at La Gorgue.

The 56th Division was now in the XIth Corps area, under orders to relieve the 61st Division in the Neuve Chapelle-Moated Grange-Fauquissart sector. The 1/8th went first into the line, taking over trenches in the Moated Grange sub-sector on the 28th October. On the 30th the Battalion lost its C.O., Lieut.-Colonel P. L. Ingpen, who had been appointed to command the 56th Divisional School. Lieut.-Colonel F. W. D. Bendall then assumed command of the Battalion. But for the remainder of the year the diaries of the 1/8th Battalion contain nothing of more than ordinary interest, and only one officer casualty is recorded—2/Lieut. C. V. Evans, attached 167th T.M.B., wounded. It should not be assumed, however, that the Battalion had an easy, quiet time. Trench warfare was vigorous, and conditions in the front line extremely bad. The shell-hole posts out in front of the trenches were little more than shell holes, muddy, and with practically no shelter from the weather. Trench-mortaring was of a violent nature—both sides were active and always on the alert. As a test of nerves and endurance that period of trench warfare in front of Estaires and Laventie was hardly equalled on any other occasion. The 1/8th were in the trenches on Christmas Day, but on 27th December were relieved and moved back to Laventie, where, on the 30th, Christmas dinners were eaten.

The 1/7th Middlesex took over front-line trenches in the Moated Grange sub-sector on 2nd November. In moving up into the line 2/Lieut. A. E. Fontaine was wounded. Until the 30th of the month the Battalion had a comparatively quiet time, and very welcome it was, as the 1/7th had left the Somme terribly weak. New officers arrived and large drafts of other ranks, and these had to be absorbed and trained, for some of them had received but little training. The periods, therefore, when there was "nothing doing" were very welcome.

1/7TH AND 1/8TH BATTALIONS.

On 30th, however, the enemy raided the 1/7th. A portion of the line held by the Battalion at this time lay between St. Tilleloy communication trench and Duck's Bill Sap (both inclusive), and here from 3 p.m. to 3.45 p.m. the Germans put down a heavy bombardment from heavy and medium trench mortars, and plastered the line with shrapnel shell. The sector was held by "A" Company (Major Emery). At 4 p.m. the bombardment recommenced, being specially heavy on the Duck's Bill Crater and Sap. The Duck's Bill was a fortified mine crater near Neuve Chapelle, connected by a communication trench with the front line, and only 40 yards from the enemy. "It never served any useful purpose," said the C.O. of the 1/7th, "and every battalion commander who ever held it desired to fill in the communication trench and evacuate it. But for some reason difficult to understand it was dearly loved by the Staff. The place was a perfect death-trap. Its garrison consisted of 12 men. Hardly a day passed without casualties, and altogether some hundreds of men must have been killed or wounded in it every year." Indeed, early on the 30th, before the enemy's raid took place, Major S. King, who had returned to the Battalion from hospital a few days previously, was making an inspection of the Duck's Bill when he was wounded by a trench-mortar shell which fell in the Crater, killing or wounding also most of the garrison.

Half an hour after the bombardment of the Duck's Bill had recommenced, *i.e.*, at 4.30, Major Emery received a message from one of his officers in the line saying that, owing to the heavy bombardment, the garrisons of the Crater and Sap had been withdrawn. Accompanied by Private Gregory and another man, Major Emery went up the line immediately and found the Crater under a very heavy bombardment from hostile trench mortars. Sending back the second man to his Company, ordering the garrison of the Duck's Bill to reoccupy their posts, the Major and Private Gregory then occupied Post "A" in the Crater. About 5.30 p.m. the bombardment ceased and the Germans advanced. A party of about 14 was seen on the southern lip of the Crater, and, after throwing bombs at them, Major Emery

1/7TH AND 1/8TH BATTALIONS.

and Gregory retired to the junction of the Crater and the Sap. Here the gallant Major, having sent his man back for reinforcements, held up the enemy by throwing bombs and with his revolver. But gradually he was forced back until just in the nick of time a reinforcing party of the Company came along, and with these men he again forced the enemy back and advanced and re-entered the Crater. This affair cost the Battalion Lieut. R. M. Wheeler and 5 men killed, and 6 wounded, all the result of the bombardment. One man was missing after the raid, which, had not Major Emery acted with promptness, might have been more serious. For the remainder of the year there is nothing of further outstanding interest in the diaries of the 1/7th Battalion.

1ST JANUARY, 1917.

The principal item of interest in the Diary of the 1/7th Middlesex for January, 1917, is a copy of the report sent to the G.O.C. on the services of the Battalion from the beginning of the War. These services have already been dealt with, but items of interest not hitherto stated are the Strength and Casualty Returns concerning the period. The Battalion on leaving England in 1914 had a strength of 934. In 1915 drafts numbered 293, and, in 1916, 1,616—total, 2,843. Casualties up to the 1st January were 1,506, transfers 95, commissions 22, and discharges 117—total, 1,740.

Study of the Diaries of the Battalions (1/7th and 1/8th) for the first three months of 1917 reveals little which need be retold. The 56th Division held the Fauquissart-La Ventie sector until the beginning of March, and was then relieved by the 49th Division. The two Battalions of Middlesex were next on the move until the second week in March, when they settled down to a period of training for the Arras Battles, the 1/7th at Dainville and the 1/8th at Sus-St.-Leger. On the 6th March, at La Gorgue, Lieut.-Colonel P. L. Ingpen rejoined the 1/8th and assumed command of the Battalion once more.

The 56th Division had been transferred to the VIIth Corps, and on leaving the Laventie area moved down to Arras, taking over a sector south-east of that town and facing Beaurains, then in German occupation. But on the 17th March the enemy evacuated the latter village and fell back to the Hindenburg Line, which along the Divisional front included Neuville Vitasse, Telegraph Hill and the Harp, all very strongly defended. But neither the 1/7th nor the 1/8th Middlesex went into the front line during March, both Battalions being engaged in training or making preparations for the coming offensive.

1/7TH AND 1/8TH BATTALIONS.

On the 1st April, however, the 1/8th moved from Monchiet (167th Brigade area) to Beaurains, taking over the front line from the 2nd London Regt., east of the village. One officer (2/Lieut. S. W. Varrail) and three other ranks were wounded, and three other ranks killed on the first day in the line. On the 4th the Battalion was relieved and moved back to the trenches at Agny to continue final preparations for the great attack of 9th April. The 1/7th, however, did not go into the front-line trenches before moving up to their assembly trenches on the night of the 8th, but were billeted at Agny, mostly engaged in digging assembly and communication trenches and in practising the attack.

8TH APRIL.

The 11th Middlesex, who as part of the 36th Brigade (12th Division) were to attack the enemy between the Arras–Cambrai road and the Arras–Douai Railway on 9th April, had left the Somme area on 21st October, 1916, and moved in stages north of Arras, the 36th Brigade taking over the Agny sector on 26th. But the Middlesex did not go into the line until 1st November. Although the line was noisy, heavy and light trench mortars being always more or less active, casualties were not heavy, and for several weeks trench warfare was normal. On the 10th December the 36th Brigade was relieved by a brigade of the 14th Division, and the 11th Middlesex moved by stages to Buneville, where a period of training began and continued until the 19th January, 1917, when the Battalion moved again, this time to Wanquetin. On 23rd the 11th marched to Arras, where billets were found in cellars. A fortnight was then spent in furnishing working parties to dig trenches and communications and generally help in preparing for the Spring operations. On the 7th February the Battalion took over front-line trenches east of Arras, but the tour was uneventful and came to an end on 11th. On 14th, Lieut.-Colonel Pargiter was invalided to England, and Major T. S. Wollocombe assumed command of the Battalion.

11TH BATTALION.

7TH FEBRUARY.

On the 20th February "D" Company and two platoons of "A" Company, under Captain Maynard, began training for a raid on the enemy's trenches. This raid was carried out on 26th at 8.30 a.m. It was a splendid success, the raiders bringing back no less than 25 German prisoners, some 10 of whom were slightly wounded. One officer (2/Lieut. D. R. Gillman) and 4 other ranks were killed and 1 officer (2/Lieut. V. H. Castle) and 14

11TH BATTALION.
4TH MARCH.

other ranks were wounded during the raid. But numerous other Germans were killed and their dug-outs bombed. On the 4th March the Battalion (in Brigade) marched out of Arras for Izel lez-Hameau, where training and practising the attack occupied the Middlesex men until 21st. On the latter date the move back towards the front line began, the Battalion marching first to Montenescourt, where all ranks were busily employed in getting ready for the forthcoming operations. The final move before taking up their assembly positions for the attack took place on the 2nd and 3rd, when the 11th Battalion moved again to Arras. On the night of 4th April "B" and "C" Companies moved up into dug-outs in "I" and the support line; "A" and "D" Companies had moved into cellars in Rue Gustave Colin near the Station. All companies were, however, still engaged in making final preparations for the attack. Bomb and grenade dumps were formed, ladders and bridges carried up to the line, and picks and shovels were drawn. They were busy days and nights, for the enemy's line had also to be patrolled and the conditions of his wire carefully noted and reported, for the guns were wire cutting. Both on the 6th and 7th April patrols went across No Man's Land to examine the enemy's wire and trenches. About midnight on 8th "A" and "D" Companies joined "B" and "C" in the dug-outs and in "I" support lines, all final preparations having been made.

8TH APRIL.

13TH BATTALION.

At the northern extremity of the Vimy Ridge the 13th Middlesex (24th Division), although not actually in the front line during the initial attack on 9th April, held the fire trenches from Boyau Brisson to the Souchez River on the night 8th/9th, when the Canadians (who were to make the assault) relieved them, and again on the night of 9th/10th, when they relieved the Canadians.

The 13th Battalion was last mentioned as being quartered in Kemmel Shelters at the end of June, 1916. At the end of July the 24th Division was transferred to the Somme, the Middlesex arriving at Corbie on 31st.* On the 17th August the Battalion moved up to the trenches at Arrow Head Copse. On the way Lieut. Molesworth was wounded. The 18th witnessed a succession of officer casualties in the Battalion. Lieut. W. J. Burt was first wounded and then killed while going down to the dressing

* The deaths of two officers are announced in the July Diary: 2/Lieut. V. Wheldon-Williams (6th) and 2/Lieut. O. W. Foulkes-Winks (20th).

station, 2/Lieut. de Pass was wounded in the shoulder by a shell splinter; finally, three officers—Captains Middleton and Reeves and Lieut. Parkes—were buried in Teale Trench by a shell burst, but were dug out and the two senior officers sent to hospital.

That afternoon the Battalion attacked the Guillemont trenches, but were held up by very heavy machine-gun fire from a strong point on the right which enfiladed the attack. Forced to seek shelter in shell holes, the unfortunate Middlesex then became a mark for the enemy's guns and again sustained severe casualties. Captains D. B. Reed, B. A. James and E. J. S. Vaughan, and 2/Lieuts. J. R. Adam, C. P. Black and C. L. Burch were killed, and Lieuts. Allen, King, Trower, Nicholson and Smith were wounded. In other ranks the losses were about 340 killed, wounded and missing. At nightfall, after that disastrous day, the Battalion was withdrawn to the Briqueterie for the night, and on the 19th to the Craters. Here the Middlesex men remained until the 22nd, when they marched back to Sandpits Camp. On the 30th, however, they again went into the line, moving up in orderly line through trenches knee-deep in mud, where eventually, in a deplorable condition (outwardly) they relieved the Suffolks in Tea Trench, Worcester Trench, Pont Street and Orchard Trench, the relief not being completed until 7.30 a.m. on 31st. An hour later the enemy's guns opened fire on the whole sector, the storm of shell increasing in fury until 2 p.m., when his infantry attacked the Middlesex. " B " Company was driven out of Tea Trench and " A " Company back up Worcester Trench to Macdougal C.T. and Pont Street. The Germans reached Orchard Trench, but here they were met by 2/Lieut. Green, who, with about 12 men of " D " Company and a Lewis gun, held up the enemy. This little party was not strong enough, however, to withstand the pressure of numbers, but were able to keep the enemy to his ground until supports came up. " A " Company, with the remnants of " B " and one platoon from " D " and " C " Companies, were then withdrawn from Pont Street to Carlton Trench. Casualties on 31st are not given in the Diary, but the month's losses were 9 officers killed and 17 wounded. In other ranks the losses were 563 killed, wounded and missing.

On 1st September the Battalion was relieved and in stages were withdrawn from the line, finding billets in Mouflers on 6th,

13TH BATTALION.

where, until 19th, training was carried out. The 13th then moved to Bruay (19th), where they went into the Carency trenches on 23rd. But for several weeks onwards there is little of interest in the diaries. Casualties were small (October, 3 other ranks; November, 15 other ranks; December, 13 other ranks). The last day of the year found the Battalion in the left sector of the Loos sector.

A successful raid on the enemy was carried out by the Battalion on 21st January, 1917. Many dug-outs containing Germans were blown up, 6 were killed in the trenches, and 3 brought back prisoners. Casualties suffered by the Battalion were 2/Lieut. H. O. Williams and 1 other rank killed and 3 other ranks wounded. Captain J. Norquoy was wounded on 10th February. On 5th March the 13th Middlesex (the 24th Division having moved from the Loos sector) took over front-line trenches in the left sub-sector of the Souchez II sector.

On the 1st April an advanced party of the Battalion marched from billets in Fosse II to the Carency sector to take over the line from the Canadians. On this day 2/Lieut. A. E. Megson was wounded. The portion of the line taken over by the Middlesex men ran from Boyau Brisson to the Souchez River. These trenches were in a very poor condition, and when on the 2nd April the preliminary bombardment of the enemy trenches opened, and heavy retaliation followed, the trenches became deplorable.*

8TH/9TH APRIL On the night 8th/9th April, " A " and " D " Companies proceeded to Château de la Haie, their places in the line being taken over by the 44th and 46th Canadians, who were to make the assault next morning.

(I) THE FIRST BATTLE OF THE SCARPE, 1917, AND VIMY RIDGE:

9th–14th April.

The heavy bombardment to which the enemy's trenches had for three weeks prior to the 9th April been subjected, culminated in a terrific tornado of shell fire at 5.30 a.m. on Zero day, when, closely following on the heels of a most effective barrage, the infantry of the Third and First Armies swept across No Man's Land like an irresistible tidal wave.

* Lieut. D. W. Parkes was wounded on 8th April.

The front attacked extended from just north of Croisilles 11TH BATTALION. (south-east of Arras) to immediately south of Givenchy-en-Gohelle on the northern point of the Vimy Ridge—a distance of nearly 15 miles. This front included some 4 or 5 miles of the northern end of the newly constructed Hindenburg Line. The official despatches state that the " general attack " was launched at 5.30 a.m., but it was not until two hours later (7.30 a.m.) that the right of the Third Army (VIIth Corps, formed of 21st, 30th, 56th and 14th Divisions, in that order from right to left) joined in the operations in what was apparently the second phase of the battle. The first battalion of the Middlesex Regiment to come to grips with the enemy was, therefore, the 11th, of the 12th Division, upon whom had fallen the difficult task of wresting Observation Ridge, with its very powerful defences, from the Germans. Apart from three distinct lines of trenches to be taken, there was the Feuchy Switch, which ran back from the German forward lines to the western edge of Feuchy. In all these trenches there were a number of " Works "—strongly defended positions, heavily wired and fully garrisoned. No easy task lay before the 12th Division.

The 37th Brigade was attacking on the right and the 36th (to which the 11th Middlesex belonged) on the left. Of the latter Brigade the Middlesex was the right attacking Battalion and the 7th Royal Sussex the left. The 12th Division had on its right the 3rd Division, and on its left the 15th Division.

The frontage attacked by the 11th Middlesex (Lieut.-Colonel T. S. Wollocombe) ran from Sap 20 (a German sap about half-way between the railway and the Arras-Cambrai road), thence some 200 yards southwards. Portions of Guildford and Hertford Trenches and of Henley Lane were also in the Battalion's objective.

At midnight, 8th/9th April, the Battalion was in its assembly 8TH/9TH APRIL positions in " I " Lines and the support trenches, and formed up in three waves for the attack. No details of the strength of the Battalion in " other ranks " are given, but there were only 20 officers—4 to each Company, the C.O., Adjutant, Lewis-gun Officer and Signalling Officer. Throughout the Army drastic orders were in vogue at this period detailing a number of officers, N.C.Os. and men from each battalion to the Transport Lines during a battle. The second-in-command always took charge of the nucleus, so that a battalion was never in danger of losing both

B 3

11TH BATTALION.
9TH APRIL.

its senior officers, and, if practically wiped out in the front line, still had a skeleton of trained officers and men to fall back upon.

As Zero hour approached Lewis-gun teams crept out into No Man's Land, taking up selected positions from which to deal with hostile machine guns and snipers should they become troublesome. Five minutes before Zero the order was given to "fix bayonets." As the thunder of the barrage broke over the German trenches at 5.30 a.m., the waiting troops followed quickly in its train, keeping as close to the screen of fire as possible. The Diary of the 11th Battalion, though not very full, is nevertheless to the point. It states that at 5.30 a.m. "the Battalion went over the top as practised on the training ground. The artillery work was splendid and never really gave the Bosche a chance." [A sporting phrase that—a chivalrous sentiment.] "Our fellows took full advantage of the different barrages and quickly captured their objective, *i.e.*, the Black Line (Hertford Trench). So far casualties had been wonderfully slight and all ranks behaved splendidly."

General Ludendorff blames some of his divisions for giving way before the fury of that first attack, but from letters taken from dead Germans and German prisoners it is evident that the terrific bombardment to which they had been subjected had deprived numbers of the enemy's troops of all power of resistance: stupefied and terror-stricken, they could no longer resist. Thus the first objective (Black Line) fell without much resistance. But the Germans were no mean opponents, and by the time the 8th and 9th Royal Fusiliers passed through the 11th Middlesex and Sussex in order to capture the second objective (the Blue Line), the enemy's defence was beginning to harden. But so far as the first day of the Battle was concerned, the 11th Middlesex had done their job—done it thoroughly, too. They consolidated the ground won and formed a strong point in Hertford Trench, which was manned by "D" Company. During the afternoon "B," "C" and "A" Companies went forward to support the 5th Royal Berks, and by nightfall on 9th the 12th Division had reached the Feuchy Chapel–Feuchy Road. During the afternoon a dug-out near Battalion Headquarters blew up (probably a delay-action mine) and about 20 H.Q. details, including Sergeant Hunter and all the signallers, were killed. Three or four more dug-outs "went up" shortly afterwards. Headquarters and "D" Company then moved back to the old British line, where they were joined in the evening by "B," "C" and "D" 11TH BATTALION. Companies. The losses of the Battalion during the day were: 2/Lieuts. H. G. Wright and G. Sinclair killed, 2/Lieuts. Holman, 9TH APRIL. Newman, Smallwood and Tatham wounded, and about 100 other ranks killed, wounded and missing.

To return to the morning of 9th: At Zero plus two hours (7.30 a.m.) the 14th Division, on the left of the 56th Division, launched its attack against Telegram Hill and the Harp, and 15 minutes later the latter Division attacked Neuville Vitasse, the 167th Brigade on the right and 168th Brigade on the left.

Of the 167th Brigade the 3rd London Regt. was on the right 1/7TH AND 1/8TH and the 1/8th Middlesex (Lieut.-Colonel P. L. Ingpen) on the BATTALIONS. left, the 1st London Regt. being in support and the 1/7th Middlesex in reserve during the initial attack on the first objective.

Two objectives were allotted to the 56th Division—the Blue Line, which ran roughly round the eastern exits (and including) Neuville Vitasse, from the Sugar Factory on the south to a point where the railway (and sunken road) crossed the Hindenburg Line north-east of the village. From this objective the support and reserve troops would, after capturing that part of the Hindenburg Line east of Neuville Vitasse, attack the second objective (the Brown Line)—Niger Trench, part of the Henin-Wancourt Line.

The 3rd Londons were to advance in three waves and the 1/8th Middlesex in four waves, a different objective being allotted to each wave. When the capture of the Blue Line had been signalled the 1st Londons were to advance and go through the troops on the first objective and attack the Hindenburg Line. The latter having been secured the 1/7th Middlesex were to leap-frog the 1st Londons and assault the Brown Line.

After the German Retreat to the Hindenburg Line the British front had been pushed forward to within (approximately) 300–400 yards of Neuville Vitasse. The German defences of the village ran in a semicircle round the western exits, Neuville Work being a particularly strong point. The trenches were defended by three belts of wire entanglements. The village was somewhat straggly, divided into two parts, the northern half of which was again protected by semicircular trenches and more thick belts of wire. Just east of the village (and connected with the latter by communication trenches) the Hindenburg Line ran in a north-westerly to south-easterly direction.

1/7TH AND 1/8TH BATTALIONS.

From Agny, where the Battalion had spent several days in preparing for the attack on Zero Day, the 1/8th Middlesex moved on 7th April into the Beaurains left sector, and at 9 p.m. on 8th went forward to the assembly trenches just west of Neuville Vitasse. A new trench, specially dug for the operations, between the front and support lines, was taken over by "A" Company, "B" Company took over the support line, and "D" Company the Marrow Trench. "C" Company apparently held the front line, which had been taken over on 7th.

The 1/7th Middlesex (Lieut.-Colonel E. J. King), which similarly had been at Agny engaged in making final preparations, moved up to the assembly trenches at 8 p.m. on the 8th, "A" Company taking over Max Trench, "B" Company Margate Trench, "C" and "D" Companies with Battlion Headquarters in the old German front line south-west of Beaurains. The battle strength of the Battalion was 20 officers and 580 other ranks.

9TH APRIL.

As Zero hour approached on morning of 9th all ranks were full of excitement. All ladders and bridges, for the passage of the troops into No Man's Land, were in position, gaps in the wire had been cut, and the sections of tanks detailed to accompany the 56th Division into action were drawn up ready to advance. From the north rumours of big successes had already begun to filter through. At last, punctually at 7.45 a.m., as the synchronised watches touched the three-quarters and the barrage fell on the German front line, the attacking troops left their trenches and advanced rapidly across No Man's Land.

In this sector also, the German troops holding the hostile front line were dazed and demoralised, and offered but feeble resistance. So that by 8.5 a.m. "C" Company of the 1/8th Middlesex had taken the first objective allotted to that Company with 12 prisoners. Passing through "C" Company, "A" Company at 8.44 a.m. was held up in front of its objective by violent machine-gun fire and a fully-manned trench in front of which the wire had not been cut. For nearly two hours "A" fought the trench and finally captured it at 10.10 a.m. Sending back 68 prisoners, the Company then began to consolidate the trench. German heavy shells now began to fall in Neuville Vitasse. After heavy fighting "B" Company, which had leap-frogged "C" and "A," gained the third objective at about 2.15 p.m., and by 4 p.m. "D" Company had cleared the enemy out of the fourth objective, immediately in front of the Hindenburg Line. Thus the Blue Line had fallen to the 1/8th Middlesex and 3rd Londons, who had similarly gained their objectives.

1/7TH AND 1/8TH BATTALIONS. 9TH APRIL.

Throughout the fighting the enemy's shell fire had gradually increased in intensity. His machine guns swept the captured area with a tornado of bullets, and snipers were everywhere busy. Eighty prisoners and seven machine guns had been captured by the 1/8th Middlesex during the day. At night (9 p.m.) "A" Company was withdrawn from its objective and moved back to the old British front line in front of Neuville Vitasse. Casualties during the day were two officers (2/Lieuts. R. H. Attwater and C. H. Askew) killed, five officers (2/Lieuts. A. Small, A. Atkinson, F. Herbert, L. H. Maudling and R. S. C. Hallett) wounded; 17 other ranks killed, 121 wounded and 3 missing.

In the meantime the attack of the 1/7th Middlesex had not met with that measure of success which had been anticipated. At Zero hour, as the leading troops of the 167th Brigade dashed forward to attack Neuville Vitasse, their trenches had been occupied by the 1st Londons, who had been ordered to go through the two leading battalions and capture the Hindenburg Line,* east of the village. The 1/7th Middlesex had then moved forward to the trenches vacated by the 1st Londons. At 11 a.m. the latter reported that they were advancing on Neuville Vitasse in order to attack the Hindenburg Line beyond the village. This was the signal for the advance of the 1/7th Middlesex.

The 1/7th Battalion moved forward in four lines of platoons, in fours at 150 paces distance. The first two lines were formed of "A" (Hampstead and Highgate) and "B" (Barnet and Enfield) Companies, each with two platoons in the first line and two in the second. "C" Company (Hornsey) formed the third line and "D" Company (Tottenham) the fourth.†

The destination of the Battalion was the sunken road on the far side of Neuville Vitasse, leading to St. Martin-sur-Cojeul, where a halt was to be made and reorganisation for the next phase of the operations take place.

The advance was carried out with extraordinarily few casualties, though just before reaching Neuville Vitasse a barrage of high-explosive shell had to be passed through. There were, however, gaps in this barrage, and by carefully watching the

* Known also as the Cojeul Switch Line.
† Company Commanders: "A," Capt. J. W. Cater; "B," Capt. C. W. Neighbour; "C," 2/Lieut. H. G. Vickerage; "D," 2/Lieut. D. T. Cousins.

fall of the shells officers got their platoons through with very little loss.

It was about 1 p.m. when the 1/7th Middlesex were assembled in four lines in the sunken road, Colonel King having established his Headquarters in the ruined Sugar Factory on the southern outskirts of Neuville Vitasse.

But now a very disquieting situation revealed itself. The 1st Londons had failed to carry their objective—the Cojeul Switch Line—their C.O. was mortally wounded, and Captain Eiloart, who had temporarily taken command of the Battalion, reported to Colonel King that his Battalion had suffered very heavy casualties, was very disorganised, and had only four company officers left.

The C.O., 1/7th Middlesex ordered Captain Eiloart to reorganise his men (who were in the sunken road and the German front-line trench, known as Neuville Vitasse Trench) and deliver a fresh attack on the Hindenburg Line (Cojeul Switch) at once in order to clear a way for the attack on the Henin-Wancourt Line. The time was 1.45 p.m. Colonel King then ordered Captain Cater (" A," Hampstead and Highgate) and Captain Neighbour (" B," Barnet and Enfield) to advance with their Companies and drive the attack home. Tottenham (" D " Company, under 2/Lieut. Cousins) was to support the attack, and Hornsey (" C " Company, under 2/Lieut. Vickerage) was to remain in reserve.

Carrying the 1st Londons along with them, the 1/7th Middlesex, working their way gradually forward through the thick mud which on all sides impeded rapid progress, succeeded in capturing Telegraph Hill Trench, the first of the trenches of the Hindenburg Line (Cojeul Switch). They had accomplished this by 3 p.m., and at that hour were reorganising. But their position was very insecure, for, at about 2.30 p.m., a liaison officer from the 21st Brigade (30th Division), on the immediate right of the Middlesex, reported that the 18th King's Regt. (of that Brigade) had failed to capture the German front-line trenches, being held up by uncut wire, and were digging in with the 18th Manchesters in support. Apparently, therefore, there were no prospects from that quarter of a fresh attack on the enemy.

This news revealed a grave situation.

The 1/7th Middlesex were now in the midst of the German system of trenches on the extreme right of the British line, touch had not yet been obtained with the Battalion on the left, and the right flank was not only exposed, but in immediate contact with the Germans, actually sharing the same trench with them.

1/7TH BATTALION. 9TH APRIL.

In front of Telegraph Hill Trench were three communication trenches (Thumb, Nail and Pore) leading to the Ibex Trench, the latter the last trench in the Cojeul Switch system. Between the two trenches was a thick belt of wire. On the right of one, at right angles to the Middlesex, was a long communication trench from Neuville Vitasse Trench to Ibex Trench, known as Lion Lane. South-east of Lion Lane there was a perfect maze of trenches leading to the Henin-Wancourt Line, and in this maze was a German strong point known as " The Egg." From the eastern portion of Lion Lane the enemy was able to enfilade Telegraph Hill Trench and any advance thence to Ibex Trench.

It was evident, therefore, that as soon as the enemy realised the position he would not be long in launching heavy counter-attacks against the exposed right of the Middlesex. Colonel King decided that the best plan to adopt (in order to deny the enemy time in which to organise a counter-attack) was to hit hard *at once*. Accordingly he issued orders to the 1st Londons to cover the right flank by occupying Lion Lane, and get into touch with the 18th King's Regt., whilst " A," " B " and " D " Companies of the Middlesex attacked Ibex Trench. But as the 1st Londons were still in a disorganised state, " C " Company of the Middlesex was ordered to remain in Neuville Vitasse Trench and establish a block at its junction with Lion Lane.

No sooner had the three attacking companies of Middlesex advanced to the assault of Ibex Trench than a murderous machine-gun fire, in enfilade, swept their ranks. The " going " was terrible, and it was only with the utmost difficulty that the troops could drag themselves through the glue-like mud which clung to them fast and held them back.

This attack was a failure.

It was obvious that, as long as those cursed machine guns on the right remained in action the capture of Ibex Trench was impossible. A fresh attack was ordered. " A," " B " and " D " Companies were to send strong bombing parties simultaneously down all communication trenches, backing up the bombers with the full strength of the companies. This second attack was ordered at 7.55 p.m., and it took time to reorganise companies after the first attack.

1/7TH BATTALION.
9TH APRIL.

The second attack was launched, and also failed, mainly owing to the dense masses of mud which clogged the trenches and formed an almost impassable obstacle. So thick and adhesive was the mud that only with the greatest difficulty was it possible to drag men out.

But the Middlesex men were undaunted : they *would* have that trench. All through the night, therefore, carrying parties were employed in bringing up fresh supplies of bombs, and preparations were made for a third attempt at 3 a.m. on 10th.

10TH APRIL.

This time the attack was a complete success, the bombing parties successfully forced their way down the communication trenches, and Ibex Trench was cleared of the enemy, 52 unwounded prisoners and three trench mortars being captured. Shortly afterwards touch with the London Scottish was obtained on the left, just north of the Wancourt Road. Casualties during these attacks had been unusually light owing to the absence of shell fire, but 2/Lieut. R. P. Perry was killed and Captain Neighbour and Lieuts. Bentliff and Monroe were wounded.

With the capture of the eastern end of the Cojeul Switch (in the early hours of 10th April) the 1/7th Middlesex had cleared their immediate front and offensive action was now possible on the threatened right flank.

It is, however, necessary to leave for a while the story of the attack down the Cojeul Switch and revert to the 9th, upon which date other battalions of the Regiment entered into the battlefield.

4TH BATTALION.

The third system of German trenches, known as the Feuchy Line (running northwards from Feuchy Chapel to the Scarpe, just east of Feuchy village) had been already broken by the 15th Division when the 37th Division passed through to widen the breach and attack Monchy le Preux. The 111th and 112th Brigades of the Division were, however, to make the initial attack, the 63rd Brigade (which contained the 4th Middlesex) was to be in Divisional Reserve.

9TH APRIL.

The 4th Battalion (Lieut.-Colonel W. I. Webb-Bowen), having drawn tools and equipment, had billeted the night of 8th April in Duisans. At 5.30 a.m. on the 9th the " Die-Hards," in a heavy rain, with other units of the 63rd Brigade, took the road to Arras. The column was delayed for about an hour and a-half on the St. Pol-Arras road between Dainville and Arras, but by 11 a.m. was moving through the town to its assembly positions. Before reaching the latter, however, a stroke of bad luck robbed the Middlesex of their C.O. *4TH BATTALION.*

The Battalion had reached Arras Station when suddenly there was a roar, followed by numerous detonations; splinters and projectiles hurtled through the air, and for a few moments pandemonium reigned. A large dump of ammunition beneath the railway bridge and about 200 yards from the Middlesex had exploded. Lieut.-Colonel Webb-Bowen was wounded and several other casualties incurred. The Battalion, being so near the dump, was fortunate in escaping heavier casualties, though the loss of its C.O. was serious enough. Captain and Adjutant Boden then assumed command until Major A. G. Dawson arrived from the transport lines. *9TH APRIL.*

By about 12.30 p.m. the Middlesex had reached their assembly positions, with Battalion Headquarters at the junction of Ivy Street and Duplicate Reserve line. Here, until mid-afternoon, the Battalion waited in reserve, but at that hour the whole Brigade advanced to Battery Valley (west of Feuchy village and Broken Mill), where by 6 p.m. all units were in position and awaiting orders to make a further advance.

At about 7.30 p.m. the Brigade moved forward to Orange Hill, the 8th Somersets and 8th Lincolns on the right and left respectively, the 4th Middlesex in support of both Battalions and 10th Y. and L. in reserve.

Late that night the situation of the 63rd Brigade was as follows :—Somersets digging in on Orange Hill, with 8th Lincolns on their left ; 4th Middlesex in support along the track south of Broken Mill ; 10th Y. and L. in Battery Valley.

Just after midnight the Middlesex received orders to move up on the left of the Lincolns along the sunken road north-east of Orange Hill. Two hours later the Y. and L. came up on the left of the Middlesex. Such was the position when dawn broke on the 10th. *10TH APRIL.*

Of the part taken by the 13th Middlesex (Lieut.-Colonel J. Greene) there are no records. Presumably the Battalion was in support or reserve until the night 9th/10th, for the Battalion Diary has only the following entry on 9th April : " At 5.30 a.m. the Canadians attacked from Kennedy Crater southwards. On the night of 9th/10th April ' A ' and ' D ' Companies returned from the Château de la Haie and relieved the 44th and 46th Canadians." The next entry in the Battalion Diary is dated 11th April. *13TH BATTALION. 9TH/10TH APRIL. 11TH APRIL.*

1/7TH BATTALION.

The general results of the first day of the battle are thus described in the despatches: "At the end of the day, therefore, our troops were established deeply in the enemy's positions on the whole front of attack. We had gained a firm footing in the enemy's third line on both banks of the Scarpe, and had made an important breach in the enemy's last fully completed line of defence."

South of the Scarpe the villages of St. Martin-sur-Cojeul, Neuville Vitasse, Tilloy and Feuchy had been wrested from the enemy, whilst north of the river the line ran from east of Fampoux round (and including) the Hyderabad Redoubt in a north-westerly direction, taking in at least half of the Vimy Ridge before it rejoined the old Canadian front line west of Petit Vimy. Many powerfully defended localities had been stormed and captured, and the Hindenburg Line from Neuville Vitasse northwards had fallen.

Such, approximately, was the position when the advance was continued on the morning of the 10th April.

Throughout the night 9th/10th carrying parties were employed in fetching up fresh supplies of bombs for the attack on Ibex Trench to be launched by the 1/7th Middlesex at 3 a.m. on the morning of 10th.

10TH APRIL.

There was no half-heartedness about this attack. The bombing parties, moving simultaneously down all communication trenches as before, took no denial. They bombed the enemy back, killing or taking prisoner those who showed fight or refused to surrender. This time—the third attempt—Ibex Trench was cleared right out of the enemy, 52 unwounded Germans being sent back to the prisoners' cages; three trench mortars were also captured. The capture of Ibex Trench had cleared the way for offensive action down the Cojeul Switch towards the Henin-Wancourt Line—the final objective. But before reaching the latter a powerful system of trenches had to be cleared.

The position merits description.

With the capture of Ibex Trench the 1/7th Middlesex now faced north-east and south-east, *i.e.*, Ibex Trench and Lion Lane respectively. Nepal Trench, the front trench of the Henin-Wancourt Line, ran from north-east to south-west, and between Nepal Trench and Lion Lane there was a regular maze of main and communication trenches, clustered about a strong point known as The Egg. This strong point, with the trenches about it, of which the principal (leading from Lion Lane to Nepal Trench) was the Zoo Trench, dangerously threatened the right flank of the Middlesex, who throughout the night had momentarily expected a heavy counter-attack, seeing that the enemy was only some 30 or 40 yards away. Had the Germans counter-attacked before the capture of Ibex Trench the consequences must have been serious. But they did not—they were either too worn-out or else did not appreciate the situation before them. At intervals they fired bursts of rifle and machine-gun fire, but that was all.   1/7TH AND 1/8TH BATTALIONS.

About 7.30 a.m. on 10th a warning order was received from 167th Brigade Headquarters that at 12 noon the attack was to be made down the Cojeul Switch towards Nepal Trench. The same warning stated that the 9th London Regiment, placed at the disposal of the 167th Brigade, was advancing to co-operate by prolonging the right of the 1/7th Middlesex. The 1/8th Middlesex had apparently also received the warning order, for their Diary states that at 11 a.m. "the Battalion moved into position for the attack on Nepal Trench." The C.O. of the 1/7th, however, seems (reasonably enough) to have regarded the Brigade warning as meaning that only his Battalion and the 9th Londons were to attack at noon, and he made his dispositions accordingly.   10TH APRIL.

Two Companies were to assemble in Lion Lane with two in support in a small trench just behind and parallel with it. Tottenham (" D " Company) on the right, with Hornsey (" C " Company) in support, was to move down Zoo Trench (as the continuation of Telegraph Hill Trench was called), whilst Hampstead and Highgate (" A " Company), with Barnet and Enfield (" B " Company) in support, was to advance down Ibex Trench.

At 11.30 a.m. further detailed orders for the attack arrived from Brigade Headquarters. These orders stated that, preceded by a heavy bombardment, five Battalions, 9th Londons on the right, then the 1/7th Middlesex, 1/8th Middlesex, and 3rd Londons on the left, with the 1st Londons in support, the attack would be delivered across the open. But the runner who had brought these orders having to advance through shell fire, had taken so long to reach the 1/7th Battalion that it was too late to modify the instructions already given to company commanders without delaying the whole attack and so losing the benefit of the bombardment. Colonel King therefore considered he was

1/7TH BATTALION.
10TH APRIL.

justified in abiding by the orders previously received at 7.30 a.m., especially as at noon only the 9th Londons were to be seen.

At 12 noon, therefore, the 1/7th began their attack. Lieut. Cousins, with the Tottenham men, began bombing a way down Zoo Trench; Captain Cater, with Hampstead and Highgate, similarly set out down Ibex Trench; the 9th Londons advanced down Neuville Vitasse Trench. None of them got very far. Apart from the murderous hail of machine-gun and rifle bullets (principally from The Egg and the network of trenches about this strong point), the thick, clinging mud was a serious obstacle: how serious may be judged from the fact that Lieut. Whisson, who was now commanding Barnet and Enfield, became bogged and it took two hours to get him out.

This first attempt was unsuccessful. That deadly machine-gun fire had broken up the attack. Colonel King then moved a Light Trench-mortar Section (under Lieut. Evans), which had been attached to the Battalion to deal with this menace. This officer succeeded in a lucky burst of fire in dumping his shells right into the German machine-gun position, killing every man in it.

At 2.15 p.m. the C.O. ordered another bombing attack down Ibex and Zoo Trenches. Pressed with great vigour, the German resistance gradually crumbled away. With bomb and bayonet the Die-Hard Territorials drove the enemy out, one after the other, of the four communication trenches that linked Zoo and Ibex together, and by 4.20 p.m. Companies were consolidating a shallow trench just in front of the barbed wire in front of Nepal Trench, *i.e.*, the Henin-Wancourt Line.

They had almost annihilated the German Regiment (31st) opposed to them, for to the 52 prisoners already sent back another 198, including five officers, were added. The Middlesex men had left behind them trenches and dug-outs full of German dead —the place was a horrible shambles. "As the first batch of prisoners came up," said Colonel King, "a young soldier at the head of the escort, his sense of discipline overcome by the excitement of the moment, called out, ' We have brought you 50 of the blighters, Sir, and there are heaps more to follow.' "

Fighting for possession of The Egg had been desperate. Protected by wire entanglements, in places 40 feet wide, with trenches cleverly concealed, the capture of this fort (or strong point) was a fine piece of work. The artillery had first of all bombarded it, making it Hades for the defenders. Then Tottenham, led by Lieut. Cousins, bombed their way into it, joining hands in the centre with a party of 9th Londons. But no sooner had the British artillery ceased shelling the point than the Germans, probably realising that the position was as good as lost, began in turn to shell it vigorously. It was here that Lieut. Cousins had his left arm smashed by a bullet and refused to go back and have his wound dressed until he had seen his Company complete its task. Later in the day he was superintending the consolidation of the final position of the Company when he fell dead, shot through the head by a sniper. A very gallant officer, a true Die-Hard, of whom his C.O. said, " There was no finer spirit in the 1/7th." ^{1/7TH AND 1/8TH BATTALIONS. 10TH APRIL.}

In the meantime the 1/8th Middlesex *had* not only moved into position at 11 a.m., but at 12 noon, in accordance with Brigade orders, began their advance. Hostile machine-gun fire on the cross roads east of Ibex Trench had, however, held up the attack. Nevertheless, " B " and " D " Companies got within 200 yards of Nepal Trench, where they dug in with " A " and " C " Companies in support in a short trench about 200 yards in rear. Shell fire during the advance had been heavy, and no sooner had the Battalion dug in than the enemy's snipers got to work with deadly effect. In this position the 1/8th remained throughout the remainder of the 10th.

The 11th Middlesex (12th Division) remained in the old British front line throughout the whole of the 10th and did not move forward again until the morning of 11th April. 11TH BATTALION. 11TH APRIL.

At 10.30 a.m. on 10th the 4th Middlesex, in common with other battalions of the 63rd brigade (37th Division) received verbal orders to advance to Lone Copse Valley, east of Orange Hill. The order of advance, from right to left, was to be Somersets, Lincolns, Middlesex and York. and Lancs. Regiments. 4TH BATTALION. 10TH APRIL.

It took an hour to organise the troops for the advance, but many more hours before the objective was reached, for the enemy had put down a very heavy barrage on Orange Hill, while artillery and machine-gun fire from the direction of Fampoux swept the ground over which the advance was to take place.

It was 11.30 a.m. when the troops moved forward. Taking advantage of every shell hole and every bit of cover available, that advance was a tortuous business. So accurate was the enemy's fire and so necessary was it to shelter wherever the

> **4TH BATTALION.**
> **10TH APRIL.**

ground offered possibilities, that at 3.30 p.m. only two companies of the Somersets on the right, two of Lincolns, and a half company of Middlesex on the left had arrived in Lone Copse Valley. The Y. and L., who were to go forward on the left of the Middlesex, were held up altogether, and the latter therefore had an exposed flank open not only to fire from Fampoux, but to counter-attack.

By 6 p.m. the Lincolns had pushed on beyond Lone Copse Valley to about 800 yards north-west of Monchy, but the enemy's fire was too deadly and costly, and they withdrew again to the valley, where, in conjunction with the Somersets and Middlesex, a line was consolidated running along the crest of the ridge, the Die-Hards (on the left) forming a defensive flank across the valley. At about 6.30 p.m. the Germans made a half-hearted attempt to counter-attack, but they were soon beaten off. The last entry in the Battalion Diary on 10th April states that at 8.30 p.m. all battalions were re-forming and reorganising owing to casualties.

At nightfall on the 10th April the general situation along the whole front was that during the day the capture of the last remaining elements of the enemy's third-line defences south of the Scarpe had been completed. On the left bank of the River little further progress had been made; that portion of Hill 145 on the Vimy Ridge, which had hitherto held up the Canadians, was swept clear by the latter, who took over 200 prisoners.

> **1/7TH AND 1/8TH BATTALIONS.**
> **11TH APRIL.**

At about 2 a.m. on 11th the 1/7th Middlesex received orders that a lodgment must be effected in the Henin-Wancourt Line, in order to enable the 1/8th to pass through and bomb their way up Nepal Trench in a north-easterly direction.

Orders were accordingly issued to " C " and " A " Companies of the 1/7th to bomb down Puma and Ibex Trenches and establish posts at their junction with Nepal Trench. The bombing attack began, and by 5 a.m. the posts were successfully established, the intervening portions of the two trenches being cleared of the enemy. A series of small counter-attacks were easily beaten off.

The bombing attack by the 1/7th had yielded no less than 118 more prisoners, though 60 of them had to be handed over to the 9th Londons, as men could not be spared for escort duty.

At about 5.30 a.m. a bombing party of the 1/8th arrived at the junction of Puma and Ibex Trenches with Nepal Trench, *i.e.*, where the 1/7th had established a block.

At 7 a.m. the 1/8th began to bomb their way up Nepal Trench, but the enemy's snipers were extremely active, and this first attempt was held up until the 1/7th brought a Lewis gun into action, which effectively kept down hostile rifle fire. The second attempt at about 8.15 a.m. was successful, the 1/8th capturing 20 prisoners and a machine gun, while many Germans were killed. All day long the gallant bombers of the 1/8th stuck to their job, taking a further 23 prisoners, and at last, at 4.15 p.m., the Battalion reported that Nepal Trench was clear of the enemy. At 9 p.m. that night the 1/8th Middlesex were relieved and marched back to trenches in the neighbourhood of Beurains. The 1/7th had already been relieved and had moved back to Agny.

1/7TH AND 1/8TH BATTALIONS. 11TH APRIL.

During the three days (9th–11th April) the 1/7th had lost 2 officers killed—2/Lieuts. Cousins and Perry—and 8 wounded. In other ranks their losses were 25 killed, 88 wounded and 1 missing, but as the C.O. said: " Never did the Battalion fight a finer fight, nor with greater good fortune or more brilliant success, and the men were justly proud of the good work they had accomplished. . . . The 7th Middlesex fought continuously for two days and two nights, destroying the 31st Regiment, and afterwards attacking the 86th Regiment and taking from it 118 prisoners."

The losses of the 1/8th Battalion for the same period were 2 officers killed and 7 officers wounded; in other ranks their casualties were 28 killed, 135 wounded, and 7 missing.

For the 4th Middlesex the 11th April was a day of discomfort. Although the Battalion made no direct attack upon the enemy, hostile shell fire, machine-gun and rifle fire were severe, and all movement was carried out under great difficulties.

4TH BATTALION. 11TH APRIL.

Midnight, 10th/11th April, found the 63rd Brigade on a line in Lone Copse Valley, a map with the 37th G.S. Diary placing the Battalions in the following order, from right to left: 8th Somersets, 8th Lincolns, 4th Middlesex and 10th Y. and L. Regiment.

At 3 a.m. on 11th the C.O. of the 4th Middlesex received orders which stated that the advance was to continue at 5 a.m., the 3rd Division on the right and the 15th Division on the left of the 37th Division. Of the latter the 112th Brigade would be on the right and the 111th Brigade on the left; the 63rd Brigade would assemble in Divisional Reserve when the 15th Division had passed through the Green Line.

4TH BATTALION.
11TH APRIL.

No movement of the 63rd Brigade took place until 11 a.m., when just before that hour Brigade Headquarters, having received a report that the 15th Division had reached the line Keeling Copse–Pelves, all four Battalions of the Brigade were ordered to move forward to the high ground at Bois des Aubepines and just south of it. The 10th Y. and L. were to form the advanced guard, the Middlesex, Lincolns and Somersets following in that order, the latter Battalion in Brigade Reserve, the Middlesex to prolong the line of the Y. and L. to the left, and the Lincolns to support the two forward Battalions.

The advance began at 11 a.m., but the Y. and L. could not get forward. Machine-gun fire swept the line of advance, the country being very open. Half an hour later the Middlesex deployed in rear of the Y. and L., ready to go forward. For about an hour they held this position, but at 12.30 p.m., under orders from the Brigade, moved to the right of the Y. and L. along the side of the road running south-west to Monchy. The advance was by platoons in file along the road, the latter being almost entirely devoid of cover. The movement was observed by the enemy, who immediately put down a very heavy artillery and machine-gun barrage. But eventually, by advancing in short rushes in parties of 12, the Battalion got through with comparatively few casualties. There was a high wind at the time which deflected the enemy's rifle and machine-gun fire.

Arrived in Monchy, the C.O. of the Middlesex was informed by the C.O. Cavalry (who were then in the village) that he was expecting a counter-attack on his right, and that he required assistance. A platoon of 20 men of the Middlesex, with two Lewis guns, was therefore sent off to the south-west corner of the village. Officer patrols pushed out failed to find the flanks of the preceding Brigade (111th), and the defence of Monchy was therefore organised in a series of posts which were established by about 3 p.m. All this while the enemy heavily bombarded the village, and all men who were not actually engaged in digging took refuge in cellars. At 5.30 p.m. another officer patrol reconnoitred the whole of the village and outskirts, but still it appeared that neither the 111th nor 112th Brigades had advanced east of Monchy. All posts were therefore consolidated and all approaches from east of the village were patrolled. Excepting for intermittent shell fire nothing happened during the night, and at 11 p.m. the Middlesex were relieved and moved back to Battery Valley, where the Battalion remained until 2 p.m. on 12th, returning at 4TH BATTALION. that hour to Arras. On the 13th the Middlesex men marched 14TH APRIL. to Doisans, and on 14th to Agnez-les-Duisans.*

The records of the 11th Middlesex for the 11th and 12th April 11TH BATTALION. are of a similar character to those of the 4th Battalion.

The 11th Middlesex passed the night, 10th/11th April, in the old British line, but at 9.30 a.m. on 11th, led by the Adjutant, 11TH APRIL. the Battalion moved forward to Halifax Trench, astride the Cambrai road, two companies on each side of the road. At 8 p.m. the Battalion again moved forward, taking over a somewhat hazy outpost line between Monchy and Guemappe from 112th Brigade (37th Division) ; the 36th Brigade had been ordered to relieve the former. In moving forward a " Crump " fell in the middle of a platoon of " D " Company, causing about a dozen casualties.

The night was comparatively quiet, and throughout the 12th 12TH APRIL. little of importance occurred. At 8 p.m. orders were received that the Battalion would be relieved, but it was 7 a.m. before the relief was complete, after which the tired Middlesex men marched back to the Caves at Ronville, where they slept throughout the 13th. On the 14th at 7.30 a.m. the Battalion (in Brigade) 14TH APRIL. marched off westwards, billeting for the night in Habarcq. Their casualties throughout the operations were about 196, of which number 50 were killed, 120 wounded and 20 missing.

Both the 16th (29th Division) and the 17th Middlesex (2nd 16TH AND Division) moved into the battle area during the operations 17TH BATTALIONS. between 9th and 14th April, but neither took part in the fighting. 9TH TO 14TH The 16th relieved the 2nd Hants in Monchy on the night of 14th. APRIL. The 17th were at Ecurie.

The 13th Middlesex (24th Division) at 9 a.m. on 14th moved 13TH BATTALION. to Aix Noulette, and then advanced *via* Arras road and Ration 14TH APRIL. Trenches over the open in artillery formation under shell fire to Angres, to form Brigade Reserve in the advance on Lens.

(II) THE SECOND BATTLE OF THE SCARPE, 1917:
23rd–24th April.

The results of the First Battle of the Scarpe had been to push the British line 4 miles further east : wide stretches of territory

* No casualties are given in the Battalion Diary.

13TH BATTALION.

as well as all the dominating features forming the immediate object of the attack had been gained, together with thousands of prisoners and guns, and a large number of German divisions had been drawn to the battle area which otherwise would have been diverted further south against the French on the Aisne.

The French offensive, originally planned to follow the British offensive within two or three days, had to be postponed owing to weather conditions. It was, however, due to take place on 16th April.

In order to assist our Allies the British pressure had to be maintained, and accordingly the First Battle of the Scarpe had scarcely ended when preparations were made for the next operations. But bad weather, the strength already developed by the enemy, and the time necessary to complete artillery dispositions, interfered with an immediate resumption of the offensive, and it was 23rd April before the next great attack (originally planned for 21st, but postponed) took place.

At 4.45 a.m., on a front of about 9 miles from Croisilles to Gavrelle, the German trenches were again stormed after they had been subjected to a perfect tornado of shell fire.

In the meantime, the Canadian Corps (to which the 24th Division was still attached) was engaged in pushing on towards Lens.

14TH APRIL.

It will be remembered that on the night of 14th April the 13th Middlesex had moved to Angres to form the Brigade Reserve in the advance on Lens. At 7 a.m. the next morning operation orders were received, and the Battalion advanced in small parties to the front line, then to the eastern edge of the Bois de Riavmont. This wood was held by two companies of the 12th Royal Fusiliers, through whom the 13th Middlesex were to advance, with the suburbs of Lens as their final objective. This advance, however, was not to be pushed in the face of serious opposition. At 9.15 a.m. a patrol of 12 men under 2/Lieut. Cartledge debouched from the wood, but at once came under heavy machine-gun fire from houses and trenches in Cite Riavmont. The officer in charge of the patrol was wounded and seven other ranks were killed or wounded. Patrols from "A" Company on the right and "C" Company on the left, however, pushed on and made progress in face of steady opposition. A footing was obtained in the northern end of Cite Riavmont, where advanced posts were established. At dusk, however, they were ordered to

withdraw by the G.O.C. Division, who had visited the front line, 13TH
and they fell back to the line of the wood. On this day the BATTALION.
Battalion lost a popular young officer—2/Lieut. F. D. Yates— 15TH APRIL.
" an excellent officer liked by everyone," as well as 50 other
casualties.

On the 16th, after artillery preparation, the operations were
resumed and progress was again made, but " A " Company on
the right came up against a strong position practically undamaged
by the artillery fire. One officer—2/Lieut. L. C. Vogan*—was
severely wounded on this day and about 20 other ranks were also
casualties.

In the evening the Battalion was relieved and marched back
to Souchez in Brigade Support. On the 19th the 13th Middlesex
marched to Marles-les-Mines, thence on the following day to
Flechin. They were not again engaged in the Battles of Arras,
1917, nor in the minor operations on 22nd south-west of Lens. 22ND APRIL.

In the battle which opened on 23rd April the four sectors of 1ST BATTALION.
the line of special interest to Middlesex men were (i) south-west
of Cherisy, where the 1st Battalion with other troops of the
33rd Division attacked the enemy, (ii) east of Monchy, west of
Infantry Hill, the 29th Division attacking in that part of the
line, (iii) north of the Scarpe, west of Rœux, where the infantry
of the 37th Division fought their way towards Greenland Hill,
and (iv) just north-west of Gavrelle, where the 2nd Division,
by fire demonstration, assisted the 63rd Naval Division in the
attack on that place.

During the First Battle of the Scarpe the 33rd Division was
in reserve. On the 12th the 98th Brigade moved into the Cojeul
Valley in close support, relieving the 19th Brigade in the Hindenburg Line on 16th, the 1st Middlesex and 4th Suffolks moving
up into the front line, though, owing to faulty guides, it was the
17th before the Middlesex were able to relieve two companies 17TH APRIL.
of the 20th Royal Fusiliers in some isolated trenches (" mere
ditches," the Diary calls them). But the Battalion was relieved
on 20th and 21st, and on 22nd was in the sunken road between 22ND APRIL.
Henin-sur-Cojeul and Neuville Vitasse preparing for the operations on 23rd.

The men were issued with bombs, rifle grenades, Véry lights,
ground flares and sandbags, and at 4.30 p.m. the Battalion again
marched off to the front line, relieving the Cameronians. These

* Died of wounds, 28th April, 1917.

1ST BATTALION. 22ND APRIL.
trenches were some 1,500 yards south-east of Heninel, not quite half-way between that village and Fontaine-lez-Croisilles. "A" Company was on the right and "C" on the left, "B" and "D" (right and left respectively) occupying trenches in rear of the front line. At 11.30 p.m. the two latter Companies moved into their assembly trenches just behind the front line.

By 1.30 a.m. all companies had taken up their allotted positions, "A" and "C" the first wave, "B" and "D" the second wave. Zero hour was 4.45 a.m.

18TH BATTALION.
The 18th Middlesex (Pioneers of the 33rd Division) were at Boyelles. They had for days been at work on the roads and communications. Their orders were to keep two companies ("B" and "D") in bivouacs ready to move at short notice from 4.45 a.m. on 23rd for work on the communications in the areas of the 98th and 100th Infantry Brigades respectively, in the event of the operations being successful. The remaining companies were in Divisional Reserve under the C.R.E.

1ST AND 18TH BATTALIONS. 23RD APRIL.
Under cover of the barrage, described in the diaries as "excellent," the 98th Brigade attacked the enemy at 4.45 a.m. (23rd), 4th Suffolks on the right, 2nd A. and S. Highlanders in the centre, and 1st Middlesex on the left. There were two separate final objectives, different means being necessary to reach each. The Suffolks had to bomb down the Hindenburg Line to the Sensée, whilst the Highlanders and the Middlesex made a frontal attack across the open; the centre of their first objective was a small oblong copse.

The attack of the Suffolks proceeded well down both trenches of the Hindenburg Line, but the Highlanders, in the centre, and "A" and "B" Companies of the Middlesex, were hung up in front of the small copse. The two left Companies of the latter Battalion ("C" and "D"), however, reached their first objective without much opposition, where 30 prisoners were taken and sent back. They then pressed on to their final objective, which they reached successfully and dug themselves in. Here they were joined by "A" Company of the Highlanders, who had fought their way past the copse. But now, unfortunately, a serious position presented itself to these three Companies, for it appeared that they were not only in the air, but the enemy was still between them and their original "jumping-off" line. Captain Beesham, therefore, made his way back along the Hindenburg Line in order to report the situation to Brigade Headquarters. But whilst he was away the enemy counter-attacked and succeeded in cutting off a portion of the Hindenburg Line, thus completely cutting off all communication with "C" and "D" Companies in their forward exposed position. To make matters worse, troops on the left of these two Companies fell back, taking with them a small party of Middlesex "moppers-up" which had taken possession of that portion of the first objective captured by "C" and "D."

1ST BATTALION. 23RD APRIL.

The position as it affected the 1st Middlesex now stood as follows: The enemy was again in full possession of his original front line; "A" and "B" Companies of the Battalion were held up in front of the copse, i.e., the line of the first objective, and were digging themselves in; the left flank of the Battalion was absolutely in the air; the enemy had regained a portion of the Hindenburg Line; "C" and "D" Companies had broken through and had reached their final objective, but were entirely cut off, the enemy being in front and behind them.

At 12 noon all units of the 98th Brigade, with the exception of "A" Company of the 2nd A. and S. Highlanders and "C" and "D" Companies of the 1st Middlesex, were back in their original lines. Indeed, it is with these very gallant fellows who, though surrounded and subjected to violent efforts to dislodge them and capture them, resisted every attempt and bloodily repulsed the enemy again and again, that the story is chiefly concerned. The old Die-Hard spirit once more shone clearly, and the indomitable pluck of the Middlesex and their Highland comrades added yet another splendid incident to their already glorious Regimental history.

Another attack by the 98th Brigade was ordered for 6.24 p.m., to be preceded by, and under cover of, a heavy barrage. Only a very slight advance was made, and by this time orderlies, signallers and officers' servants had all been pressed into the thin line.

At 8 p.m. news was received at Battalion Headquarters, 1st Middlesex, that the enemy had formed a barricade in the Hindenburg Line and was advancing towards Brigade Headquarters, but he was first held up and then driven back to his original position by the Suffolks.

Under cover of darkness, men who had been lying out all day in shell holes crawled back, and the front line of the Brigade now consisted of about 300 men from 1st Middlesex, 2nd R.W. Fusiliers and 1st Cameronians.

1ST BATTALION.

But no word was received of the gallant fellows who were surrounded. The barrage for the attack at 6.24 p.m. had passed over them, but apart from knocking their trenches about considerably had fortunately inflicted very few casualties.

The night 23rd/24th passed quietly, though the enemy was obviously nervous, for he continually fired Véry lights.

24TH APRIL.

As dawn broke on the 24th, certain movements on the part of the enemy gave rise to the suspicion that he had vacated his position. Patrols were sent out and returned with the information that the Germans had fallen back. The 1st Middlesex, therefore, advanced at once and took possession of the hostile front-line trenches, pushing out other patrols to discover the extent of the enemy's retirement. A message now came in from the two forward Companies (" C " and " D ") : they were still holding on to their position, they had even taken a few prisoners, but both officers had been wounded.

During the morning the 1st Middlesex were relieved by the 20th Royal Fusiliers, but owing to the enemy's activity it was deemed unwise to withdraw " C " and " D " Companies until nightfall. But as soon as possible after darkness had fallen the intrepid Die-Hards and Highlanders were relieved, after a 40-hours' fight, completely surrounded, and reached the sunken roads at 11 p.m. It is interesting to note that of the 16 Lewis guns which the two Companies had with them, all were brought back, only one having been damaged.

25TH APRIL.

The Battalion was now once more united, and on the 25th marched back from the sunken roads, through Henin-sur-Cojeul, to Grosville. Before the Die-Hards left the line, however, the G.O.C. Division visited the Battalion and personally congratulated the two Companies on their tenacity and success. These congratulations were followed later (on 1st May) by a letter from the Third Army Commander—General Sir E. H. H. Allenby—who had been furnished with a report of that gallant fight: " I have read this account with great pride and admiration. I congratulate all ranks in the 2nd Battalion Argyll and Sutherland Highlanders and the 1st Battalion Middlesex Regiment on the staunchness and bravery of their two splendid companies."*

16TH BATTALION.
23RD APRIL.

East of Monchy-le-Preux the 29th Division, at Zero on 23rd, had attacked Infantry Hill, and although the 16th Middlesex (Major T. W. O'Reilly commanding) were not in the assault, the

* There were three altogether.

Battalion was attached to the 88th Brigade and manned the defences of Monchy. [margin: 16TH BATTALION.]

After the Public School Battalion had taken over front-line trenches in Monchy from the 2nd Hants on the night of 14th April, several days were spent in making new defences in the village. This tour was not without heavy casualties, for 1 officer was killed, another wounded, and in other ranks the losses were 7 killed, 59 wounded and 3 missing. On relief the Battalion moved back to Ronville, again moving forward on the night of 22nd/23rd to positions between Orange Hill and Monchy for the operations due to begin on the latter date.

Heavy fighting was still going on when, about noon on 23rd, the 16th Battalion moved to the following positions: Battalion Headquarters about half a mile west of La Bergere and just north of the Arras-Cambrai road, " B " Company to the junction of Spring, Pick and Shovel Trenches, " A " Company garrisoned a line of strong points astride the sunken road leading south-east of Monchy and about a mile from the village, " D " Company was in Shrapnel Trench; two platoons of " C " Company held a position from the small square copse west of Bois du Vert to a trench south of that point, the remaining two platoons being in the sunken road already mentioned. A heavy counter-attack developed during the day against the small square copse, but the Lewis guns of " B " Company helped to beat off the assault. [margin: 23RD APRIL.]

On the night 24th/25th the Battalion was relieved and moved back to Arras, having lost during the operations 6 officers wounded, 13 other ranks killed, 75 wounded and 10 missing.* North of the Scarpe the 37th Division had at Zero hour on 23rd attacked Greenland Hill, the final objective of the Division, crossing the hill in a north-to-south direction. The 37th Division had on the 18th April been ordered to take part in the operations instead of the 4th Division, which was to be withdrawn. All units of the former, therefore, moved up on the night of 20th/21st to relieve the latter, the 63rd Brigade taking over the divisional front line, which ran from (and including) the Hyderabad Redoubt on the south to a point south-west of Gavrelle, where the left divisional boundary joined up with the right of the 63rd (Naval) Division. [margin: 24TH/25TH APRIL.]

The attack was carried out by the 63rd Brigade on the right and 111th Brigade on the left, and at Zero hour (4.45 a.m.) on

---

* No names are given, and both the Battalion Diary and Brigade Headquarters Diary are lacking in details of an interesting nature.

4TH BATTALION.
23RD APRIL.

23rd the units of the former were disposed in the following positions: The 4th Middlesex (Lieut.-Colonel A. G. Dawson commanding), the right attacking Battalion of the 63rd Brigade, held the Hyderabad Redoubt and an oblique line, the right facing almost north (in Clyde Trench), the left facing east (in a portion of Harrow Trench); the 10th Y. and L. were on the left, facing north-east; the 8th S.L.I. supported the Middlesex and the 8th Lincolns the Yorks. and Lancs.

When Zero hour arrived the morning was dull, and the smoke which was used in the 18-pdr. barrage obscured the first objective from the troops as they advanced. The first objective was Chile Trench, which ran obliquely across the front of attack. But in spite of the difficulties of that advance and in maintaining direction, the first objective was captured and the attacking troops pushed on to the Blue Line (second objective), which was roughly the line of the Roeux-Gavrelle road, crossing the Brigade front. The Middlesex by 6.30 a.m. had succeeded in reaching a line 200 yards east of this road, but then came under a murderous enfilade fire from both flanks, which were exposed, and were forced to take whatever shelter was possible. At 7 a.m. the C.O., Lieut.-Colonel Dawson, fell dead, killed by a machine-gun bullet. The Adjutant, Captain J. Boden, then took command, but at 9 a.m. he was badly wounded by shrapnel, and command of the Battalion then passed on to 2/Lieut. P. W. Smith. On the left of the Middlesex the 10th Y. and L. were so severely handled that they had been unable to reach Chile Trench, a misfortune which accounted for the heavy enfilade fire from that flank. This check had, however, been observed by the Lincolns, who, passing on through the Y. and L., attacked Chile Trench, where a party of some 50 or 60 Germans at first offered a stout resistance until their flank was turned. Chile Trench was taken by the Lincolns at about 10.30 a.m. But still the 63rd Brigade was held up.

At noon the enemy was seen forming up on the crest of Greenland Hill for a counter-attack, and shortly afterwards his infantry advanced down the western slopes in extended order and in artillery formation. But the Lewis guns, aided by rifle fire and the machine guns of the 63rd M.G.C., tore gaps in the advancing Germans, and soon their lines wavered and finally gave up the attempt, leaving the ground littered with dead and wounded. Their losses here were very heavy.

From noon onwards until 9 p.m. that night the 4th Middlesex worked hard at consolidating their position, which was by no means comfortable. Shelled all day and still subjected to machine-gun fire, work was difficult and was not carried out without further losses. At 9 p.m. they were relieved by troops of the 112th Brigade, three battalions of which should have been sent up to relieve the 63rd Brigade, which had been fighting hard all day. The Middlesex then fell back to the sunken road and during the night consolidated their line. Throughout the 24th the Battalion, shelled heavily at intervals, hung on to the position until 11 p.m., when two companies of the 9th Leicesters came up and the Middlesex men withdrew to Halo Trench, where they remained until 27th.

4TH BATTALION.
23RD APRIL.

27TH APRIL.

North of the 37th Division the 63rd Division had attacked and captured Gavrelle. In this successful operation the Naval Division had, on its left, the assistance of the 2nd Division, then occupying a line in front of Oppy Wood. The 17th Middlesex, however, were not involved in the operations on 23rd April to any serious extent, but what they saw is interesting: " The Division on our right attacked and took the village of Gavrelle. The situation on our Brigade front remained quiet until about 10.45 a.m., when the enemy started to shell heavily the whole of the front; the enemy were reported massing for counter-attack against the village of Gavrelle. The Battalion took up defensive line on railway embankment, which was shelled heavily. . . . The enemy made five counter-attacks against our right; all were repulsed with heavy losses to the enemy by our heavy artillery. The enemy could be seen easily from O.P. at Battalion Headquarters, and the whole of his counter-attacks were seen and reported on. At 7.30 p.m. the situation was reported normal again, and Battalion took up its original position. At 9.30 p.m. the Battalion was sent out to dig a defensive trench in front of railway embankment. 2/Lieut. B. H. Last killed."

17TH BATTALION.
23RD APRIL.

On the 24th the enemy again attacked the Naval Division, but on each occasion was bloodily repulsed. On this date the 17th Middlesex moved back to a camp at Roclincourt, where next day they began preparations for the next battle.

24TH APRIL.

The results of the Second Battle of the Scarpe may be summed up as follows: The villages of Guemappe and Gavrelle had been captured, as well as the whole of the high ground overlooking Fontaine-lez-Croisilles and Cherisy, and good progress had been made east of Monchy, on the left bank of the Scarpe, and on Greenland Hill.

But in order to assist the French, who were attacking on the Aisne, the British Commander-in-Chief arranged to continue the offensive at Arras until the former had attained their object. The operations east of Arras had, however, taken on the characteristics of a " wearing-out " battle.

(III) THE BATTLE OF ARLEUX,

28th-29th April.

From the strength of the enemy's resistance (which was on the increase and not diminishing) it was clear that the continued British attacks at Arras were having the desired effect—the German reserves were being drawn to that part of the line and away from the French front.

On the 28th April, on a front of about 8 miles north of Monchy-le-Preux, the enemy was again attacked by troops of the Third and First Armies. The 12th Division made progress between Monchy and the Scarpe, the 37th Division gained a little more ground on Greenland Hill, and the 2nd Division captured portions of the enemy's line in the neighbourhood of Oppy.

Zero hour was at 4.25 a.m., when both British and Canadian troops made a heavy assault on the enemy. The two days' fighting which followed the initial attack was fierce in the extreme, counter-attack after counter-attack being launched by the enemy with a lavish expenditure of men, as terrible as it was useless! The German losses in prisoners and guns were small compared with the number they lost in killed and wounded.

4TH, 1/8TH, 11TH AND 17TH BATTALIONS.

From a Regimental point of view, the chief interest in the battle centres chiefly round the 17th Battalion of the 2nd Division, for the 4th Middlesex of the 37th Division were in close support, while the 11th Battalion of the 12th Division was in reserve in the Railway Triangle east of Arras. One other Battalion—1/8th, of the 56th Division—held front-line trenches south of the Arras-Cambrai road and east of Wancourt, but they were outside the area of the operations. It is, therefore, to that fierce struggle in and around Oppy Wood and its defences that this story turns —a story full of heroic, hard fighting, but of heavy losses; an intense struggle in which the 17th Middlesex, with other units of the 2nd Division, were matched against some of the finest fighting troops then in the German Army.

11TH BATTALION.

As the 36th Brigade was in reserve, the 11th Middlesex (Lieut.-Colonel T. S. Wollocombe) were not engaged with the enemy, though both on 28th and 29th April parties of officers and men were at work digging a new line on Orange Hill.

28TH/29TH APRIL.

The 4th Middlesex (Lieut.-Colonel G. A. Bridgman) also were not in the first line of the attack on Greenland Hill. Two companies of the Battalion at 11 p.m. on 27th had moved up to Clasp Trench, the assembly trench, the other two companies in Chile Trench; the former were in close support and the latter in reserve.

4TH BATTALION.

27TH APRIL.

At Zero hour on 28th the two support companies moved forward in rear of the right attacking battalion—8th Somerset Light Infantry, of the 63rd Brigade. The darkness was intense, and it was almost impossible to see beyond 20 yards. A few minutes after Zero the enemy's guns put down a very heavy barrage, and the smoke and dust added to the difficulties experienced in keeping direction. It appears also that very soon after the advance most of the officers became casualties. The result was that all units of the Brigade lost direction and went too far to the left. Cuthbert Trench, full of Germans, was not attacked at all, and these gave a lot of trouble, as they were able to pour a heavy enfilade fire into the advancing waves of the 63rd Brigade. Parties of all battalions became separated and pushed on, some almost reaching Railway Copse, others reaching Wick Trench. During this advance they captured some prisoners, who were sent back, but three or four of these parties were recaptured by the Germans in and about Cuthbert Trench. At 6.30 p.m. the position of the Brigade was that parties of all battalions were in Whip Trench and others about 300 yards east of Cuthbert Trench. Here they dug in and remained throughout the day. At night the two reserve companies of Middlesex were sent up to reconnoitre and, if possible, turn the Germans out of Cuthbert Trench. But the latter was strongly held with machine guns, and owing to the weakness of the two companies (they totalled in all only about 80 men) it was inadvisable to attack the enemy. They therefore dug-in in front of the trench.

During the night of 28th/29th the 63rd Brigade was relieved and the 4th Middlesex moved back to the Transport Lines at St. Nicholas, thence to Manin.

28TH/29TH APRIL.

4TH BATTALION. 29TH APRIL.

April had been a disastrous month for the 4th Battalion. In the Monchy-le-Preux operations the losses were 201 killed, wounded and missing, and in the operations from 23rd to 29th the number was 281.

17TH BATTALION.

The 17th Middlesex (Lieut.-Colonel G. C. Kelly) were the left attacking Battalion of the 6th Infantry Brigade (2nd Division). They had the 13th Essex (also of the 6th Brigade) on their right, and the 2nd H.L.I. of the 5th Brigade on their left. The objectives of the former Brigade were Oppy Wood and village and the area south of both. The 5th Brigade was to capture the enemy's trenches which lay between the objectives of the 6th Brigade and extended almost to the village of Arleux. The latter was to be attacked by the Canadians.

At this period Oppy Wood was but a scorched and shell-blasted mass of tree stumps, while the villages of Oppy and Arleux were in ruins, the enemy troops sheltering beneath the tumbled bricks and masonry in deep dug-outs. Nor were the British areas less shell-torn, for in places scarce one brick stood upon another, and shelter for a dog could hardly be found. For days the opposing guns had been engaged in mercilessly shelling one another and in subjecting the front-line and communication trenches to such a storm of shell that it was a wonder that any living thing could emerge from that terrible holocaust. There were, indeed, instances of men becoming insane under that awful fire, and German prisoners when taken were not infrequently still shaking violently from the ordeal through which they had passed.

The first objective of the 6th Infantry Brigade—the Blue Line—ran north and south at the eastern exits of Oppy Wood. The second objective—the Green Line—followed the eastern outskirts of the village, and the third objective—the Brown Line—the line of Oppy Support Trench.

To the 17th Middlesex had been allotted the capture of Oppy Wood and Village; "mopping-up" parties were attached to the Battalion to "mop up" Oppy when taken.

To the uninitiated it might be explained that the term "mop up" meant the clearing out of dug-outs, buildings, etc., in which hostile troops had taken shelter during the infantry attack. It had been found that the attacking waves of infantry, if they had to clear out lurking Germans from ruins, etc., lost time. Special troops (moppers-up) were therefore detailed to carry out that task, leaving the attackers free to go through to the next objective.

In view of the fact that the 17th Middlesex were " Service " men, *i.e.*, a Service Battalion, and, though first-class fighting men, were disbanded early in 1918 (a regrettable necessity, which will be explained later), the story of the great fight at Oppy is given in full, just as related by the Battalion : " The Battalion marched from Roclincourt on the evening of the 27th and formed up in its battle formation on the front allotted to the Battalion opposite Oppy Wood and village of Oppy. The forming up was carried out without hitch and in perfect silence in spite of steady shelling of the front area. The attached 2nd South Staffordshire Company formed up also in their respective places, either as 'moppers-up' or strong-point parties, and the carrying parties were provided by the South Staffords formed up in rear. Touch was established with the 13th Essex on the right and 2nd H.L.I. on the left. The Battalion was formed up on a four-company front and in three waves, each wave having its own " moppers-up " immediately behind it. The five Vickers guns attached to the Battalion took posts, two behind the right flank and three behind the left flank of the last wave. These guns were allotted duties of covering the flanks during the advance until they should have reached the strong points which they were ordered to garrison. The two Stokes mortars had instructions to move up behind the right flank. The order of companies from right to left was ' D,' ' B,' ' C,' ' A ' Companies."

From the above clear description of a battalion formed up for battle it is almost possible to see the line of troops waiting for the signal to advance.

" At 4.25 a.m. our barrage came down and at 4.33 a.m. the leading wave entered the enemy's front-line trench. Wire was found to be perfectly cut and the trench practically empty. The Battalion pressed forward behind the creeping barrage, and the first objective (the eastern exits of Oppy Wood) was reached with only few casualties. Shortly after the advance commenced the O.C., ' A ' Company, on the left, noticed that the battalion on our left had either lost touch or had been unable to make progress. He therefore placed a Lewis-gun section and some bombers in the enemy front-line trench, with instructions to block the trench and prevent any movement of the enemy against the left flank. The right flank during the advance to the first objective appears to have kept well in touch with the 13th Essex. Fighting became much heavier on reaching the line of the first objective, very heavy machine-gun and rifle fire being opened from the houses in the village. Captain Parfitt, of 'D' Company, had been specially charged with the consolidation of the first objective, and this was taken in hand by the first wave, while remainder pressed on towards the second objective (the eastern outskirts of the village). Very heavy fighting now ensued on the right, but on the left the German trench running north and south through C.7.c (east of the Crucifix, which was just north-west of Oppy village) was reached. The fighting had now become so serious that both the second and third waves were fully involved in the struggle for the second objective, while the first objective was being consolidated. Up to this juncture reports from wounded and reports by runners had been received, confirming the capture of the first objective and of the struggle for the second objective, but owing to the hostile shelling all reports were somewhat late in reaching Battalion Headquarters, and the situation on the left did not seem clear, as although 'A' Company were known to have gained ground, a report came in from the H.L.I. on our left to the effect that they were hung up by fire in the sunken road in the neighbourhood of the Crucifix. A senior officer was now sent from Battalion Headquarters to clear up the situation on the left and to locate a suitable forward position for Battalion Headquarters to move to.

"It was now very nearly 8 o'clock, and a few minutes later a report came in from O.C. 'A' Company (the left company) to say that the enemy was working round both his flanks. The only available reserve inside the Battalion, viz., the 'moppers-up' of the first objective (who had reported the completion of their task) had already been sent forward to strengthen the right in the hopes that the second objective might still be reached. Captain Edwards, the officer who had been sent out to clear up the situation, found that the enemy had pressed down in strength from the north, both down the German front-line trench and by the Crucifix Road on the flanks of our two left companies and had driven them back through the wood to the enemy front-line trench. Here these two companies were making a stand, but had by now sustained very heavy losses. The enemy also appear to have counter-attacked against the front and right flank as well and had succeeded in re-entering the wood and getting in between the troops consolidating on the first objective and those who had been driven back to the Oppy Trench. The enemy had also worked up Oppy Trench from the south and were bombing up from that direction. All communication with the remnants of the troops in the first objective was now cut off, and runners who attempted to get through to the troops still holding the Oppy Trench were either killed or wounded.

" Lieut.-Colonel Martin, 13th Essex Regiment, commanding, sent forward a company of the 1st R. Berks. Regiment to endeavour to relieve the situation, but these could not get beyond the O.B. line (old British front line). The remnants of the two companies still holding on to the Oppy Trench finally exhausted all their bombs, and when reduced to about 10 all told, made a dash for the O.B. line. One officer and three men succeeded in getting through. The troops on the first objective were not heard of again until a wounded officer succeeded in making his way back during the night. His evidence made it clear that these troops had fought till they were practically exterminated by the superior pressure of the enemy, the few survivors probably surrendered. The few remaining men of the Battalion, with some of the South Stafford carrying party, remained for the rest of the day in the O.B. line until relieved at night by the 23rd R. Fusiliers.

" Of the troops who 'went over the top' in the morning, 1 officer and 41 unwounded men eventually found their way back, while 3 wounded officers and 106 wounded other ranks were able to get back in the early stages of the fight.

" Had the flanks remained secure it is believed that the first objective could have been held against counter-attack, and possibly the second objective would have been gained in its entirety, although in view of the strength of the enemy in the village this may be doubtful. As it was, the sudden onrush of the enemy from both flanks, which enabled them to re-occupy the wood, combined with their vigorous counter-attack in front, was disastrous, and in the confused nature of the fighting it was impossible to know where to ask for fresh artillery barrages to be placed."

The 17th Middlesex lost in this attack 11 officers and 451 killed, wounded and missing, but again the Die-Hard spirit was demonstrated in the stubborn resistance against superior numbers of the enemy and in the grim manner in which both officers and men fought to the very last.

17TH BATTALION.
29TH APRIL.

On the 29th April the Battalion was at Roclincourt, reorganising, but moved on the 30th to a camp by Ecurie Wood.

The general results of the Battle of Arleux have already been given in the early pages of this chapter.

(IV) THE THIRD BATTLE OF THE SCARPE,

3rd–4th May, 1917.

On the 3rd May another attack was made by the Fifth, Third and First Armies (in that order from right to left) between Bullecourt and Fresnoy, *i.e.*, roughly on a front of about 16 miles. The French were to launch their offensive against the Chemin de Dames on 5th May, and in order to assist them Sir Douglas Haig had extended his battle front to include the Hindenburg Line in the neighbourhood of Bullecourt.

12TH, 1/7TH, 1/8TH AND 11TH BATTALIONS.

But the sectors of the front of special interest to the Middlesex Regiment were Cherisy, Monchy-le-Preux, and just south of the Scarpe west of Pelves. In these three sectors the 12th, 1/7th, 1/8th, and 11th Battalions of the Regiment were engaged.

12TH BATTALION.

The 12th Middlesex (18th Division) had not previously been engaged in the Arras Offensive. They had been out of the front line for a month, training, but on 29th April arrived in the support area in the neighbourhood of Heninel and Neuville Vitasse. Here they bivouacked until the 1st May, when they took over front-line trenches before Cherisy Village, which the 18th Division had been ordered to capture on 3rd May; the 21st Division, with Fontaine-lez-Croisilles as its objective, and the 14th Division, with orders to capture the enemy's trenches west of Vis-en-Artois, were on the right and left respectively of the 18th Division. Of the latter the 54th Brigade was to attack on the right and the 55th on the left.

1ST MAY.

The two assaulting Battalions of the 54th Brigade were 7th Bedfords on the right and 12th Middlesex on the left; the 11th Royal Fusiliers were in support of both assaulting Battalions. Cherisy was a long, straggling village built upon the forward slopes of a ridge. The northern half lay in the area to be attacked by the 55th Brigade, the southern half was the objective of the 12th Middlesex. The front of the village was strongly protected by Fontaine Trench, the latter defended by thick belts of wire entanglements. At the eastern outskirts of the southern half was an orchard full of machine guns. Sunken roads on all sides lent themselves to the defence of the village. All officers and N.C.Os. were well acquainted with the plan of operations, and the men knew exactly what to do and where to go, and had the original intention—to attack at dawn, when the objectives could be seen—been adhered to, all might have gone well. But Zero hour was put back to 3.45 a.m., and the attack was to be made in pitch darkness. Probably Army Headquarters had good reasons for altering the time, but the change was disastrous, as will be seen.

The first objective was the sloping ground just east of the Sensée River, which flowed from north-east to south-west on the farther side of the village; the second objective was the summit of the ridge beyond.

The 12th Middlesex (Lieut.-Colonel W. H. Johnston) formed up on a two-company front, " D " on the right, " C " on the left, with " B " and " A " Companies (respectively) in support.

At 3.45 a.m. on 3rd the British barrage fell, and five minutes later the enemy put down a very heavy " H.E." barrage west of our own. The Companies went forward immediately the Divisional guns opened fire, but in the inky darkness touch was quickly lost with the flanking troops and the former " went on their own." " D " Company swerved to its right across the front of the 7th Bedfords, one of the supporting platoons of " B " Company following suit. To make matters worse, a tank which had gone forward on the right of the Bedfords circled to its left and came back through the advancing troops. Stumbling on as best they could, the latter found themselves in front of the wire protecting Fontaine Trench, only to find it uncut. At this critical stage the Bedfords, with " D " Company and a platoon of " B " Company of the Middlesex, began to retire. " This," records the Battalion Diary, " was due to someone on the right having shouted ' retire.' " They were sent forward again with the exception of " B " Company men, who were kept in reserve in case of counter-attack. But both the Bedfords and " D " Company had lost touch with the barrage and could get no further than a line in front of Fontaine Trench.

The two left companies, however, kept better direction, and " C " got through to the Sensée and formed a line along the western banks of the river. " A " Company could not get beyond the village, but established themselves in ruins and formed a strong point at the southern end. This strong point was

12TH BATTALION.
3RD MAY.

garrisoned by 50 men, who were, the Battalion Diary again records, " eventually reduced to eight and a sergeant, of whom five and the sergeant eventually got back."

Meanwhile, the 11th Fusiliers had been ordered to reinforce the front line, but No Man's Land was an inferno, hostile shell and machine-gun fire terrific, and the Battalion could not get across.

Next a message, carried most gallantly by a runner (Pte. Fox), who had to run the gauntlet the whole way back under very heavy fire, reached the C.O., stating that " C " Company still held on to its line along the river bank, and that it was in touch with " A " Company on its right and the Buffs of the 55th Brigade on its left. But the latter were forced to fall back, and the Middlesex and Bedfords, seeing what was happening on their left, came back also. " A " Company still held on, but was gradually reduced in numbers until the remnants made a dash and got away to their own lines.

The casualties in this affair were very heavy. All the officers, both C.S.Ms. and all N.C.Os., with the exception of the sergeant in charge of the strong point already mentioned, had gone down. At night the 6th Northants, who had been in reserve, attacked again with the object of relieving men of the 18th Division who were believed to be still holding out in Cherisy, but it is impossible to say how far the object was gained, for the Battalion was back again on its " jumping-off " line by 10.15 p.m. Many men of " B " and " D " Companies of the Middlesex Regiment, who had been lying out in shell holes all day, came back with the Northants.

The 12th Battalion in this attack lost 14 officers and 304 other ranks in killed and wounded and missing. The officers killed were Capt. H. Perks, Lieuts. L. J. Gore and R. P. Pyman, and 2/Lieuts. J. H. Stephens, J. A. Hatton, J. A. D. Coleman and W. H. Walker.

4TH MAY.
12TH MAY.

On the 4th May the Battalion moved back to a shell-hole area close to Neuville Vitasse until 11th, when another move was made, on 12th, to bivouacs near Henin Vinage; here pleasant grass land was very welcome after the noisome shell holes.

On the left of the VIIth Corps (21st, 18th and 14th Divisions) the VIth Corps (56th, 3rd and 12th Divisions in that order from right to left) had on 3rd May attacked the enemy's positions from the Arras–Cambrai road to the southern banks of the Scarpe.

1917 "Caked with Mud, Dirty, Unshaven" 71

After the First Battle of the Scarpe the 1/7th and 1/8th Middlesex had been withdrawn (with other units of the 167th Brigade) into support. On the 18th the former Battalion moved back to Arras, getting into billets at midnight. The following morning a fleet of London motor 'buses arrived, and, caked with mud from head to foot, dirty and unshaven, and worn out from continued discomfort and sleepless nights (for the bitter cold had rendered sleep impossible) the 1/7th, still in the best of spirits, were carried to La Cauchie for a 10 days' rest; the 1/8th followed on 20th to Berles. *1/7TH AND 1/8TH BATTALIONS.*

But the 28th found the 1/8th back again in the front-line trenches east of Wancourt, the 1/7th being in support south of La Fosses Farm.

On 30th April warning orders for the attack due to take place on 3rd May were circulated, and after various changes had taken place on the divisional front, the 167th Brigade on 2nd May held the left sub-sector of the divisional front south-east of Monchy, *i.e.*, from the Arras–Cambrai road to a small copse, with the 1st Londons on the right and the 1/7th Middlesex on the left, with the 1/8th Middlesex in support in the Wancourt line and the 3rd Londons in Brigade Reserve.

The line occupied by the 1st Londons and 1/7th Middlesex was a newly-dug trench just east of Knife Trench; the Germans were in Tool Trench—the distance between the opposing lines varied from about 100 to 200 yards.

On the right of the 167th Brigade the 169th held the Guemappe sector.

The objectives of the former Brigade on 3rd May were, first, Tool Trench; second, Lanyard Trench to the southern end of Bois du Vert; the third objective was Spur Trench, east of Lanyard.

Along the front to be attacked by the Middlesex there was one particularly awkward feature: the German trenches were sited on the reverse side of a slight rise in the ground, and it was impossible for the Divisional Artillery to obtain direct observation of the results of their registration. As there was no prolonged preliminary bombardment, it was impossible for patrols to find out whether the guns had successfully cut the wire and generally demolished the enemy's trenches.

On the morning of 2nd May the 1/7th were disposed in the following positions: " C " and " D " Companies (right and left   *2ND MAY.*

c 4

1/7TH AND 1/8TH BATTALIONS. 2ND MAY.

respectively) in the first line, with two platoons in Knife Trench and two in Saddle Trench; "B" Company in String and Dragoon Trenches, and "A" in trenches south of La Fosses Farm.

During the afternoon the enemy's guns heavily bombarded the line; "B" Company was severely shelled and had 58 casualties, of whom 7 were killed. The whole Company was badly shaken and had to be withdrawn to reorganise. Finally, it was combined with "A" Company to form the third wave of the attack, "A" Company of the 3rd Londons being added to the Battalion to form the fourth wave.

3RD MAY.

At Zero hour (3.45 a.m., 3rd May) the Battalion was ready formed up for the attack in the following order: "C" and "D," right and left front attacking Companies; "B" and "A," right and left, in support in a nameless trench behind Saddle Trench.

The 1/8th Middlesex were in Brigade Reserve in the Wancourt line. The same adverse conditions which had so seriously interfered with the attack of the 12th Middlesex further south, *i.e.*, the unfortunate change in Zero hour, similarly affected the attack of the 1/7th Middlesex and their comrades of the 56th Division. The peculiar lie of the ground was also another factor.

At Zero the Divisional barrage fell, and the troops at once advanced to the attack. "As soon as the first wave topped the ridge between Knife and Tool Trenches," records the Battalion Diary, "it was obvious that the enemy's front line had never been adequately dealt with by the artillery and had apparently escaped the barrage, as it was full of infantry, standing shoulder to shoulder, ready for our infantry to come on."

The unfortunate Middlesex men must have shown up clearly against the sky-line in spite of the darkness, for as each line reached the rising ground it was swept away by a withering fire from rifles and machine guns. Survivors stated that, as they advanced, it seemed as if the whole German line burst into a sheet of flame.

The result was that the Battalion was pinned down into shell holes, from which the men were unable to emerge, having to pass the day in that desperate position until darkness fell again and they were able to crawl back singly or in small parties. There were reports that isolated parties had penetrated Tool Trench and that one body of men had even reached a support line just beyond Tool Trench, but these gallant fellows must have been wiped out. The C.O. (Lieut.-Colonel E. J. King) reported afterwards that the enemy's shell fire was " terrific " and " such as

I have never witnessed before." This from one who had been through the Somme Battles of 1916 is sufficient evidence of the awful gruelling the troops had to endure during the 3rd May.

1/7TH AND 1/8TH BATTALIONS.
3RD MAY.

At 6.10 p.m. orders were received from Brigade Headquarters, stating that the 3rd Londons would take over the front-line and support trenches, with the 1/8th Middlesex in close support. The relief was completed by 9.30 p.m., the worn-out 1/7th being by that time in the Wancourt line.

The losses of the 1/7th were severe. Tottenham ("D" Company) were the heaviest sufferers: Captain J. O. Taylor and 2/Lieut. B. A. Kemp had been killed. "C," the right Company (Hornsey) had Captain N. A. Weston and 2/Lieut. L. Troughton wounded. The gallant Captain Cater, one of the hardest fighting officers who ever served with the Battalion, had made a determined attempt with Hampstead and Highgate to push through, fell, badly wounded, was captured by the Germans, and died in a German hospital on 9th July, 1917. Other casualties amongst the officers were: 2/Lieuts. R. H. Hartley, S. W. J. Bishop, B. Wright and C. M. Snith killed, and Captain C. R. Rintoul and 2/Lieut. W. H. Wisson wounded. In other ranks the losses were 25 killed, 106 wounded, and 59 missing—in all a total of 11 officers and 190 other ranks.

During the evening of the 4th the Battalion moved back to Tilloy.

4TH MAY.

The 1/7th had failed, but not for want of gallant efforts. From the list of "Recommendations for Immediate Award" the following accounts of brave deeds are taken—they are evidence of the fighting spirit of the Battalion. Of one subaltern (2/Lieut. A. A. Riley) the record states: "When the assault had failed and the bulk of the officers were casualties, he collected what was left of his own Company and men of other units in his neighbourhood, occupied a line of shell holes, linked them up, reorganised his men in them, and presented a strong front to any possible counter-attack. The example of this young officer had a fine effect on all ranks." Next comes the story of L/Cpl. J. H. Ward, a stretcher-bearer: "In the performance of his duties this man showed personal bravery of an exceptionally high order. In daylight, under heavy rifle and machine-gun fire, he repeatedly crossed the rise in front of Tool Trench to bring in badly wounded men. In all he brought in 12 men, one being shot dead in his arms, and his gallant conduct is the talk of all who witnessed it."*

* He was recommended for the Victoria Cross, but awarded the D.C.M.

1/8TH BATTALION.
3RD MAY.

The 1/8th Battalion was in support during the action on 3rd and moved back to the Wancourt line on 4th. Their casualties during the operations were three other ranks killed and eight wounded.

11TH BATTALION.
3RD MAY.

During the attack by the 36th Brigade, 12th Division, the 11th Middlesex were in reserve to the Fusiliers in their attack on the first divisional objective—the Brown Line (Gun Trench). The Middlesex were in Bayonet Trench, their final duty being the clearing of Pelves. The attack, however, failed, and after darkness

4TH/5TH MAY.

had fallen on the night 4th/5th the 11th Battalion took over the front line from the 8th and 9th Royal Fusiliers, who had lost very heavily. The Middlesex occupied Scabbard, New, Rifle and Bayonet Trenches, portions of which were unrecognisable, having been blown to bits by hostile shell fire. Hard work during the night resulted in a decent amount of cover when dawn broke on 5th. Throughout the remainder of 5th and on the 6th and 7th the defences were strengthened. The Battalion was relieved on night 7th/8th and moved back to the Orange Line.* Before the relief, however, a hostile party of about 50

7TH MAY.

Germans had, very early in the morning of 7th, advanced against "A" Company, the records narrating this adventure in the following sarcastic terms: "About 3 a.m. a part of about 50 of the enemy were observed to be crossing No Man's Land, *apparently with the idea of relieving "A" Company in Scabbard Trench.* Two Lewis guns and rifles effectively dealt with this party, at least two-thirds of which were observed to fall, the remainder doubling back."

The close of the Third Battle of the Scarpe concluded the Battles of Arras, 1917, but there were two subsequent operations —the capture of Roeux (13th–14th May) and the capture of Oppy Wood (28th June), and in the first of these the 11th Middlesex were again engaged.

The Capture of Roeux,
13th–14th May.

The 11th Middlesex, with other units of the 36th Brigade, were out of the front line until the night of 10th May, when the

* The 11th Battalion during this period had 3 officers wounded and 65 other ranks killed and wounded.

Brigade relieved the 35th Brigade in the right sub-sector of the 12th Divisional front.   11TH BATTALION.

At this period the divisional front line (which was immediately south of the Scarpe and south-west of Roeux) ran from Rifle Farm along Rifle Trench and Scabbard Trench to the southern banks of the river. On the right the 3rd Division held Monchy, while across the Scarpe, on the left, the 4th Division was just west of the famous Chemical Works and Roeux Cemetery.   10TH MAY.

The dividing line between the 36th and 37th Brigades (the latter being on the left of the former) was a point where the extension of Curb Lane joined Halberd Trench.

The front line was very irregular and in places the opposing trenches were close to one another. Along the 36th Brigade front the enemy was very strongly posted in Devil's Trench, in rear of which lay another equally powerful line—Gun Trench.

On the evening of 11th May, at 7.30 p.m., the 4th Division, across the water, attacked the Chemical Works and Roeux Cemetery, the guns of the 12th Division co-operating. This attack was continued throughout the 12th and was completely successful.

Meanwhile, during the night 11th/12th, the 11th Middlesex had relieved the 9th and part of the 8th Royal Fusiliers in the front line, and by 2.30 a.m. on 12th the Battalion held the front-line trenches, "A" Company on the right in Chain Trench from Bit Lane to Harness Lane, "B" Company in Rifle Trench from the junction to Harness Lane, "C" Company in Halberd Trench and in the forward piece of Rifle Trench, and "D" Company (in support) between Musket Trench and Orange Lane, and on each side of the junction Curb Lane and Rifle Trench.   12TH MAY.

At 7.30 a.m. a shell fell just to the right of the junction of Curb Lane and Rifle Trench, killing 2/Lieut. A. A. Keogh; two other ranks were also killed and two wounded.

During the day companies lay low and rested, the enemy also being very quiet. But an attack on Devil's Trench had been ordered for 6 p.m.

At Zero hour a three-minute heavy bombardment of Devil's Trench took place, under cover of which both the 3rd and 12th Divisions attacked the enemy. Heavy machine-gun and rifle fire met the troops as they rushed towards the German trenches, and for a while the situation became obscure. At 7.30 p.m., when the position became clearer, it was found that, with the

11TH BATTALION.
12TH MAY.

exception that we occupied a small portion of Arrow Trench on the right of the Brigade boundary and to the north of Bit Lane, the attack generally had been a failure. Reports, however, reached the 11th Middlesex that the King's Regiment (the left attacking Battalion of the 3rd Division) had gained their objective, and, in the words of the Battalion Diary, " it was determined to carry Devil's Trench at all costs."

Gallant resolution, but how difficult to carry out! Up to this period three more officers—2/Lieuts. H. A. Godfrey, R. V. Morrison, and A. C. C. Towgood—had been killed, and 2/Lieut. Gardener wounded; the casualties in other ranks were also heavy.

Meanwhile, immediately the situation became known at 7.30 p.m., 2/Lieut. Wilkins was sent out with his platoon to form a defensive flank on the Battalion right, parallel with and 50 yards from Bit Lane.

The second attack, which took place at 9.45 p.m., after a short preliminary bombardment, again failed, though the gallant fellows who rushed towards Devil's Trench got within 40 yards of it. But the position was too strongly held.

13TH MAY.

When dawn of 13th broke that portion of Arrow Trench won on the previous day was still held by Captain Anderson (" A " Company) and his men. All companies had lost heavily, " C " and " B " being especially weak. The enemy's barrage was particularly heavy: Monchy Trench and Curb Lane were swept by a perfect tornado, and about Battalion Headquarters the shells were falling and bursting with terrifying frequency. The Battalion Diary records that " the work of the orderlies, which had always been good during the recent fighting, was worthy of the highest praise."

In the second attack on Devil's Trench 2 more officers (2/Lieuts. W. H. L. Bartlett and A. W. Carter, both of " B " Company) were killed, the total casualties suffered by the Battalion being now 6 officers killed and 1 wounded; 26 other ranks killed, 66 wounded, and 20 missing, believed killed.

The final positions held by all companies were: Captain Anderson with about 40 other ranks of " A " Company in Arrow Trench; " B " Company in Rifle Trench; " C " Company in Halberd Trench and the forward piece of Rifle Trench; " D " Company in Chain Trench. Throughout the 13th the Germans were quiet—they were just as worn out as the Middlesex men. Only the guns were occasionally active.

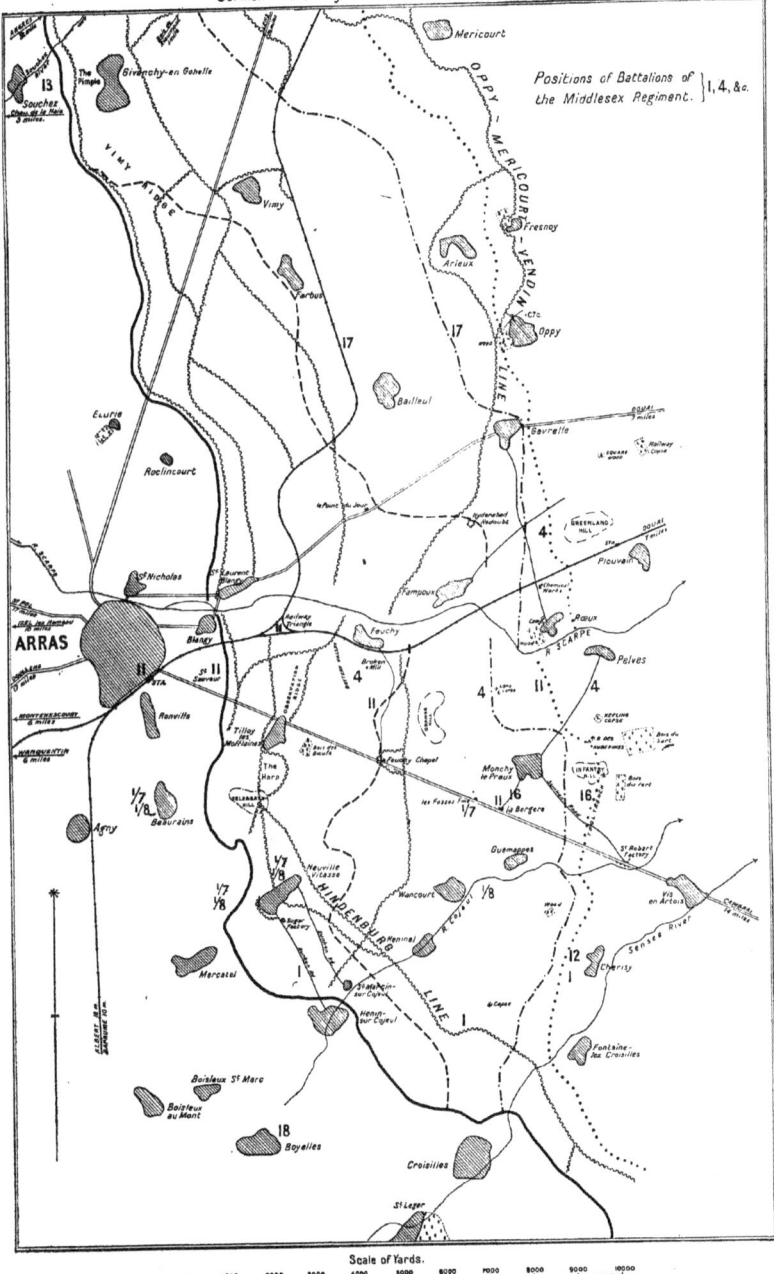

At 10 p.m. the company commander of a relieving battalion 11TH BATTALION. arrived to reconnoitre the line. Captain Anderson, who had most gallantly maintained his position in Arrow Trench, was 13TH MAY. ordered to withdraw his men to his original front line: " this was carried out very much against his will."

By 3 a.m. on 14th May the relief was complete and the 11th 14TH MAY. Middlesex had moved back into support. On 15th they marched back to billets in Arras.

The attacks by the 12th and 3rd Divisions south of the Scarpe were no doubt intended to assist the 4th Division in capturing Roeux, for although the official despatches state that the village was taken by the 51st Division, when the Scotsmen relieved the 4th Division on the night 12th/13th the latter already held half of the village, and the enemy then evacuated the other half, for during the 13th the German guns shelled the eastern outskirts of Roeux.

In all no less than 10 battalions of the Middlesex Regiment fought in the Battles of Arras, 1917: from the northern extremities of the Vimy Ridge to the Cojeul River, south of the Arras–Cambrai road, the Die-Hards had wrested many a trench from the enemy. The villages of Neuville Vitasse, Thilloy, Monchy, Cherisy and Oppy, the slopes of Observation and Telegraph Ridges, Infantry and Greenland Hills—all were stained with the blood of Middlesex men. And some there are who lie there still, now that the awful sounds of battle are over and the plains of Picardy once more silent.

CHAPTER XXIX.

The Flanders Offensive: I.

THE BATTLE OF MESSINES, 1917,

7th–14th June.

IT would be difficult to point to a more successful limited attack during the Great War than the operations between the 7th and 14th June, known as the Battle of Messines, 1917. This battle was necessary before the extensive operations in Flanders known as the Battles of Ypres, 1917, could be undertaken: for possession of the Messines–Wytschaete Ridge was essential in order to deny the enemy observation over the British lines during the attack east of Ypres. The official despatches give the following excellent description of the front:—

" The group of hills known as the Messines–Wytschaete Ridge lies about midway between the towns of Armentières and Ypres. Situated at the eastern end of the range of abrupt, isolated hills which divides the valleys of the River Lys and the River Yser, it links up that range with the line of rising ground which from Wytschaete stretches north-eastwards to the Ypres–Menin road, and then northwards past Passchendaele to Staden.

" The village of Messines, situated on the southern spur of the ridge, commands a wide view of the valley of the Lys, and enfiladed the British lines to the south. North-west of Messines the village of Wytschaete, situated at the point of the salient and on the highest part of the ridge, from its height of about 260 feet, commands even more completely the town of Ypres and the whole of the British positions in the Ypres salient.

" The German front line skirted the western foot of the ridge in a deep curve from the River Lys opposite Frelinghien to a point just short of the Menin road. The line of trenches then turned north-west past Hooge and Wieltje, following the slight rise known as the Pilckem Ridge to the Yser Canal at Boesinghe. The enemy's second-line system followed the crest of the Messines–Wytschaete Ridge, forming an inner curve. In addition to the defences of the ridge itself, two chord positions had been constructed across the base of the salient from south to north. The first lay slightly to the east of the hamlet of Oosttaverne and was known as the Oosttaverne Line. The second chord position, known as the Warneton Line, crossed the Lys at Warneton and ran roughly parallel to the Oosttaverne Line, a little more than a mile to the east of it."

13TH, 19TH AND 23RD BATTALIONS.

Thus the terrain of the battlefield-to-be; where also Middlesex men were to go forward and assist in capturing the German positions, for in this battle the 13th Battalion (24th Division) and 19th and 23rd Battalions (41st Division) were engaged.

The front of attack selected extended from St. Yves, north of "Plugstreet" Wood, to Mount Sorrel (north of the Ypres–Comines Canal) inclusive—a distance of about 9 miles. The final objective was to be the Oosttaverne Line already described. Three Corps (IInd Anzac, IXth and Xth), each of four divisions (three divisions in line and one in reserve), were to make the attack, the front-line Divisions, from right to left, being 3rd Australian, New Zealand, 25th, 36th, 16th, 19th, 41st, 47th and 23rd. The reserves were 4th Australian, 11th and 24th Divisions. The Xth Corps, on the left, disposed the 41st Division on the right in the St. Eloi sector, the 47th just north of the Ypres–Comines Canal, the 23rd on the left of the 47th and the 24th just east of Kruisstraathoek, in reserve.

Preparations for the battle were extraordinarily difficult, for the enemy had direct observation over the British front-line and reserve positions. Labour and material had been scanty, for the prior demands of the Arras offensive left little for the Messines front. Yet, with the means at his disposal, Sir Herbert Plumer (who commanded the Second Army) proceeded steadily to prepare for the first phase of the Battle of Ypres. Railways were built, huge dumps of ammunition and stores formed, roads made and pipe lines laid to carry water forward to the area of the battle.

But the most interesting feature of the battle was the construction and explosion of 19 deep mines at the moment of assault. This was a feature unique in warfare; unique even in a war which had witnessed the birth of countless inventions undreamed of in pre-war days.

Ever since the formation, in the late autumn of 1916, of definite plans for the offensives of 1917, our miners and tunnellers had been at work on these mines. In all 24 were constructed, but four were outside the scope of the present operation, and one was lost as the result of a mine blown by the enemy.

Some of the 19, however, had been constructed as long as 12 months, and the care and anxious work necessary to ensure their safety was a great strain on those whose duty it was to guard them constantly. As an instance: for over 10 months preceding the Battle of Messines, 1917, almost continuous underground fighting (mining) was in progress, and only the greatest skill and splendid disregard for their own safety by our tunnelmen saved two large mines in this area from destruction.

In the construction of these mines 8,000 yards of mine galleries had been driven into the earth and over 1,000,000 pounds of explosives had been used as charges. Such mining was without parallel.

The front of attack of the Xth Corps extended from the Diependaal Beek, south-west of St. Eloi, to Observatory Ridge, north of the Ypres–Comines Canal. The 41st Division, holding the right sector of the Corps front, disposed the 124th Brigade on the right from the Diependaal Beek to O.3.2. (or opposite Oasis Street, which was in the German lines), and the 123rd Brigade on the left from O.3.2. to Triangular Wood. The ruins of St. Eloi were in about the centre of the Divisional sector and just behind the front-line trenches.

Since the Battle of Le Transloy in October, 1916 (during which the 41st Division was in reserve), neither the 19th (Pioneers) nor the 23rd Battalions of the Middlesex Regiment had been engaged in operations on a large scale. The Division moved from the Somme area towards the close of the year, and when the New Year of 1917 dawned was holding the St. Eloi sector and did not move south to take part in the Battles of Arras. *19TH AND 23RD BATTALIONS.*

Strenuous as were the five months from January to May, inclusive, for all Battalions, in addition to their trench duties, had to supply large working parties for R.E. work, no incident of outstanding importance is recorded either in the diary of the 23rd or 19th Middlesex. Trench warfare went on night and day ceaselessly, shell fire, bombing, patrol work, digging, sniping, and a hundred and one things connected with the work of maintaining the line, kept all ranks on the go, and when out of the line practice attacks and marching seemed never-ending. It was hard going all the time. And it was better so, for work kept men from thinking too much of the awfulness of war.

23RD BATTALION.

One incident alone in all those five months may be mentioned. It is a story which will bear re-telling over and over again.

About the middle of February wiring parties were very busy putting out new entanglements and repairing those already out.

21ST FEBRUARY. The enemy was similarly engaged. On the night of 21st the officer-in-charge of a wiring party of 23rd Middlesex and a corporal went out into No Man's Land in order to reconnoitre wire supposed to have been put up already. Both lost their way and, wandering about, found themselves at last in the German thin wire and only five yards from the enemy's parapet. For half an hour they remained in this position, reconnoitring the enemy's wire and generally taking notes of the construction of his trenches and gathering any other information they could. But apparently their voices were heard by the enemy, who threw a volley of bombs in the direction of the officer and his N.C.O. Both, slightly wounded, set out on the perilous task of crawling back through the enemy's wire. Three times the gallant N.C.O. went back and released his officer, who had been caught in the entanglements. Nevertheless, the two succeeded in reaching their own trenches after an exciting and dangerous adventure. No names are given in the official reports of this small affair. It is mentioned in a matter-of-fact way just like any other item, but it is to be hoped that the wonderful devotion of the N.C.O. met with a well-deserved award.

After this little incident the wiring party went on with its work and placed no less than 47 coils of wire in position.

That offensive operations were going to take place in the near future was obvious from the nature of the work allotted the Battalion, and the manner of their training when out of the front-line trenches. On the 2nd April the Battalion Diary of the 23rd Middlesex records: " Signs of preparation for offensive action in our sub-sector noticed." The signs were portentous: working parties of R.F.A. began to build new gun emplacements at the junction of Convent Lane and the Bollartbeek, while parties of R.A.M.C. set to work to construct new Aid Posts and dig deep oblong holes in the ground.*

---

* Casualties among officers of 23rd Middlesex from 1st January to the end of May, 1917, were as follows: 2/Lieut. A. S. Hutchinson, wounded 8.1.17; 2/Lieut. A. Bedingham, killed 24.2.17; 2/Lieut. F. Gore, died of wounds 25.3.17; 2/Lieut. R. B. McGuire, accidentally killed 30.4.17.

On the 6th May we find a company of the Middlesex doing garrison duty at one of the mine shafts, which were now more closely guarded than ever. *19TH AND 23RD BATTALIONS. 6TH MAY.*

As late as the 3rd and 4th June the Battalion was practising assembling for the attack and advancing ("quick" and "slow" advance) behind the barrage. The 5th June was "X" day, on which the 23rd moved forward to their assembly trenches.

The records of the 19th Middlesex (Pioneers) from January to May, 1917, make poor reading. It is a pity, for the nature of their work is known and it is not as bare of interest as the Battalion diaries would have one believe. Everyone knows what good fellows the Pioneers were and how splendidly they did their work: "Work on C.Ts. (communication trenches), tramways and roads" is sufficient for them to record, but the reader is left to guess the remainder. If he did not serve in France or Flanders during the War he will never know how, at all times of the day and night, the Pioneers stuck to their duty with a devotion which will never be forgotten.

On the 4th June the 123rd M.G. Company relieved the 122nd M.G. Company in the front-line trenches in the St. Eloi sector, the relief being completed during the early hours of 5th. The 5th was "X" day, during which all battalions of the 123rd Brigade moved forward to their assembly positions. *4TH JUNE.*

The 123rd Brigade was to attack with the 23rd Middlesex (Lieut.-Colonel A. R. Haig-Brown) on the right, the 10th R.W. Kents in the centre, and the 11th R. West Surrey Regiment on the left. At 10 a.m. one company of the Middlesex marched off from Chippewa Camp and took over Old French Trench on the right of Convent Lane. At 10 p.m. that night the three remaining companies moved forward, one platoon to Gordon Lane, five platoons in Voormezeele Switch, and one company in Old French Trench: Battalion Headquarters were in the latter. One platoon went up to the front line (referred to as "Locality" in the diaries) and, creeping out into No Man's Land, cut the wire in front of their trenches in order to facilitate the forming-up operations. Steps in the parapet were also made and a patrol went out and reconnoitred the enemy's front line, finding it but lightly held. *23RD BATTALION.*

Throughout the 6th all final preparations were made. Rations and water for two days were drawn from G.H.Q. Line Dump, and S.A.A., bombs, and Véry lights from the Convent Lane *6TH JUNE.*

23RD BATTALION. 6TH JUNE.

Dump. The day was comparatively quiet in the front-line trenches until about 10 p.m., when the enemy, obviously nervous, opened fire with field guns on Voormezeele Switch, Old French Trench and the assembly areas. At 10.30 p.m., when tapes were being laid on the assembly ground, Lieut. T. W. Purves was killed by a shell.

Between 11 p.m. and midnight companies moved off to assembly positions in platoons. There was slight shelling at the time, but no more casualties were suffered, and just after midnight the 23rd Middlesex were in the front-line trenches. The trench strength of the Battalion was 16 officers and 550 other ranks.

The attack was to be made on a two-platoon frontage, "C" Company on the right, "A" on the left, "B" in rear of "C," and "D" in rear of "A," each company on a three-platoon basis. There were six waves.

The enemy's trenches in front of the 123rd Brigade were a portion of Oasis Trench (right) and Oar Trench (left); Oasis Support and Oar Support; Oasis Reserve and Oar Reserve. His communication trenches between the above were Oasis Street, Oar Avenue, Oar Street and Oar Alley.

The particular trenches allotted to the Middlesex lay between Oasis Street on the right (inclusive) to Oar Avenue on the left (exclusive).

There were three objectives, though only two were allotted to the 123rd Brigade: the 122nd Brigade was to pass through both the 124th and 123rd Brigades and capture the final objective.

The first objective was the Red Line (described as an "imaginary" line), varying from 80 to 150 yards beyond the enemy's front line, but it included Oosthoek Estaminet and Eikhof Farm. The second objective, the Blue Line, was the line of the Damm Strasse, in front of which a line of advanced posts were to be formed.

The method of attack is also interesting, for although the present generation will probably know it, there will be in the years to come a race of young soldiers who know nothing of the manner in which attacks were made during the Great War.

At Zero hour (3.10 a.m.) the whole Battalion was to "go over the parapet and advance, if possible, to within 75 yards of the enemy's trenches and lie down." While this move was in progress the guns would be pounding the enemy's front line in order to force him to take cover so that the advancing troops would not be detected. The first wave of the attack, however, was to crawl as far forward from its original 75 yards as possible, and as close to the barrage as was consistent with safety.

23RD BATTALION. 6TH JUNE.

As soon as the guns lifted off the enemy's front line the first wave, followed by the whole Battalion, was to dash towards the hostile trenches and on to the support line, where the first wave was to halt and "mop up" until the arrival of the 20th D.L.I. who had been detailed as "moppers-up." The first wave, after handing over to the Durhams, were to follow on in rear of the second, third, fourth, fifth and sixth waves, which in the meantime would have gone on to the Red Line.

The second wave was to halt on the Red Line and "mop up," the third, fourth, fifth and sixth waves going on to the Blue Line, on which the barrage would be falling, the assault of the Damm Strasse taking place as soon as the guns lifted off it.

Up to the enemy's support trenches the fifth wave was to carry water, bombs and sandbags, then dump them in the support trenches and proceed with the other waves as described.

Finally, the sixth wave and (if present) the first wave were to form the line of posts just east of the Blue Line.

In addition to their revolvers, all officers were to carry a "knobkerry" (a stick with a heavy knob, such as the Zulus used). Each man, as well as his equipment and 200 rounds of ammunition, was to carry a shovel (instead of the entrenching tool), two sandbags, two bombs and two ground flares.

In rear of the Battalion the Battalion Pioneers were to go forward, finally joining the sixth wave and helping in the work of consolidation.

Such are some of the details of an attack in the summer of 1917.

For weeks the British guns had pounded the enemy's trenches —the Damm Strasse and Pheasant Wood receiving special attention. His first-line support trenches had also been subjected to heavy trench-mortar fire, and gas had been released when the wind was in a favourable direction. To all of which the enemy had replied vigorously.

But the Germans had no knowledge of the surprise awaiting them in the form of those 19 mines. In fact, General Ludendorff said : "The heights of Wytschaete and Messines had been the site of active mine warfare in the early days of the War. For a long time past, however, both sides had ceased to use such tactics ; all had been quiet and no sound of underground work on the

23RD BATTALION.

part of the enemy could be heard at our listening posts. The mines must, therefore, have been in position long before." Some were, others were not, and yet it is difficult to believe that the Germans were entirely ignorant of our mining operations, for in February he had exploded several heavy mines and camouflets in an endeavour to interfere with our mines.

7TH JUNE.

At 2.45 a.m. on 7th the Middlesex, climbing the trench parapets by means of ladders, entered silently into No Man's Land and moved across to within 70 yards of the enemy's trenches. Wave followed wave and lay down one behind the other. Excitement was intense. Wonder and curiosity, not without a certain amount of dread, was centred on the explosion of the mines—so soon to take place. Behind the front-line trenches points of vantage had their watchers, intent upon witnessing what should be the greatest and most awe-inspiring sight ever witnessed upon a battlefield.

At five minutes past three a solitary golden-rain rocket, evidently fired from the Ruined Farm which lay between Oar Trench and Oar Support in the German lines, soared up into the sky and burst, throwing a shower of brilliant sparks over the grim battlefield, threatening to disclose the lines of waiting troops out in No Man's Land. But no action followed and everyone breathed afresh.

Seconds now seemed like hours, for in two minutes' time (at 3.7 a.m.) the mines were due to " go up."

Along the whole of the Messines front watchers were now gazing with scarce-controlled emotions at that dread space between the lines of opposing trenches, so soon to be turned into an inferno.

The synchronised watches touched Zero hour and immediately there was a roar such as no man had ever heard, and a sight which can only be likened to Etna and Vesuvius disgorging their volumes of flame and smoke and lava into luckless Herculaneum. First there was a rumbling and strange groanings from the very bowels of the earth; the ground shook, lurid tongues of flame and smoke, clouds of dust and *débris* shot up into the air, as if Satan and his legions had at last broken through the bonds which bound them, as if the inferno of Dante had indeed become a reality, and Hell let loose.

To the awful explosion of the mines was added the terrifying roar of the British barrage as it fell upon the German front-line trenches, blasting the broken defences to still further confusion, 23RD BATTALION. creating havoc on havoc, so that men shivered at the awful grandeur of that appalling bombardment. It would be a miracle 7TH JUNE. if any living thing still remained in the German front-line trenches.

The barrage lifted from Oasis and Oar Trenches and at once the waiting line of troops got to their feet and rushed towards the enemy's lines. No Man's Land was still thick with smoke and dust, and difficulty was experienced in keeping touch on the flanks, but there was little to fear from the German front line. Oasis and Oar Trenches existed now in name only. Broken and battered almost beyond recognition, the ruined trenches were incapable of offering cover to the few Germans who clung to the tumbled earth. And they, poor fellows, were too nerve-shattered to offer any resistance, but could only fling their shaking hands above their heads and cry out, " Mercy, Kamerad, Mercy ! "

The enemy's support line fell as quickly, but it was in moving towards the Damm Strasse from the support line that most of the Middlesex casualties occurred, for the Blue Line was strongly held, though the occupants had also been much shattered by the terrific bombardment to which they had been subjected.

By 4.5 a.m., however, the Damm Strasse had been stormed and captured, and the 23rd Battalion had collected about 80 prisoners. Advanced posts were now pushed out about 80 yards in front of the Blue Line and the Battalion consolidated a line about 50 yards south of it.

Thereafter the battle on the 41st Divisional front concerns chiefly the 122nd Brigade, which at 6.30 a.m., followed by tanks, passed through the 123rd and 124th Brigades and continued the attack to the Black Line, including portions of Ravine and Denys Woods, both of which were captured.

At 2.40 p.m. the 24th Division (the Reserve Division of the 13TH BATTALION. Xth Corps) passed through the 41st Division in order to assault the final objective, *i.e.*, the Green Line, running approximately 7TH JUNE. along the line of Odyssey Trench northwards through Rose Wood and past the eastern side of Delbske Farm. As will be seen later, the 13th Middlesex, one of the attacking battalions of the 73rd Brigade (24th Division) give their objective in the Green Line as " from the front (eastern) edge of Ravine Wood on the right, *via* Olive Trench to the Hollebeke road on the left."

For the time being, therefore, it is necessary to leave the 23rd Middlesex consolidating their position (from 4.30 a.m. to 6 p.m.)

13TH BATTALION. 7TH JUNE.

on the Blue Line (Damm Strasse) and follow the fortunes of the 13th Battalion to the final objective of the attack.

From Flechin, where the 13th Middlesex had arrived on 25th April, the Battalion (in Brigade) moved in stages by route march northwards to the Ypres area, and on 12th May reached Steenvoorde. On 14th a move was made to the Dickebusch area. The following day the whole of the 73rd Brigade was placed at the disposal of the C.E., Xth Corps, for work, and thereafter until the end of the month the Middlesex men were engaged mostly in digging and in assisting in preparing for the coming offensive.

From 1st to 4th June the Battalion practised the attack over trenches just north of Steenvoorde, moving to their assembly trenches at midnight on the 6th. These trenches were situated between Swan Château and Château Segard.*

The assembly trenches were reached at about 2 a.m. on 7th, but not until 11.30 a.m. was another move made, and then to Ecluse Trench and Old French Trench. News filtered through of the capture of all the objectives allotted to the 41st Division, and at 1.30 p.m. the 13th Battalion moved up to the Black Line, *i.e.*, the present front line and "jumping-off" line, from which the 24th Division was to attack the Green Line, the final objective.

Zero hour for the attack of the 24th Division was 3.10 p.m., and it was nearly that before the 9th R. Sussex and 13th Middlesex, the two assaulting Battalions of the 73rd Brigade, reached their "jumping-off" line, for the Diary of the latter records that: "Within a few minutes of arrival the Battalion went over the top (3.10 p.m.) under an excellent barrage." "B" Company (Capt. R. S. Dove) was on the right, "A" Company (Capt. F. J. Stratton) on the left, the right and left supporting Companies ("D" and "C" respectively) being commanded by 2/Lieut. Dawkins and Lieut. Roberts. The "moppers-up," furnished by "D" and "B" Companies, were under 2/Lieuts. C. W. Wallis and R. W. Phillips.

The objective of the Battalion, in the Green Line, was from the front edge of Ravine Wood on the right, *via* Olive Trench, to the Hollebeke road on the left.

By this time the enemy had been very badly shaken, for our guns had shelled him unmercifully all day long, so that without

* The Diary gives the name "Château Cigare"—the Chateau Segard was probably meant.

much opposition the Green Line was reached and taken, " B " 13TH
Company consolidating well in front of Ravine Wood and BATTALIO:
Verhaest Farm. On the left, however, " A " Company had to 7TH JUNE.
throw back its left flank, for the 47th Division, on the left of the
24th, had failed to make sufficient progress on its right flank.
The Middlesex men, therefore, were only able to consolidate the
left half of Olive Trench, " C " Company assisting " A " in this
operation and in forming a defensive flank. About 100 wounded
and 20 unwounded Germans had been captured, mostly in the
Ravine, also five machine guns, trench mortars and a large quantity
of material.

Comparative quietude reigned during the remainder of the
day, the enemy's fire being erratic. The chief discomfort felt
by the Battalion was the want of water, and it was not until
darkness had fallen that rations and water were brought up.

A quiet morning on 8th was succeeded by heavy reciprocal 8TH JUNE
shelling at night, but no attacks were made by either side.

On the 9th an attempt to gain that portion of Olive Trench
held by the enemy, by means of strong fighting patrols, pushed
out in conjunction with patrols from the 47th Division, failed
owing to the strength of the position. In this attempt 2/Lieut.
E. N. Makeham was wounded and reported missing.*

The 10th was an " artillery day," both sides shelling each other 10TH JUN
heavily at intervals, but no infantry action followed, and on the
night of 11th/12th the 73rd Brigade was relieved by the 124th
and the 13th Middlesex moved back to Dominion Camp, and on
13th to Micmac Camp, well satisfied with their part in the
Messines Battle.

Meanwhile, the 23rd Battalion had experienced an uncom- 23RD
fortable time in the Blue Line. The enemy's line north of the BATTALIO
Damm Strasse, *i.e.*, in the Salient, was farther west than the
latter, and he was therefore able to enfilade the trenches of
the Middlesex, which he did in a most annoying fashion. Nevertheless, the work of consolidating the line continued, and when
the Battalion was relieved on the night of 11th June a fairly 11TH JUN
strong position had been formed, the parapet reversed, and much
wire put out to form a good second line. At 8.30 p.m. the
Battalion moved back to the Reserve Line. All ranks were tired
out, but in good spirits, though their losses had been heavy, the
roll call showing only 8 officers and 298 other ranks who had

* Died in German hands on 28th August, 1917.

19TH AND 23RD BATTALIONS.

marched out of the Blue Line; the Battalion had lost about half its numbers.

The 23rd Middlesex did not take any further part in the battle, which concluded on 14th June.

Of the 19th Middlesex (Pioneers of the 41st Division) during the Battle of Messines there is little to record, " general work on the C.Ts. (communication trenches) " being the only comment.*

14TH JUNE.

By the close of the battle on 14th June the British line had been pushed forward to and included the Oostaverne line. Messines and Wytschaete (mere ruins) and the whole of the Salient from north of " Plugstreet " Wood, northwards across the Ypres–Comines Canal to Armagh Wood, had been " pinched off." All the high ground so necessary to the coming operations in the Ypres Salient was ours; 7,200 prisoners, 67 guns, 94 trench mortars, and nearly 300 machine guns had also been taken from the enemy.

---

* It may be interesting to note how difficult it was to obtain information concerning the three Battalions of the Middlesex Regiment who were present at the Battle of Messines, 1917. The 23rd Battalion's narrative of the actual attack on 7th June consists of exactly 112 words; the 13th Battalion takes nearly 200 words, and the 19th Battalion only five words.

CHAPTER XXX.

The Flanders Offensive: II.

THE BATTLES OF YPRES, 1917,

31st July–10th November.

INTRODUCTION.

TO give an intelligent pen-picture of the Battles of Ypres, 1917, without first briefly discussing the general situation and the plans and intentions of the Allied Commanders-in-Chief, is impossible. Neither is it desirable from a Regimental point of view to omit such vital matters, otherwise the operations become merely a series of battles without reason. Moreover, a comprehensive knowledge of the general situation and plans of operations assists the reader in appreciating the success or failure of an attack by any particular battalion: and that is one of the true functions of regimental history.

At a conference of military representatives of *all* the Allied Powers (France, Great Britain, Italy, Russia, Belgium, etc.), held at Chantilly in November, 1916, the scheme of operations agreed to " comprised a series of offensives *on all fronts* " (France and Flanders, Italy, and Russia), " so timed as to assist each other by depriving the enemy of the power of weakening anyone of his fronts in order to reinforce another." So far as the British Army was concerned, the first attack (from the Ancre to the Scarpe) was to take place early in 1917, after the French had attacked farther south. But Fate intervened and in several ways interfered with these plans. Marshal Joffre was superseded in December, 1916, by General Nivelle, who produced fresh plans for a great French offensive in the Spring of 1917, whereby Sir Douglas Haig was to attack a few days before his Ally so as to draw off the German reserves and artillery to the British front, after which Nivelle was to launch his great offensive. Then came the German retreat to the Hindenburg Line in March and April, which again forced

Sir Douglas Haig to modify his plans. The Arras Battles (as already described) began on 11th April; on the 16th the French offensive was launched, resulting in little gain and enormous casualties. To assist the French our offensive was continued at Arras, and in May the French again attacked. The losses on the French front in April and May caused mutinies of a very dangerous nature to break out in the French Army. Immediately it became clear that, in order to prevent the Germans gaining the initiative, Sir Douglas Haig must continue his offensive, *i.e.*, in other words, carry out the plans of a series of offensives on his front so as to deprive the enemy of the opportunity of attacking the French. The offensive at Arras was stopped and the attack transferred to Flanders, where the Battle of Messines was fought as a preliminary operation to the Battles of Ypres.

Meanwhile, Russia was in a state of revolution and as an Ally could give but little assistance, thus releasing fresh German divisions for the Western Front. Italy was depending on the offensive along the Western Front to contain the Germans and prevent them transferring troops to the assistance of the Austrians. America, though now in the War, was, as it were, "not yet in sight." The brunt of the fighting therefore fell upon the British. As a military writer in *The Times* said: "Great Britain had to put forth her whole power in 1917 in Belgium and France to save the situation; it was a stupendous task—the task of engaging the whole German Army and preventing its employment elsewhere."

Such, briefly, was the general situation.*

The "intentions" of the British Commander-in-Chief in the Battles of Ypres, 1917, were as follows: The Fifth Army was to attack the enemy on a seven and a-half mile front from Klein Zillebeke (south of the Menin Road) to Boesinghe, *i.e.*, from a south-to-north line through Sanctuary Wood, thence just west of Hooge, through Wieltje to the Yser Canal, by the Ypres–Langemarck railway, and along the eastern bank of the Canal to a point in front of Boesinghe. The Second Army, on the right of the Fifth, was to cover the right flank of the latter and advance only a short distance, forcing the enemy to distribute his artillery fire. On the left of the Fifth Army the First French Army was to advance its right in close touch with the British forces and so

---

* The intensely interesting situation in France and Flanders in 1917 may be studied further in the "Official Despatches," "Sir Douglas Haig's Command, 1915–1918" (Boraston and Dewar), and "My War Memories" (Ludendorff).

secure them from counter-attack from the north. The Belgians were on the left of the First French Army, from Noordschoote to St. George's, from where the Fourth British Army carried the line to the Belgian Coast at Nieuport. The enemy became nervous of the latter, fearing (rightly) a British attack along the Belgian coast, which had, indeed, been the original plan in order to get at the German submarine base.

After several days' postponement to suit the French, " Z " day was definitely fixed and final preparations made for the opening attack to begin at 3.50 a.m. on 31st July. At that hour the disposition of the attacking troops of the Fifth Army were, from south to north : 24th, 30th, a brigade of the 18th, 8th, 15th, 55th, 39th, 51st, 38th and Guards' Divisions. The 24th Division was just west of Shrewsbury Forest and the Guards east of Bixschoote, on the eastern side of the Yser Canal. On the right of the Fifth Army the right flanking division of the Second Army was the 41st, astride the Ypres–Comines Canal, north of Hollebeke, which at the opening of the attack was in German hands.

In the first of the Battles of Ypres, 1917 (the Battle of Pilkem Ridge) the sectors of the front of foremost interest to the Middlesex Regiment were on the right of the attack, *i.e.*, from the Ypres-Comines Canal (inclusive) to the Ypres–Roulers Railway, north of Hooge. Here, of the 41st, 24th, 30th and 8th Divisions, in that order from right to left, the first, second and fourth-named formations contained battalions of the Regiment; another battalion formed part of the 18th Division, in IInd Corps Reserve.

The 23rd and 19th Battalions were in the 41st Division, the 13th in the 24th Division, the 2nd Battalion in the 8th Division, and the 12th in the 18th Division : five battalions in all, so that the Regiment is well entitled to name " Ypres, 1917," among its Battle Honours. Indeed, ere those weary weeks and months of fierce fighting amidst awful surroundings were over, ending with " Bloody Passchendaele," there was not a single operation of the eight battles, which go to form the larger title, in which Middlesex men were not engaged. _{2ND, 12TH, 13TH, 19TH AND 23RD BATTALIONS.}

Both the 23rd and 19th Battalions of the 41st Division, and the 13th Battalion of the 24th Division, had recently been engaged in the Battle of Messines, but had been moved out of that sector further north. The 12th Battalion had not taken part in any major operations since early May, and the 2nd Middlesex, after

23RD, 19TH, 13TH AND 2ND BATTALIONS.

23RD BATTALION.

following the retreating enemy to the Hindenburg Line on the Somme, were for some time engaged in trench warfare before moving up to the Ypres Salient.

The 23rd Middlesex (Lieut.-Colonel A. R. Haig Brown), with other units of the 123rd Brigade (41st Division), were, at the end of June, in the Chippewa area, but on the 2nd July moved to the Berthen area, where training and practice for the forthcoming operations took place until the 22nd. On the latter date the move back to the first line began, and on 25th/26th the 123rd Brigade relieved the 142nd Brigade in the line from Klein Zillebeke road to the Ypres–Comines Canal, the 23rd Middlesex remaining in reserve in Ridge Wood until "Y.Z." night (30th July).

30TH JULY.

19TH BATTALION.

The 19th Middlesex (Pioneers of the 41st Division), under Lieut.-Colonel A. Irons, were similarly out of the line "at rest" until the 11th July, when they moved to Mille Kruis for work on tramways, roads, tracks and gun positions: they were in Ridge Wood from 24th to the night of 30th, when they moved up to position east of the Vierstraat–Ypres road, in readiness to go forward and carry out their part in the operations which were to begin next day.

30TH JULY.

13TH BATTALION.

The 13th Middlesex (Lieut.-Colonel L. H. Dawson), after the Battle of Messines, had moved to Micmac Camp, thence on 19th June to the front line from Railway Embankment, in Battle Wood, to the Ypres–Comines Canal. Persistent heavy shelling characterised this tour in the line, and on 22nd two officers—2/Lieuts. R. S. Harris and Webb—were both wounded by the same shell, the former dying of his wounds on 24th. On relief on 24th the Battalion marched back to Micmac Camp. The 24th Division was now out of the line and all units of the 73rd Brigade moved to the Lumbres area, the 13th Middlesex to billets near Nielle. From 1st to 17th July training for the coming attack was carried out, and then a move was made back to the forward area; by the 23rd the Battalion had arrived in camp at Dickebusch, relieving the 9th East Surreys in the support area (Larch Wood and Scottish Wood) of the 73rd Brigade sub-sector. On this date Colonel Dawson was sent into hospital and Major S. R. Frend assumed temporary command.

23RD JULY.

2ND BATTALION.

The 2nd Middlesex were last mentioned as moving back to Moislains on 1st April after the capture of Heudicourt during the advance to the Hindenburg Line. On the 11th the Battalion marched to Lieramont, near the front line, but in Brigade

Reserve. The following day the 2nd Scottish Rifles attacked 2ND BATTALION. Quentin Mill and Gauche Wood, " B " and " D " Companies of the Middlesex supporting the attack. The Scotsmen were completely successful in their attack, and the two companies of Middlesex were withdrawn on the morning of 13th without having suffered a single casualty.

Throughout the remainder of April and well on into May the 8th Division continued to fight its way forward towards the Hindenburg Line. At times in support and reserve, at others in the front line of the attack, the 2nd Middlesex took their fair share of the fighting. Casualties were numerous, especially among officers. The full story of those strenuous days is hidden behind all too brief entries in the Battalion Diary: they are sadly epitomised. But from what can be gathered from the documents the following gives some idea of the work of the 2nd Middlesex.

The Battalion went into the front-line sector in front of Vaucelette Farm on 14th April: the " line " was a line of posts only, each containing from three to twelve men. On 15th 2/Lieut. F. T. S. Lillywhite was wounded.* Three days later the 2nd West Yorkshires attacked Villers-Guislain, passing through " C " Company of the Middlesex, whilst " B " Company, in conjunction with the attack, advanced to a line south-east of the village, subsequently handing over the line to the West Yorkshiremen. On 21st the Middlesex took over from the West Yorkshires a line east of the village, but the tour, which ended on 23rd, was apparently uneventful, and the Battalion moved again to Heudicourt.

The next front-line sub-sector into which the 2nd Battalion moved (on 1st May) was in front of Gonnelieu, which had been captured by the 25th Brigade on 21st April. " D " and " B " Companies took over the forward trenches, whilst " C " and " A " were in support north-west of the village. On 5th May the 2nd Middlesex, in conjunction with the 2nd Scottish Rifles, raided the enemy's outworks of the Hindenburg Line, north and south of the Gouzeaucourt–Cambrai road. Zero hour was 11 p.m., and, under cover of a creeping barrage, the two Battalions advanced, the Middlesex reaching the neighbourhood of Sonnet Farm, where, however, they were held up. At 1 a.m. the withdrawal signal was given. The casualties in this raid were 4 officers (2/Lieuts. O. P. Beaumont, O. C. McCaw, W. H. Taggart and

* Died of wounds, 25.5.17.

S. E. Barrat) wounded, 4 other ranks killed, 48 wounded and 3 missing. On the 6th Capt. H. B. W. Savile was wounded. A final tour in the first line (from 11th to 13th May, east of Gonnelieu) preceded a march back to Lieramont, followed by a move by route-march to Curlu. For the time being the 8th Division had done with the Somme.

On the 3rd June the Battalion, in Brigade, entrained at Edge Hill Station, arriving at Bailleul about 4 a.m. on 4th. The 11th June found the Battalion in billets outside Hazebrouck, the 13th in Vancouver Camp, Vlamertinghe, and the 18th in Ypres.

From the 19th to 24th the Middlesex men were in Ypres (first in the Cavalry Barracks and then at the Lille Gate). The salient at this period was in an uproar: shell fire was continuous and heavy, both sides shelling each other furiously. On 19th 14 other ranks were wounded, on 20th 3 other ranks, on 21st 1 other rank was killed, 6 wounded, 5 sustained shell shock and 1 was missing; on 22nd 5 more were wounded and 1 suffered shell shock. On 23rd the casualties were even heavier: Capt. H. B. W. Savile, 2/Lieuts. E. L. Taggart and G. H. C. Pennycook and 2/Lieut. J. H. Frew (attached 23rd T.M.B.) and 6 other ranks were wounded; the 24th added 7 more other ranks to the list of wounded. These casualties occurred during the time the Battalion was in support, for it was not until the 25th that the 2nd Middlesex relieved the 2nd West Yorkshires in the left subsector of the front line. The 8th Division had assumed command of the sector between the Ypres–Roulers railway and Zouave Wood, the 23rd Brigade taking over the left of the Divisional front, *i.e.*, from the Ypres–Roulers railway to the Bellewaardebeck inclusive.

Of the tour, which began on 25th June and ended on the 30th, nothing is recorded but four other rank casualties—all wounded. The whole of July, with the exception of the last day or two, was spent out of the line in hard training, but at 9 p.m. on 30th July the 2nd Middlesex moved forward to their assembly trenches in Railway Wood, ready for the assault at dawn on 31st.

Mention of the 13th Middlesex was last made on 12th May, when, having been withdrawn from the line after the Third Battle of the Scarpe, they bivouacked amidst pleasant grass lands near Henin Vinage. The Battalion at this period was terribly weak and could muster all told only six platoons, each numbering about 30 men. For several days training was carried out, and then a move was made to Boileux St. Marc on the Cojeul River. On the evening of the 9th June the Middlesex men marched back again into the front-line trenches in front of Heninel. This tour ended on 17th, on which date relief came, and on the two following days the Battalion (in Brigade) marched to Pas, where, until 3rd July, further training was carried out.

13TH BATTALION.

But the 18th Division was already under orders for the Ypres Salient—no pleasant prospect—and on 3rd July the 12th Middlesex, with other units of the 54th Brigade, entrained for Godewaersvelde, and on arrival marched out to billets near Steenvoorde, the Brigade having taken over the Watou area. Three days later the Battalion moved to Dickebusch Huts, but even on the back areas the enemy's shell fire was so severe that, after 48 hours in their huts, the Middlesex were compelled to move back to Ottawa Camp, near Ouderdom.

For the next fortnight large working parties were supplied for work in the neighbourhood of Zillebeke, where preparations for the coming offensive were in full swing. Long marches every night from the camp to work and back again were, however, cheerfully carried out by all units. The Battalion Diary records that " for a gallant rescue of a wounded man one night Sergeant Moss, of " D " Company, was awarded the Military Medal."

At last, on 26th, the Battalion was relieved from work and marched back to Steenvoorde, where all ranks were given a three days' rest. On 29th the 54th Brigade marched to the Dickebusch area, the 12th Middlesex to Cornwall Camp, near Ouderdom, thence to Château Segard, just behind the line. In this position they awaited the opening of the attack on the morning of 31st July.

26TH JULY.

(I) THE BATTLE OF PILKEM RIDGE:

31st July–2nd August.

Although the front of the Allied attack on 31st July extended from the Lys River opposite Deulemont northwards to beyond Steenstraat, a distance of about 15 miles, it is with the main operations from the Zillebeke–Zandvoorde road to Boesinghe that this narrative principally deals, and with the attack of the 41st Division of the Second Army astride the Ypres–Comines

D

19TH AND 23RD BATTALIONS. Canal, detailed to cover the right of the Fifth Army during the advance of the latter.

" Preceded . . . by discharges of thermit and oil drums and covered by an accurate artillery barrage from a great number of guns,"* reads the official narrative, " the Allied infantry at Zero hour, 5.30 a.m. on the morning of 31st July, entered the German lines at all points. The enemy's barrage was late and weak."

It is, however, that portion of the battle front which lay between the Ypres–Comines Canal and the Menin Road which interests Middlesex men most, for on that part only of the front of the first of the Battles of Ypres, 1917, were battalions of the Regiment engaged. Of the six divisions engaged in this part of the line—41st, 24th, 30th, 8th, 18th and 25th—all, with the exception of the 30th and 25th, contained Middlesex men.

The front of attack of the 41st Division was from 500 yards west of Forret Farm on the right (south of Hollebeke) to the north-east corner of Battle Wood on the Klein–Zillebeke road on the left; of the 24th Division from the Klein–Zillebeke road on the right to Observatory Ridge and the south-west corner of Sanctuary Wood on the left; of the 30th Division from the left of 24th Division to Zouave Wood; of the 8th Division from the south-east corner of Zouave Wood, thence across the Menin Road to, and including, Railway Wood to the railway.

The 41st Division attacked with two brigades in the front line, *i.e.*, the 122nd south of the Ypres–Comines Canal and the 123rd north of it. The assaulting Battalions of the latter were 23rd Middlesex on the right (two companies on a one-company frontage, two companies in support), 11th Queen's right centre, 10th Royal West Kents left centre, 20th D.L.I. left.

19TH BATTALION. The 19th Middlesex with 124th Brigade were in reserve.

23RD BATTALION. The " jumping-off " line of the 23rd Middlesex lay between the Canal on the right and the Ypres–Comines railway on the left, so that the left of the Battalion would have to cross the latter in their advance on the Red Line—the first objective. The Red Line ran from Hollebeke (south of the Canal) on the right along Optic Support to Oblique Trench, thence across the Canal through Oaf† Keep and along Imperial Trench to the Klein–Zillebeke road.

* They had employed such quantities of artillery and ammunition as had been rare, even in the West." (General Ludendorff in " My War Memories.")
† In some maps " Oaf Keep," in others " Opaque Keep."

"A" and "D" Companies had been detailed as the attacking Companies, "A" forming the first two waves and "D" the second two waves; "B" and "C" were in support.

The Battalion had a difficult task before it. The advance from the "jumping-off" line was into a bottle-neck, which would narrow as the attacking companies reached their first objective. The left flank would have to cross the railway embankment, which, just where it joined the German front-line trench, Opaque (or Oaf) Keep, was about 25 feet high. It was certain this embankment would be honeycombed with dug-outs and machine guns were known to be in position between the embankment and the Canal.

At 8.30 p.m. on the night of 30th July the Battalion left Ridge Wood for the shelter trenches prior to forming up for the attack. At about 2 a.m. on 31st "A" and "D" Companies moved forward to their assembly positions immediately in front of Battle Wood. These two Companies approached their allotted position in the line of attack under heavy shell fire, which, with increasing intensity, was sweeping the whole area, Buffs Bank and the Canal forward of Iron Bridge receiving marked attention. So difficult was the approach march of "A" and "D" Companies that they did not arrive in position until just before Zero hour. Two Vickers guns with their teams assembled with "A" Company, but the third gun had gone astray.

At 3.50 a.m. the barrage opened on the German lines and the advance began. But almost immediately "A" and "D" Companies were in trouble. The ground between the Canal and the railway embankment was waterlogged and impassable. The advance took place, therefore, along the embankment, and by 3.54 a.m. (four minutes after Zero and according to time-table) the Red Line had been captured. The second objective—the Blue Line—lay between 300 and 400 yards in rear of the Red Line, the railway embankment running obliquely across the intervening space. The capture of the Blue Line was timed to take place by Zero plus 28 minutes, *i.e.*, 4.18 a.m. But the ground was in a shocking state, and in the inky darkness progress was very slow, so that the barrage, which was moving too quickly for the advance, got ahead. Clear of the Red Line, the first, third and fourth waves of the attack came under heavy machine-gun fire from dug-outs in the railway embankment and from the crest of a hill 500 yards on the left flank. Here 2/Lieut. J. L.

23RD BATTALION.
31ST JULY.

Sutherland was shot down and killed and numerous other casualties were suffered. Lieut. N. Shoobert was killed by a bomb thrown from another of those accursed dug-outs, for although the wire had been cut, sufficient remained around the waterlogged shell holes to impede the Middlesex men as they strove gallantly to reach the railway embankment. An expanse of ground from 10 to 35 yards wide was under water, which prevented the attackers from rushing the dug-outs from all sides. At Zero plus 45 minutes the situation was roughly as follows: Lieuts. Inwood, Heney and Goulding and 40 other ranks with three Lewis guns were digging in on the Blue Line at O.6.c.9.5.0,* in touch with the Queen's on the left, but not in touch with the 122nd Brigade south of the Canal. Another officer (Lieut. Humphrey), with 20 other ranks, were also digging themselves in on the Red Line north-east of the embankment, also in touch with men of the Queen's Regiment on the left. Two dug-outs on the railway embankment between the Red and Blue Lines still held out and were being attacked from the southern side with Vickers guns. Eventually, L/Cpl. Taylor and Pte. Thompsett, arming themselves with bombs, dropped down the embankment and crept along towards the dug-outs from the south-west. They reached the dug-outs uninjured and hurled their bombs at the enemy. With a crash the bombs broke through the dug-out windows, and the discomfited Germans, about 40 in number, were compelled to surrender, and the majority were sent back under escort, a few having been detained for stretcher bearing. By 5.30 a.m. the C.O. had established his forward Headquarters in one of these dug-outs.

By 6 a.m. the Blue Line had been reconnoitred and had been patrolled to the Canal bank without encountering a single German.

But there were still two enemy dug-outs between the Blue and Green Lines and just astride the Middlesex area to the north-east, which were causing considerable trouble. From this direction heavy machine-gun fire swept both the Red and Blue Lines and the railway embankment, and no movement except by men singly could take place. Hostile aeroplanes were now busy and soon the enemy's artillery was accurately shelling the captured positions.

Throughout the remainder of 31st, during the night of 31st/1st August, and during the daylight hours of the latter,

* It is impossible to give any other disposition or location, there being no object whereby to describe the position.

Water Knee-deep

"A" and "D" Companies held on to their positions, but when darkness fell they were relieved by "B" Company. On the afternoon of 31st rain had fallen heavily, and soon the newly-dug trenches both on the Red and Blue Lines were knee-deep in water, the garrison of the former being forced to seek shelter in dug-outs on the railway embankment. [23RD BATTALION. 31ST JULY.]

No further fighting took place on the Battalion front, and late on the night of 3rd August the 23rd Middlesex were relieved by the 10th Queens and moved back, first to support trenches, and then on 4th to Elzenwalle Château. The casualties in the operations on 31st were three officers killed,* one wounded, 14 other ranks killed, 121 wounded and four missing. [4TH AUGUST.]

The Pioneers (19th Middlesex), as usual, describe their part in the Battle in terse and unilluminating phrases: " ' A ' Company worked on Oaf Avenue, ' B ' Company on Optic Avenue, ' C ' Company on tramways, ' D ' Company on transport tracks"; that is the sum total of the description of many hours of splendid work carried out under shell fire amidst horrible surroundings, and without a ghost of a chance of letting off a rifle to relieve their pent-up feelings. For a fortnight they were at work on the same jobs until, on 14th August, they were relieved and marched back to a "rest" area, there to work just as hard as when in the front-line areas. [19TH BATTALION. 31ST JULY. 14TH AUGUST.]

The Official Despatches thus sum up the result of the attack by the 41st Division on 31st July and up to the night of 2nd August: "On the left English troops (41st Division) had captured Hollebeke and the difficult ground north of the bend of the Ypres-Comines Canal and east of Battle Wood. Between these two points our line had been advanced on the whole front for distances varying from 200 to 800 yards."

On the left of the 41st Division, the right division of the Fifth Army, *i.e.*, the 24th Division, had fought its way through practically the whole of Shrewsbury Forest, though the enemy still clung to the eastern edges.

The 24th Division attacked, with the 72nd Brigade on the right, 73rd in the centre, and 17th on the left. The assaulting battalions of the 73rd Brigade were the 7th Northants on the right and 2nd Leinsters on the left; the 13th Middlesex were in support, "D" Company in close support of the Northants, and "B" acting in a similar capacity to the Leinsters. The 73rd [13TH BATTALION.]

* 2/Lieut. J. H. Devereux, in addition to the two already given.

13TH BATTALION.
31ST JULY.

Brigade was to assault the enemy's trenches from Immediate Avenue on the right to Iliad Avenue on the left.

The Middlesex assembled in Larch Wood and neighbourhood, and although the enemy kept up his usual practice of shelling the Divisional area from midnight onwards, very few casualties were suffered.

At 3.50 a.m. the barrage fell and in inky darkness the troops advanced, but immediately found great difficulty in keeping direction. Opposite the 73rd Brigade a rocket burst in the sky, throwing out two red stars, and at once the enemy's barrage fell heavily at about 50 to 100 yards in front of the advancing troops. Casualties became heavy, especially among the Northants. A few Germans were captured in shell holes about 100 yards in front of the British line. In Iliad and Iliad Reserve the Leinsters met stiff opposition, but overcame it and took about 20 more prisoners. The enemy's main line of resistance, however, was in Lower Star Post and along the ridge running north and south of it. The Post was in the centre of Shrewsbury Forest and had a large clearing in front of it. All the ground in this area was strongly garrisoned and the defences were concealed and well protected. Fire positions provided a clear sweep down the valley and within a few minutes of Zero hour the advancing troops came under a galling fire from the ridge. The " going " was very bad, especially in the low-lying parts of the Forest. The volume of machine-gun fire was so great as to force a division in the attack, the Northants veering off to the right and the Leinsters to the left. At 6.45 a.m. the first objective (Blue Line) was reported as having been taken, but the position was obscure and information scanty, walking wounded supplying most of the reports.

At this period the Northants put their reserve company of Middlesex (" D ") into the line to fill the gap between the former Battalion and the Leinsters. By about 1 p.m. the Leinsters had reached the Blue Line north of the Lower Star Post, but there still existed a gap of about 400 yards between the two assaulting Battalions of the 73rd Brigade. The Leinsters then put in their reserve company (" B ") of the Middlesex to fill the gap, but still Lower Star Post defied capture.

" D " Company, attached to the Northants, had already lost heavily. All the company officers had gone down, 2/Lieut. C. W. Wallis being killed and 2/Lieuts. J. B. Faulkner and G. G. Holt gassed.

Attack by 2nd Middlesex

At 6 p.m. orders were received from Brigade Headquarters to consolidate the Blue Line, and the 13th Middlesex (less "D" Company) were ordered to take over the line. The relief took place during the night 31st July/1st August, "D" Company moving back to the transport lines in Micmac Camp. The other three Companies ("A," "C" and "B") took over the front line, and throughout the 1st and 2nd August consolidated their position. Other officer casualties were 2/Lieut. H. Rogerson killed, and 2/Lieuts. H. E. Marriott and N. Blackall wounded. There are no records of other rank casualties during the Battle, but at the end of the month of August the losses are recorded as 254 killed, wounded and missing. [13TH BATTALION. 31ST JULY.] [2ND AUGUST.]

The 8th Division attacked from the line—eastern edge of Zouave Wood—north-west corner of Railway Wood, immediately south of the Ypres–Roulers railway; the 24th Brigade was on the right and the 23rd Brigade on the left. These two Brigades were to capture the first and second objectives, *i.e.*, Blue and Black Lines; the 25th Brigade was then to pass through and capture the third objective—the Green Line.

The 23rd Brigade attack on the Blue Line was to be carried out by the 2nd West Yorks on the right and the 2nd Devons on the left; the Black Line was to be attacked by the 2nd Scottish Rifles on the right and 2nd Middlesex (Lieut.-Colonel J. H. Hall) on the left. The Brigade front ran from the south-east corner of "Y" Wood to the north-west corner of Railway Wood. [2ND BATTALION. 31ST JULY.]

Zero hour was 3.50 a.m.

Under an excellent barrage the attack on the Blue Line was successful, very little opposition being encountered by the West Yorks and Devons. At Zero plus 30 minutes the Scottish Rifles and 2nd Middlesex, who were to attack the Black Line, crossed the enemy's front line, and right up to the line of the second objective the enemy's resistance was not very strong; even up to the line of the artillery protective barrage the troops advanced without serious opposition. But as soon as consolidation of the Black Line had begun " the enemy " (so the Battalion narrative has it) " stopped running away and then opened fire with machine guns from an enclosure on the railway and from the neighbourhood of Sans Souci. Gradually also his snipers crept closer and began their deadly work.

The German trenches on the Westhoek Ridge, along the Battalion front, had been captured by "A" Company of the

2ND BATTALION.
31ST JULY.

Middlesex on the right and "D" on the left; "C" on the right and "B" on the left then pushed through to positions on the eastern slopes of the ridge, where they dug themselves in and held on. About 8 a.m. a hostile aeroplane, with streamers attached, passed close over the Black Line and dropped a white light. This was followed by very heavy shelling.

The situation at 5.45 a.m. was that the 25th Brigade had reached the Black Line, but the 24th Brigade, on the right, could not get quite as far and had had to form a defensive flank on the right to the south-west.

The 25th Brigade, which was to attack and capture the third objective—the Green Line—was held up and little progress was made.

The dearth of anything in the way of a detailed narrative of the fighting on 31st July and 1st August robs the story of the Battle, from the point of view of the 2nd Middlesex, of its chief interest. Of the several counter-attacks made by the enemy, but repulsed with heavy losses to the attackers, or of the intensely heavy shell fire to which the gallant troops were subjected and under which they clung with great tenacity to their gains, there is little information. But the Die-Hards did their job well, though they suffered for it, for when they were withdrawn from

1ST AUGUST. the line on the 1st August (the 23rd Brigade having been relieved by a Brigade of the 25th Division, which relieved the 8th Division) to Dominion Camp, they had lost many gallant officers and men. Captain W. C. Dobbs and Lieut. W. M. von Winckler and 2/Lieut. G. C. Storkey had been killed; 2/Lieut. E. Gordon-Jones was wounded and died of his wounds; 2/Lieuts. C. H. Fuller, K. T. A. Anderson, J. H. Clowes, G. D. Cowie, O. G. Johnson, C. F. J. Blake and R. A. Watson had been wounded. In other ranks the losses were 28 killed, 201 wounded, and 38 missing. On the 31st July the strength of the Battalion had been 28 officers and 830 other ranks.

12TH BATTALION.
31ST JULY.

The 12th Middlesex (54th Brigade, 18th Division) saw little of the fighting in the front line on the 31st July and 1st August. Their Division was, with the 25th Division, detailed to go through the 30th Division when the latter had captured the Black Line (second objective) and take the third objective—the Green Line.

"The functions of the Battalion," records the Diary, "as laid down in operation orders for the offensive on July 31st, were varied. Twelve platoons were detailed as garrisons for strong points and one company for carrying work. As it turned out, the line on which the strong points were to have been made was not taken, and in consequence the Battalion returned to Château Segard, with the exception of the 'carrying company' ('C'), which did some admirable and valuable work and was especially complimented by the Brigadier."

12TH BATTALION.

On 2nd August the 12th Middlesex relieved the 2nd Bedford in Sanctuary Wood, and on the night of 3rd went forward to relieve the 17th King's Regiment in the front line, with Battalion Headquarters in the tunnel under the Menin Road, near Stirling Castle.

2ND AUGUST.

The main area of the battle has been described, but there yet remains an attack by the 19th and 37th Divisions immediately south of Hollebeke, to which no reference is made in the official despatches, nor is it included in the Battle Honours of the Regiment: an attack in which the 4th Battalion took part and acquitted itself with considerable gallantry, so that the G.O.C., 37th Division, said of them that "they have fully maintained their name of 'Die-Hards.'"

4TH BATTALION.

The 4th Middlesex had arrived in the Kemmel area towards the end of June and went into trenches near Zero Wood on 28th, one officer—2/Lieut. J. G. Lyal—being wounded on the following day. Their next tour was in the Torreken Farm area, where, on 18th July, they had their first experience of "Tear Shells." On moving back to Beaver Camp training began, and in view of the forthcoming operations practice attacks were made over model trenches. On the night 29th/30th the Battalion moved forward again and relieved the 13th Rifle Brigade in the front line of the Kemmel Hill trenches.

At 3.50 a.m. on the 31st July the 19th and 37th Divisions, in conjunction with the main operations north of the Ypres–Comines Canal, attacked the German trenches from Beek Farm northwards to the road junction just south of Bee Farm (O.23.b.2.4). The operations were in two phases: (i) from July Farm northwards by the 19th Division, to whom for the operations up to Zero plus 3 hours the 63rd Brigade (less two battalions) was attached; (ii) at Zero plus 4 hours by the 37th Division, the 63rd Brigade having again come under the orders of its own divisional commander, and to which one battalion of the 112th Brigade was attached. Again the records are somewhat difficult to follow,

31ST JULY.

4TH BATTALION.
31ST JULY.

for these words occur in the Battalion Diary of the 4th Middlesex : " The best evidence is still not available."

The order of advance of the Battalion was " C " Company on the right, " D " on the left, " A " supporting " C," and " B " in reserve. The objectives of the Battalion were July Farm and Rifle Farm.

At 3.50 a.m. the attacking troops left their trenches and formed up parallel with the barrage then falling on the enemy's line. Darkness was just giving way to dawn. " C " Company had to form up on the eastern side of May Farm, and as the Middlesex passed over this area a German, crying " Kamerad," ran forward with hands up and surrendered.

During the first stages of the advance " D " Company lost touch with the right unit of the 19th Division (7th King's Own), but regained it shortly afterwards west of Bee Farm. By Zero plus 40 (4.30 a.m.) " C " Company had reached Rifle Farm ; there was then a gap to the left, after which " D " Company carried on the line. " A " Company was behind Rifle Farm. Up to this time touch had been maintained with a company of 8th Lincolns, which had formed a defensive flank on the right from June Farm to July Farm.

At 4.30 a.m. also two platoons of " A " Company passed through " C " to reconnoitre Bar Farm. Here they found two German medical officers and eight other ranks. Almost immediately, however, a heavy counter-attack was launched by the enemy, which was gallantly repulsed. The attack had, however, drawn " C " Company into the fight, while the leading ranks of the 8th Lincolns, on the right of the Middlesex, were also drawn into the action. Severe fighting now took place at close quarters in front of Bar Farm, and apparently the enemy suffered very heavy casualties. His machine guns, however, were a source of loss to the Middlesex, for they were firing from the left front, right front and right of the Die-Hards. Another German counter-attack, on the left of " C " Company, was launched. Throwing back their left flank, the remnants of this Company " fought it out where they were until they were all killed or wounded."[*]

In the meantime, " D " Company, on the right, had advanced until its left reached Bee Farm, north of which were the 8th King's Own. This position was reached about 5 a.m. The farm was

[*] 63rd Brigade Narrative.

searched and about 40 Germans taken, but as they were being sent 4TH BATTALION. back at least half of them fell dead or wounded by hostile machine-gun fire. Between 7 and 8 a.m. the enemy's bombers appeared 31ST JULY. and attacked the right flank of " D " Company. They were dispersed and gave no further trouble.

" B " Company, meanwhile, were engaged in " mopping up " May Farm and the neighbourhood, which, owing to the darkness, had not been fully cleared of the enemy during the first advance. About eight Germans were taken prisoner, but many more were killed.

From now onwards until the Middlesex were reinforced by the East Lancashires the situation of the Battalion was obscure. Apparently the German trenches in May Farm were responsible for creating confusion in the front line, and undoubtedly they had caused heavy casualties before they were " mopped up."

The front line consolidated ran south and north through June Farm and May Farm.

The losses of the 4th Battalion on the 31st July were severe : Lieuts. P. W. Farr and L. C. Thomson and 2/Lieuts. F. J. R. Simpson, H. McDonnell and S. J. Bear were killed, 2/Lieut. A. D. Reid was wounded and died of his wounds on 8th August, 1917, Captain E. Belfield was wounded and a prisoner in German hands. In other ranks the losses were 15 killed, 97 wounded, missing believed wounded 69, missing believed killed 23—total, 8 officers and 203 other ranks.

Throughout the 1st August the Battalion remained in its position, but on the 2nd was relieved and marched back to Beaver Camp. Here the Battalion received hearty congratulations from the Divisional Commander : " The G.O.C., 37th Division, wishes to convey to the officers, N.C.Os. and men of this Battalion his appreciation of their steadfastness and gallantry during the recent operations. He considers that they have fully maintained their name of Die-Hards."

The general results of the Battle of Pilkem were promising. The British line on 2nd August ran from Hollebeke through 2ND AUGUST. Shrewsbury Forest, Stirling Castle to Westhoek (both the Belle-waarde and Westhoek Ridges being captured), thence, crossing the Ypres–Roulers railway to the eastern outskirts of Frezenberg, St. Julien and the line of the western bank of the Steenbeek to the Ypres–Staden railway, where the line joined up with the French,

So far the offensive seemed to promise great things.

(II) THE BATTLE OF LANGEMARCK, 1917:
16th–18th August.

It was strange how often the elements seemed to conspire with the enemy to bring the Allied offensives to a standstill. For, on the afternoon of 31st July, ere the Battle of Pilkhem ended, the storm clouds burst and thereafter for four days torrential rain fell without cessation. The ground, low-lying and consisting of clayey soil, torn and battered as it was by shells, already sodden with rain, was turned now into a succession of vast muddy pools. It was a horrible sight, discomfiting in the extreme to those who had to live in it, and dismaying to those who would have to make the next attack *across* it. The Steenbeek and Bassevillebeek, as well as other streams, choked and swollen by the persistent rain, overflowed their banks, filling the valleys and depressions and turning them into long stretches of bog, impassable excepting for a few well-defined tracks. These tracks soon became a mark for the enemy's artillery, yet to leave them was to court death by drowning, and not a few men and animals were lost in this way.

Thus for some days the Allies, instead of being able to resume the offensive immediately and sweep on before the enemy had time to reorganise fresh lines of defence, had perforce to wait until such time as the ground was dry enough to permit of another advance. This delay was a Heaven-sent respite to the enemy, who thus had time to prepare and bring up reinforcements to meet the next attack. He had also time to prepare a new system of tactics, or rather time to bring into operation a new idea by which he hoped to defeat the attacks of his opponents. This was the introduction of " pill boxes."

These " pill boxes " were field forts built of reinforced concrete, often many feet thick. The boggy nature of the ground, which was quite unsuitable for the making of deep dug-outs, had compelled the enemy to construct these new defences, which he had distributed all along his front. They were heavily armed with machine guns and manned by troops who had been ordered, and were determined, to hold on at all costs.

The second of the Battles of Ypres, 1917, *i.e.*, the Battle of Langemarck, 1917, began at 4.45 a.m. on the 16th August on a front extending from the north-west corner of Inverness Copse to the junction of the British and French forces south of St. Janshoek.

In this battle three Battalions of the Middlesex Regiment, 2nd, 1/7th and 1/8th, took an active part, whilst two more, the 12th and 16th, were in reserve. The story is chiefly concerned with the right flank of the attack, where the 56th and 8th Divisions, amidst appalling conditions, made great efforts to win through to their objectives.

2ND, 1/7TH, 1/8TH, 12TH AND 16TH BATTALIONS.

The 1/7th (Lieut.-Colonel F. W. D. Bendall) and 1/8th (Lieut.-Colonel P. L. Ingpen) Middlesex, of the 167th Brigade, 56th Division, were last mentioned as withdrawing to old German trenches covering Tilloy and to the Wancourt line respectively, after the operations (the Third Battle of the Scarpe) on 3rd and 4th May. Both Battalions went again into the front line on 16th, the 1/8th taking over the left sub-sector between Monchy and the Arras–Cambrai road, and the 1/7th the right sub-sector on the right of the 1/8th Battalion. The 1/7th were not engaged with the enemy, but the 1/8th made two attacks.

The 1/8th Battalion had taken over part of Tool Trench, the other portion being held by the enemy. At 9.30 p.m. on 18th the Battalion carried out a bombing attack against that portion of Tool Trench still held by the Germans. Under 2/Lieut. W. A. Pengelley 20 bombers and 20 riflemen attacked the enemy and got into the trench, but owing to the strength of the enemy could not hold it, and the position becoming untenable the party was withdrawn. The daylight hours of the 19th, save for heavy shell fire on the support and back areas, were comparatively quiet, but at 9 p.m., in conjunction with the 29th Division (on the left of the 56th) the 1/8th made a frontal attack on Tool Trench. " D " Company, with two platoons of " A," formed the attacking force. As part of the trench was already held by the Middlesex ordinary artillery fire was impossible, and only light trench mortars and rifle grenades could be used to form a barrage. About 25 men got into the German trench, and for two hours had a stiff bombing fight with the enemy, but the remainder of the attackers were held up by machine-gun fire and could not advance. Eventually the survivors of the 25 returned to their own trenches. In this affair 2/Lieut. W. A. Pengelley was killed, 2/Lieut. Ball wounded, and Captain G. W. Tremlett was reported missing. In other ranks the losses of the Battalion were 3 killed, 32 wounded and 15 missing.

On relief, both the 1/7th and 1/8th Middlesex moved back to the Montescourt area for training and rest, and if ever troops

1/7TH, 1/8TH
AND 16TH
BATTALIONS.

deserved the latter they were these two Territorial Battalions. On the 10th June, however, the 1/7th moved back into the line to trenches on Telegraph Hill, the 1/8th taking over support trenches 1,000 yards north of Neuville Vitasse. On 19th both the 1/7th and 1/8th moved to the Wancourt Line in support, the two Battalion Headquarters sharing one dug-out, but on the 1st July they were again withdrawn. Several weeks of training followed before the move to the Ypres area, where, on 7th August, the 1/7th and 1/8th reached Ouderdom and went into camp. On 12th/13th August the 56th Division relieved parts of the 25th and 18th Divisions in the line on the Westhoek Ridge in preparation for the attack due to take place on 16th.

The 16th Middlesex (of the 86th Brigade, 29th Division), after relief in Shrapnel Trench on the 24th/25th April, moved to Arras and thence to Souastre, where several days were spent resting and training. May was a disastrous month for the Battalion. On 2nd the 16th were once more in Arras. There is then no entry in the diary until it is recorded that "the Battalion is ordered to dig strong points at N.6.C. (west of Monchy-le-Preux)." There then follows a casualty list giving 2 officers killed and 1 wounded, and 1 other rank killed, 25 wounded and 1 missing. Relief was followed by another tour, and on the night of 28th/29th the Battalion took over the right Battalion sector of 86th Brigade front, two and a-half companies moving into Hill Trench and one and a-half companies into Dale Trench.

On the following morning 11 officers and 230 other ranks, in conjunction with the 1st Lancashire Fusiliers in the centre, and 8th East Lancashires on the right, attacked Hook Trench under an artillery barrage. The left of the attack failed to get in, though two and a-half companies gained their objective. Of the centre battalion only a few men reached their objective; the right battalion failed to reach its objective. In a heavy counter-attack all the attacking force, with the exception of two officers and some 30 men of the 16th Middlesex, was driven back to its "jumping-off" line. These gallant fellows held out until about midday on the 31st, when, owing to lack of bombs and ammunition, and with no hope of immediate relief, they were forced to surrender. In this disastrous attack the 16th Battalion lost 8 officers 1 killed, 3 wounded, 2 missing, and 2 missing believed prisoners), and, if the figures given in the diary are accurate, practically all other ranks engaged in the attack were killed, wounded or missing. The remnants of the Battalion were withdrawn on 31st to Arras. *16TH BATTALION.*

June was spent out of the line in training, and towards the end of the month the 29th Division moved north to the Ypres area. The 16th Middlesex arrived at Rexpoede on 27th and marched to billets south-west of Proven in divisional reserve.

On 5th July the 16th Battalion arrived in camp west of Elverdinghe and on the following day moved to support positions about 1,200 yards south of Boesinghe, west of the Yser Canal. The enemy's shell fire was heavy, for even in support the Middlesex lost 10 other ranks wounded on 7th and 1 killed and 7 wounded on 10th. On the 13th the Battalion moved south to a wood, but even here bad luck seems to have dogged them, for on 15th they had one other rank killed and 12 wounded.

In the meantime (on 12th) other units of the 86th Brigade had taken over front-line trenches in the Swanhof sector, east of the Canal, and here the 16th Middlesex relieved the 2nd Royal Fusiliers on 17th. No actual fighting was done by the Battalion during this four days' tour, but when they came out of the line they had suffered 4 officers wounded, 9 other ranks killed and 48 wounded.* On relief on 20th July the 86th Brigade moved back to Corps Reserve, and when the first of the Battles of Ypres, 1917, was launched was located in the Proven area.

After the Battle of Pilkem the 29th Division relieved the Guards Division astride the Ypres–Staden railway, south-west of Langemarck, early in August, the 16th Middlesex going into the front line on the 9th/10th west of the Steenbeek, with Battalion Headquarters at Fourche Farm (U.20.C.9.3.); the front line was close to the western banks of the stream. On 10th/11th the Battalion pushed outposts across the stream in touch with French troops on the left and the 1st Lancashire Fusiliers on the right. In this small operation 22 unwounded and 3 wounded prisoners were taken. *10TH/11TH AUGUST.*

This attack was made, under Corps orders, by three platoons of " A " Company of the Middlesex and three platoons of Lancashire Fusiliers. The platoons formed up in three lines west of the Steenbeek, and at 4.20 a.m., under a " pocket barrage,"†

---

* Heavy enemy retaliation for a heavy barrage put down by the 29th Divisional artillery was apparently responsible, the Diary of the 86th T.M. Battery reporting : " Heavy casualties amongst regiments holding the line."

† A barrage put down round the objective.

16TH BATTALION.

Passerelle Farm, east of the stream, was attacked. The attack was successful and, besides the prisoners already stated, two machine guns and a howitzer were captured. The Battalion Diary states that the position was "consolidated and held," but the Brigade Diary records that a second attack was necessary, during which the farm was recaptured, three more wounded prisoners being taken. On the night of 12th/13th the 16th Middlesex were relieved and marched back to camp, north-west of Elverdinghe.

12TH/13TH AUGUST.

Casualties during this tour were again heavy: 2/Lieuts. L. H. Smith and C. W. Bishop and 30 other ranks had been killed, and 2/Lieuts. Mumford, Simpson, Lewis and Harrison and 83 other ranks wounded.

The Battalion had, however, done good work in capturing the crossings over the Steenbeek—a necessary preliminary operation to the battle which opened on 16th.

The line taken over by the 56th Division on the night 12th/13th August extended roughly from Stirling Castle on the south, northwards to Clapham Junction, along the western edge of Glencorse Wood, and along the Westhoek Ridge to the Westhoek–Zonnebeke Road. The 18th Division was on the right of the 56th and the 8th on the left. The 169th Brigade held the right and the 167th Brigade the left sectors of the 56th Divisional front.

1/7TH AND 1/8TH BATTALIONS.

In the battle which opened on the 16th the 1/8th Middlesex were to be on the right, 1st Londons on the left, the 3rd Londons in support, and 1/7th Middlesex in reserve. The objective allotted to the Division was the high ground eastwards which lay between the Westhoek–Zonnebeke Road, on the north, and a line along the southern edge of Glencorse Wood, Black Watch Corner (at the south-west corner of the Polygon Wood), and the western point of Polygon Wood. Thus Glencorse Wood and the Nonne Bosschen Wood lay in the line of advance and hard fighting was expected. Some 600 yards north-west of the Polygon Wood was a German strong point—Iron Cross Redoubt—(in the 8th Divisional area), from which stout resistance might be looked for. But the thing most likely to oppose the attack was the appalling conditions of the ground. The "woods," as such, had long since disappeared—only black and broken tree stumps remaining to show where pleasant arbours had once been. Gaping shell holes, full of water, were everywhere, and the ground all around was soft and spongy, while the recent rains had, in places, left sheets of water, through which the troops were bound to flounder to their objectives. The Westhoek Ridge itself, upon which the troops of the 167th Brigade would assemble for the attack was but 40 to 50 feet high, and here the trenches were thick in mud. No pleasant prospect, to say nothing of the fact that, owing to the short time they had been in the line, the assaulting troops had had little or no opportunity for making a reconnaissance.

On the night of 14th August " B " and " C " Companies of the 1/8th Middlesex (Lieut.-Colonel P. L. Ingpen) moved up from Canal Reserve Camp and took over the front line south of Westhoek, *i.e.*, the right sub-sector of the 167th Brigade sector ; " A " and " D " Companies were in reserve. On the 15th Captain E. B. Reynolds was wounded. At 8 p.m. on the latter date " A " and " D " Companies advanced to their assembly positions, joining " B " and " C." During the assembly operations the German " S.O.S." went up and a heavy barrage fell on the British lines, causing a great deal of confusion. Two other ranks were killed, 25 wounded, and 1 was missing from the German artillery fire.

At Zero hour—4.45 a.m.—the attack began. The 1/8th Middlesex advanced in three waves, " B " Company leading, followed by " C " and " A " ; " D " Company remained in reserve. One company of the 3rd Londons was attached to the Middlesex as " moppers-up."

Between the British and German trenches there was a valley, and as the troops reached the low ground they were brought up suddenly : a broad belt of mud lay before them. This belt was said to be about 30 yards broad, from 4 to 5 feet deep, covered with from 6 inches to a foot of water. As it was impossible to get through this sea of mud and water, " B " Company was forced to edge off to the left, while the left battalion of the 169th Brigade, also encountering the same obstacle, had no option but to bear off to the right. When, therefore, the O.C., " B " Company, reached the southern edge of the Nonne Bosschen Wood he found he had lost touch with the right flanking unit, which he could see advancing over the ground to the south-east. By this time he had lost touch with the barrage. Moreover, hostile machine-gun and rifle fire across the valley, as well as the mud, prevented him getting any further. After several vain attempts to advance, " B " and " C " Companies tried to consolidate their position, but were prevented by the mud. Light

1/8TH BATTALION.
16TH AUGUST.

trench mortars were sent for, but before they could reach the forward companies of the Middlesex the teams were shot down. At 7 a.m. troops of the 169th Brigade could be seen falling back, but the situation of the 1/8th Middlesex remained unchanged. At 10 a.m., however, as the flanks of the Battalion were exposed, the first line of the Middlesex was withdrawn to a position about half-way between Jabber Trench (the "jumping-off" line) and the eastern edge of the Nonne Bosschen Wood, the position being covered by posts in front. But there was little security in this line, for at least a dozen German aeroplanes were in the air above the Middlesex, some flying low down and machine-gunning the troops as they crouched in their posts. One was brought down by Lewis-gun fire. A 1 p.m. the enemy's guns opened fire on the Middlesex heavily, and many casualties were suffered. This fire continued until 3 p.m. The Germans were then seen massing on the left front of the Brigade. At 4 p.m. they advanced and the Divisional guns placed a barrage on the line of the Hannebeke stream. The enemy was, however, probably intent on gaining his former positions only, as it was just as impossible for him to cross the sea of mud as it had been for the troops of the 167th Brigade to pass through it.

Just before 6 p.m. numbers of troops of all units who were retiring were collected by Lieut.-Colonel Ingpen, who, forming them into two waves, led them forward again to the original front line of the 1/8th Middlesex. In doing this he was wounded.

1/7TH BATTALION.
17TH AUGUST.

Early on the 17th the remnants of the 1/8th were relieved by the 1/7th, the former moving back to Half-Way House.

The 1/7th (Lieut.-Colonel Bendall, temporarily in command, Lieut.-Colonel E. J. King being in hospital), though not engaged in the attack, had a strenuous day on 16th. At 7.30 a.m. Barnet and Enfield Company was ordered to take up bombs and S.A.A. from the Menin road to Westhoek Ridge. Next, at 8.30 a.m., Hampstead and Highgate advanced in support and were placed under the orders of the 3rd Londons. At 10.45 Tottenham was ordered to follow Hampstead and Highgate.

At 5 p.m., as the enemy was thought to be counter-attacking, "A" and "C" Companies were ordered up to the Westhoek Ridge and told to hold on at all costs. By 6 p.m. "C" was already in position and digging in on the reverse slope, and at 7 a.m. Battalion Headquarters began to move forward. It was during this move that Lieut.-Colonel Bendall was wounded and

Major P. C. Kay, who had just arrived, assumed command. At midnight, the 1/7th was ordered to relieve remnants of the three other Battalions of the Brigade, and by 6 a.m. "B" and "D" Companies held the front line, with "A" and "C" in support. *1/7TH BATTALION. 17TH AUGUST.*

"After passing a horrible day amidst the most ghastly conditions, with masses of badly wounded men on all sides, whom it was impossible to evacuate and for whom practically nothing could be done until after dark, the Battalion was relieved by the 9th Rifle Brigade."*

The 1/7th returned to Château Segard, and at 10 a.m. on the 18th proceeded to the Steenvoorde area, where also the 1/8th were by now located.

So far as the 56th Division was concerned, only about 400 yards of ground had been won, but the Division had not been give a fair chance. It had been moved up hurriedly into the line, the attacking troops had had no time in which to reconnoitre the ground, form dumps or make other necessary preparations.

The losses of the 1/7th and 1/8th Middlesex were very heavy. Both C.O.s had been wounded. Eight other officers of the 1/7th were also wounded (Captain Ashby and 2/Lieuts. Edwards, McIntyre, Meynell, Fisher, Thurston, Kimber and Stott). In other ranks the Battalion had lost 28 killed, 166 wounded and 9 missing. Three officers and 52 other ranks were also evacuated sick to hospital. The 1/8th reported their losses as 2/Lieuts. A. E. Duffield, F. W. Andre, and 31 other ranks killed, Lieut.-Colonel P. L. Ingpen,† Capts. G. R. G. Byham, T. M. Peake and C. V. Burder, and 2/Lieuts. Smart, Henderson, Sudbury, C. H. King and R. H. A. Batchelor and 114 other ranks wounded, 64 other ranks missing, and 14 wounded "at duty." *1/7TH AND 1/8TH BATTALIONS. 18TH AUGUST.*

The story of the operations on 16th–18th August now turns to the 8th Division, on the immediate left flank of the 56th Division. The Divisional front ran in a north-westerly direction from where Jabber Reserve Trench cut the Westhoek–Zonnebeke road, to the Ypres–Roulers railway, just south of Railway Dump.

The attack of the 8th Division on 16th August was carried out by the 25th Brigade on the right and the 23rd Brigade on

---

* From "The History of the 7th Battalion Middlesex Regiment," Lieut.-Colonel E. J. King, C.M.G.

† On 17th Major P. de St. Q. Isaacson assumed command of the Battalion, vice Lieut.-Colonel P. L. Ingpen, wounded. On 19th Major C. H. Pank took over command from Major Isaacson.

2ND BATTALION.

the left. Of the latter the 2nd West Yorkshires were on the right and the 2nd Middlesex (Lieut.-Colonel J. H. Hall, commanding) on the left, the dividing line between the two Battalions being the Sexton House–Sans Souci road.

After the heavy fighting of 31st July and 1st August the 2nd Middlesex had marched back to Dominion Camp, where for a fortnight training was carried out. Even in camp they suffered casualties, for at 2.30 a.m. on 12th hostile aircraft dropped bombs, killing 4 and wounding no less than 62 other ranks. On the night of 15th the Battalion moved forward again to the Westhoek Ridge in preparation for the attack to take place at 4.45 the following morning.

16TH AUGUST. The records of the attack are brief and do not make interesting reading. The 2nd Battalion formed up on the assembly tapes, Companies being in position by 2.45 a.m. The Divisional artillery put down an excellent creeping barrage at Zero hour, the troops following close on the screen of fire. Five minutes later the enemy's barrage fell on lines two and three of the assembly tapes and, although causing heavy losses, did not interfere with the attack. All went well until the left of the Battalion reached an enclosure north of Sans Souci, lying close up alongside the railway, and here machine-gun fire held the advancing troops to their ground. Apparently the left Division (16th) had not got on very well, for heavy fire was coming from north of the railway line and from Potsdam. A few more yards were gained, but the left flank was again held up. The right flank of the Battalion was similarly held up by machine-gun fire from the left and could get no further than the south-west corner of the enclosure mentioned above. Meanwhile the West Yorkshires were reported in Zonnebeke Redoubt, while the 25th Brigade had captured Anzac and Iron Cross Redoubt. But by this time all the attacking waves had become much thinned, having suffered very heavy casualties. The fact of the 56th Division, on the right of the 8th, being held up exposed the flank of the latter to violent enfilade fire from the Nonne Bosschen and Polygon Wood, while north of the railway the advance of the 16th Division had not gone well. Thus both flanks of the 8th Division were opened to enfilade and a withdrawal was essential. Heavy counter-attacks were made by the enemy, and the final line occupied by the Division ran roughly along the western bank of the Hannebeek stream.

Late that night the 2nd Middlesex were relieved by the 2nd Scottish Rifles and marched back first to Swan Château and on 18th to Halifax Camp. Their losses in the operation of 16th were 2/Lieut. F. J. Bilby killed, Capt. S. F. W. M. del Court and 2/Lieuts. E. S. Mathews, P. Cunningham, C. T. M. Hall and A. E. Turton wounded, and 2/Lieut. W. G. R. Smith missing. In other ranks their losses were 11 killed, 151 wounded and 23 missing. [2ND BATTALION 16TH AUGUST.]

The 12th Middlesex (Lieut.-Colonel Johnston), of the 54th Brigade, were not one of the assaulting battalions of the 18th Division. The Battalion was attached to the 53rd Brigade, which, with the 55th, attacked Glencorse Wood–Inverness Copse area on the morning of 16th. [12TH BATTALION.]

At 6.30 p.m. on 15th "A" Company moved to Jack Trench, behind Stirling Castle, "B" and "D" to Crab Crawl, near Sanctuary Wood, while "C" Company, attached to the 4th Londons, went to the Menin Road. The *rôle* of the Middlesex was to support the Londons and Bedfords, who were attacking the above woods. At about 3 a.m. on 16th "A" Company was sent off to the Menin Road Tunnel, "D" Company taking over their position in Jam Trench. It was not, however, until the night of 16th/17th that the Battalion relieved the 4th Londons and two platoons of the Royal Berks in the front line on the western edge, and south of Glencorse Wood. The 17th was a comparatively quiet day, and at night the Middlesex were relieved and marched back to Dickebusch, where they entrained for Arneque, rejoining the 54th Brigade in the Buysscheure area. [16TH/17TH AUGUST. 17TH AUGUST.]

It will be obvious from the foregoing narrative of the Battle of Langemarck that the advance on the right flank was of a very limited nature. The conditions of the ground and weather prohibited any extensive gain of ground. Moreover, the enemy had developed his main strength against the British right. On the left the attack had gone well and all objectives were gained, with the exception of a small section of trench north-east of Langemarck. The general results of the battle were that a wide gap had been driven into the German third-line system. General Ludendorff said of the Battle of Langemarck: "On the 16th we sustained another great blow. The English pressed on beyond Poelcapelle* and, even with an extreme exertion of strength on our part, could only be pushed back a short distance."

* Not Poelcapelle : Langemarck was probably meant.

An eloquent tribute in itself to the fine fighting qualities of the British troops.

(III) THE BATTLE OF THE MENIN ROAD RIDGE:

20th–25th September.

A month passed before the next attack was launched upon the enemy: a month during which rain again fell in torrents, making the Ypres Salient more desolate than ever. How men kept body and soul together amidst all the horrors and discomforts of those terrible weeks was a marvel. That troops could endure and yet be fit in such awful surroundings—mud, and gaping shell holes and craters full of filthy, putrid water, the whole countryside waterlogged and with scarce a dry rag to their bodies, or an inch of dry ground anywhere—speaks volumes for their grit, determination and endurance.

The third battle began on 20th September, the front selected extending from the Ypres–Comines Canal, north of Hollebeke, to the Ypres–Staden railway north of Langemarck. The average depth of the objectives was 1,000 yards, but in the neighbourhood of the Menin Road the ground to be won was about a mile in depth.

Before Zero hour on 20th, however, certain rearrangements in the British front had taken place, which included a modification of artillery tactics to meet the situation created by the change in the enemy's methods of defence. The new system adopted by the enemy (which, it must be admitted, had met with a certain amount of success in the previous battles) consisted in manning his forward trenches with just sufficient troops to disorganise an attack, the bulk of his forces lying in close reserve ready to deliver a powerful and immediate blow which might recover his lost positions before the British had time to consolidate their gains. Sir Douglas Haig's method of dealing with the new German system of defence was to limit the depth of objectives and reorganise the artillery so as to deal effectively with hostile concentrations and counter-attacks.

The wretched state of the weather since the battle of 16th–18th August made a long wait necessary in order to give the ground time to dry after the heavy rains. The weather improved at the beginning of September, and artillery and other preparations proceeded steadily. Nevertheless, it was the third week in the month before the next attack was possible.

19TH, 23RD, 1ST, 18TH, 4TH AND 16TH BATTALIONS.

The left flank of the Second Army was extended northwards, the objectives in front of it now including the high ground crossed by the Menin Road. This change necessitated a similar change in the dispositions of some of the divisions under Sir Herbert Plumer (the Army Commander), amongst which was the 41st Division, containing the 19th and 23rd Middlesex. Of the 12 divisions in the front line of battle on the morning of 20th September only one (the 41st) contained Middlesex men. There were two divisions of the Second Army in reserve—the 33rd and 37th—and one of the Fifth Army—the 29th—which also contained battalions of the Regiment, *i.e.*, the 1st and 18th (33rd Division), 4th (37th Division), and 16th (29th Division).

The chief interest in the battle, from a regimental point of view, is, however, centred in the 23rd and 1st Battalions, the former (of the 123rd Brigade, 41st Division) attacking the enemy at 6.30 p.m. on 20th, and the latter putting up a truly magnificent fight when the enemy counter-attacked on 25th September.

Of the 23rd Battalion, between the 4th August and the night of 19th September, there is little to record. The only event which might have been interesting is thus described in the Battalion Diary on the 10th of the former month: "German dug-outs at O.6.B.35 raided; 19 prisoners captured." The Battalion was then holding the line in Battle Wood. No one captured 19 Germans in 1917 without fighting, and it is a pity that the narrative is missing from the Brigade Headquarters Diary, though the latter states "see report attached." On the night of 19th September, at 8.30 p.m., the Battalion paraded and marched to Larch Wood (from shelters in Ridge Wood) and took up positions in readiness for the operations the next day. The 41st Division was attacking with the 124th Brigade on the right and 122nd on the left. The 123rd Brigade was placed in reserve to go through and capture the final objective, or reinforce the two assaulting Brigades, as the situation demanded. The 39th Division was on the right and the 23rd on the left.

23RD BATTALION.

19TH SEPT.

The Divisional front line ran from Shrewsbury Forest in a northerly direction through Bodmin Copse. In front of this

23RD
BATTALION.
19TH SEPT.

line the enemy trenches were, from right to left, Jehu, Java, Java Drive, Java Avenue and Jap Trench, all powerfully defended with machine guns, mostly mounted in concrete emplacements. The Basseville Beek crossed the Divisional front from north to south at about 800 yards' distance from the front-line trenches. The enemy's defences beyond the stream were Joist Trench and Tower Trench. The first objective (Red Line) included Jehu and Java Trenches, then a line north about 150 yards west of the Basseville Beek to the gap between the Dumbarton Lakes. The second objective (the Blue Line), with the exception of about 300 yards on the right, was east of the stream and ran through " wooded " country. The third objective (Green Line) was the line of Joist and Tower Trenches; it also included Tower Hamlets.

20TH SEPT.

The barrage opened at 5.40 a.m. on 20th and the advance began. The 124th Brigade was held up between the Red and Blue Lines; the 122nd Brigade reached the Green Line, but owing to lack of support had to fall back to the Blue Line.

About mid-day the 123rd Brigade was ordered to reinforce the firing line and take the final objective (Green Line). The 23rd Middlesex were to attack on the right, Royal West Kents in the centre, and Durham Light Infantry on the left.

At 1 p.m. the Middlesex moved forward from the trenches in Larch Wood and an hour later arrived at Canada Tunnels (Canada Street area). The Brigadier held a conference at 3.20 p.m. and explained the plan of attack to the C.Os. of the attacking battalions. Operation orders were issued at 4 p.m. Zero hour was 6.30 p.m.

In artillery formation the Middlesex advanced at 4.30 p.m. *via* Lower Star Point to Java Trench. Here they were met by machine-gun fire from in front and from the right flank, and sheltered as best they could in trenches which had been much battered by the fire of the guns of both sides. No easy task lay before the Battalion; the enemy was well posted on a ridge, and his snipers and machine guns were extremely active, the slightest movement drawing fire. But at 6.30, under a new barrage, which reached the ridge and concrete dug-outs, " B " and " C " Companies advanced. In extended formation, and in short rushes, these gallant fellows reached the Blue Line, which, in front of the Middlesex, was west of the Basseville Beek. Over ground swept and much cut up by shell fire these two companies secured their objective, but they found themselves opposed to a 23RD BATTALION. merciless hail of bullets and shells, and being too weak in numbers to push on to the final objective, were forced to consolidate their 20TH SEPT. position as best they might. During the advance three dug-outs, encountered in the valley before the men pushed on up the ridge, were captured and "mopped up." The records from this stage are somewhat confusing, for the Battalion Diary speaks of the "rear company being on the western bank of the Basseville Beek with orders to hold all positions until daybreak" (21st September), whereas there is no mention of the exact position of the Middlesex until 8.30, when the Brigade Narrative says, "G.O.C., 41st Division, stated that the 23rd Middlesex were believed to be on the Green Line on the right and the 122nd Infantry Brigade on the left." The "position map," however, places the German line just west of the stream. At about 8 p.m. the Germans were observed concentrating on a ridge in front of the Battalion, but Lewis-gun and rifle fire soon dispersed them. Patrols sent out at 10 p.m. reported the Blue Line "all clear." At midnight orders were received from Divisional Headquarters to resume the attack at 9.30 a.m. on 21st. The R.W. Kents were to attack on the right and the D.L.I. on the left; the Middlesex were to attack from their positions along the Basseville Beek. The general direction of the attack was Jager Trench (right)—Joist Trench (left).

The frontal attack by the R.W. Kents and Durhams made 21ST SEPT. slight progress, but not sufficient to enable the O.C., Middlesex, to join in the attack, for had he done so his line of advance would have exposed his men to enfilade fire from both flanks. He was, therfore, bound to wait until the advance of the other attacking battalions silenced the machine guns on his left. This, however, did not happen, the main attack being held up short of the objective. The story of the attack as contained in the Diary of the Middlesex is as follows: "' C,' ' D ' and ' A ' Companies advanced in short rushes, taking cover in shell holes, until the copse on the Basseville Beek was reached; hostile machine-gun fire was very intense and casualties numerous.* The ground from here forward was found to be practically a quagmire, and further advance was impossible without entailing enormous casualties.

* The Battalion's losses on the 20th had been 10 other ranks killed, 71 wounded and 21 missing; on the 21st they were 1 officer killed, 3 wounded, 4 other ranks killed, 47 wounded and 2 missing.

23RD BATTALION.
21ST SEPT.

An advanced line was then pushed forward and the Battalion dug in."

There was, apparently, a forward party of Middlesex just across the stream, for the Brigade Narrative states that they were attacked by the enemy. During the afternoon the German artillery fire had been very heavy and several counter-attacks were launched, all of which were, however, repulsed with terrible losses to the enemy. At 5.30 p.m. the hostile barrage on the front line of the 123rd Brigade was intense, and the valley of the Basseville Beek was like a seething furnace of bursting shells. Just before 7 p.m. the barrage lifted and the enemy again attempted to attack the R.W. Kents and Durhams, but were beaten back with heavy losses.

It was about this time (7 p.m.) that the Middlesex were heavily attacked by the enemy, whose troops advanced in five lines. An S.O.S. was sent up, the while the Middlesex, firing as hard as they could with rifles and Lewis guns, held the enemy. Then the barrage came down, and when it ceased no living thing was visible on the ground over which those five lines of Germans had been seen advancing.

22ND SEPT.

Throughout the 22nd and 23rd the Middlesex clung to their positions, and at 3 a.m. on 24th the Herts arrived to relieve the remnants of the Battalion. By 5 a.m. the last company had been relieved and the Battalion then proceeded to Micmac Camp.

19TH BATTALION.
20TH–25TH SEPTEMBER.

All that the 19th Battalion (Pioneers) record in their Diary during the operations from 20th to 25th September is that: " Division attacked at 5.40 a.m. 'A' and 'B' Companies duckboarded track, 'C' Company tramways, 'D' Company mule track," and " ditto, ' ditto ' during the remaining days of the battle."

4TH BATTALION.
20TH SEPT.

The 4th Middlesex (63rd Brigade, 37th Division) moved up to Irish House between 4 and 5 p.m. on 20th, to be (with other units of the Division) in closer support to the 19th Division, which had attacked the enemy from just north of the Ypres–Comines Canal. But the Battalion did not go into action, and on 21st moved back to Mont Kokereele, remaining there until 27th September, when they moved into front-line trenches in front of Shrewsbury Forest.

27TH SEPT.

16TH BATT.
20TH SEPT.

The 16th Middlesex (86th Brigade, 29th Division) were in tents, bivouacs and dug-outs in Charterhouse Camp on 20th

September, but were not called upon to go forward to the fighting line. After relief from the line on 12th/13th August they had marched back to their camp. On the 14th Lieut.-Colonel T. W. O'Reilly was posted to the Corps Depot and Lieut.-Colonel F. G. G. Morris assumed command of the Battalion. At 2 p.m. the 16th again moved forward, and after dark took over the Blue Line, with posts north-west and south-east of Montmirail Farm, Denain Farm, Martin Hill and on the railway. That night (16th/17th) Lieut.-Colonel Morris was killed in action. The next day Major J. Forbes-Robertson arrived and took over command of the Battalion. On relief on 19th/20th the 16th Middlesex, though they had not been in action, had lost 1 officer (the C.O.) killed and 1 wounded, 15 other ranks killed, and 66 wounded. The remainder of August and September until 20th were uneventful. On the 21st of the latter month a squadron of hostile areoplanes dropped about 20 bombs on Charterhouse Camp, but only wounded one other rank. For several days the Battalion was then engaged in salvage work.

But to return to the operations on 20th September.

By nightfall the whole British line from the Ypres–Comines Canal to the Ypres–Staden railway had been advanced, the greatest depth of ground won being astride the Menin Road and including the whole of the high ground covered by the road, and for which much heavy fighting had taken place during the previous attack.

But the enemy did not abandon their important positions without desperate efforts to regain them. The afternoon and evening of 20th saw no less than eleven heavy counter-attacks against various parts of the line; all were broken up and the enemy repulsed.

From the 21st September onwards until and including the 25th September very heavy counter-attacks were launched by the Germans on wide fronts between Tower Hamlets and the Polygon Wood, and north-east of St. Julien.

"All these attacks," record the official despatches, " were repulsed except that, on the 25th September, parties of German infantry succeeded in entering our lines north of the Menin Road. Heavy and confused fighting took place in this area throughout the day, in which English, Scottish and Australian troops (33rd Division and 5th Australian Division) gradually drove the enemy from the limited foothold he had gained."

1ST BATTALION.   In this fighting the 1st Middlesex, of the 33rd Division, gained
22ND SEPT.   fresh honours for the Regiment.* The Battalion had received
orders on 22nd to proceed up the line on 23rd and immediately
made preparations for the move. Just after 11 a.m. on the
latter date the Middlesex men left camp and, marching *via*
Rosenhill, Dickebusch, Kruisstraathoek and Trois Rois, reached
dug-outs in the railway embankment and the banks of the Zillebeke
Lake, the Battalion being settled in by 4.30 p.m. At 10 a.m.
24TH SEPT.   on the morning of 24th Major H. A. Hanley, temporarily in
command of the Battalion, Lieut.-Colonel Elgee,† the C.O.,
being then at Berthen in command of the 98th Brigade Depot
Battalion),‡ accompanied by one officer and one N.C.O. from
each company, went up to reconnoitre the line which the Battalion
was to take over that evening from a battalion of the York and
Lancs Regiment, prior to an attack to be launched (in conjunction
with a general attack) on the morning of 26th.

This line lay between the Polygon Wood (just east of Black
Watch Corner) and the Reutelbeek. It had been but a day or
two in our possession and was still in the course of consolidation.
The defences consisted of shell-hole posts connected by short
lengths of trench; all around were huge craters. Just behind
the centre of the line was Carlisle Farm. The German defences
were stronger than our own; they had a fairly continuous line
of trenches in front (west) of Cameron House and Jut Farm,
with numerous shell-hole defences, and here and there several

* Between the 25th April (upon which date the gallant Die-Hards, having suffered grievous losses in the Second Battle of the Scarpe, coming out of the line with only 8 officers and 230 other ranks) and the 24th September there is little to record of outstanding interest concerning the 1st Middlesex. The Battalion, on the former date, reached Grosville, and until early in May were out of the line, absorbing drafts, training and getting ready for the next battle. At the end of July the Battalion entrained at Pont Remy for Adinkerke, and in August went into trenches in the St. George's sector, east of Nieupoort. On 1st September a move was made to Moulle, thence on 15th to Nord Peene. On 20th the Battalion, being then billeted in Roukleshelle, moved off at 4.30 a.m. through Berthen, Hensken and Reninghelst to Alberta Camp.

† Lieut.-Colonel J. W. L. Elgee had recently returned to the Battalion. He had been evacuated sick to England in March. Lieut.-Colonel Hanley tells this fine story of Lieut.-Colonel Elgee: " On rejoining the Battalion (about 20th September), he learned that we were going into the next show at Ypres. He at once said that, as I had had the Battalion for the last six months or so, and had had all the trouble of training it, etc., I should have the honour of commanding it in the battle affair, but that he would go in with us and serve under me. He even suggested this to the Division, who decided, however, that it would not be practicable, but that Elgee should stand down and let me take the Battalion in. This, just to show the fine soldierly spirit of Elgee ! "

‡ The Depot Battalion was formed of a percentage of officers, N.C.Os. and men from each battalion of the Brigade when the latter was engaged in battle operations.

ruined buildings, which served as machine-gun posts. About
midway between the opposing lines of trenches, and in front of
the northern sub-sector of the Brigade line, was another farm
(Jerk House), also in possession of the enemy. It was this line
(570 yards in length), hardly consolidated, and so difficult to
distinguish in places, that men going to and from the line frequently lost their way amidst the maze of craters and shell holes,
subjected all the while in a more or less severe degree to heavy
shell fire, that the Middlesex were to take over before the next
battle. The records describe it briefly as consisting " mainly
of short, isolated lengths of trench dug amongst the shell holes,
with supporting lines in rear."

<small>1ST BATTALION.
24TH SEPT.</small>

Major Hanley and his officers returned from their reconnaissance, and at 6.30 that night the 1st Middlesex left the railway
dug-outs, south-west of Zillebeke Lake, and, proceeding by
sections at 100 yards intervals, moved up *via* Dormy House and
Yeomanry Track to the front line. Guides met the various
platoons at the starting point, and the relief was carried through
to the accompaniment of a good deal of shell fire. One shell fell
amidst a platoon of " B " Company, killing one man and wounding
the platoon commander—2/Lieut. Buttle—and 10 other ranks.

Battalion Headquarters had moved up to the southern edge of
Glencorse Wood, where news of the relief was anxiously awaited.
But reports were slow in coming in, many of the guides losing
their way in the crater area, whilst the enemy's shell fire was
increasing in intensity. " D " Company was the first to report
" relief complete," but it was 11.40 p.m. before that news reached
Battalion Headquarters. For some hours no further news was
received, all telephone wires having been cut by hostile shell fire.
" A " Company, which was in position before 10 p.m., was the
last to report. The Company Commander had sent several
orderlies with reports (other communication being impossible),
and hours passed before at last one got through. Eventually,
by means of officer patrols, all companies were, at 4.30 a.m. on
25th, accounted for as being in position—" A " Company on the
right, " B " on the left, " D " supporting " A," and " C " supporting " B."

<small>25TH SEPT.</small>

Once in position, the two forward companies sent out patrols
and covered their fronts with a series of posts.

The right sub-sector of the 33rd Divisional front was held by
the 100th Infantry Brigade, whose line extended from the southern

1ST BATTALION. 25TH SEPT.

bank of the Reutelbeek southwards to the Ypres–Menin Road. The 5th Australian Division was on the left of the 98th Brigade.

At about 5.30 a.m. the enemy suddenly placed a very violent barrage on the front, support and reserve lines of the 33rd and Australian Divisions. Some indication of the intensity of this barrage may be gathered from the fact that the Germans employed no less than 27 batteries of field artillery, 17 field howitzer batteries, 15 heavy howitzer batteries, and 5 batteries of H.V. long-range guns; indeed, an officer of the Middlesex stated that it was "one of the heaviest bombardments of the War." Gas and heavy shrapnel were largely used. There was a thick morning mist when the bombardment opened, under cover of which and the fire of their guns, the enemy attacked the Australians' right, the 1st Middlesex and the 100th Brigade south-west of Reutelbeek.

From captured documents it is possible to give quotations from the orders issued to the two German battalions—3rd Battalion, 229th R.I.R., and 2nd Battalion, 230th R.I.R.—which attacked the 33rd Divisional front. These orders were issued on 24th September and, after detailing the two battalions (already mentioned) as the assaulting troops, states that they "will attack the enemy opposite them to-morrow (September 25th, 1917) and will eject him from his present position." The sector of attack is given next: the 3rd Battalion, 229th R.I.R., from the southern edge of Polygon Wood to the Reutelbach (Reutelbeek), *i.e.*, Veldhoek Trench (called by the Germans the Wilhem Stellung), Carlisle Farm, and the 3rd Battalion, 230th R.I.R., from the stream southwards. Light machine guns were to be in the front line, heavy machine guns were to accompany the first, second and third waves of the attack, one platoon of heavy machine gunners to be attached to each company.

The Assault Battalion (a special formation then in vogue in the German Armies) of the Fourth German Army was to take a prominent part in the attack.

As soon as the barrage opened (referred to as the "destructive fire") the Germans were to "work closer to the enemy" . . . "touch must be kept." Other instructions were: "The companies will attack with strong first waves immediately the barrage lifts in order not to give the enemy any time to collect his wits." Finally, "troops must be in position by 4.40 a.m. Destructive fire (barrage) starts at 5.15 a.m. Fall in for the attack 5.45 a.m."

It will therefore be gathered from the above German orders 1ST BATTALION. that, ere ever they had time to acquaint themselves with the 25TH SEPT. nature of the ground in front of them or their surroundings, the 1st Middlesex would be heavily attacked.

The story of this attack and the way it was met is one of the proudest memories of all Die-Hards.

Curtained by the thick mist and under cover of the merciless barrage his guns were putting down on the front, support and reserve lines of his opponents, the enemy advanced at about 6 a.m. His troops, in considerable strength, swarmed across No Man's Land. The brunt of the first attack seems to have fallen on three platoons in the centre and on the right of " B " Company. Handicapped by the fact that they had never seen their front in daylight, and that the Yorks and Lancs, whom they had relieved, had been unable to give them very much information (that unit only having held the sector for about 24 hours), these platoons nevertheless held their ground for some time. But, aided by their knowledge of the ground and (to them) the friendly mist, the German troops worked their way through and between the posts and took them in rear. " These three platoons," states the narrative, " seem to have made a good fight, one post being seen entirely surrounded, but offering a fierce resistance."

On the right, " A " Company (and the 100th Brigade on their flank) was attacked from behind a small ridge in front. But with Lewis-gun and rifle fire the enemy was completely repulsed, and as his troops fell back they were subjected to a severe flanking fire. Here at least he made no progress.

About 6.30 a.m. the enemy launched another attack. Five waves of Germans with supports came on unhindered by a practice barrage which had been placed along the whole German front that morning by order of Second Army Headquarters.*

The attack came from the direction of Jerk House. The first attack had cut a gap between " A " and " B " Companies, and through this gap the Germans, gradually closing in, worked from shell hole to shell hole. Desperate fighting, much of a hand-to-hand nature, now took place. " A " Company was losing heavily, and eventually the enemy entered Veldhoek Trench from the left, bombing along it in a southerly direction. Finally, the

* Lieut.-Colonel Hanley states : " When the heavy ' gunning ' started out over the front line it was thought to be merely our own side having their 'furious joy,' and no notice was taken. Owing to the thick mist, nothing could be seen of any attack."

1ST BATTALION. remnants of the Company fell back about 150 yards. In the
25TH SEPT. fighting the Company Commander—Captain S. Preston—was
killed, also 2/Lieut. T. J. Young, of "B" Company, who had
been acting as liaison officer between the two Companies. All
the officers of these two front Companies were either killed or
missing.

Remnants of both "A" and "B" Companies were by now
making their way back to the support line, where "C" and "D"
Companies, unable to see owing to the thick mist and kept down in
their trenches by the two heavy barrages and hostile machine-gun
barrage, were in ignorance of what had been happening in the
front line. But as soon as they learned the situation steps were
taken to check the enemy's advance. Lewis guns were pushed
out to cover the gap in the centre, and groups of men dashed
forward into shell holes. On came the enemy, but now he met
comparatively fresh troops and at once sustained a check.

"D," the right support Company, endeavoured to get into
touch with the left of the 100th Brigade, but owing to the marshy
ground failed to do so. The mist lifted and troops of the 100th
Brigade were seen falling back, thus uncovering the flank of the
Middlesex. In the distance the enemy in large numbers was
observed crossing the ridge in front, and heavy fire was brought to
bear on him. Once again the grey waves were checked. But
all the while enemy aeroplanes, flying low down over the Middlesex
trenches, harassed the Die-Hards with machine-gun fire.

Battalion Headquarters had by now received news that the
enemy had penetrated the front line, and Major Hanley prepared
his position for defence should the Germans break through the
supporting companies. The situation was reported to 98th
Brigade Headquarters, and the latter ordered the 2nd Argyll and
Sutherland Highlanders to place one company at the disposal of
the O.C., 1st Middlesex. At about 8 a.m. this Company ("C")
was in a trench behind Battalion Headquarters of the Middlesex.
But presently a platoon from the Highlanders was sent to fill a
gap between the right of the Australians and the left of "C"
Company (the left front company) of the Middlesex.

It was about this time that a corporal staggered into Battalion
Headquarters and reported that No. 6 Platoon of "B" Company,
under Sergeant Martin, was still holding on to its original
position, in touch with the Australians on their left. These
gallant fellows were on the extreme left of the Middlesex front

line and, although exposed to frontal fire and enfiladed from their right, had refused to surrender and were clinging grimly, with extraordinary tenacity and courage, to their position. As soon as this information reached the C.O. he sent a message to Brigade Headquarters asking for the barrage to be put down on that flank.

Arrangements were being made to fill the gap between " D " and " C " Companies when orders arrived at Battalion Headquarters from Brigade Headquarters with details of an attack to be made in order to regain the original front line. The time was then about 12.30 p.m.

At 1.15 p.m. Battalion Orders for the attack were issued. The first paragraph reads : " The enemy has gained possession of our front line running J.15.d.4.8 to J.9.d.4.0, with the exception of one platoon on the extreme north of the sector, which still holds its position." The attack was to be made by the 1st Middlesex and " A " and " C " Companies of the Argyll and Sutherland Highlanders, to regain the lost line. " C " Company of the Middlesex was to attack on the left on a front of 180 yards, " A " Company of the Highlanders in the centre on a frontage of 200 yards, and " B " Company on the right also on a front of 180 yards. Three platoons of " C " Company of the Highlanders were to support the attack and dig in 200 yards in rear when the original front line had been reorganised. Zero hour was to be 2 p.m.

The situation of the 1st Middlesex when these orders were issued was that " D " Company (right), with remnants of " A " and " B " Companies, and " C " (left), were holding a support line roughly about 200 yards behind the original front line. There was a gap between these two Companies very thinly held by one or two posts some 50 to 80 yards apart. Orders to the A. and S. Highlanders stated that their " A " Company was to advance on a front of 180 yards and endeavour to fill the gap, and when level with the Middlesex both Battalions were to advance to the original front line and consolidate it, afterwards pushing out posts to their front.

The barrage started well in front of the line held by " D " and " C " Companies of the Middlesex, the Highlanders having, therefore, to start without its assistance. " A " Company of the latter Battalion left the " jumping-off " line at 1.55, followed at 200 yards distance by " C " Company. The whole movement was, however, visible to the enemy, who put down a heavy barrage

E

1ST BATTALION. in front of the attack. In spite of the barrage the Highlanders
25TH SEPT. pushed on and came up level with the Middlesex. But now a hurricane of machine-gun bullets swept the whole line and neither the Middlesex nor the Highlanders could move. They therefore consolidated the ground held, forming once more a continuous line across the Brigade front. A message, despatched to Battalion Headquarters, asking for a further barrage, did not reach its destination. In the meantime, consolidation proceeded.

Towards evening the Germans again advanced and heavy fire was opened upon them. The enemy, however, occupied some concrete emplacements on the right centre of the line and put up Red Cross flags. As they were observed strengthening their position no notice was taken of the flags, and both Middlesex and Highlanders kept the enemy under heavy fire.

26TH SEPT. The situation remained the same until the third phase of the attack took place at dawn on 26th, when other units of the Brigade, passing through the now worn-out Die-Hards, not only gained the original line, but a line running north and south from Jut Farm to Cameron House. The Middlesex and Highlanders were then withdrawn during the afternoon of that date,* when it was definitely established that a new line had been gained and consolidated. Then, also, the gallant fellows—the survivors of No. 6 Platoon, " B " Company—who all alone had held out on the extreme left flank of the original line, were relieved. How many they numbered, how many were killed and wounded, it is not possible to say, but their fine devotion to duty was typical of the splendid spirit of the Regiment.

On vacating the position they had held with so much staunchness, the 1st Middlesex made their way back to Clapham Junction (along the Menin Road), where for a little while they took shelter in some reserve trenches. They then marched back to the Railway Dug-outs south and south-west of Zillebeke Lake.

The losses of the 1st Battalion from 24th to 26th September, inclusive, were heavy : 4 officers were killed,† 3 wounded and 2

* There is a mistake in the official despatches concerning the action of the Middlesex and Argyll and Sutherland Highlanders. In describing the Battle of Polygon Wood, 26th September–3rd October, the despatches state that the advancing troops " effected the relief of two companies of the Argyll and Sutherland Highlanders who, with great courage and resolution, had held out in our forward line all night, although isolated from the rest of our troops." From the foregoing account it will be seen that it was No. 6 Platoon of " B " Company of the 1st Middlesex who was isolated and held out.

† In addition to the two officers already given, Lieut. E. N. Whyte and 2/Lieut. W. G. Rapley were amongst the killed—all on 25th September.

missing; in other ranks the losses were 37 killed, 69 wounded, 131 missing, and 12 missing believed prisoners—in all a total of 9 officers and 249 other ranks. {1ST BATTALION. 26TH SEPT.}

The 18th Middlesex (Pioneers of the 33rd Division) had a most strenuous time during the above operations. More than once they "stood to," as there was a likelihood of employment as infantry, but mostly their time was put in in digging communication trenches and clearing the roads, though they furnished carrying parties also. They had 1 officer wounded, 3 other ranks killed, and 30 wounded during the operations which ended on 26th. {18TH BATTALION. 20TH–25TH SEPTEMBER.}

On 28th the 23rd Division relieved the 33rd, the latter moving back to the Blaringhem area for rest, but the hard-worked Pioneers stayed in the line—their services were too valuable to be dispensed with.

(IV) THE BATTLE OF POLYGON WOOD:

26th September–3rd October.

The heavy fighting which had taken place after the successful advance on 23rd September was not allowed to interfere with the plans made for an attack by the Second and Fifth Armies (on 26th September) from south of Tower Hamlets to north-east of St. Julien—a front of just under 6 miles. South of the Menin Road only a short advance was intended, and north of the road the objective was a position from which a direct assault could be made upon that portion of the main ridge between Noordemhoek and Broodseinde, traversed by the Becelaere–Passchendaele Road.

The battle began at 5.50 a.m. and, as already described, the attacking units of the 33rd Division passed through the line of the 1st Middlesex, relieving a platoon of "B" Company, who, with great courage and resolution, had held out, though isolated from the remainder of the line. The 1st Battalion was, however, not engaged in the battle and had indeed seen its last action in the Battles of Ypres, 1917. {1ST BATTALION.}

Although they were in the area of the battle, neither the 4th Middlesex (37th Division) nor the 16th Middlesex (29th Division) attacked the enemy. {4TH AND 16TH BATTALIONS.}

4TH BATTALION.
27TH SEPT.

On 27th September the 4th Battalion moved during the evening to Bus House, where they were met by guides from the 1st Cambridgeshire Regiment and led up to the line in front of Shrewsbury Forest and east of the Bassevillebeek Valley, where they remained until relieved by the 8th Lincolns on 1st October. Although the enemy's shell fire during the tour had been heavy, the only casualties reported were two other ranks killed and two wounded. On relief the Battalion moved to the support trenches at Mont Sorrel. On the night of 3rd/4th October " B " and " C " Companies moved up east of the Bassevillebeek into close support of the 8th Lincolns, who were to attack the enemy on the following morning.

3RD/4TH OCT.

16TH BATTALION.
29TH/30TH SEPTEMBER.

The 16th Battalion (less " C " and " D " Companies) moved up from Charterhouse Camp on the night 29th/30th September, relieving the 1st Royal Dublin Fusiliers in the front line, *i.e.*, the right sub-sector of the Langemarck sector; " C " and " D " Companies moved to Dulwich Camp. On 1st October the latter Companies relieved " A " and " B," the latter marching back to camp. On the night 3rd/4th " C " and " D " were relieved by the 1st Royal Dublin Fusiliers, who were to attack the enemy on the 4th. Two platoons of " B " Company (2 officers and 80 other ranks) were, however, attached to the Fusiliers as liaison party on the right flank with the 4th Division, and moved up to the front line during the night.

3RD/4TH OCT.

3/10TH BATTALION.
3RD/4TH OCT.

On the night 3rd/4th October also another Battalion of the Middlesex Regiment was moving up to take part in the battle of 4th October. This was the 3/10th—a third-line Territorial Battalion under the command of Lieut.-Colonel C. H. Cautley.

Only a very few third-line Territorial battalions saw service overseas, but the 3/10th Middlesex was one of them. The Battalion had embarked at Southampton (33 officers and 974 N.C.Os. and men) on 31st May, 1917, and reached Havre on the following day. From Havre a move was made by train on 2nd June to Hesdin, marching on detrainment to Le Parcq. On the 6th the Battalion moved finally to Duisans, where the Middlesex men went to hutments. They were now attached to the South African Brigade of the 9th Division. Ten days were spent in the hutments, and then the Battalion proceeded to Blangy, where, having encamped in the old German front line, companies were split up for wiring and digging, under the R.E., on the Corps line, and the communication and support trenches over a front extending roughly from Pont du Jour to Monchy. Six other ranks (the first casualties suffered by the Battalion) were wounded during this work, two men subsequently dying of their wounds. On the 27th June two companies went into the front-line trenches, between Fampoux and Monchy, for their first instruction in trench warfare; they were attached to the 4th Division. The other two companies went into the line for a similar purpose on 10th and 11th July and were attached to the 17th Division. The total casualties suffered by the Battalion for June were 1 officer killed (Lieut. W. F. Wolley) and 22 other ranks killed and wounded. On 23rd July the 3/10th Middlesex were definitely posted to the 4th Division and joined the 10th Brigade, being brigaded with the 1st Royal Warwicks, 2nd Seaforth Highlanders and the Household Battalion.

The front of the 10th Brigade at this period ran north from the left bank of the Scarpe River, and from the eastern outskirts of Roeux, the ruined village being included in the Brigade area. The German front line was Carrot and Cyprus Trenches in front of Hausa and Delbar Woods.

August was a comparatively quiet month, but some good work was done by the Battalion in patrol work. At 5 a.m. on 14th Major O'Neill* and three other ranks went out to reconnoitre a German post on the Canal. The post was occupied by two of the enemy, who were wounded and brought back as prisoners, and from whom much useful information was obtained. At 1.30 a.m. on 15th a German patrol approached a wiring party of the Middlesex. The latter withdrew and were replaced by a fighting patrol, which opened fire on the Germans. Cries and groans were heard, but in the morning no bodies could be found.

In September the 4th Division left the Arras front and moved up to the Ypres area, the 3/10th Middlesex entraining at Saulty on 19th for Proven, where 10 days' training was carried out. On 29th a move was made to a camp at Elverdinghe preparatory to marching up to the line for operations on 4th October. The same night, at 11.45 p.m., a German aeroplane dropped a bomb on the camp, with the result that 7 other ranks were killed and 42 wounded. On the night of 3rd/4th the Battalion left camp for the front line north-east of Langemarck, from which sector the 4th Division was to attack the enemy.

* Awarded the M.C. for his good work on this occasion.

(V) THE BATTLE OF BROODSEINDE:
4th October.

It is always interesting to see what the other side (the enemy) thought of the operations in the Ypres Salient in 1917, and of the Battle of Broodseinde. General Ludendorff writes: "Early in October the artillery actions revived, and on the 2nd and 3rd artillery engagements of great violence took place. The infantry battle commenced on the morning of the 4th. It was extraordinarily severe, *and again we only came through it with enormous loss.* It was evident that the idea of holding the front line more densely, adopted on my last visit to the front in September, was not the remedy."

But he says nothing of the way in which the elements again favoured his defence for on the very evening before the battle opened the spell of fine weather, so welcome and so necessary, broke, and a heavy gale of wind with rain blew up from the south-west, making the terrain of the battlefield-to-be worse than before.

The attack began at 6 a.m. on 4th October, with the main line of the ridge east of Zonnebeke as the principal objective. The main attack extended from the Menin Road to the Ypres-Staden Railway, a front of about 7 miles. South of the Menin Road only a limited advance was undertaken with the object of capturing certain strong points.

The enemy was in great strength, for he had brought up three fresh divisions (in addition to those already in his front line) which were to launch an attack for the purpose of retrieving his losses of 26th September. The British attack anticipated the enemy's offensive by ten minutes only, and the artillery of the former caught the Germans as they were forming up for the attack: the slaughter was terrible—little wonder that General Ludendorff said : " We only came through it with enormous loss."

Only the extreme flanks of the attack are, however, of interest to the Middlesex Regiment, *i.e.*, on the south the attack of the 37th Division just east of Dumbarton Lakes and on the Menin Road, and in the north the attacks of the 29th Division astride the Ypres–Staden Railway, and of the 4th Division on the right flank of the 29th Division.

4TH BATTALION.

The 8th Lincolns were the attacking Battalion of the 63rd Brigade (37th Division), and although " B " and " C " Companies of the 4th Middlesex waited in support east of the Bassevillebeek they were not called upon to move forward. Throughout the day the whole of the valley in front of Mount Sorrel was violently shelled by the enemy, and although Battalion Headquarters came in for a great deal of attention, only two other ranks were wounded. Throughout the 5th the Battalion remained in the same position, moving back by lorry on the 6th to a camp near Hallebast Corner. <small>4TH BATTALION.</small>

<small>5TH OCTOBER.</small>

The attack of the 4th Division in the Battle of Broodseinde is of special interest to the Regiment, for it was the first big battle in which the 3/10th (Territorial) Battalion was engaged. <small>3/10TH BATTALION.</small>

The 4th Division attacked on a two-brigade front—the 11th on the right, 10th on the left. The 2nd Seaforth Highlanders was the assaulting Battalion of the latter Brigade, the 3/10th Middlesex being in support, and the 1st Royal Warwicks and the Household Battalion in reserve.

The forming-up line for the attack was just east of Eagle Trench, north-east of Langemarck. The first objective on the 10th Brigade front was the line of a road on the farther side of 19 Metre Hill : the second objective was only about one thousand yards east of the Hill.

By 4 a.m. on 4th, the Seaforths were in position east of Eagle Trench : the 3/10th Middlesex had two companies (" B " and " C ") along the road in rear of Eagle Trench, two platoons of " B " having been told off to move in between the left flank of the Seaforths in order to keep touch with the 87th Brigade (29th Division) attacking on the left of the 4th Division. The remaining companies of the Middlesex were north of Davies Street and between Au Bon Gite and Langemarck. <small>4TH OCTOBER.</small>

The advance was over difficult, heavily shelled ground, and a distance of 1,200 yards had to be covered before the first objective was reached.

At Zero (6 a.m.) there was just enough light to see, but the skies were heavy in clouds and a slight drizzly rain was falling. The barrage fell, and at once the two companies of Middlesex under the Seaforth Highlanders moved up to Eagle Trench, followed by " D " and " A " Companies at about 8 a.m. Battalion Headquarters, which had been at Au Bon Gite when the attack began, were on the move up to Eagle Trench when the C.O. ((Lieut.-Colonel Cautley) was knocked down by a shell splinter, and Lieut. H. K. Smith, the Battalion Intelligence Officer, was wounded in the wrist. On the C.O. recovering Battalion Headquarters moved to Eagle Trench.

3/10TH BATTALION.
4TH OCTOBER.

The narrative of the battle, contained in the Battalion Diary of the 3/10th Middlesex, is disappointing, nor is there much more than the usual bald report of operations in the Brigade Diary. The only account which gives any idea of the fighting is a report by the O.C., " D " Company, Middlesex (Lieut. Day), which also gives a better idea of the position of the front assaulting Battalion, *i.e.*, the 2nd Seaforth Highlanders.

Lieut. Day had taken up his position with his company in B.3 area (immediately west of Langemarck, the road on the western side of the village being the eastern limit of the area) on the night 3rd/4th. At Zero hour next morning he moved his company forward to B.2, the left moving along the Langemarck–Schreiboom Road, to direct. In the move forward the commanders of Nos. 15 and 16 Platoons became casualties. " A " Company was close behind " D." Having rallied his company, Lieut. Day moved to B.1, just behind Eagle Trench, reorganized, and then moved on again to the trench. Here he reported to the O.C., Seaforths, who ordered him to reinforce " C " Company of the Highlanders on the right of the latter Battalion. Again reorganizing his company, the O.C., " D " pressed forward to Beek Street (about half-way between the jumping-off line of the 10th Brigade and 19 Metre Hill) and reported to the O.C., " C " Company, Seaforths, whose men were then about 150 yards in front, fighting their way forward towards the first objective. Lieut. Day was then ordered to take the right flank of the attack forward. Suffering heavily from machine-gun fire, and pushing on from shell hole to shell hole, the line appears to have reached a position roughly about Imbros Houses where a firm stand was taken. Patrols were then sent off to the left where, from a concrete house, hostile machine-gun fire was doing terrible damage. The O.C., " C " Company, Seaforths, now told Lieut. Day to hold on to his position while he and another officer reinforced the left, *i.e.*, the concrete house which had been captured by the Middlesex.

The position at 9.30 a.m. was roughly as follows : the concrete house was held by a mixed party of " D " Company of the Middlesex and Seaforth Highlanders : " B " and " C " Companies of the former battalion were in the rear of the house. A thin line of Seaforths was holding shell holes about eighty yards down the forward slope of 19 Metre Hill and 2/Lieut. Gooch, with about twelve men of the Middlesex, was holding shell holes on the southeastern slope of the Hill.

No messages had reached Lieut. Day from forward or flank positions, so with his batman—Private Hardimann, he set out to reconnoitre the position with the result already explained. The enemy's machine-gun fire was so deadly, however, that beyond obtaining the above information he could do no more: he therefore returned to his former position on 19 Metre Hill and with his men consolidated, sending out a small party under C.S.M. Heather about fifty yards to the right. At this period Lieut. Day had with him Nos. 14 and 16 Lewis guns, a few men of each team, and signallers under L/Cpl. Porter who, with two runners, were doing good work. Other men in outlying shell holes tried to reach the O.C., "D" Company, but on each occasion were shot down by the enemy's machine-gun fire. Orders were therefore signalled to the remainder to consolidate their shell holes and dig through to their C.O.

3/10TH BATTALION. 4TH OCTOBER.

Difficulties now arose in getting word through to his C.O. giving his position. At 10.15 a.m. a runner—Private Cutles—set out with a message. It was a perilous task and meant running from shell hole to shell hole, and he had scarcely started when he was shot down. At 12 noon another runner—Private Cutt—in the next shell hole was crossing over to get the message when he, too, was hit.

For nearly three hours, during which consolidation was pushed on, a storm of machine-gun bullets swept the shell holes held by the little band of Middlesex men and then, just before 3 p.m., parties of troops, under 2/Lieut. Kirby, were observed withdrawing from their forward positions: they came back and joined up on the left with Lieut. Day and his men.

The enemy now counter-attacked. He came on in strong lines advancing from the front and right: on the left his attempt to break through were repulsed with heavy loss. But his machine guns were subjecting the gallant fellows on the Hill to a terrific fire, during which several men were shot whilst firing. One of these was Private Hardimann, who, shot through the hand as he was filling magazines for the Lewis gun team, carried on with his work.

The Lewis gun team, under Corporal Ames and Private Rathbone fought their guns splendidly. A German machine-gun team had pushed up to within one hundred yards, but were all knocked out.

The situation now began to look desperate. The Germans had advanced to within about eighty yards of Lieut. Day's

3/10TH BATTALION.
4TH OCTOBER.

position. They were coming on from the right in rushes. He therefore destroyed his maps and records and the little band prepared to sell their lives dearly. Ammunition was now reduced to 35 rounds, this despite the fact that men had crawled out and taken ammunition from the bodies of the poor fellows who had been killed.*

At 4 p.m. the enemy having been held, another runner—Private Lester—was sent off to Battalion Headquarters stating the position and asking for ammunition. Then at 5 p.m. the enemy appeared to be assembling for another counter-attack, but presently the guns came to the rescue and broke up the threatened attack. By 6 p.m. Private Lester not having returned, Private Cook was sent off on a similar errand.

About 7 p.m. an officer of the Rifle Brigade told Lieut. Day that he had supports coming up in rear and that he would send up some ammunition. But two more hours passed without supports or ammunition and at 9 p.m. 2/Lieut. Kirby went back to explain the situation and desperate need for ammunition. At 10 p.m. a subaltern of the Seaforths with a few men near Lieut. Day reported that he also was practically without ammunition, and half an hour later, having no news of previous runners and still in the same predicament, L/Cpl. Porter and another man were sent back to Battalion Headquarters asking the C.O. for ammunition and reinforcements, the strength of the little party being now reduced to about twenty-five other ranks.

5TH OCTOBER.

At last, at 3.15 a.m. on 5th, L/Cpl. Porter returned with 2/Lieut. May and his No. 13 Platoon, and the much-needed ammunition. The latter then reinforced Lieut. Day's right and got into touch with the Hampshires of the 11th Brigade. Throughout the remainder of the day and night of 5th the position was held, but the enemy were comparatively quiet. The wounded, lying out, were tended as far as possible, and what little water the party had was given to them.

In the meantime, the little party of 3/10th down the forward slope of 19 Metre Hill, under 2/Lieut. Gooch (" C " Company), had with the utmost gallantry continued to hold their position though several men had been wounded and a hurricane of bullets swept the position.

* Lieut. Day has the following note in his narrative : " During the counter-attack I saw an officer on my left with a group of Dogged (Seaforths) and Dove (3/10th Middlesex) doing splendid work, though twice wounded. I afterwards found him to be Lieut. Best (?), Durham Field Coy., R.E."

At about 12.15 a.m. on 6th October, Lieut. Day was relieved by the Warwicks. But before moving off he called for volunteers to carry down the wounded who had been lying out for many hours unable to walk back themselves: the Warwicks promised to look after those whom Lieut. Day and his men could not take back.

3/10TH BATTALION. 6TH OCTOBER.

Thus ended the first big battle in which the 3/10th Middlesex were engaged. Only a limited view of the operations has been given for, as already explained, Lieut. Day's narrative is the only record giving anything of the true nature of the fighting.

The 3/10th Battalion lost heavily in this operation. Their casualties on 4th and 5th totalled 12 officers* and 365 other ranks; they had gone into the battle with a strength of 30 officers and 492 other ranks.

The 16th Middlesex of the 29th Division (on the immediate left of the 4th Division) thus describe their part in the Battle of Broodseinde: " 3rd/4th October. 'C' and 'D' Companies relieved by 1st Royal Dublin Fusiliers in front line. Two platoons 'B' Company (strength: Lieut. B. Foster, 2/Lieut. R. W. P. Mitchell, 80 other ranks) attached to 1st R.D.F. as liason party on right flank with 4th Division and moved up to front line with them for offensive operations on 4th. Casualties: Lieut. Foster and 2/Lieut. Mitchell wounded. Other ranks: killed 9, wounded 25, missing 6."†

16TH BATTALION. 3RD/4TH OCT.

The general results of the Battle of Broodseinde were that our line was pushed forward to Polderhoek Château—Reutel—Noordemhoek—Broodseinde—Abraham Heights and thence to the northern outskirts of Poelcapelle: the ridge which we had hoped to capture was for the most part in our hands.

(VI) THE BATTLE OF POELCAPELLE:

9th October.

The general situation after the successful operations of the 4th October is of extreme interest, for as the official despatches

---

* Killed: Capts. H. C. Lewis and L. A. Ball. Wounded: Capt. H. T. Egerton, Lieut. H. K. Seth-Smith, 2/Lieuts. W. H. Dixon, P. F. Jones, H. G. R. Kirby, H. Woodnoth, J. F. Williamson, D. H. Towers and R. E. Gundry. Missing: Lieut. J. P. Watson.

† Throughout the War the diaries of the 16th (Public Schools Battalion) Middlesex were consistently brief and in no way explain the heavy fighting done by that Battalion. The 16th were a very gallant "crowd," and it is a pity their records are so incomplete.

state: "the operations marked a definite step in the development of our advance." From the starting-point, near Mount Sorrel, a line had been established some nine thousand yards forward and from the farthest point reached the "well-marked Gravenstafel Spur offered a defensible feature along which our line could be bent back from the ridge."

But the year was far spent and with the ground in such a deplorable state from the holocaust of shells and the incessant rain, making movement extremely difficult, it was doubtful whether the remainder of the ridge could be captured before the winter finally settled in. On the other hand, the enemy's losses had been terrible and his new system of defence a failure: discouragement and confusion were rife among the German troops.

The above conditions might be sufficient in themselves to induce any commander to continue the offensive, but there were others even more pressing and they are given because, from the regimental point of view, when troops have been called upon to persevere with a seemingly hopeless task (and Heaven knows that the Battles of Ypres, 1917, seemed hopeless enough to those who took part in them) it is desirable to explain why it was necessary to keep on attacking even in the midst of those awful seas of mud and under such appalling conditions.

The paramount need at that period was for the Allies to retain the initiative in their own hands, but the only allied army capable of conducting serious offensive operations was the British. The Russian Armies had ceased to be a fighting force: Italy was hard pressed and on the defensive: the French Armies in the south were in a state of grave internal trouble—mutiny: the Americans were not yet in a position to give any help on land. The Russian collapse had set free large numbers of German troops who were being transferred rapidly to the Western Front. To retain the initiative, therefore, it was necessary for the British Armies to keep on attacking in order that the Germans might be prevented from attacking the Allied line where it was weakest with probable grave results, and until the winter put an end to the possibilities of a German counter-stroke.

Such were the conditions which induced Sir Douglas Haig to go on with that ghastly dual struggle—against the enemy and against the foulest weather—in which an army ever had to fight. And to his undying glory be it said that the British soldier, with indomitable pluck and endurance, carried out his orders to the bitter end, though they often seemed hard and (to not a few) purposeless: through those seas of mud he fought his way forward, death sometimes would have been highly welcome.

The next attack was to be launched at 5.20 a.m. on 9th October on a front of over six miles from a point east of Zonnebeke to the junction of the British and French trenches north-west of Langemarck. On the left, French troops were to prolong the front of the British attack to a point opposite Draaibank, and minor operations were to take place on the right of the main attack, east and south-east of the Polygon Wood. These operations are now known as the Battle of Poelcapelle 1917.

On the 7th rain fell heavily, continuing throughout the 8th, so that when the hour came for the troops to move forward to their assembly positions the slippery state of the ground (to put it in mild terms), combined with an exceptionally dark night, made movement extremely difficult.

The part of the line which, however, concerns the Middlesex Regiment was that alongside the Ypres–Staden Railway, where the 4th and 29th Divisions attacked the enemy and secured a line well to the east of the Poelcapelle–Houthulst road.

The 16th Middlesex of the latter division had been detailed as counter-attack Battalion in the operations of the 86th Brigade. At 2 a.m. (9th) the Battalion, less two platoons of " B " Company, moved off from Harrow Camp, Elverdinghe, to the Pilkem Ridge, where they dug in round the guns. Battalion Headquarters were at Cork House.

16TH BATTALION. 9TH OCTOBER.

At 5.20 a.m. the 86th Brigade attacked the enemy's position. The 1st Lancashire Fusiliers capturing the first and second objectives and the 2nd Royal Dublin Fusiliers the final objective. At 8 a.m. the Middlesex were ordered forward and advanced in artillery formation, " C " Company leading followed by " D," " A," and " B." They moved forward through Langemarck to a blockhouse in Broombeek Street, given in co-ordinates as U.18.c.4.5, where they dug in: no casualties occurred during the advance. During the afternoon the Battalion was called upon to reinforce the front line as the Germans were counterattacking. The Middlesex were on the point of starting when the order to move was cancelled as the counter-attack had been dealt with by the troops in the front line. A little later the Battalion moved forward and dug in in front of Conde Houses (U.13.a.2.9). In the evening the Battalion took over the right

16TH BATTALION.
10TH/11TH OCTOBER.

half of the Brigade front, and although the brigade on the left of the 86th Brigade was attacked by the enemy who crossed the Broonbeek Stream, the attack did not reach the Middlesex. On the night of 10th/11th the Battalion was relieved and moved back first to Olga House and later to Elverdinghe Château. Casualties during the 9th were 2/Lieut. C. Eddy and 5 other ranks killed, 62 wounded and 2 missing.

3/10TH BATTALION.
9TH OCTOBER.

The 3/10th Middlesex remained at Bridge Camp, only one corporal and nine men being attached to the 234th Machine-Gun Company for carrying ammunition to the front line, and 3 officers and 97 other ranks to the 9th Field Company R.E. for laying duck boards and carrying duties. Of the former party the corporal and 2 other ranks were wounded and of the latter 5 men were wounded. On the 12th the 3/10th moved to Poll Hill Camp, near Proven.

12TH OCTOBER.

(VII) FIRST BATTLE OF PASSCHENDAELE:

12th October, 1917.

In the two Battles of Passchendaele (10th October and 26th October–10th November) no battalion of the Middlesex Regiment was actually engaged with the enemy, yet more than one held trenches in the battle area and are therefore fully entitled to those battle honours: to have to endure all the horrors of holding the front line, even though no attack was launched upon the enemy, or being in support or reserve, is sufficient justification for claiming the distinction of having been present during the battle.

4TH BATTALION.

The 4th Middlesex (37th Division) was the only one in the area of the First Battle of Passchendaele.

6TH OCTOBER.

From the 6th October (when the Battalion arrived at Hallebast Corner) they remained in camp until 3 p.m. on the 10th, but at that hour "enbusse" in the Milky Way and arrived at Shrapnel Corner (east of Ypres) at 5.30 p.m. They then marched to Canada Tunnels (near the Menin Road) and were guided by men from the 11th Royal Warwicks, who led them to the Support Battalion Headquarters (8th East Lancashire Regt.). Here guides from the East Lancashires guided the Middlesex to the front line just south of Veldhoek, the left flank of the latter Battalion resting on the Menin Road.

The way up to the line had not been without loss. The enemy's guns were very active and as the Battalion passed Mont Sorrel the shell fire was particularly heavy. Two officers (2/Lieuts. A. W. Bays and E. H. Swallow) and 6 other ranks were killed and 5 other ranks wounded. *(4TH BATTALION.)*

The 11th and 12th (the day of the battle) were comparatively quiet, and the worst discomfort during these two days was the non-arrival of the customary ration party. The 13th was also a quiet day. On the 15th the Battalion was relieved and moved back in lorries to Mont Kokereele. From the latter place the 4th Battalion on 21st marched to a billeting area south of Meteren where training was begun. *(12TH OCTOBER. 21ST OCTOBER.)*

(VIII) THE SECOND BATTLE OF PASSCHENDAELE:

26th October–10th November, 1917.

In the operations which began on 26th October the 12th Middlesex (18th Division) were in the battle area, but not until the 10th November did the Battalion move up towards the front line. On that date they relieved the 8th Suffolks at Boesinghe, where canal dug-outs were taken over. On the 11th the Battalion furnished carrying parties for the front line and on the 12th the Middlesex relieved the 6th Northants in the front line. *(12TH BATTALION. 10TH Nov. 12TH Nov.)*

In the final battle the village of Passchendaele and the high ground north and north-west of it had been captured, but the whole of the ridge had not been taken when the Battles of Ypres, 1917, closed.

A critical study of the general situation on all fronts will reveal the fact that not only was Sir Douglas Haig compelled to continue with his offensive, but had also to bear practically the whole Allied burden on his shoulders. To prevent the Germans attacking the French and the German-Austrian Forces launching further heavy attacks on the Italians was of vital importance. Those gallant souls who gave their lives in the Ypres Salient in 1917 did not give them in vain, for not only had the enemy lost very heavily, but General Ludendorff said: "Our wastage had been so high as to cause grave misgiving." Over 20,000 Germans were taken prisoners: many guns, machine guns and trench mortars were also captured.

CHAPTER XXXI.

THE BATTLE OF CAMBRAI, 1917:

20th November–3rd December.

" We were expecting a continuation of the attack in Flanders and on the French front when, on the 20th November, we were surprised by a fresh blow at Cambrai."—GENERAL LUDENDORFF.

WHILE the Flanders operations were in progress other parts of the enemy's line had been under close observation and investigation in order to discover the strength with which he was holding them : for the Battles of Ypres had compelled the Germans to concentrate large forces in that area and weaken other portions of their line. The weak spot was found south-west of Cambrai which was held chiefly by tired divisions resting after withdrawal from the Ypres Salient.

The object of the attack was to gain a local success by a sudden assault at a point where the enemy did not expect it and the Cambrai front was the most suitable, for here not only was the enemy weak in numbers, but the ground was favourable for the employment of tanks, of which large numbers were to be employed.

The success of the German-Austrian offensive in Italy was also an important factor in determining the attack, for it was still necessary to compel the enemy to deflect reinforcements which were to be used against the hard-pressed Italians, to the Western Front.

The general plan of attack was to dispense with previous artillery preparation and to depend upon the tanks to break through the enemy's wire of which great quantities protected his trenches. As soon as the advance of the tanks and infantry, working in close co-operation, began, the guns were to assist with counter-battery and barrage fire, but no previous registration of guns for this purpose could be permitted for fear of rousing the enemy's suspicions. Everything depended upon the observance of the utmost secrecy, and extraordinary precautions were adopted to keep preparations from becoming known.

The German defences on the Cambrai front comprised three main systems of resistance. The first of these, containing part of the famous Hindenburg Line, ran in a general north-westerly direction for a distance of six miles from the Canal de l'Escaut (or Scheldt Canal) at Banteaux to Havrincourt. At the latter place it turned abruptly north along the line of the Canal du Nord for a distance of four miles to Moeuvres, forming a pronounced salient in the German front. In advance of the Hindenburg Line the enemy had built a series of forward positions of considerable strength, including La Vacquerie on the north-eastern corner of Havrincourt Wood. Behind the Hindenburg Line, and at varying distances lay the second and third main German defences known as the Hindenburg Support Line and the Beaurevoir, Masnieres and Marquion Lines.

The operations subsequently divided themselves into three phases (i) the Tank Attack (20th-21st November), (ii) Capture of Bourlon Wood (23rd-28th November), and (iii) the German Counter-Attacks (30th November-3rd December).

Several Battalions of the Middlesex took part in these operations and one—the 17th—gained another Victoria Cross for the Regiment, Captain A. M. C. McReady-Diarmid of that Battalion carrying out what was probably the finest bombing feat of the Great War.

1/7TH, 1/8TH, 11TH, 13TH, 16TH, 17TH, 20TH AND 21ST BATTALIONS. The Battalions engaged in the battle, or within the battle area, were 1/7th and 1/8th (56th Division), 11th (12th Division), 13th (24th Division), 16th (29th Division), 17th (2nd Division), and 20th and 21st (40th Division).

1/7TH AND 1/8TH BATTALIONS. After the Battle of Langemarck the 1/7th and 1/8th Middlesex with other units of the 167th Brigade, had moved back to Steenvoorde, where five days' rest gave all ranks the opportunity for scraping themselves clean of mud and in resting after the operations. But on 23rd August the Brigade moved by train and marches to the Watten area where, after a further week's rest, both Battalions marched to St. Omer and entrained for Bapaume; the 56th Division was again destined for the Somme country. On arrival at Bapaume on 31st August the 1/7th and 1/8th (in Brigade) moved to Barastre as the 56th Division was relieving the 3rd Division in the line, *i.e.*, the Morchies, Lagnicourt and Louverval sectors.

During the night 6th/7th September the 167th Brigade took over the Morchies sector from the 76th Brigade, 3rd Division, the 1/7th Middlesex (Lieut.-Colonel E. J. King) relieving the 2nd Suffolks. The system in vogue was eight days in the trenches, eight in support, another eight in the front line and then a rest in Divisional Reserve. The line was, however, very quiet. [1/7TH AND 1/8TH BATTALIONS. 6TH/7TH SEPT.]

On the 14th the 1/8th Middlesex (Lieut.-Colonel C. H. Pank) relieved the 1/7th Battalion.

September and October and the early days of November were passed almost without incident. Although every night fighting patrols were sent out the enemy was passive and no encounters took place. One unfortunate incident happened on the night of the 8th/9th October to the 1/7th Battalion. An officer (2/Lieut. H. G. Blaxall) with two scouts went out to reconnoitre a supposed German sap-head and none of the party returned. They probably got too close to the enemy's trenches and were shot down.

On the 23rd October Lieut.-Colonel E. J. King regretfully relinquished command of the Battalion. Constant exposure in the trenches and the hard life of the front line had broken his health and at last there was nothing for it but to give up command of the Battalion he had done so much to make into a first-class fighting unit. He was very much missed by all ranks of the Battalion. Lieut.-Colonel P. C. Kay, a young officer of only twenty-nine years of age, then assumed command. Colonel Kay had becoming Acting Major and Second-in-Command in April, 1917, and in that capacity was present during the three Battles of Arras in which the 1/7th were engaged and the Battle of Langemarck. He was destined to command the Battalion in every subsequent battle in which it took part to the end of the War, with the exception of the latter half of the Battle of the Scarpe, 1918. [23RD OCTOBER.]

Lieut.-Colonel C. H. Pank, another gallant officer, had some time previously taken over command of the 1/8th Middlesex from Lieut.-Colonel P. L. Ingpen, an officer of great experience and much war service.

On the 20th November when the Tank Attack, in the Battle of Cambrai, opened, the 1/8th Middlesex held front-line trenches in the Morchies sector, while the 1/7th Battalion held the forward trenches on the right sub-section of the Lagnicourt sector.* [20TH NOV.]

* Lieut. D. R. Glendinning was killed on 16th November by a sniper. He had only joined the 1/7th on 11th November.

11TH BATTALION.
16TH MAY.

We left the 11th Middlesex at midnight 15th May billeted in Arras. The next day—16th—was Albuhera Day, but the Diary records that "owing to the exigencies of the situation" it was impossible to celebrate it in the usual way. The remainder of May and the better half of June were spent out of the line, training and resting, but on the 19th the Battalion moved back into the forward areas taking over support trenches in the Monchy defences on that date, and front-line trenches on the night of 23rd. But British and German guns were seldom silent and the records contain daily casualties in killed and wounded. On 24th 2/Lieut. Ogilvie was wounded and on 27th a shell from a trench mortar badly wounded 2/Lieut. Strong. On 25th July 2/Lieut. G. F. Kidds was killed in Tool Trench by a trench-mortar shell. Apart from the usual amount of hard work on the defences when in the front line, work which had to be carried out often under shell fire, and the training when in back areas, August, September, and the first three weeks of October were not signalized by any special incidents. On 23rd of the latter month the 24th Division relieved the 12th and the 11th Middlesex (in Brigade) moved to Magnicourt-sur-Canche. The next move was to Fillievres on

16TH NOV.
29th, where several days were spent in training. On 16th November the Battalion marched to Frevent and there entrained for Péronne, the 12th Division having been ordered south to take part in the Cambrai operations. On reaching Péronne the 11th Middlesex marched to Moislains and on 17th to Equancourt.

18TH NOV.
On 18th the Battalion proceeded to the reserve trenches, Gonnelieu, with two companies of the 8th Royal Fusiliers attached to hold the support line. The 12th King's were then holding the outpost line as a screen behind which the final preparations for the attack on 20th were being made.

16TH BATTALION.
The 16th Middlesex, after the Battle of Poelcapelle on 9th October, had moved back on the night 10th/11th to Elverdinghe Château, where a few hours were spent. On the morning of 11th the Battalion entrained for the Proven area, but their stay in the latter was short, for, on 16th, the 29th Division was transferred to the Third Army and proceeded by train to the Somme country.

17TH OCTOBER.
The Middlesex arrived at Beaumetz early on 17th October and marched to camp at Heudecourt, where they were billeted in huts and carried out training until the 16th November. On the night 17th/18th they left Heudecourt and marched to Boislieux-au-Mont where they entrained for Péronne. At the latter place

(like the 11th Battalion) they detrained and marched to Equancourt at 1 a.m. on 19th.

16TH BATTALION.
19TH Nov.

The Tank Attack:

20th–21st November, 1917.

Of the four Battalions of the Middlesex Regiment (1/7th, 1/8th, 11th and 16th) engaged on the first day of the Cambrai operations, the 11th of the 12th Division at Zero hour, was on the right at Gonnelieu, the 16th at Equancourt waiting to "go through" when the first and second German lines had been captured, and the 1/7th and 1/8th on the extreme left, the 56th Division having been ordered to make a demonstration with gas, smoke and artillery, in order to assist the main attack from Gonnelieu to the Canal du Nord opposite Hermies—a front of about six miles.

1/7TH, 1/8TH, 11TH AND 16TH BATTALIONS.

The 12th Division had been ordered to attack the enemy on the Gonnelieu–Bonavis ridge, and for this purpose the 35th Brigade, on the right, and the 36th Brigade, on the left, were to assemble on both sides of Gonnelieu, Sonnet Road being the dividing line between Brigades. There were three objectives: (i) the Black Line, which (on the Divisional front) ran from Bleak Support to Village Line; (ii) the Blue Line, which varied at from 900 to 1,500 yards north-east of the Black Line and (iii) the Brown Line, which included Lateau Wood and the Hindenburg Support Line as far as Vacquerie Valley. The Black and Blue Lines were allotted to the 35th and 36th Brigades: the Brown Line was to be captured by the 37th Brigade (right) and the 36th Brigade (left). The 55th Division was on the right of the 12th and the 20th Division on the left.*

Seventy-two tanks were allotted to the 12th Division, *i.e.*, 48 for the Blue Line and 24 for the Brown Line. They were to form up 1,000 yards from the German front line and the infantry behind them. Of the dispositions of the battalions of the 36th Brigade and the task allotted to each it is not possible to write, but the story of the attack as related in the Diary of the 11th Middlesex (Lieut.-Colonel T. S. Wollocombe) is given in full.

11TH BATTALION.

* The Diary of 36th Infantry Brigade Headquarters for November, 1917, is missing from the official records and the Divisional Narrative is very poor. It is therefore impossible to give more than a very brief account of the part taken in the attack by the 11th Middlesex.

11TH BATTALION.
20TH Nov.

Every precaution to prevent the enemy obtaining information concerning the impending attack had been taken and extraordinary measures resorted to to keep the operations secret.

"Zero" was at 6.20 a.m. on 20th November and at that hour the tanks, moving forward in advance of the infantry, literally fell upon the enemy's wire, tearing great lines in it through which the troops passed. Protected by smoke barrages which "blinded" the enemy's artillery, the tanks rolled on across the German trenches, smashing up the enemy's machine guns and driving his troops to ground. The British infantry, following close behind the tanks, cleared the Germans from their dug-outs and shelters, whilst the tanks patrolled the line of hostile trenches. The surprise of the enemy was complete. Both the main Hindenburg Line and its outer defences were quickly overrun, and the attack then swept on to the Hindenburg Support Line.

The 11th Middlesex thus relate their part in the attack: "Formed up behind our tanks—12 per battalion—'C' and 'B' Companies in the first wave, 'A' and 'D' in the second, all ready by 3.45 a.m. The Battalion attacked the furthest objective (Brown Line apparently) and formed up 800 yards in rear of leading battalions." (Dispositions of latter unobtainable). "Zero, minus ten minutes, tanks and infantry moved off. No excitement on the part of the Huns except one M.G. Our guns started off at Zero (6.20 a.m.). Battalion Headquarters in Gun Support. 2/Lieut. Chippenfield went off to find a new Battalion Headquarters 8.25 a.m. 9.25 a.m.—No news from Chippenfield. Moved off in three parties to find a new Battalion Headquarters. Eventually found a suitable dug-out in the Hindenburg Line, R.16.d.6.1. Battalion started one tank short, one tank also stuck in our old front line. Battalion gained all its objectives well up to time, and reorganization and consolidation taken in hand at once. Total captures about 150 prisoners, including a regimental commander and several officers, 6 machine guns all in working order, two handed over to a tank and taken on to Masnieres, various Granatternwerfer and ammunition and materials, a dug-out containing quartermaster's stores, etc. Bosche headquarters, probably near Cambrai, were still ringing up to this dug-out several hours after we had gained our objective. Casualties: Capt. E. A. Moore, Capt. G. T. Whinney, Lieut. Hedgecock, 2/Lieut. Sewell, 2/Lieut. Angrave wounded, and about 90 other ranks. Reorganization of the line to be in support to 9th Royal Fusiliers, facing south-east, completed 11.30 p.m. No lights permitted at all during the night."

11TH BATTALION. 20TH NOV.

Such was the 11th Battalion's account of the 20th November. It is not very illuminating.

The 29th Division had been detailed to pass through the Brown Line (when captured by the 12th, 20th and 6th Divisions, in that order from right to left), force the crossings over the Canal at Marcoing and Masnieres and capture both those places: the cavalry were then to pass through in the third phase of the attack.

The 86th Brigade was to capture Nine Wood and the trenches east of it to the St. Quentin Canal, the 6th Division, on the left of the Brigade, forming a defensive flank up to Premy Chapel Hill.

The objectives allotted to the 16th Middlesex (Lieut.-Colonel J. Forbes-Robertson) were as follows: " C " Company the southern edge of Nine Wood, Escaut Trench and Escaut Support, on the eastern side of the wood; " A " Company the quarry outside the south-western edge of Nine Wood and then push on to the road junction at the north-eastern edge of the wood; " B " Company the quarry south of the quarry attacked by " A " Company and the German strong point north-east of Marcoing (in L.17 a) and to assist, by covering fire, the Royal Fusiliers who were attacking on the north side of Marcoing; " D " Company to wheel round the south-eastern corner of Nine Wood and also to attack Escaut Trench and Escaut Support. " A " Company was to supply the " mopping-up " party for the Escaut Trench.

16TH BATTALION. 20TH NOV.

At Zero hour the 86th Brigade advanced to the old British front line where the Middlesex occupied Plough Trench and Plough Support, having the Royal Fusiliers on their right and the Royal Guernsey Light Infantry on their left. Here the Brigade waited until the Hindenburg Main and Support Lines had been captured.

At 10.40 a.m. the Middlesex were ordered to move forward as advanced guard of the 86th Brigade. The Battalion advanced in diamond formation, " C " Company leading, with " B " Company right and " A " Company left flank guards: " D " Company was the main guard. At 11.30 a.m. the Hindenburg Support Line was forced when the Battalion slowed down in order to allow the Royal Fusiliers and R.G.L.I. to close up on the right and left respectively. The advance on Nine Wood then began.

16TH BATTALION.
20TH NOV.

Hitherto there had been no opposition and very little shell fire, but as the Middlesex moved up the slopes of Premy Chapel Hill the enemy opened rifle fire on the advancing troops and the Germans could be seen reinforcing their line from Marcoing. Firing and advancing by platoons and afterwards by sectional rushes the attack was pushed home with as little checking as possible. "A" Company, led by Captain J. A. W. Wilson, made progress rapidly in the direction of the south-western side of Nine Wood. "C" Company, under Captain D. B. Tuck, having driven back the enemy's outposts, reorganised in a quarry and then attacked the southern edges of the wood. "D" Company (2/Lieut. A. L. Bobby), which by then had come up into line and together with "B" Company was skirting the south-eastern corner of the wood, attacked Escaut Trench and Escaut Support.

On the right of the Middlesex, the Royal Fusiliers, attacking the northern edge of Marcoing, were checked by heavy machine-gun fire from the German strong point north-east of the village. Major F. R. Hill (commanding "B" Company) had dropped a platoon under Lieut. H. M. Trower to protect his right flank. Lieut. Trower then attacked the strong point and captured it, bayoneting a crew of eight Germans who were working the gun: the Royal Fusiliers were then able to continue their advance. Escaut Trench and Escaut Support were captured without great difficulty, the Royal Fusiliers coming up on the right of the Middlesex. "A" Company, dashing through the wood, emerged from the eastern side and occupied a portion of the sunken road just north of Escaut Support.

By 1.30 p.m. all the objectives allotted to the Middlesex had been won: the Royal Fusiliers, on the right, and the R.G.L.I., on the left, had also captured the line allotted to them. The tanks had again done splendid work, rendering great assistance to the attacking infantry whom they stood by until all the objectives had been captured. Consolidation was then begun and patrols were pushed out to Noyelles.

The work of these patrols was particularly good: a platoon under 2/Lieut. Morris, with the assistance of a tank, made for the cross roads north of Noyelles. This officer with his men advanced through the village and reported it clear of the enemy. Another platoon, under 2/Lieut. Whittington, pushed on to the crossing over the canal, north-east of the village. The bridge had been blown up, but the light railway bridge was still intact and, a little later, this bridge head was handed over to the Royal Fusiliers who, 16TH BATTALION. in the meantime, had come up, Lieut. Whittington returning to the Battalion. A third platoon (of "C" Company), under 20TH Nov. 2/Lieut. Green, went out to the cross roads north-west of Noyelles and there established and consolidated a post, and later another platoon of the same Company established a post about 250 yards east of the former.

The Battalion Diary then records that "conflicting reports and rumours kept coming in as to the position on the right of Noyelles," *i.e.*, at the crossing over the canal. A post of snipers was then placed on the light railway bridge where they sniped the enemy from the bridge. But what is not clear is the reason why the whole line was not pushed forward to include Noyelles, which had already been reported clear of the enemy.

Throughout the day the 29th Division had made splendid progress, Masnieres and Marcoing and (as already shown) Nine Wood had been captured and the passage of the canal had been secured at both villages. There is, however, a point in the official despatches concerning Noyelles which is not apparently quite correct. They state that patrols of the 6th Division had entered the village, whereas it has been shown that these patrols were Middlesex men of the 29th Division, and in the records of the latter there is no mention of troops of the former Division having been seen. Cavalry *had* been seen in Noyelles, and at about 3 p.m. mounted troops had come up to Nine Wood, passing through in the direction of Cantaing whence they returned just before darkness set in.

On the front of the Middlesex the night of 20th/21st passed quietly. 20TH/21ST NOVEMBER.

In the meantime the 56th Division, on the far left of the battle front, had carried out a vigorous demonstration in order to hold the attention of the enemy. The 169th and 167th Brigades, on the right and left respectively, held the Divisional front line, the left flank of the latter extending to the Hirondelle River.

This demonstration was not only effective, but interesting and amusing: for the British soldier loves nothing as much as "fooling" the enemy. A dozen full-sized dummy tanks and some 250 dummy figures were constructed to the great amusement of the troops. The tanks were placed into No Man's Land during the night of the 19th, and at 6.30 a.m. on 20th, when the real attack was being made further east, smoke bombs were thrown by

1/7TH AND 1/8TH BATTALIONS. 20TH Nov.

specially detailed parties of troops of the 56th Division in order that the enemy could see the tanks but dimly through the clouds of vapour which hung over No Man's Land. The dummy figures of men were then moved up and down in order to give the idea that an attack was launched. This masquerade was a great success. German machine guns and artillery opened fire and until midday the dummy tanks were shelled vigorously. Both the 1/7th and 1/8th Middlesex were holding front-line trenches during the demonstration, but only a few casualties were suffered by the former, and only one other rank was wounded in the latter.

The attack of the 20th had resulted in the breaking of three German systems of defence to a depth of some four and a half miles on a wide front, and 5,000 prisoners had been captured. But one of the most important bridges along the front of advance had been wrecked, and the 51st Division had been held up in front of Flesquieres: these two set-backs had serious effects upon the whole operation.

On the morning of 21st the attack was resumed. By 8 a.m. Flesquieres had been turned from the north-west and captured.*

At 11 a.m. the Beaurevoir-Masnieres line was attacked and positions in the line north and east of Masnieres were established.

11TH BATTALION. 21ST Nov.

The 11th Middlesex of the 12th Division apparently made no move on 21st. The Battalion was slightly shelled during the morning, but the work of organising the trenches and making fire steps was carried on. Nothing unusual happened during the afternoon, and certain trenches to be used as communication trenches were cleared.

16TH BATTALION. 21ST Nov.

West of the Canal de l'Escaut the 29th Division and the cavalry were engaged all day at Noyelles, but all attacks were beaten off, though apparently the enemy remained in possession of the village.

At daybreak about five hundred Germans attacked the Middlesex posts north-west of the village and drove in the two platoons. The latter retired down the sunken road to Nine Wood and, finding a gap in the line of the R.G.L.I., filled up and con-

---

* It is difficult to understand why this was not done on 20th, seeing that on both flanks of the 51st Division the 6th and 62nd Divisions had advanced far ahead.

solidated their position there, the process of consolidation being 16TH BATTALION. 21ST Nov.
interrupted by a party of the enemy from a ditch just west of
Noyelles. But 2/Lieut. Kirkham went out alone and with a
Lewis gun drove them off and there was no more trouble from
that direction.

At 12.50 p.m. the enemy developed a counter-attack from
Noyelles against Nine Wood which was successfully beaten off.
Eventually the posts at the cross roads were removed and handed
over to the 2nd Yorks and Lancs who relieved the 16th Middlesex
on the night of the 21st.

Along the front of the 56th Division, with the exception of 1/7TH AND 1/8TH BATTALIONS. 21ST Nov.
the right flank which, keeping touch with the left Brigade of the
36th Division west of the Canal du Nord, had advanced slightly,
no movement was made. Both the 1/7th and 1/8th Middlesex
sent out patrols but found the enemy still occupied his front line
in strength. 2/Lieut. J. Kimber of the 1/7th was wounded
on one of these patrols.

On the evening of the second day of the battle the British
front line ran approximately as follows : the right flank lay along
the eastern slope of the Bonavis Ridge, thence passed east of
Lateau Wood, striking the Masnieres–Beaurevoir line north of the
Canal de l'Escaut at a point about half-way between Crevecœur
and Masnieres, thence roughly north-west past and including
Masnieres, Noyelles and Cantaing to Fontaine, also inclusive :
from Fontaine (where it made a sharp salient round the village)
the line bent back to the south, running in a general westerly
direction along the southern edge of Bourlon Wood to the Canal
du Nord, south-east of Mœuvres : from the latter the line linked
up with the old British front line about midway between Boursies
and Pronville.

The general situation was now, however, of great interest.
The tank attack had been a great surprise, but had not resulted in
the capture of Bourlon Village and Wood, nor of that important
tactical feature—the Bourlon Ridge : also the forty-eight hours
after which it had been calculated the enemy's reserves would
begin to arrive, had expired. But without the possession of the
Ridge the other ground would be difficult to hold. Sir Douglas
Haig decided to continue the attack.*

---

* For the full reasons which decided Sir Douglas the Official Despatches should be studied.

THE CAPTURE OF BOURLON WOOD:

23rd–28th November.

20TH AND 21ST
BATTALIONS.

In the operations which took place from the 23rd to 28th November (both dates included) seven Battalions of the Middlesex Regiment were either engaged with the enemy or were in close support.

On the 21st November the 40th Division* arrived in the Beaumetz area, having been out of the front line for some time engaged in training for the Cambrai operations. At a conference held at Divisional Headquarters on 22nd the general outline of the attack to be carried out on Bourlon Wood and Village was discussed, and the relief of the 62nd Division north of Graincourt ordered: the 119th and 121st Brigades were to relieve the West Riding Troops on the night 22nd/23rd.

The front line of the 62nd Division to be taken over by the 40th Division ran from the German system of trenches between Nine Wood and the south-west corner of Bourlon Wood, at a point from 1,000 yards due east of Anneux, north-east of the latter village to Anneux Chapel, thence in a north-westerly direction along a sunken road to E.17.c.8.3 (a point about 1,500

* The 40th Division remained on the Somme after the German Retreat to the Hindenburg Line throughout the spring, summer and autumn of 1917, and from the records of the 121st Brigade and 20th and 21st Middlesex it is evident that no attacks of importance were made on or by the enemy during that period, i.e., along the Divisional front. Of raids and patrol encounters there were many, and the minor activities of trench warfare kept the troops fully engaged when in the front line and training when out of it.

On the 6th April the 121st Brigade took over the front line between Gouzeaucourt and the south-east corner of Havrincourt Wood. The guns of both sides were continually active and there are frequent mentions of casualties.

The 21st Middlesex (Lieut.-Colonel W. H. Samuel) had taken over the left of the Brigade front in front of Gouzeaucourt Wood. The guns of both sides were very active, and on the 8th the Battalion had 30 odd casualties, Lieut. C. R. Bourke and 2/Lieut. J. D. Green being amongst the wounded. The next night—the 21st—the Battalion carried out a small operation and successfully advanced the line about 1,000 yards which drew congratulations from Corps H.Qs. Their casualties were, however, heavy— 26 other ranks killed and 38 wounded. The line was continually on the move, as it was essential to clear the enemy out of the ground he held in front of the Hindenburg Line and compel him to seek shelter in his new defensive position. By the end of April the British line ran across Highland Ridge, north of Villers-Plouich.

The 20th Battalion (Lieut.-Colonel F. S. B. Johnson) relieved the 21st on 10th April, but there are no special items of interest to record during the month. On the 5th May the Battalion co-operated in a raid by the Suffolk and Welch Regiments. In this affair 2/Lieut. H. C. Greenhalgh and 3 other ranks were killed, and Major C. H. Morris and 2/Lieuts. S. U. Sheppard and F. S. Perryman and 38 other ranks were wounded. 2/Lieut. G. F. Wallace was wounded on 23rd May.

yards north of the Sugar Factory on the Bapaume–Cambrai road), then falling back sharply south-west to roughly the sunken road running north-west from the Sugar Factory. The 119th Brigade was to be on the right and the 121st Brigade on the left, the cross roads west of Anneux Chapel and north of the Quarry being approximately the dividing point between the two Brigades. On the right of the 40th Division the 51st Division was to attack Fontaine Notre Dame, and on the left the 36th Division Quarry Wood and Inchy. 20TH AND 21ST BATTALIONS.

The relief of the 62nd Division was completed at midnight on 22nd by the 119th and 121st Brigades.

Of the 121st Brigade the 20th Middlesex were to attack on the right and the 13th Yorks on the left, the 21st Middlesex to move in echelon to the Yorkshires and be prepared to form a defensive flank on the left: the 12th Suffolks were in Brigade Reserve.

" A " Company on the right and " B " on the left of the 20th Battalion had taken over the front line from the cross road to E.17.d.4.1. (there is no other way of describing the position): " C " was in support in trenches north-east of the Sugar Factory and " D " in reserve at the Factory. 20TH BATTALION.

At 10.30 a.m. on 23rd (Zero hour) the Divisional barrage fell on the enemy's positions south and south-west of Bourlon Wood 23RD Nov.

On 26th the 21st Battalion had just taken over the front line when, three minutes later, they were raided by the enemy, and in the fight which ensued 2/Lieut. B. J. Lamb and 5 other ranks were wounded.

The 20th Battalion took over trenches in the Gonnelieu sector on 11th June and repulsed a hostile raid on 12th; 2/Lieut. W. P. Nash was wounded and 4 other ranks killed or wounded. The remainder of June was comparatively quiet. On 3rd June Lieut.-Colonel F. P. Dunlop assumed command of the 20th Middlesex. For the 21st Battalion also June was a quiet month.

The whole period from the spring to the autumn on the Somme was practically spent in digging more trenches and establishing ourselves in front of the Hindenburg Line, during which the enemy tried to interfere with the work. He was, however, unsuccessful, and, as the year advanced, formidable trenches and defences everywhere sprang up in front of the enemy's position. Casualties, mostly sustained during patrols or raids, were fairly heavy. Of the 20th Battalion, Lieut. N. T. Watson was wounded on 12th July, which seems to have been the only officer casualty up to the end of October, when the Battalion was at Warluzel in training.

The Diary of the 21st Middlesex of 7th July has the following interesting citation of the award of two Military Medals :—

" On night 28th/29th May, 1917, while covering the withdrawal of a patrol, L/Cpl. Empson and Private Bailey, with a sergeant in charge, were attacked by a hostile patrol of about 12 men. The sergeant was overpowered and disarmed by the enemy. L/Cpl. Empson and Pte. Bailey charged the enemy, rescued the sergeant, and drove the enemy back to his lines." 2/Lieut. W. Lacey was gassed on 25th July and 2/Lieut. C. Raynham was wounded on 29th July. At the end of October the 21st Middlesex were at Sombrin, engaged in training.

20TH BATTALION.
23RD NOV.

and, preceded by tanks, the infantry advanced to the attack. On the right of the Divisional front the 119th Brigade entered Bourlon Wood, but on the left the 121st Brigade had all the difficulties of heavy machine-gun fire from the high ground to contend with*. It was 11.30 a.m. therefore before the spur west of the Wood and south of the Village was reached by "A" Company. "B" Company, on the left, suffered very heavy casualties, but the O.C. at 12.25 p.m. reported that he was working round the left of the Village. Apparently a few men actually entered the Village, but after hours of hard fighting, and the position of the forward companies of Middlesex at 5.30 that evening was on the south-western outskirts of the Village (described in co-ordinates as E.18.a.9.9.—E.12.c.4.3.—E.12.c.0.3.) and late that night "C" and "D" Companies held the front line with "A" and "B" in reserve in the sunken road from which the attack had started.

21ST BATTALION.
23RD NOV.

The 21st Middlesex, on the left, who had been ordered to advance in echelon and to protect the left flank of the Yorkshires, were also met by violent machine-gun fire. A German strong point on the extreme left of the Brigade front caught the Middlesex in enfilade and many casualties were suffered. Captain F. S. Bryan "B" Company, was killed and 2/Lieut. R. P. Grey wounded. C.S.M. Hall of "B" Company, after Captain Bryan had fallen, took over command of the Company, though shot through both arms. At 12.20 p.m. a Battalion of Royal Irish, on the left of the 21st Middlesex, reported that they had attacked the strong point and had captured it but were driven out again by a fierce counter-attack. A second gallant attempt to capture the strong point failed. At 1.10 p.m. Captain E. W. Evers was killed. At 3.20 p.m. another attack on the strong point shared the same fate, heavy machine-gun fire beating back the attackers. The day's fighting seems to have centred round this German stronghold for there are yet further references to other attempts to capture it. Finally, a British aeroplane flew low over the strong point, the observer firing his Lewis gun at the German garrison. A storm of bullets greeted the first attempt. Again the machine flew over the point even lower, but the Germans on this occasion aimed more truly and the aeroplane "crashed."

---

* There are no narratives of operations either with the 40th Division G.S. Diary, or 121st Bde. H.Q. Diary, and the Diary of 20th Middlesex is mainly a time-table of events.

The right companies of the 21st Battalion made but little progress, though small parties were dribbled up to join the Yorkshires who had reached a point on the high ground west of the village. 20TH AND 21ST BATTALIONS.

At about midnight dismounted cavalry arrived and relieved the 21st Middlesex who then moved back to the Sugar Factory and neighbourhood.

Thus at midnight on 23rd two companies of the 20th Middlesex were near the south-west corner of Bourlon Village, and two in support: the 21st Middlesex were at the Sugar Factory in reserve. 23RD NOV.

Meanwhile on the right and left of the line other Battalions of the Middlesex Regiment, though in the line, had very little fighting, Bourlon Wood remaining always the centre of the great struggle.

The 11th Middlesex (12th Division) made no attack, and in the evening received orders to supply 1½ companies to support the 8th Royal Fusiliers in an attack on Quarry Post—Bleak Quarry on 24th. 11TH BATTALION. 24TH NOV.

The 16th Middlesex (29th Division), who had taken over the centre sector of the 86th Brigade front, north-east of Masnieres, remained in this position throughout the 23rd and 24th, and on the latter date were consolidating trenches south-east of the town. 16TH BATTALION. 24TH NOV.

On the extreme left the 56th Division again attacked the Hindenburg Line in the direction of Tadpole Copse, but as the 168th and 169th Brigades were the attacking troops, the 1/7th and 1/8th Middlesex of the 167th Brigade co-operated only by a fresh feint attack with gas and dummy figures. 1/7TH AND 1/8TH BATTALIONS.

In this part of the line neither of these Battalions were involved in the fighting, and it was not until the 30th that the latter became involved with the Germans during the heavy counter-attack on that date.

The 24th was a day of hard fighting. Twice the enemy attacked the 119th Brigade in Bourlon Wood and at the second attempt drove in the latter at the north-east corner of the Wood: an immediate counter-attack, however, restored the position. At 7 a.m. the 20th Middlesex had received warning that the enemy would probably counter-attack from the village. Preparations were made to meet the attack, but whether it was made it is impossible to say. At 5.15 p.m. the remnants of " A," " B " and " C " Companies held the spur south-west of the Village, and " D " 20TH BATTALION. 24TH NOV.

20TH BATTALION.
24TH Nov.

Company was with a Battalion of the Suffolks, retiring with the latter at 6.45 p.m. to the old front line. The shell fire and machine-gun fire throughout the day had been extremely heavy and, when at 3 a.m. on 25th " A," and " B " and " C " Companies were relieved, they moved back to the neighbourhood of the Sugar Factory, well pleased to get out of the inferno in the front line. " D " Company, with the Suffolks, were not relieved until the early hours of 26th when the whole Battalion marched back to Bertincourt, arriving at that village at 4. p.m.

21ST BATTALION.
24TH–26TH NOVEMBER.

The 21st Middlesex, in the meantime, had remained in the rear and in front of the Sugar Factory throughout the 24th and 25th and on 26th were relieved and marched back to the Hindenburg Support Line, near Havrincourt, whence on 27th they also marched to Bertincourt.

The whole of the 40th Division had been relieved on the 25th/26th after a splendid fight, in which both Bourlon Wood and Village had been captured, but when the Division handed over the Village had been lost and the line pressed back slightly on the northern outskirts of the Wood.

16TH BATTALION.
24TH–27TH NOVEMBER.

Throughout these days (24th—27th) the 16th Middlesex made no attack on the enemy, but remained strengthening their position at Masnieres.

11TH BATTALION.
27TH Nov.

The 11th Battalion on 27th marched back to Egypt Camp, Heudicourt.

THE GERMAN COUNTER-ATTACKS:

30th November–3rd December.

The general results of the Tank Attack on the 21st November, and the capture of Bourlon Wood 23rd–28th November, had been to push forward the British line to west of Vendhuille, Banteaux, Lateau Wood, Masnieres, Noyelles-sur-Escaut, Cantaing, thence to Bourlon Wood (the greater portion of which remained in our hands) whence the line bent back in a S.W. direction to where the Canal du Nord crossed the Bapaume–Cambrai Road, thence N.W. to just south of Mœuvres and south of Tadpole Copse.

But towards the end of November, from the increasing activity of the enemy's artillery in registering targets, and from the movements of transport and German troops behind the hostile lines, it was obvious that counter-attacks were imminent. Preparations were therefore made to meet whatever attacks were launched by the enemy. From opposite Vendhuille to Cantaing there were five British divisions in line: 55th (opposite the former village), 12th (between Gonnelieu and Banteaux), 20th (at Lateau Wood), 29th (holding Masnieres), 6th (Noyelles) and 59th (Cantaing). These Divisions were weak and held extended fronts, but though tired with heavy fighting G.H.Q. considered that they would be able to beat off any attacks. North of Cantaing the 47th Division had taken over Bourlon Wood, and the 2nd Division had come into line on the left of the former Division, from the left of the Wood to south of Mœuvres: the 56th Division still remained in the line south of Tadpole Copse.

Thus five Battalions of the Middlesex were involved in the operations of the 30th November and succeeding days, *i.e.*, 11th (12th Division), 16th (29th Division), 17th (2nd Division) and 1/7th and 1/8th (56th Division). 11TH, 16TH, 17TH, 1/7TH AND 1/8TH BATTALIONS.

The 2nd Division had relieved the 36th Division in the Mœuvres–Bourlon Wood front on the night 26th/27th November, the 17th Middlesex (Lieut.-Colonel R. S. H. Stafford)* taking over a portion of the line from Lock 5 to a point about two hundred yards south of Mœuvres: but the Battalion was relieved by the 1st King's on 29th and moved back into support, south of the Bapaume–Cambrai road, "A" Company being at the immediate disposal of the King's if necessary. 17TH BATTALION. 26TH/27TH NOVEMBER.

On the morning of 30th November, between the hours of 7 and 8 o'clock, the enemy suddenly opened an intense bombard- 30TH Nov.

* After their heavy losses in the severe fighting of 28th April at Oppy, the 17th Middlesex (Lieut.-Colonel C. Kelly) moved back to Roclincourt, Marœuil and Dieval. They were not engaged in the Third Battle of the Scarpe, being too weak (12 officers and 120 other ranks), but were at Marœuil reorganising and training, and it was not until 3rd June that the Battalion, organised into two double companies, went into the front line in the Fresnoy sector. On 6th, 2/Lieut. S. A. Kempster, who had been out visiting listening posts, was killed by a bomb. About the middle of June the 2nd Division was relieved and moved north to the XIth Corps area, taking over trenches in the Givenchy sector about 20th. Active trench warfare was in vogue in this sector, raids on and by the enemy were frequent, and the guns and trench mortars of both sides indulged in frequent bombardments. Corporal Searle distinguished himself on the 7th July when out reconnoitring on this date during a raid. August and September were months of normal activity, though on the 24th the enemy raided the Battalion's trenches, inflicting 17 casualties (all wounded) on the Middlesex men. On the 6th/7th October the 2nd Division was relieved and moved back to the Auchel area for training, the 17th Middlesex billeting in Burbure. During this period of training the Division not only completely renewed its lost strength, but benefited greatly, and when it went into the line on the Cambrai front the rifle fire of the infantrymen was so good that they had again reached the "15 aimed shots a minute" of pre-war standard.

F

ment. Had this continued the troops holding the front line would have been warned, but the bombardment was of short duration; owing also to smoke shells and bombs it was difficult for the troops to see what was going on in other parts of the front and the approach of the German Infantry. The latter, in strong assault companies, swarmed across No Man's Land, whilst great numbers of low-flying German aeroplanes rained machine-gun fire down upon our troops.

The attack began first from Vendhuille to Masnieres (the opening attack) and two hours later from Fontaine Notre Dame to Tadpole Copse (the main attack).

In the opening attack the rapidity with which the enemy advanced after his short hurricane bombardment secured him the northern end of Bonavis Ridge and Gonnelieu, the latter village with Villers-Guislain being turned from the flanks.

Of the 12th Division, holding the line between Gonnelieu and Banteaux, many officers and men were captured, having been surrounded almost before they were aware of the attack. The 11th Middlesex (Lieut.-Colonel T. S. Wollocombe) were, however, out of the line at Heudicourt when the attack began, but at 7.50 a.m. received orders to be prepared to move at short notice. The story of that great day of fighting as contained in the Battalion Diary is as follows: "9.15 a.m. Orders to proceed to St. Quentin Mill, south-east of Gouzeaucourt and to deal with the situation as it arises. Head of column, the advanced guard at about two hundred yards clear of Revelon Farm, went into action on the high ground and checked the advance of the enemy. Every available man called out, details from all battalions and divisions. Cavalry came up, some dismounted, and filled gap on our left, other cavalry went into action mounted. Sixteen tanks came up to attack Gouzeaucourt.*

"Companies in position in valley near railway, in touch with Guards on the left and Queen's on the right. 'A,' 'B' and 'C' Companies W.6.b.4.8 to W.6.d.6.1. (about six hundred yards south of Gouzeaucourt) consolidating a line east of sunken road in touch with Guards on the left and 20th Hussars on right in touch with Queen's. 'D' Company digging in six hundred yards

---

* The enemy was prevented from entering Gouzeaucourt by the very gallant action of transport details of 1st West Yorks and D.L.I. of the 6th Division; they held the Germans off until troops of the 29th Division came to their assistance, and later the Guards, who reoccupied the village.

Heavy Fighting at Masnieres

north-east of Revelon Farm with a platoon about three hundred yards north-east of Farm in touch on right with Northants. 2/Lieut. Booth and 2/Lieut. Challon wounded. Three other ranks killed and about twenty wounded." 11TH BATTALION. 30TH Nov.

The scene now shifts to Masnieres, where, with fine gallantry, troops of the 29th Division were maintaining their line intact.

The 16th Middlesex (Lieut.-Colonel J. Forbes-Robertson) held a line covering the south-eastern outskirts of Masnieres, with an outpost at Mon Plaisir Farm. From very early morning on 30th the enemy had shelled the back areas, but at 7 a.m. put down a heavy barrage on the village. At 7.30 a.m. his machine-gun barrage began. From 7.40 to 7.45 a.m. there was a lull in the firing and then for ten minutes the German guns placed a heavy fire upon the front-line trenches of the Battalion, lifting again at the latter hour on to Masnieres for twenty minutes. 16TH BATTALION. 30TH Nov.

At 8.15 a.m. German infantry advanced to the attack. Their lines of skirmishers advanced down the hill between Crevecœur and Rumilly: they were followed by thicker waves. From their trenches the Middlesex could see that south of the Canal, and on their right flank, the enemy was advancing in the same formation against the 20th Division. Lewis guns and rifles then got to work, the hostile infantry providing fine targets as they swarmed down the slopes towards Masnieres. The deadly fire of the Middlesex was, however, too much for the Germans and at about 400–500 yards range they were checked and forced to seek whatever cover the ground afforded. The advanced post at Mon Plaisir was, however, driven in. An S.O.S. call sent up by the Middlesex to the divisional artillery produced no response. The 20th Division having been driven back altogether, the 16th Battalion then brought up more platoons and posted them at the Lock bridge south-east of the village and also on the small foot-bridge, while snipers were posted in the house south of the Lock. About 10 a.m. two companies of Royal Fusiliers reported to the O.C., Middlesex, as reinforcements, and they were ordered to cross the Canal and occupy the cross-roads south of Les Rues Vertes and the southern edge of the latter. But the enemy had already reached the cross-roads and the Fusiliers were driven back across the Canal into Masnieres. In the meantime, seeing that the capture of Les Rues Vertes was likely, Colonel Forbes-Robertson had sent the Adjutant with a few men to the Brigade Dump with orders to shift as much ammunition as possible to the northern side of the Canal. The dump was in the possession of the enemy, but he was driven off temporarily and some of the ammunition saved. At about 11 a.m. Captain E. Featherstone, who was establishing the bridge-head post at the Lock, was wounded.

Incessant shell fire swept the position held by the Middlesex all the morning and early afternoon, but still, with fine pluck, the Battalion maintained its position. "B," "C" and "D" Companies, in their original front line, were badly enfiladed by field guns at close range and from time to time the German infantry endeavoured to advance, but were shot down and all their efforts came to naught. Hostile aeroplanes flew over the trenches all day long and were fired on, but none were brought down.

When night fell the line was still held intact, but the Battalion had suffered heavy losses: "Lieut. A. L. Bobby and 28 other ranks had been killed, Colonel Forbes-Robertson, Captain Featherstone, 2/Lieuts. A. G. Whittington, A. K. Mellenfield, J. B. Newman, C. H. Larkins,* S. L. Davies, T. L. Deeves, A. Gosden and G. F. Wicksteed were wounded, while 2/Lieut. T. W. Lane was missing. The Battalion M.O.—Captain B. Knowles—had also been wounded, but with the C.O. remained 'At duty.' 110 other ranks had also been wounded and 38 were missing."

A heavy toll indeed, but the Middlesex had maintained their line. The enemy had failed to dislodge the 29th Division from Masnieres.

In the northern area of the battle, *i.e.*, from Fontaine Notre Dame to Tadpole Copse, the enemy's infantry did not advance to the attack until 9 a.m., after a heavy preliminary bombardment. But at that hour, to the intense astonishment of our troops, wave after wave of Germans in close formation advanced against the positions held by the 47th, 2nd and 56th Divisions. The sheer madness of that advance made our men gasp. Utterly regardless of life, the German Staff flung thousands of troops against our line in an endeavour to break down the defence by weight of numbers. It was then that the "15 aimed shots a minute" of the 2nd Division Infantry made itself felt: the slaughter of the enemy was enormous. Into ten successive waves of Germans one battery of machine guns alone fired no less than 70,000 rounds of ammunition:

* D. of W., 21.11.17. The "officers'" casualties given above evidently cover a number of days.

they fell in scores, in hundreds. Line after line, caught in enfilade by our machine-gun fire, fell as they advanced. Our artillery had such targets as they had not seen for many a month and did enormous execution, many guns firing at short range.

16TH BATTALION.

The 17th Middlesex (Lieut.-Colonel R. S. Stafford), when the enemy's bombardment opened at 8.30 a.m., were back in support on the western side of the Canal du Nord and just south of the Bapaume–Cambrai road. The Battalion had been relieved on the night of 29th by the 1st King's. " A " and " C " Companies were in dug-outs just south of the road, " D " Company in dug-outs in rear of " A " and " C," and " B " Company in reserve in dug-outs near Lock 6.

17TH BATTALION.

At 9 a.m. companies were ordered to " stand to " without packs (in order to move lightly), each man to carry two bombs. The order to carry bombs did not, unfortunately, reach " A " Company before it was called upon by the King's. " D " Company then moved forward to replace " A," and " B " to take " D's " place. The latter had just settled down just south of the road when two enemy *Flammenwerfer* were seen in action north-east of Lock 5. They were promptly knocked out by Lewis-gun fire. A little later " C " Company was also moved up to the 1st King's Headquarters. Meanwhile, the King's had been heavily attacked, their left company being almost cut up. The enemy then penetrated down the trenches almost to the Bapaume–Cambrai road, but a spirited attack by " D " Company, under Captain McReady-Diarmid, drove him back and, besides leaving many dead and wounded behind he also lost some 27 men taken prisoners. At 2 p.m. " D " Company was established some five hundred yards south-west of Lock 5, but further advance was impossible owing to lack of bombs. " B " Company was now just south of " D."

30TH NOV.

Of what happened on 30th to " A " and " C " Companies with the 1st King's there are no records, but at nightfall the gain of a few hundred yards of trenches along the front of the 6th Brigade (and the whole of the 2nd Division, was all the enemy had to show for the loss of thousands of men killed and wounded. His losses had been prodigious.

At 9 p.m. " B " Company relieved " D." The former had orders to push on to the sunken road south of Mœuvres in which a gallant company of 13th Essex were reported to be holding out though surrounded by the enemy. The O.C., 1st King's, took

F 3

17TH BATTALION.
30TH Nov.

over command of the whole front line west of the Canal and an attack on the bridge-head just south of Lock 5 failed.

During the night several attempts by the enemy to drive the Middlesex back were successfully beaten off.

1/8TH BATTALION.
30TH Nov.

In the Tadpole Copse sector the enemy opened his attack with a heavy trench mortar and artillery barrage at 10 a.m. Here " A," " B " and " C " Companies of the 1/8th Middlesex (Lieut.-Colonel C. H. Pank) were holding the old Hindenburg Support Line, " D " Company being in support in Tadpole Reserve. At 10.25 a.m. an urgent message reached Colonel Pank from the O.C., " C " Company, asking for reinforcements of bombers. About half an hour later news reached Battalion Headquarters that the Germans, having broken through the front line held by the Battalion on the right had reached the old Hindenburg Support Line, and were even then advancing down the communication trenches towards Battalion Headquarters, 1/8th Middlesex. Hastily gathering the personnel of Battalion Headquarters Colonel Pank gave orders for the trench to be manned, and with a few men managed to get up the dug-out shaft as the enemy approached but, unfortunately, the remainder could not do so as almost immediately the Germans threw several bombs down the shaft. Colonel Pank reached Tadpole Reserve and, hurriedly organising a counter-attack, took forward a party of " D " Company, who not only bombed the enemy back but recaptured Battalion Headquarters, though only after heavy fighting. A line was then established in the old Hindenburg Front Line with a bombing block about 150 yards up a communication trench. But communication could not be re-established with " A," " B " or " C " Companies who had been surrounded during the first attack.

At about 9 p.m. Battalion Headquarters moved back to Barbican and there Colonel Pank, who had been wounded, reorganised the line with " D " Company and a company of the 13th Londons which had been sent up as reinforcements.

The casualties suffered by the 1/8th on 30th November were very heavy : Lieut. J. W. Johnson and 2/Lieut. J. H. Pattrick and 11 other ranks had been killed,* Lieut.-Colonel C. H. Pank, Captain J. D. White, Lieut. C. V. Burder and 40 other ranks wounded : Lieuts. H. C. Vaux, G. D. Dowty, J. E. Bayliss,

* The Battalion Diary also records Lieut. V. H. L. Meyers amongst the casualties, but does not state whether killed, wounded or missing.

W. J. S. Simpson, 2/Lieuts. C. J. M. Jeffreys, C. H. Jackson, C. R. Bird, R. W. Smart and 162 other ranks " missing, believed prisoners of war," and 18 other ranks missing. [1/7TH AND 1/8TH BATTALIONS.]

The 1/7th Middlesex (Lieut.-Colonel P. C. Kay) were not engaged on 30th. The Battalion was in camp at Fremicourt, but at 2 p.m. moved forward to Beugny in support, and later took up another position south of Louverval Wood. [30TH NOV.]

Fierce fighting continued along the whole front throughout the 1st December. The 11th Middlesex were, however, not engaged with the enemy and spent the day consolidating their line. The Battalion Diary records that the Guards and cavalry captured Gauche Wood, and in the afternoon cavalry captured Chapel Crossing. The Diary ends with the words " No further excitement to-day." [11TH BATTALION. 1ST DECEMBER.]

At Masnieres, during the afternoon and evening, at least nine separate attacks were beaten off by the 29th Division. Along the front held by the 16th Middlesex the enemy began a heavy attack (preceded by a bombardment) on Les Rues Vertes at 7.30 a.m., but the Battalion caught the attack in enfilade and " did much good work ! " German aeroplanes were again very active and the diary records that " none of ours visible." About 11 a.m. a German battery of field guns, firing in enfilade, caused fourteen casualties. " B " Company was also shelled by a heavy trench mortar firing from behind Mon Plaisir Farm, while a Stokes gun which the Middlesex had brought up during the night was destroyed. At intervals until the afternoon the enemy launched infantry attacks against the Battalion, but they were all completely checked, and nowhere did the Germans get closer than 200 yards from the Middlesex trenches. At 3 p.m., however, the Battalion outposts in the houses across the Lock Bridge were driven in, and by 5.30 p.m. the enemy in strength was in occupation of the Canal bank at the bridge. [16TH BATTALION. 1ST DECEMBER.]

At 9 p.m. that night orders were received from Brigade Headquarters to evacuate Masnieres and take up a position in support in the Hindenburg Support Line : the evacuation was begun at 11 p.m. The Middlesex " filed out being checked by the Adjutant at the Sugar Factory at 11.45 p.m." The men came out complete with arms and ammunition, and everything but a very small proportion of tools was brought away. The Battalion then fell back to Welsh Ridge, about 1,000 yards south of Marcoing.

In the meantime the enemy had launched heavy attacks

against the left sub-sector (Mœuvres) of the 2nd Divisional front. Here the line was held by the 17th Middlesex on the right and the 1st King's (both 6th Brigade) on the left. Throughout the night the enemy tried to bomb his way down both sides of the Canal du Nord and down the trenches of the Hindenburg Line, west of the Canal, but was repulsed.

17th Battalion. 1st December.

Just before 5 a.m. a particularly heavy attack was made down Edda Weg, but owing to the prompt action of C.S.M. Jackson and a party of " C " Company of the Middlesex he was beaten back without occupying a foot of ground. At 8 a.m. the enemy began a series of strong bombing attacks along the front of the sub-sector. One of these was made on " B " Company (Captain Stansfield). Full details of this attack and the very gallant efforts of the Company Commander and his men to stem the German rush are unavailable, but apparently the enemy made progress. Bombs again gave out, and with none to keep the enemy back the Company was forced to give ground, the enemy advancing 300 yards and attempting to cut off Battalion Headquarters, 1st King's Regiment. " A " Company of the Middlesex, however, with Lewis-gun fire checked this attempt. By now all " B " Company's officers were missing and the men tired and shaken.

It was at this critical stage that what was probably the finest bombing feat of the War took place.

Captain A. M. C. McReady Diarmid of " D " Company (17th Middlesex), seeing the position, called for volunteers from his Company. Arming himself with a plentiful supply of bombs he rushed forward and attacked the enemy. With extraordinary coolness and gallantry he flung bomb after bomb at the Germans with splendid accuracy. Back up the trench he drove the enemy regaining every foot of the 300 yards lost. Every bomb he had thrown himself, but alas! just as he had regained all the lost ground he was killed by an enemy bomb at the very moment of his triumph. Single-handed he had killed and otherwise disposed of 94 of the enemy—67 dead and 27 wounded were actually counted after the recapture of the trench " a feat which can hardly, if ever, have been equalled in the past."* All who saw him were inspired by his wonderful action and he was rightly awarded the Victoria Cross.

During the night of 1st the 2nd Highland Light Infantry

---

* From the " London Gazette " of 15th March, 1918.

relieved "B" and "D" Companies of the Middlesex who, exhausted by the hard day's fighting, moved back into support to trenches west of the Canal near the Bapaume–Cambrai road. {17TH BATTALION. 1ST DECEMBER.}

The two Companies ("A" and "C") attached to the 1st King's had also seen heavy fighting during the day.

"A" Company, under Lieut. F. J. Nunn, cleared the Germans out of Ernst Weg with great dash, regaining 300 yards. The covering fire of the Lewis gunners was especially good and kept the enemy's machine-gun fire down. Four German machine guns and two prisoners were captured and forty of the enemy's dead were found in the trench. After defeating several determined counter-attacks "A" Company moved back into support of the H.L.I. and remained there until relieved on the 3rd December.

"C" Company, under Captain C. Gregory, was sent by the O.C., 1st King's, to garrison the old support line of that Battalion in the neighbourhood of Donner Weg. One platoon bombed its way up Edda Weg driving the enemy back some distance. At 3 a.m. (1st December) the Company was relieved and moved back to dug-outs just south of the Canal du Nord. At 9 a.m., however, as the enemy was again counter-attacking, three platoons were ordered to carry up bombs and to reinforce "B" and "D" Companies. The other platoon reinforced the 1st King's in Ernst Weg and remained there until relieved at 2 a.m. on the 2nd.

This practically concludes the actions of the 17th Middlesex from 30th November to 2nd/3rd December (inclusive). Their casualties had been heavy. Captains A. M. C. McReady Diarmid and F. N. Stansfield and 40 other ranks had been killed; Captain J. M. Matheson, R.A.M.C. and 2/Lieuts. P. R. Hislop, E. J. Frances, C. G. Gunn, W. Fricker and 138 other ranks wounded and two other ranks missing. The Battalion had captured 27 prisoners and four machine guns. {2ND/3RD DEC.}

Neither the 1/7th nor the 1/8th Middlesex went again into the front line after the 30th November. The 56th Division was relieved by the 51st on 2nd/3rd December, and the former after withdrawal from the line, moved north to the XIIIth Corps area east of Arras where the Londoners relieved the 31st Division in the Arleux sector on 8th. {1/7TH AND 1/8TH BATTALIONS. 8TH DEC.}

The 11th Battalion, after the excitements of 1st December about Chapel Crossing, had a quiet day on 2nd, during which consolidation was carried on. On the 3rd 2/Lieut. Smith and six other ranks were wounded by shell fire. On the 4th the {11TH BATTALION. 4TH DEC.}

16TH BATTALION.
2ND DEC.

Battalion withdrew to Brusle and on the following day to Dernancourt, the 6th being spent in cleaning up.

6TH DEC.

The 16th Middlesex on the morning of 2nd December marched back to Ribecourt, thence on the 3rd to Havrincourt Wood and on the 4th to Fins. From the latter village, after a march on 5th to Etricourt, the Battalion moved by train to Petit Houvin, thence by march to Maizieres where on the 6th December they billeted.

17TH BATTALION.
6TH DEC.

The 17th Middlesex, after relief on the night 3rd/4th December, moved to trenches north of Hermies and marched on 4th to billets in Lebucquiere where on the 6th the C.O. read out to all companies congratulatory messages to the 2nd Division from Sir Douglas Haig.

20TH AND 21ST BATTALIONS.

Neither the 20th nor the 21st Battalions of the 40th Division were again engaged in the Cambrai operations after the 27th November. The 121st Brigade withdrew to Bailleulmont on 28th, remaining there until 1st December, when the Brigade Group moved to Hamelincourt and Erviller, in divisional reserve to the 16th Division, relieving the 49th Brigade in the left sector of the Divisional front on 2nd.

2ND DEC.

At the conclusion of the German counter-attacks which began on 30th November the British line formed such a dangerous salient that Sir Douglas Haig decided on a withdrawal from certain parts of the line, and on the 4th/5th December the evacuation of portions of the front most gallantly won began. By the 7th the new line corresponded roughly with the old Hindenburg Reserve Line, " and ran from a point about 1½ miles north by east of La Vacquerie, north of Ribecourt and Flesquieres to the Canal du Nord, about 1½ miles north of Havrincourt, *i.e.*, between two and two and a-half miles in front of the line held by us prior to the attack of the 20th November."

" Cambrai, 1917 " was a great battle and it was a pity that the splendid gains by the infantry were not fully exploited by the cavalry. The tanks had proved their worth and the artillery was magnificent in the support lent to the hard-fighting troops in the front line.

On the Western Front the campaign of the memorable year of 1917 was over. The British Army had suffered great losses, for the bulk of the fighting had fallen to Sir Douglas Haig's gallant troops, whose endeavours were bent upon the difficult task of preventing the enemy from gaining the initiative : in which they were successful.

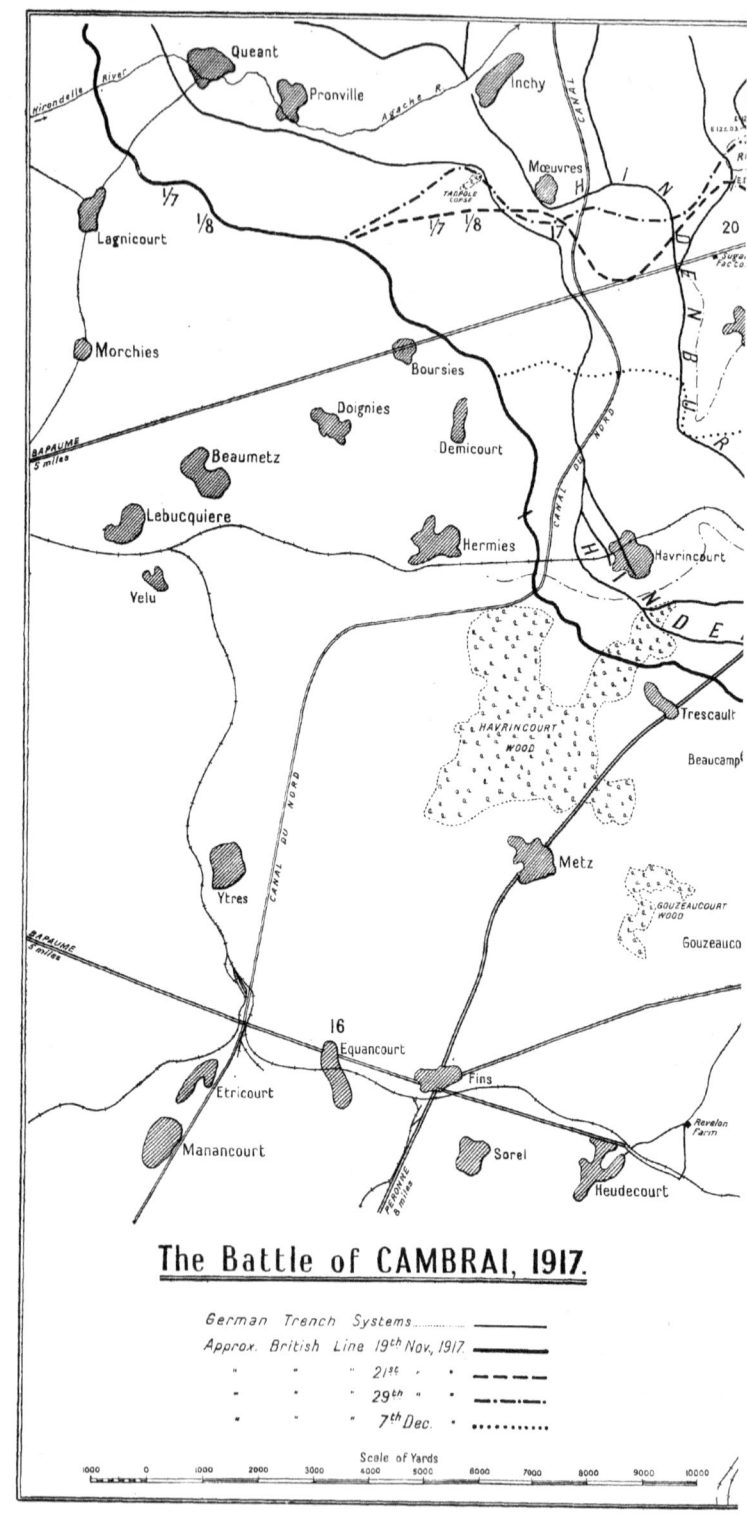

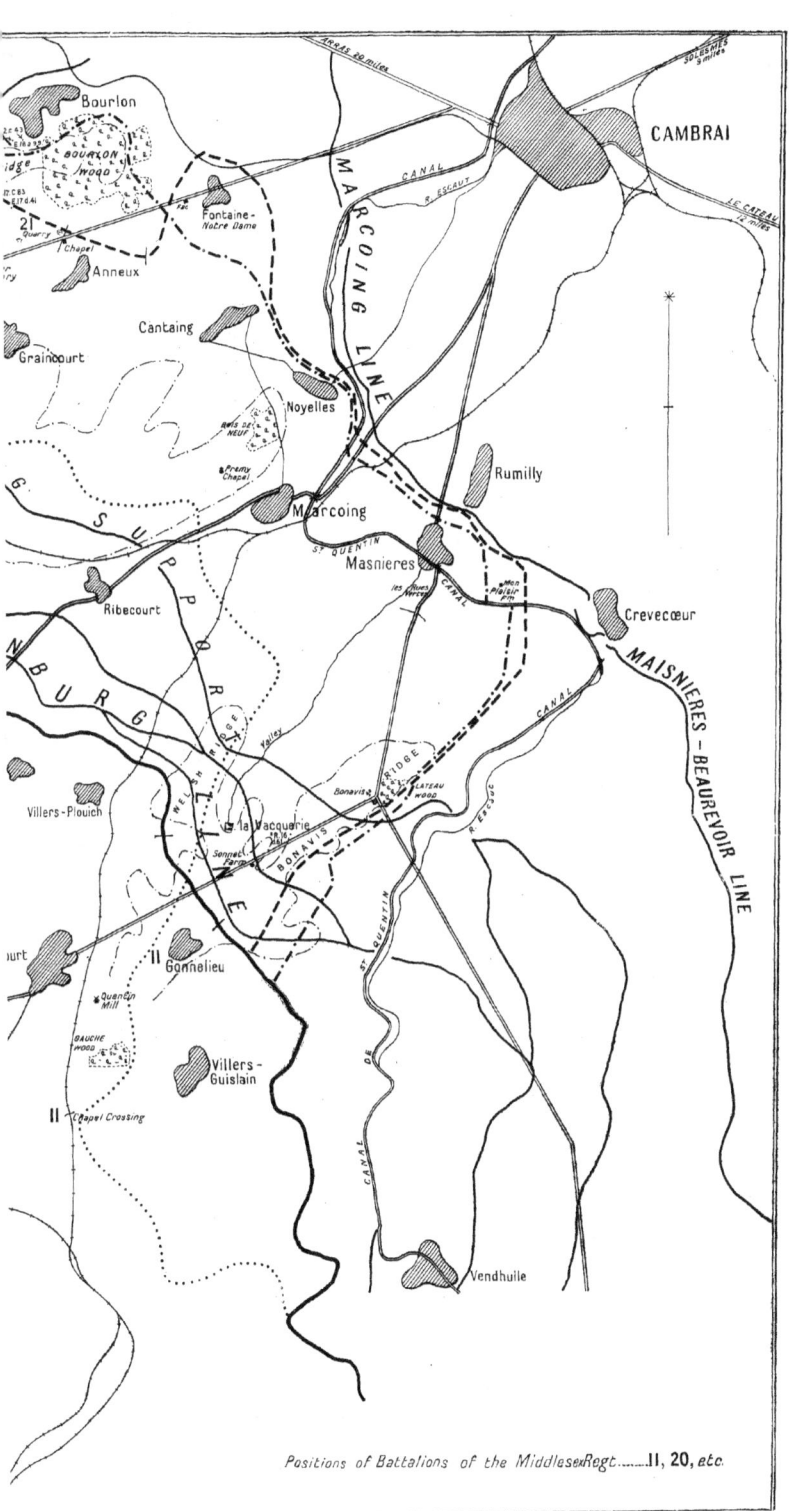

Positions of Battalions of the Middlesex Regt .... II, 20, etc.

To face page 170.

CHAPTER XXXII.

The Last Winter in the Trenches
TO THE EVE OF THE GREAT GERMAN OFFENSIVE:
21st March, 1918.

I. TO THE END OF 1917.

FROM the foregoing pages it will be seen that the majority of the Battalions of the Middlesex Regiment in France and Flanders during the year 1917 had been engaged in the desperate fighting of that year. Some had gone into battle at full strength and had emerged from the trenches sorely depleted in numbers: others, already weakened, came out of the inferno still weaker, and in order to regain their strength had to spend lengthy periods out of the line absorbing reinforcements and training them to take their place in the front-line trenches. Between times, *i.e.*, when major operations were not in progress, raids on the enemy and constant vigilance in the front line, kept all ranks busy. War had become a highly scientific business: indeed, when men had time to compare the conditions in the trenches in those early months of the War in 1914 with conditions prevailing towards the end of 1917, they never ceased wondering at the marvellous changes which had taken place. Things unheard of, even undreamt of, in 1914 were now an everyday occurrence: the very means of carrying on warfare—gas, bombs, guns of enormous calibre, tanks, wonderful underground dug-outs, the use of camouflage, to mention only a few—all were the results of over three years of warfare such as no military nation had ever conceived in those Elysian days before war broke out in August, 1914.

From the sanguinary fighting east of Ypres towards the end of September, the 1st Middlesex (98th Brigade, 33rd Division) had come out of the line with a loss of 249 all ranks between the 24th

1ST BATTALION.

1ST BATTALION. and 26th of that month. The first four days of October were spent
26TH SEPT. out of the line at Ebblinghem, but on the 5th the Battalion moved
to Esquerdes, and on the 6th to Bailleul where the Die-Hards
billeted in canteen huts. They were now for the time being
attached to their old Brigade, the 19th, and on the 8th took over
front-line trenches in the Ploegsteert area, Battalion Headquarters
being at Bristol Castle. Of this tour there are no incidents to
14TH OCTOBER. record. On the 14th the Middlesex were relieved and marched
back to Weale Camp, near Neuve Eglise, where they came again
under the orders of the 98th Brigade. The remainder of October
and the whole of November and December were comparatively
uneventful, and when the year closed the 1st Middlesex were in
billets in the Convent, Poperinghe. Lieut.-Colonel J. W. L. Elgee
still commanded the Battalion.

31ST DEC. The 18th Middlesex (Pioneers) of the 33rd Division (Lieut.-
18TH Colonel H. Storr, commanding), " carried on," though other units
BATTALION. of the 33rd Division had been withdrawn from the line, about the
Menin Road. Their work was always hazardous, and in reading
their records it is evident that not only were they constantly at
work digging trenches but were also used as " carrying parties "
while the Lewis gunners held posts near Zillebeke Lake. Their
Headquarters until the 6th October were near Dickebusch: they
moved to Westoutre on 7th and to Gable Farm, Wulverghem, on
8th. The 18th November saw the Pioneers at St. Jean, the 33rd
Division having moved up to the Ypres Salient where conditions
were hardly describable. Across seas of mud they moved to their
work. They repaired a mule track between Zonnebeke Station
and Seine, worked on the tramways, repaired duck board tracks
and horse and R.A.M.C. tracks: night and day they carried on,
shelled most of the while. Their Lewis guns were put into the
line and their gunners suffered casualties. The lives these Pioneers
led were infinitely trying: many were killed or wounded. When
the year closed they were still in the Salient, at Savile Row.

31ST DEC. The 2nd Middlesex (23rd Brigade, 8th Division), after arrival
2ND at Halifax Camp on 18th August, stayed in the Cæstre area
BATTALION. absorbing drafts and training until the 27th, when the Battalion
paraded and moved by route-march to north-west of Armentières,
and on the 31st relieved New Zealand troops in the front line. On
6TH SEPT. the 6th September the Middlesex were relieved and moved back
to billets in Pont Nieppe. One officer—Major A. G. Cade—
was slightly wounded during this tour. On the 5th October,

while in these same billets, the whole area was shelled by the enemy, Major Cade being again wounded, while 7 other ranks were killed and 27 wounded. Two officers (2/Lieuts. C. Everett and W. Cheeseman) were " gassed " while the Battalion was holding trenches opposite the village of Frelinghien. Another officer (Capt. and Adjutant F. G. Shakle) was killed on 20th November whilst the Battalion was in Outskirt Farm, Poperinghe. On the 23rd the Battalion marched up to the front line and took over trenches north-west of Passchendaele, in the Mosselmarckt area. This area was still under violent artillery fire from the sullen enemy. On the first day 2/Lieut. J. C. Oliver was wounded. On the 24th 2/Lieut. A. P. King and 5 other ranks were killed, and 2/Lieuts. A. Brown and G. C. Miller and 1 other rank wounded. The next day 8 more ranks were killed and 16 wounded. On this day also the C.O., Lieut.-Colonel J. H. Hall, proceeded to England to fill a six month's appointment at home, and Major C. D. Drew assumed command of the Battalion. On the 30th the Battalion moved back to St. Jean. Between the 26th and 30th (inclusive) the casualties were 19 other ranks killed and 46 wounded. An expensive tour. But that was life in the Ypres Salient; day and night the opposing guns were seldom silent. On the 2nd December Major C. A. S. Page assumed command of the 2nd Middlesex, Major Drew reverting to second-in-command. At 9 a.m. on 2nd December the Battalion entrained at St. Jean for the Wizernes area, thence moved to billets at Quelmes where, until the 27th, training was carried out. The 31st of the month saw the Middlesex back again at St. Jean.

The 4th Middlesex (of the 37th Division) arrived at Meteren on 21st October: they were there, training hard, until the 10th November when they marched to Beggar's Rest, which aptly described their new camp, for it was a very poor place, the ground being from five to six inches deep in mud. The Battalion did not go into line, but provided working parties which were employed around Molen Dump and Spoil Bank, carrying material for a new reserve line. Another move took place on the 17th to Curragh Camp, where training and the furnishing of working parties occupied the Battalion until at last on 25th the Middlesex relieved a battalion in the front line in front of the Hollebeke sector. On the 26th Lieut.-Colonel H. A. O. Hanley joined the Battalion. The 31st December found the Battalion in dug-outs at the Spoil Bank.

After the severe fighting in the Cambrai operations the 1/7th (Lieut.-Colonel P. C. Kay) and 1/8th Middlesex (Lieut.-Colonel C. H. Pank) moved north with the 50th Division, and early in December were holding front-line trenches in the Arleux-Oppy sector. There was but little doing towards the end of the month, and on 31st the Diary of the 1/7th thus describes the life of the Battalion: " Battalion holding front line. Situation very quiet. Work impossible owing to severe frost. Casualties to date—nil!" The fighting strength of the 1/7th Middlesex was then only 21 officers and 384 other ranks. The 1/8th were in support of the 1/7th, engaged in providing working parties.

From Dernancourt the 11th Middlesex (Lieut.-Colonel T. S. Wollocombe) of the 12th Division, marched to Edge Hill Station on 8th December, and there entrained for the Wittes area. At the latter place the Battalion Diary records that " We learnt with much regret that 2/Lieut. P. E. Booth had succumbed to his wounds. We thereby lose a very promising young officer."* A move was made to Tannay on 23rd December where Christmas was spent. The last entry for the year in the Battalion Diary states that: " The Drums played the New Year in at midnight."

Of the 12th Battalion (18th Division) there is little to record between 21st November and 31st December with the exception of details of an accidental explosion of trench-mortar ammunition whilst the Trench-Mortar Battery was practising fire against low-flying aeroplanes. The Battalion was then at Vimy Camp, Haringe. In the explosion Major H. Podmore and six other ranks were killed, and Major G. L. Harrison wounded. Captain G. C. Moran, the senior officer, took over command of the Battalion.

After the Battles of Pilkhem and Langemarck 1917, the 13th Middlesex (73rd Brigade, 24th Division) were not again engaged in the Battles of Ypres, 1917. The Battalion reached the Dickebusch area on the night of 15th August and there spent several days in training. They went back into the front line south of Inverness Copse on the 23rd August, and on the following morning " C " and " D " Companies repelled an attempt by the enemy to recapture a dug-out which had been taken from him two nights previously. On the 27th 2/Lieut. B. Tedman was wounded. A few nights later, in wet weather, the Battalion was relieved and again moved back to the Dickebusch area. Thereafter, until the

* Died of wounds on 4th December, 1917.

third week in September, little of interest was recorded. On the 21st September the 24th Division moved down to the Somme: the 13th Middlesex entraining at Bailleuil for Bapaume. A railway accident near Achiet-le-Grand, which delayed the Battalion, also resulted in four other ranks being killed and several injured. On the 27th the Middlesex reached Bapaume and marched to Haplincourt, thence on 24th to Moislains and, by bus, on 25th to Roisel.

On the night 26th/27th the 73rd Brigade relieved the 102nd Brigade (34th Division) in the Hargicourt sector, the 13th Middlesex taking over the left sub-sector. The Battalion had come to an extraordinarily quiet part of the line and throughout the remainder of September and October and until 20th November there is little to record. On the latter date, however, the Battalion Diary mentions the bombardment by the 55th Division (on the left of the 24th Division) who attacked the enemy when the Battle of Cambrai opened on that morning. Nothing of importance, however, happened along the front of the 24th Division, and it was not until the 30th that the 13th Middlesex were moved off rather hurriedly to south-east of St. Emile to support a brigade of the 55th Division which had been driven back in the enemy's counter-attack. On the 1st December the Middlesex were relieved and moved back to Hervilly, and a few days later to Hargicourt again. Christmas Day was spent out of the line, the records testifying to the Battalion having a good time, but the last day of the Old Year found the 13th back again in the front-line trenches.

A series of moves followed the arrival of the 16th Middlesex (29th Division) at Petit Houvin on the 6th December. From Petit Houvin the Battalion marched to Maizieres and billeted in the village until the 16th. On the latter date they moved via Houvin, Frevent and Flers to Blangermont: on the 17th to Grignt and on the 18th to Renty. The latter march, a distance of about eighteen miles, was carried out in blizzards and through snow drifts, only one man falling out. In Renty the 16th Battalion spent the remainder of the year.

In Lebucquerie, whither they had withdrawn on the 4th December after their splendid fighting in the German counter-attacks at Cambrai, the 17th Middlesex (2nd Division) went into the front line again south of Mœuvres on 8th. The following morning at about 7.30 the enemy attacked the Battalion's left bombing posts with *Flammenwerfer*, causing the garrisons of the posts to fall back some 150 yards. " C " Company then went up to reinforce " A." Throughout that day continual bombing attacks took place. On the 10th Lock 7 was heavily bombarded by the enemy and the front-line and communication trenches subjected to intermittent shelling. A post on " A " Company's front was again pushed in but the enemy was driven back " apparently by Sergeant Glennie of ' C ' Company alone, who was wounded and probably captured in doing so."* Two or three days of comparative quietude followed and on the 14th the Battalion moved to Velu Wood. The 31st found the Battalion holding reserve positions at the Spoil Bank, furnishing working parties and digging new communication trenches.

From their heavy fighting in Bourlon Wood the 20th and 21st Middlesex of the 40th Division had moved back with other units of their Brigade—the 121st—to the Bailleulmont area until the 1st December when a move was made to a camp at Hamelincourt and Ervillers. The 121st Brigade was now in Divisional Reserve to the 16th Division. On the 2nd the Brigade took over front-line trenches east of Ervillers, and for the remainder of December both the 20th and 21st Middlesex held busy positions in the line where much patrol work was carried out, or else in support or reserve when the usual training had to be carried out.

The 20th Battalion was relieved in the left sub-sector of the Bullecourt sector by the 21st Battalion on the 31st December, the former moving back to L'Abbaye Mory Camp. The ground was frozen hard, and more snow fell on this day.

From Poll Hill Camp, Proven, whither they had moved after the Battle of Broodseinde, the 3/10th Middlesex (10th Brigade, 4th Division) left the Ypres area on the 18th October. The Battalion first marched to Houpoutre and there entrained for Aubigny where, on arrival, the 3/10th marched to Y Huts, near Etrun. In this camp the Battalion remained training until the 23rd when a move was made to Schramm Barracks.

On the night 24th/25th October the Battalion went into the front line, taking over the Cambrai Road sector (between Pick Avenue and Gordon Avenue). Wiring and patrol work was carried out during the tour of four days, and on relief (28th/29th) two companies moved back to Spade Reserve and two to the Caves

---

* Battalion Diary.

at Les Fosses Farm. November was a comparatively quiet month. December began with the Battalion in Arras. On the 10th the Battalion went into the Monchy sector. On the 30th they were out of the line in the Bois des Bœufs. 3/10TH BATTALION. 31ST DEC.

II. TO THE EVE OF THE GERMAN OFFENSIVE, 1918.

New Year's Day, 1918, witnessed the dawn of a year unparalleled in the military history of the nations. For three years and a little over four months the titanic struggle had been waged with a fierceness and ferocity hitherto unknown, for even in bygone ages warfare was a comparatively mild affair compared with the wholesale slaughter during those ghastly years of the Great War.

But on the 1st January, 1918, there were, at that date, no indications of the momentous things which were to take place within a few months, and it is not until early in March that it is possible from the official diaries of battalions, brigades and divisions, kept in the field, to sense the oncoming of great happenings.

Because of the necessity to conserve their strength, consistent with a vigilant watch upon the enemy's dispositions, raiding and patrol work by battalions holding front-line sectors was reduced to the lowest limits. For the first few months of the year, therefore, there is little to record, with the exception of constant work while in the line, on the defences, or training when back in the " rest " areas.

The 1st Middlesex spent a considerable portion of that period in the front line south-west of Passchendaele, though in February three weeks' training was carried out at Meringhem. On the 19th January there is an interesting note in the Battalion Diary to the effect that a party of officers of the American Expeditionary Force were attached to the Middlesex (then holding reserve positions at Seine) for instruction. In the line the enemy is described as being " very quiet," and only four other ranks were wounded during the month. In February two other ranks were killed and four more wounded. On the 6th March, however, there is an entry in the Diary which (unbeknown at that period) was really the beginning of the enemy's preparations for his great offensive. The entry is as follows: " Considerable gas shelling in the evening." The same entry is repeated on the 7th and 8th, casualties on the latter date amounting to 2 other 1ST BATTALION. 7TH MARCH.

1ST BATTALION. 9TH MARCH.	ranks killed, 12 wounded, and 14 " gassed." On the 9th 3 other ranks were killed, 7 wounded and 11 " gassed." This gas shelling was part of the German plan to " thin out " the ranks of their opponents before launching their great attack on 21st March. Gradually this " gassing " increased until on the 18th (the Battalion being then in the line south-west of Passchendaele) it is described as " very heavy," and on the night 17th/18th the 1st Middlesex had three officers (Captain H. I. E. Ripley and 2/Lieuts. Hardy and Garrett) and thirty-one other ranks " gassed." The enemy was using " mustard gas " the fumes of which were insidious, *i.e.*, those affected showing signs only after several hours. On the 19th
20TH MARCH.	and 20th the same tactics were continued by the enemy and about twenty more men were " gassed." On the latter night hostile patrols approached the Battalion posts and threw bombs : the enemy also raided the 4th King's, on the left of the 1st Middlesex, but only succeeded in leaving four prisoners behind.
18TH BATTALION.	The clearing of " pill boxes," the continuation of the Passchendaele draining and repair of tracks kept the 18th Middlesex (Pioneers of the 33rd Division) busy. They also incurred losses
20TH MARCH.	on 7th March from gas shelling, and on 20th March two large calibre shells fell in Middlesex Camp (where the Battalion was located), completely destroying the Signal Office and equipment, killing the Sergeant Signaller and wounding the operator on duty.
2ND BATTALION.	The 2nd Middlesex began the year badly. On the night of 3rd/4th January they were due to relieve the Royal Irish Rifles in the front line north-east of Passchendaele. The weather being extremely cold and frosty the duck-board tracks were slippery which hampered the relief considerably. Moreover, the enemy's guns were vigorously shelling all approaches to the front line. The result was that, although the relief was carried out, four other ranks were killed, 2/Lieut. Aitken and fourteen other ranks were wounded and one other rank was missing : not a good beginning for the year. The next day 2/Lieut. C. J. G. Livesay was killed, 2/Lieut. Shingler and seven other ranks were wounded and two more other ranks were missing. The enemy made a futile attempt
14TH JAN.	to raid " B " Company's left post at Vox Farm on 14th January, but was driven off.

The Appendices to the Battalion Diary for January contain particulars of several awards during the first tour in the line from the 3rd to 5th of the month. Captain and Adjutant W. Evans was awarded the Military Cross. This officer was at Battalion

Headquarters, situated in a concrete dug-out, which was being heavily shelled. A shell struck the roof of the dug-out and blew part of it in, but hearing that two men had been buried by the same shell in a shelter outside, he immediately went out and collecting some men succeeded in digging out one wounded man and did not desist until the second man was found, but dead. Lance-Corporal J. Markland, to whom the D.C.M. was awarded, was moving up to the trenches with his platoon under heavy shell fire: both the platoon commander and platoon sergeant had been wounded and several others had become casualties, but, although himself wounded in several places Lance-Corporal, Markland led the remainder of his platoon into the line, a distance of over a mile, under shell fire and handed over to his company commander before reporting himself wounded.

The citation in which the gallantry of Private W. Tabor is recorded is thus given in full: " Awarded Bar to Military Medal for conspicuous gallantry and unflinching devotion to duty near Passchendaele from 3rd to 5th January, 1918. On 3rd January this man, while on his way up to the line, fell heavily on the duck-board track which was slippery with ice, and fractured two ribs. He did not mention this to anyone, but as a company runner continued to carry messages, very often under machine-gun fire. On the early morning of 5th January he volunteered to accompany his Company Sergeant-Major to search for the body of an officer who had been killed in No Man's Land. On finding the body, which was close to the enemy's line, they dragged it for some forty yards, being under close and heavy machine-gun fire, until they were within ten yards of our line. Owing to the continuous fire they were unable to take the body further, but they removed all papers which might have been of value to the enemy. It was only on 7th January, after the Battalion had been relieved, that Private Tabor reported sick and the extent of his injuries discovered."

Company Sergeant-Major J. R. Ayres, whom Private Tabor had accompanied out into No Man's Land, was awarded the Divisional Commander's Parchment Certificate.*

From the night 15th/16th January until the 11th February the 2nd Middlesex were out of the line, but on the latter date relieved the 2nd Royal Fusiliers at Belle Vue in Brigade Reserve.

* The officer mentioned was 2/Lieut. C. J. G. Livesay.

180   *Eve of the German Offensive*   1918

2ND BATTALION.

The following day (12th) 2/Lieut. W. Goulden, Battalion Intelligence Officer, was killed. That the Battalion worked hard while in the line is evident from an entry in the Diary on 23rd February when it is recorded that in a recent tour the Middlesex had dug out approximately 21,580 cubic feet of earth. On the 3rd March two platoons under Lieuts. Frayne and Aitken carried out a very successful raid on the enemy's trenches at Teal Cot: two " dummy " raids, one on each side of the main raid, were made at the same time. Six Germans were brought back as prisoners and many more were killed. .The casualties of the Middlesex were only one man wounded (" at duty "). On the 20th March the Battalion was at Quelmes engaged in training.

20TH MARCH.

4TH BATTALION.

" Working parties as usual " is the first entry in the Diary of the 4th Middlesex for several days from the 1st January. The Battalion was at Spoil Bank, in the Ypres Salient, but on the 5th moved to Curragh Camp and on the 11th to Dickebusch. Towards the end of the month the Battalion moved by rail to Ebblinghem, thence by march route to La Belle Hotesse for training purposes. About the middle of February the Battalion moved forward again to the trenches, reaching Mount Sorrel on 15th. Trenches were taken over in Shrewsbury Forest and the neighbourhood. On the night of the 6th March 2/Lieut. R. A. K. Stuart, Sergeant Clark and Private Butler crawled into the enemy's line and captured a German sergeant-major and an orderly. Two days later the enemy heavily bombarded the Battalion trenches: 2/Lieut. J. H. Hedley was killed by a sniper and 1 other rank was killed, 41 wounded and 3 were missing after the bombardment. On 18th 2/Lieut. Benda was wounded: on the 21st March the Battalion held trenches east of Ypres.

21ST MARCH.

1/7TH AND 1/8TH BATTALIONS.

The 1/7th and 1/8th Middlesex of the 56th Division were holding trenches in the Oppy sector on 1st January, the former in the front line and the latter in support east of Bailleul. A gallant incident marked the advent of the New Year.

1ST JANUARY.

At 11.15 p.m. on the night of the 1st, a German patrol of five men entered No. 1 Bombing Post held by " B " Company (Barnet and Enfield) where there was a double sentry post, and attempted to kidnap one of the sentries. They knocked one sentry down and whilst two covered him with their revolvers the three other Germans attempted to attack the remaining sentry, Private G. H. Clayton. Although wounded in three places Clayton defended himself vigorously: he bayoneted two of the Germans which so

terrified the remainder that they fled leaving behind two caps and 1/7TH AND 1/8TH BATTALIONS.
a revolver. A patrol went out immediately to intercept them but they had already escaped. Clayton was awarded the D.C.M. for his gallantry.

On the 5th the 1/8th relieved the 1/7th but the tour was uneventful, and on the 9th the 56th Division was relieved by the 62nd Division and moved back to the Tinques area for training purposes. The 1/7th billeted in Chelers and the 1/8th in Tinques.

Although out of the front line both Battalions had to find large working parties—a serious hindrance to training. Indeed, the 1/7th was actually reduced at one period to 18 officers and 50 other ranks. Under such conditions it was impossible to carry out training properly. For over a month these two Battalions were out of the line but, on the 16th February the 1/7th Middlesex* took over front-line trenches in the Gavrelle sector, being relieved on the 20th by the 1/8th Battalion.

A month later (16th March) the 1/8th record casualties which show the effect of the enemy's gas shelling and attempts to thin the line. On that date the Battalion had 1 officer (2/Lieut. E. A. Muzell) and 69 other ranks "gassed": on the 17th 1 officer (2/Lieut. C. J. C. Small) and 55 other ranks: on the 18th 2 officers (Captain L. A. Higson and 2/Lieut. E. J. M. McDonnell) and 35 other ranks: on the 19th 42 other ranks, and on the 20th 20 other ranks—all "gas" casualties. On the 21st the 1/7th was back in Wakefield Camp and the 1/8th had been relieved and moved by train to St. Aubin.

There is little of outstanding interest in the Diaries of the two Territorial Battalions until the opening of the German offensive, but on 20th March the 56th Division was holding the 20TH MARCH. same sector of the line when the enemy's attack began on 21st.

Five Battalions of the Regiment, *i.e.*, the 3/10th, 11th, 12th, 3/10TH, 11TH, 16th and 17th began the New Year with every hope of " carrying 12TH, 16TH AND 17TH on " for the whole course of the War. But Fate had ordained BATTALIONS. otherwise. The strenuous efforts of the British Army during the previous year (1917) had left it weak in numbers and at a low ebb. Drafts from home had fallen off. Nervous because of the heavy casualties suffered in the great struggles of 1917, in which the British Army had practically shouldered the burdens of most

---

* On the 15th February Lieut.-Colonel M. Beevor, The Buffs, arrived and assumed command of the 1/7th Middlesex, vice Lieut.-Colonel P. C. Kay, who reverted to Second-in-Command.

3/10TH, 11TH, 12TH, 16TH AND 17TH BATTALIONS.

of the heavy fighting of that year (at Arras and at Ypres), the authorities at home kept back thousands of troops in training in England who should properly have been in France and Flanders. Faced therefore with keeping up the strength of his divisions Sir Douglas Haig (under instructions from the Army Council) had no other resource than to reduce the number of battalions in a division from 13 to 10, by disbanding numerous battalions in order to bring other units up to fighting strength. It was a bad policy, bound to affect the fighting efficiency of units, but it had to be done. As a result, in February, 1918, many splendid fighting battalions were disbanded and their personnel distributed amongst other battalions. In these changes the 3/10th (Territorial) and the 11th, 12th, 16th and 17th (Service) Battalions were involved. It was a great pity for the record of these battalions was of the best.

3/10TH BATTALION.

The 3/10th began the year at Bois des Bœufs (Monchy area) in reserve, but on the 3rd went into the front line, relieving the 1st Hants in the left sub-sector held by the right Brigade (10th) of the 4th Division. The tour was uneventful save for patrol work each night. On the 13th the Germans attempted to raid the Battalion "Sap 7" but were vigorously repulsed. The Battalion was relieved, but went back again into the front line on the night 27th/28th January for what was to be its last tour in the trenches.

The 3/10th came out of the front line on the night 1st/2nd February and occupied the Brown Line. It was there that they received orders concerning their disbandment. The 10th

27TH JANUARY. Brigade Diary records that on 27th January orders for the reorganisation of Divisions had been received whereby the 3/10th were to be disbanded. On the 6th February the Royal Scots relieved the 3/10th in the Brown Line and the Middlesex moved back to Schramm Barracks to billets. On the 8th they moved to Agnes les Duisans, but before leaving the barracks they were formed up into three sides of a square. They were then inspected and addressed by the Divisional Commander, Major-General T. G. Mattheson. The General said: "It is with very great regret that I address you this morning to bid you farewell. As you know, orders have been issued for the Battalion to be disbanded . . . You have been in the Division since August, 1917, and have well maintained your position in the 10th Infantry Brigade, a fact of which you may well be proud, when it is taken into consideration the little experience you had when you joined the Division compared with the three years' experience of the battalions then in the Division. To whatever unit it may be the lot of each one of you to be transferred, it will be with pride that you will remember that you held your own in the very difficult and strenuous fighting in the District of Flanders in October, 1917." The General then thanked all ranks for their loyalty, zeal and energy and, having told them they had done splendidly, he wished them good luck in the future. {3/10TH BATTALION.}

The 3/10th reached Agnes les Duisans about midday on 8th and were billeted in the 4th Divisional Depot Camp, where they remained until the 20th. On the latter date, however, information was received that the Battalion was not to be broken up but was to become the 11th Entrenching Battalion under the orders of the C.E., XVIIth Corps, Third Army. The C.O., Lieut.-Colonel C. H. Cautley, was appointed O.C., Third Army Group Entrenching Battalion, with Headquarters at Albert. On the 21st February the Battalion moved to Arras. The Diary of the Battalion ends on the 23rd February, and there are no records as to what happened from that date but, being Middlesex men, it is certain that they carried out their duties with the same degree of energy and loyalty as when they were fighting infantry. {8TH FEBRUARY. 23RD FEB.}

The 11th Middlesex (Lieut.-Colonel T. S. Wollocombe) on 6th January moved to Neuf Berquin on the 36th Brigade (12th Division) taking over the Estaires area, and on the 13th of the month relieved the 10th Welch Regiment in the Fleurbaix Sector, but the tour was unproductive of any item of outstanding interest. On the 29th the 11th Battalion went into the Bois Grenier Sector, and the following quotation is from the Battalion Diary : " After a lapse of 2¼ years we had come back to the sector in which we underwent our instruction shortly after coming overseas." {11TH BATTALION.}

The 11th Middlesex received orders concerning their disbandment on the 5th February : 7 officers and 150 other ranks were to be sent to each of the 1/7th and 1/8th Battalions, 10 officers and 200 other ranks to the 1st Battalion, and 15 officers and 300 other ranks to the 4th Battalion. These drafts were despatched on 7th and 8th February. Battalion Headquarters, totalling 6 officers, Medical Officer, and about 135 other ranks not disbanded moved to Doulieu on 10th. The 11th Middlesex now ceased to exist as a battalion, and on the 27th of the month the {5TH FEBRUARY. 4TH, 1/7TH AND 1/8TH BATTALIONS. 27TH FEB.}

12TH BATTALION.

Diary (the last) states that "Surplus, less transport, to be posted to No. 2 Entrenching Battalion, selected few posted to Machine-Gun Battalion."

The 12th Middlesex (18th Division) began the year at Vimy Camp, Haringhe, but on the 10th January entrained for Boesinghe, **15TH JAN.** thence marching to Abri Camp. On the 15th the Battalion took over front-line trenches astride the Ypres–Staden railway, but the enemy does not appear to have been very active in this area. On the 28th 2/Lieut. H. D. Cheeseman was wounded. Two days later the Battalion entrained at Boesinghe and proceeded to Mendinghem, marching on detrainment to a camp unnamed, but given in the Diary as at "W.24.b.5.9." It was here that on 1st February the G.O.C., 54th Brigade, addressed the Battalion on the forthcoming disbandment.

The 18th Division began to move south to join the 5th Army on the Somme on 9th February: the 12th Middlesex reached Noyon on 10th. On the 11th the Battalion moved to Muirancourt, arriving at 2.20 p.m. on 11th. The Battalion was struck **12TH FEB.** off the strength of the 54th Infantry Brigade on 12th February and from that date became the 18th Entrenching Battalion.

13TH BATTALION.

North-east of Hargicourt the 13th Middlesex held front-line trenches when the New Year dawned. They moved back to Hervilly, to support trenches, on 5th, and back to Hancourt in Brigade Reserve on 8th. These three places sum up the existence of the Battalion during January and February. The line was very quiet, though towards the end of the latter month the enemy's shell fire (chiefly with H.V. guns) began to increase. On the **20TH MARCH.** 2nd March the Battalion was at Bernes, training, and on the 20th the first hint of the forthcoming German offensive is given in the Battalion Diary which states: "Orders were received that in event of enemy attack the Battalion was to form an obligatory garrison under direct Corps orders in a line of redoubts north-east of Vermand. These positions were reconnoitred during the morning."

16TH BATTALION.
1ST JANUARY.

The 16th (Public Schools) Battalion (Lieut.-Colonel J. Forbes-Robertson) spent the 1st and 2nd January at Renty, resting and training. Then on the 3rd they moved to Setques and Fersinghem where again Battalion and Brigade training (much of it carried out in snow storms) occupied all ranks until the 16th of the month, on which date a move back to the front line was begun. On the 18th the Battalion relieved the Berkshires in shell-holes north-west of Passchendaele. One other rank 16TH BATTALION. killed and one wounded are the casualties recorded during this tour which ended on the night 19th/20th. The next, and last tour in front-line trenches (*as* the 16th Middlesex) began on 23rd and ended on 26th, on the conclusion of which the Battalion entrained at Wieltje for Brandhoek, marching thence to Red Rose Camp. One other rank killed, one wounded and two missing were the casualties in this tour, and they are given because they were the final losses in the line suffered by the Battalion.

The 16th were at work on the Gravenstafel line on 3rd 3RD FEBRUARY February when orders were received to disband the Battalion. The Middlesex then moved back on the 4th to Warrington Camp, where drafts of officers and men were dispatched to the 2nd, 18th and 20th Battalions of the Regiment. On the 11th, 11TH FEB. Battalion Headquarters and details, strength, 3 officers and 58 other ranks, marched to VIIIth Corps Reinforcement Camp at Poperinghe where disbandment was completed.

Thus passed from the roll of Battalions of the Regiment another splendid fighting unit. No more would the paved roads of France and Flanders, or the shell-torn villages through which they passed, echo to the marching song of the Public Schools Battalion :

"Left, left, left, right, left,
 Brace your broken knees up ;
Cover off your file.
Dress, dress, dress by the left,
 Pick it up, pick it up,
 Swing along in style," etc., etc.

With so fine a record behind them it surely would have been 17TH BATTALION. possible to retain the 17th Middlesex, also one of the finest Service Battalions which ever left the shores of England ! But no ; they also were thrown into the melting-pot.

From the Slag Heap, Hermies, where they were in reserve, the 17th moved on the 2nd January into the front line on the right bank of the Canal du Nord during the night 2nd/3rd January. On the following night the Battalion had, what was in reality, its final fight with the enemy.

At 4.20 p.m. on 3rd the enemy began a light trench-mortar 3RD JANUARY. ("Pineapples") bombardment of Stone, Scott and Sark Posts and Sap "A" and the Posts on the left of the Battalion, which gradually increased in intensity. On Scott and Sark Posts and Sap "A" the bombardment was especially severe. The enemy

17TH BATTALION.
3RD JANUARY.

then advanced, and after a vigorous defence, during which one officer alone—2/Lieut. Murray—threw no less than eighty bombs, the enemy succeeded in driving in the posts at the blocks and seven men were "missing, believed killed." The garrison at Sark Post was temporarily driven in, but regained their position. Scott Post was attacked by large numbers of Germans, dressed in white, in order to make themselves indistinguishable in the snow. Eleven of the garrison were wounded, nine were missing (also "believed killed"), and the remaining six made their way back to the front line. Stone Post put up a fine fight and inflicted very heavy casualties on the enemy and maintained its position with only one casualty. The result of this affair was that eight of the 17th Middlesex were killed, 21 were wounded, and 16 missing, all of the latter were "believed killed."

The Battalion was relieved on the night of 3rd/4th, and on the 4th was located in camp at Beaulencourt where, until the 24th, the Middlesex remained training. On the latter date a move was made to Etricourt and here, on the 26th, a draft of seventy men arrived. This draft showed to what extent the United Kingdom had been drained of its manhood, for the Battalion Diary describes them as "lads who had just turned nineteen years old." Yet, though they were young in years, they proved themselves fine soldiers in the time to come.

On the last day of January the 17th Middlesex relieved the 1st King's in the left sub-sector of the Vacquerie sector, but this tour was uneventful, and on the night of the 2nd/3rd February the 1st King's again took over the front line.

On completion of this tour—the last spent by the 17th Middlesex as a battalion—in the front line, the C.O. was notified of the disbandment "owing to the difficulties in obtaining reinforcements to keep all battalions up to establishment." On the night of 6th/7th the Middlesex marched back to billets west of Metz, and on the 9th to Menancourt. That night the officers of the Battalion held a "breaking-up dinner." The next day 15 officers and 300 other ranks were sent off to join the 13th Middlesex at Roisel, and on 12th a similar draft was dispatched to the 21st Middlesex at Mercatel, south of Arras. Details now remaining with the Battalion numbered four officers and about 100 other ranks. On the 22nd these details were posted to No. 6 Entrenching Battalion, under Lieut.-Colonel Collard, Vth Corps, at Barastre. On this day the 17th Middlesex ceased to exist, but those

6TH/7TH FEBRUARY.

22ND FEB.

survivors of the Battalion and those who read this history will remember their fine record: in particular their splendid defence during the German counter-attacks at Cambrai on the 20th November, 1917, and succeeding days. [margin: 20TH AND 21ST BATTALIONS.]

When the New Year dawned the 20th Middlesex (121st Brigade, 40th Division), were resting and cleaning up at Mory, while the 21st Battalion held front-line and support trenches in the Bullecourt sector, the former relieving the latter on the 4th January. On the 5th the enemy attacked the Suffolks on the right of the 20th Middlesex and entered the trenches of the former, but was eventually ejected and the line re-established. The 21st Middlesex, then in Brigade Support, were ordered to assist the Suffolks, and on the 7th (the enemy in the meantime having occupied a sap) carried out a minor operation which was extremely successful: the sap head was destroyed. On the 8th the enemy again attacked the Suffolks and penetrated 100 yards down a support trench. "D" Company of the 21st Middlesex again counter-attacked and brilliantly drove the enemy out, capturing eighteen prisoners and a *Granatenwerfer*, besides inflicting severe casualties on him. Both the Suffolks and 21st Middlesex received hearty congratulations on their fine fighting from the Army Corps, Divisional and Brigade Commanders. On the 9th the 21st Middlesex took over front-line trenches from the 20th Battalion. [margin: 5TH JANUARY.]

Inter-battalion reliefs continued throughout January at intervals of a few days, for the line was in a shocking condition. Both the Germans and the British were having great difficulty in maintaining their defences in the terrible weather. Ration parties were stuck in the trenches and could not deliver their food: in places troops of both sides moved about "over the top," for it was impossible to use the trenches. In this horrible state, during which the general routine of the front line, patrol work, and also raiding, had to be carried out, January passed, the last day of the month finding the 20th Battalion in the front line and the 21st at Mory l'Abbaye, in Brigade Reserve. Until the second week in February both Battalions remained in the Bullecourt area, but on the 12th the 20th moved to Hamelincourt and the 21st to Mercatel. A fortnight of training now ensued, and on the 28th February the 20th marched to billets in Bailleul and the 21st to Gouy-en-Artois. [margin: 28TH FEB.]

The early days of March were uneventful, save for the usual

20TH AND 21ST BATTALIONS. training, marching, the supply of working parties and the manifold duties when out of the front-line trenches. On the 20th of the month the 20th Middlesex were in the Blairville area and the 21st in the Mercatel area.

21ST MARCH. In the Diary of the 20th Middlesex, however, on the 21st March, there is the following entry: " 5 a.m. Intense firing 5 a.m. Stood to till 6.30 a.m. and continued in state of instant readiness "—the Great German Offensive of 1918, the last effort of the enemy to defeat the Allies, had begun.

CHAPTER XXXIII.

The German Offensives of 1918.

(I) THE OFFENSIVE IN PICARDY:

21st March–5th April.

THERE is no period of the War more interesting to the student of Military History than the three months—March, April and May—which witnessed the Great German Offensives of 1918 in Picardy, Flanders and Champagne: nor is there any which sheds a more glowing light upon the powers of endurance and heroic fighting qualities of the British soldier. Even the brilliance of the Allied Advance to Victory, which followed upon the failure of the enemy's great effort to win the War, pales before the vast onslaught of the grey German hordes which rose up suddenly out of the mist on the morning of the 21st March, 1918, and flung themselves in fury upon the thinly-held line of the Fifth and Third British Armies between La Fère and Croisilles. No such sight as that of seventy-six divisions (the number of German divisions flung against the Fifth and Third Armies and *more than the total number of British divisions in France and Flanders*) ranged against thirty-four divisions, which were all that Sir Douglas Haig could oppose to the formidable array pitted against him, had ever been seen in any previous war. It was prodigious. Not even a comparison between the number of British and German divisions gives a true estimate of the overwhelming power of the latter, for Sir Douglas Haig's divisions were weak in personnel: they had not only been "thinned out" by the fearful gas shelling to which they had been subjected, but even the reorganisation had failed to bring them up to establishment. On the other hand, the German divisions were at full strength, reinforced from the East after the Russian debacle: they were, moreover, fully trained and fresh, whereas the British had carried out their training under the greatest difficulties having, when out of the line, to provide large working parties constantly—a great hindrance to training. The enemy's superiority in artillery was also enormous : twenty to thirty batteries were allotted to each kilometre, which, on a thirty-mile front, amounted to between 1,000–1,500 batteries " without trench mortars " and heavy guns. Little wonder that Marshal Hindenburg admitted that " the Germans would have the advantage of numbers."

For weeks and months the enemy had been preparing for his great offensive. British aeroplanes had reported the greatest activity behind the German lines in front of the Fifth and Third Armies, and as the 21st March approached it was certain that the enemy's attack was to be made from the Sensée River southwards.*

The objectives of the three German Armies to be engaged were : Seventeenth (right)—the British line roughly from Croisilles to opposite Mœuvres ; Second (centre) and Eighteenth (left) —the line from and between Villers-Guislain and La Fere. The intervening parts of the line, between Villers-Guislain and Mœuvres, were to be attacked indirectly, but " the Seventeenth and Second (Armies) were to take the weight off each other in turn and with their inner wings cut off the enemy holding the Cambrai re-entrant " (known to us as the Flesquières Salient), " afterwards passing through between Croisilles and Peronne,"† protected on the south flank by the Eighteenth Army in conjunction with the extreme left wing of the Second.

In the middle of February the Chief of the German General Staff had informed the German Kaiser that the battle-to-be was " the greatest military task that has ever been imposed upon an army," and just before the great offensive opened he reported to the Kaiser that " the Army was assembled and well prepared to undertake the biggest task in its history."

Upon the results of this offensive the very existence of the German Empire depended : failure would be the beginning of the end.

On the 19th March it was known that the enemy's preparations on the Arras–St. Quentin front were approaching completion. About that time two of the enemy, belonging to a trench-mortar battery, opposite the French line, deserted and gave information of the date of the offensive : it was to take place on the 20th or

---

* For the reason the Germans selected this front for their offensive, " My War Memories, 1914–1918," by General Ludendorff, may be studied with advantage.
† General Ludendorff.

21st March. This information was correct, for the German orders stated that "the Michael* attack would take place on the 21st/3. The first attack on the enemy's lines is fixed for 9.40 a.m." 1/7TH, 1/8TH, 13TH, 19TH AND 23RD BATTALIONS.

Of the twenty-two divisions which held the British front line from opposite La Fere to Gavrelle, only two contained battalions of the Middlesex Regiment, *i.e.*, the 24th Division, east of Le Verguier (13th Battalion), and the 56th Division (1/7th and 1/8th Battalions) at Gavrelle: the 41st Division (containing the 19th and 23rd Middlesex) was in reserve west of Albert, having returned from Italy early in March.†

THE FIRST BATTLES OF THE SOMME, 1918.

(I) THE BATTLE OF ST. QUENTIN:

21st–23rd March.

The story turns first to the Fifth Army front where, in the neighbourhood of Pontru, the 24th Division held the front line. The 75th Brigade was in reserve at Bernes on the 20th March, but all battalions had been allotted battle positions, so that when the long-expected German offensive opened every officer and man knew what to do. The 13th Middlesex (Major A. M. Hingley, commanding) on the 20th March had reconnoitred their positions consisting of a line of redoubts covering Vermand. 13TH BATTALION.

At 10 p.m. that night the Germans opened a slow bombardment all along the British front line which continued until about 4.30 a.m. on the 21st. At the latter hour the bombardment increased to "drum fire." At 5.45 a.m. the Middlesex were 21ST MARCH.

---

* The "Michael Attack" was the German name given to the great offensive.

† Between the 1st January and the 8th March, 1918, there is little to record concerning the 19th and 23rd Middlesex in Italy. A well-organised raid on the Austrian trenches was carried out by the latter from the Montello sector on the 1st January, but from that date things were very quiet in the line. The 23rd Battalion was at Molini on the 1st March, where it was inspected prior to leaving Italy. On the 2nd the first half Battalion left for France, followed by the second half Battalion on the 3rd, and on the 8th the Middlesex, travelling via Longeau, reached Mondicourt, marching thence to billets at Coullemont. When the German offensive began the 23rd were still billeted in that village. The 19th (Pioneers) Battalion also detrained at Mondicourt on the 8th March and went into billets at Couturelle, where, until the 18th, they remained resting and training. On the 19th they marched to Arras for work on the fourth system of defence.

**13TH BATTALION.
21ST MARCH.**

ordered to man battle positions and the Battalion started on up the line.

By this time the enemy's shell fire was terrific. Gas and high-explosive shell from guns of all calibres and trench mortars rained upon our front and support lines from the Oise to the Scarpe Rivers. Even the back areas as far as St. Pol were heavily shelled.

When dawn broke the ground was covered by a thick fog through which it was impossible to see more than a few yards.

By 7.30 a.m. the Middlesex were in position, " D " Company in Yard Redoubt (at Bihucourt), and " C," " A " and " B " Companies in Woodcock, Woody and Worm Redoubts respectively. Battalion Headquarters were at Vermand Château.

At 9.45 a.m., when the enemy's attack became general along the whole front, fog still covered the battlefield and screened the advance of the hostile grey hordes as they swept across No Man's Land, overwhelming the garrisons of posts out in front of the line ere ever they had a chance of adequately defending themselves. British artillery observers and machine-gunners were unable to see S.O.S. signals sent up, so thick was the mist, and, thus blinded, it was impossible for our guns to give protection to the infantry in the front line. From Moy on the Oise to Gouzeaucourt on the southern flank of the Flesquières Salient, no less than forty German Divisions were set in motion against eleven British divisions then holding the front line.

The 13th Middlesex reported that " news of the situation in front was very scanty and unreliable throughout the day, but by 9 p.m. troops of the 17th and 72nd Infantry Brigades (of the 24th Division) were falling back, but rallied on the line of the redoubts. Enemy following up were driven back." Thus the Battalion did not come into action on the first day, though Battalion Headquarters and " D " Company in Yard Redoubt were intermittently shelled and the latter suffered some casualties.

22ND MARCH.

Dawn had no sooner broken on the 22nd than, again protected by heavy mist, the enemy continued his attacks, the grey waves sweeping on again like an angry sea. " C " and " D " Companies of the Middlesex were early in action and three times drove back determined attacks. But against the vast numbers hurled against them their positions could not long be maintained. At 2.30 p.m., therefore, under orders, as troops on the right had withdrawn, the Battalion fell back through the 50th Division, then holding the Villeveque–Boully line as the 75th Brigade had been ordered to concentrate at Meraucourt. Violent shell fire and machine-gun fire swept the companies as they fell back from their redoubts and " D " Company, in particular, had great difficulty in getting back at all. But eventually, fighting splendidly and suffering heavy casualties, the Company withdrew. The Company Commander—Captain M. S. McGahey—though wounded three times, continued to lead his men. 2/Lieuts. B. Tedman and W. J. Wallond were killed, and 2/Lieut. A. R. Hayford was wounded and missing. Eventually the Battalion got back to the crater on the Estrees cross-roads. The time was now about 5 p.m. ^{13TH BATTALION. 22ND MARCH.}

From the cross-roads the Battalion marched back to Meraucourt for the night, where the 73rd Brigade bivouacked west of the village. Owing to hostile shell fire, however, the Middlesex moved out to emergency battle positions west of the camp.

Early on the morning of the 23rd the Brigade received orders to occupy the Green Line, south of the River Ormignon, and at 5 a.m. was on the move. The Middlesex were in position by 7 a.m. without having encountered the enemy. At 9 a.m. fresh orders were received to withdraw west of the Somme by way of the bridge at Falvy. Thick mist hid this withdrawal and, having crossed the river, the Middlesex moved to Marchelepot where the Brigade was to concentrate On arrival at the latter place the Battalion was ordered back to support the 24th Brigade of the 8th Division then defending the river crossings. During the night " A " and " B " Companies were sent forward in close support of the 2nd Northants. ^{23RD MARCH.}

The 8th Division had received orders on the 21st March to be ready to move south at six hours' notice, and on the 22nd the 23rd Brigade Group entrained at Wizernes for the Somme area. At Chaulnes the Brigade detrained during a bombing raid by German aeroplanes and suffered some casualties. It was, however, 1 a.m. on the 23rd before the 2nd Middlesex (Lieut.-Colonel C. A. S. Page) left Wizernes, and the Battalion did not arrive at Chaulnes until the afternoon, marching thence to Villers-Carbonnel, in reserve to other units of the Brigade which were holding the crossings of the Somme river between St. Christ-Briost and Eterpigny. The Middlesex remained in this position during the night 23rd/24th March. ^{2ND BATTALION. 22ND MARCH. 23RD MARCH.}

Thus, south of the Somme in the Fifth Army area, the 13th Battalion of the Middlesex Regiment had been seriously involved

2ND BATTALION. with the enemy, whilst the 2nd Battalion had come up into line ready to resist the German advance.

20TH AND 21ST BATTALIONS. Meanwhile in the Third Army area, north of the Somme, the 20th and 21st Middlesex of the 40th Division and the 19th and 23rd Battalions of the 41st Division had also been engaged.

21ST MARCH. On the 21st March when the great offensive began the 20th Middlesex were at Blairville and the 21st at Boisleux-au-Mont.

Intense firing was heard at 5 a.m., and the 20th Battalion " stood to " until 6.30 a.m. At 12.30 p.m. orders came to hand to move to Hamelincourt, but on the march the destination of the Battalion was changed to the assembly point " C " (St. Leger). Scouts were sent on ahead to reconnoitre the ground and push through St. Leger while the Battalion moved across open ground in artillery formation until it reached the assembly area. Shortly afterwards the scouts returned and reported that they had reached Croisilles which (at 8 p.m.) was being heavily shelled. At about 9.15 p.m.* the Battalion received orders to move to a fresh assembly area—" B " (north of Mory Abbaye) which position was occupied by 11 p.m.

In the meantime the 21st Middlesex had left Boisleux between 5 and 6 p.m. under orders to move to assembly point " F," north of Boiry Becquerelle, to seize Henin Hill, and deny it to the enemy. The move was accomplished without opposition and the Battalion took up a position in depth on a frontage of about 1,400 yards: patrols were then pushed out in an endeavour to gain touch with

22ND MARCH. the enemy. At 3 a.m., however, on the 22nd, the 21st were ordered to march to the Sensée Valley, north-east of Ervillers, where they were to be in reserve to the 121st Brigade then holding the third system (near St. Leger), which ran across the Valley. The 13th East Surreys were on the right and some R.E. troops on the Arras-Bapaume road on the left.

The 20th Battalion on reaching the Mory Abbaye area had set to work to dig themselves in, and by 5 a.m. on the 22nd, " C " Company was in the Army Line north-east of Abbaye, " B " Company in strong points north-east and south of Abbaye, " D " Company south of Abbaye, " A " Company in reserve south-west of Abbaye and Battalion Headquarters in a cellar in Abbaye with

---

* The Diary of the 121st Brigade states that these orders were sent to the 20th Middlesex at 1 a.m. on 22nd March, actually after the Battalion had reached Mory Abbaye.

a strong point north-west of the cemetery. "C" Company had a few casualties from shell fire.

20TH AND 21ST BATTALIONS.

Shortly after 1 p.m. on the 22nd the 20th Middlesex received orders to reinforce the right flank of the Corps Line, as an enemy break-through in the direction of Vaulx Vraucourt was reported. Companies were hurried off and occupied a line of trenches 1,500 yards due north of Beugnatre (at H.5 central). The Battalion dug itself in more securely for shell fire was heavy.

22ND MARCH.

Against Croisilles the enemy had launched masses of troops, for the attack of the Seventeenth German Army on the northern flank of the Flesquières Salient was designed for the purpose of breaking through and capturing, or forcing the evacuation of the Salient.

Of the general situation and fighting during the remainder of the day it is not possible to write with certainty, the 121st Brigade Diary admitting that from 6 p.m. the situation " remained extremely obscure."

From the Battalion Diaries of the 20th and 21st Middlesex it is possible to adduce the following story :

After moving to trenches due north of Beugnatre, the 20th Middlesex reported at 7 p.m. that the Yorkshire and Suffolk Regiments on their flanks had been driven in. "C" and "D" Companies were therefore moved across to Mory in support, the former Company into trenches south-west of Abbaye with orders to gain touch with the Suffolks and place themselves under the C.O. of that Battalion," D " Company to the sunken road running south from Mory Copse under the command of the O.C., Yorkshire Regiment. Meanwhile "B" Company moved to the sunken road at "B.28 central" (running south-east from Mory) and "A" Company to old trenches in "H.4.a" (south of "B" Company). Between 9 and 10 p.m. the situation in Mory was reported as critical, scouts reporting that the enemy was on the outskirts of the village, though Abbaye was clear. "C" Company was then moved up to join "D" Company in the road south of Mory Copse. Such is the story of the 20th Middlesex to the close of the 22nd March.

Turning to the 21st Battalion: at 2 p.m. "D" Company had been ordered up to reinforce the Welch Regiment in Croisilles Switch, in the neighbourhood of Judas Farm. At 6 p.m. this Company reported that troops in front of them had been driven back, and shortly afterwards the Middlesex were engaged with

20TH AND 21ST BATTALIONS.
22ND MARCH.

the enemy's advanced troops; the latter were reported to have occupied St. Leger. The story of the 21st Battalion on the 22nd March ends here.

The Battalion Diaries of the 20th and 21st Middlesex both record counter-attacks on the enemy on the morning of the 23rd.

23RD MARCH.

The 20th Battalion records that " C " and " D " Companies, under the O.C., Suffolks, attacked on the left of the 122nd Brigade (wherever that was). The right of the attack made no progress, and the two companies were cut off and surrounded, having to fight their way through the enemy to their original position in the sunken road south of Mory Copse : in this they were badly cut up. The situation in Mory was now acute. " A " and " B " Companies of the Battalion were ordered to dig a defensive flank south of Mory from " B.27 central to B.28 central," which interpreted means an east and west line directly south of, and approximately seven hundred yards from, the southern exits of Mory. It is now clearly evident that the enemy was between the two halves of the Battalion. The enemy's shell fire continued to swamp the whole area occupied by the Middlesex, while his snipers in the village were a source of great annoyance. Noon came and saw little change in the situation. Later in the afternoon the 20th Middlesex reported that a German field gun, firing from east of Mory Copse, was enfilading Battalion Headquarters (south of the village) and that the enemy was observed massing in the sunken road south of the Copse. Where then were " C " and " D " Companies of the 20th Middlesex ? Night came on and the two Companies (" A " and " B "), south of Mory, still held their positions with some of the Hants and 14 H.L.I. on their right.

Meanwhile the 21st Battalion, in conjunction with the 13th East Surreys on their right and the 18th Welch in reserve, had attacked the enemy in order to regain Mory and the Army Line running north-east and east of the village.

When the orders (given verbally by the Brigade Major) were received at 6.20 a.m. to concentrate at once for the attack, the 21st Middlesex were widely extended along the Army Line*
across the Sensée Valley, " D " Company being still in the Croisilles

---

* The " Army Line " apparently ran from east and south-east of Hamelincourt—a south-easterly direction north of Mory Copse and round Mory itself in the direction of Vaulx-Vraucourt.

Switch. By 8 a.m., however, the Battalion was concentrated in a quarry north-east of Ervillers and company commanders were issued with orders for the attack. The hour for the attack was fixed for 8.45 a.m. as the East Surreys were seen deploying south of Ervillers. *21ST BATTALION. 23RD MARCH.*

At 8.45 a.m. the attack began, the Middlesex advancing on a two-company front: one company was in support of the right of the right company with orders to gain touch with the East Surreys, the other company was in battalion reserve. " A " and " B " Companies were in the front line, formed up on the St. Leger–Ervillers road. They moved off in artillery formation in the direction of Mory. As they topped a ridge 1,000 yards north-east of the village hostile machine-gun fire swept their ranks, though the enemy's shell-fire was not heavy. The advance, however, continued without a break: in short rushes the Middlesex approached the Army Line and found the enemy not actually occupying it but on the other side of the wire where they enfiladed the attacking troops. A report came to hand that a body of Germans was advancing from the direction of Mory Copse and the reserve company of the Middlesex was thrown in and a request made to the Brigade for reinforcements. A Company of the 18th Welch was then sent up and dug in four hundred yards in rear of the right flank of the Middlesex.

At about 11.45 a.m. the O.C., " C " Company, arrived at the Battalion Aid Post wounded, and reported that his men were very close to Mory, on the Railway Embankment, north-east of the village. The gallant fellows were not seen again.

The attack of the 21st Middlesex reached the Army Line as far as a point about two hundred to three hundred yards northeast of Mory, but by now the strength of the attacking troops had been so much reduced that it was impossible to advance further on the village. A German strong point in Mory Copse, and machine guns in Mory itself, swept the whole position occupied by the Battalion. Orders were therefore given to consolidate in depth and companies began to dig themselves in. The so-called Army Line was a shallow excavation about eighteen inches in depth, and very broad, affording little or no cover. In that desperate position, enfiladed from Mory on the right and from a communication trench on the left and under full observation by the enemy, the gallant survivors of this counter-attack made good their ground.

"The troops," recorded the C.O. in his report, "had carried out the attack in the best possible order and with magnificent dash, more as though they were on a field day than in a battle."

When dusk had fallen the consolidation of the trenches was pushed on rapidly, but despite hard work all night when dawn broke on the 24th there yet remained some fifty yards undug.

The night of 23rd/24th had passed quietly.

In the meantime the 41st Division had arrived on the Somme and had been put into the line east of Bapaume. The 23rd Middlesex (123rd Brigade) had marched to Mondicourt–Pas Station very early on the morning of the 21st March and had entrained at 7 a.m. for Albert, which place was reached at 5.45 that afternoon. The Battalion then marched to Bouzincourt and billeted for the night. The next morning the Middlesex marched via Miraumont to Achiet-le-Petit where, by the roadside, dinners were eaten, blankets dumped, and bombs and ammunition served out to companies. At 3.30 p.m. lorries carried the Battalion to a monument (just west of Favreuil) on the Arras–Bapaume road where, in a field, the Middlesex bivouacked until midnight.*

At 12.15 a.m. on the 23rd companies marched off via Fremicourt to Beugny where support positions in front of the latter village were taken up. By dawn the Battalion was disposed in shelters or in hastily dug trenches.

At 10.30 a.m. Beugny and the neighbourhood were subjected to a regular tornado of shells and the 23rd Middlesex had numerous casualties. The enemy's infantry, in great strength, then advanced to the attack and drove in the advanced battalions. The Middlesex, in order to conform to the line on their flanks, fell back west of Beugny to a new line (the Green Line) astride the Beugny–Fremicourt road. "D" Company covered the retirement of the other companies.

That night the 23rd were relieved and moved back to the aerodrome at Favreuil, having lost throughout the day 4 other ranks killed, 39 wounded and 12 missing.

The 19th Middlesex (Pioneers of the 41st Division) were working on the Fourth System of defence at Arras until the 23rd March, when they marched to Bihucourt and went into the line

---

* The Battalion Diary on this date (22nd) records the following casualties: eight other ranks killed, 2/Lieut. S. R. Hylands and 12 other ranks wounded, 2 other ranks missing," by bomb at Details Camp."

at night at Beugnatre, taking over from the 18th K.R.R. of the 122nd Brigade. For the time being the gallant Pioneers had become infantrymen.

19TH BATTALION. 23RD MARCH.

(II) THE FIRST BATTLE OF BAPAUME AND ACTIONS AT THE SOMME CROSSINGS:

24th–25th March.

On the night of the 23rd March the British line from the Oise to the Scarpe Rivers ran approximately as follows: Amigny—Viry—Noureuil—just west of Cogny—Eaucourt—Golancourt—Eppeville, thence along the western bank of the Somme Canal to one mile north of Biaches, crossing the Canal and Somme River to east of Cléry, thence just west of Bus, east of Bertincourt, bending then sharply back westwards, north of Bertincourt to about a mile east of Haplincourt, thence in a north-westerly direction just west of Beugny, east of Mory, west of St. Leger (we held Judas Farm), east of Boyelles through Henin and St. Martin to Fampoux and Roeux: north of the latter village to Avion there had been no change in the line since the 21st.

Our losses in men and material had been great and much ground had been abandoned to the enemy, but nowhere along the whole front had there been a wholesale break through such as the enemy had reasonably hoped for, and indeed had confidently expected. To the undying glory of the British soldier it may be said here that never had he fought more splendidly or more tenaciously clung to his ground, giving way only under the heaviest pressure, often not even then, for many a gallant fellow hung on and refused to leave his post, preferring death.

" They shall not pass," seemed to be the dominant thought in everyone. The spirit in which all ranks fought is well illustrated in a story of a very gallant signaller of the 21st Middlesex:

21ST BATTALION.

The 21st Battalion, it will be remembered, had spent the night of the 23rd/24th March digging in on the outskirts of Mory, on ground won by their counter-attack in order to recover the Army line and (if possible) the village. They had, when dawn broke on the 24th, dug themselves in, in all but fifty yards of the line won. On the 24th they were shelled by a trench-mortar battery (which the enemy had brought up), but the Divisional

24TH MARCH.

G 4

21ST BATTALION.
24TH MARCH.

artillery eventually dealt with this battery. Several times during the day the guns also shelled Mory Copse and moving German troops. A daylight patrol, under Sergeant Hickman, brought in a prisoner from near Mory Copse.

Nothing really vital happened until about 10.30 that night when suddenly there was an ugly rush of German troops who broke through the spot where the trench had been left undug. They came on and through the gap in massed formation, spread over either flank and surrounded several parties of the Middlesex. It was then that the incident of the signaller took place. This gallant fellow (his name is unrecorded) saw the enemy when they reached the wire and immediately rang up headquarters: he then sent up the S.O.S. signal until it was answered. Being by this time surrounded he smashed his Fullerphone and joined in the fighting. Thanks to his efforts the Divisional barrage came down with extraordinary rapidity and though for a short while it fell on friend and foe alike, the enemy's casualties were very heavy.

Taken in rear, many small parties of Middlesex had to give way, but for the most part they succeeded in fighting their way through and rejoined their companies. It was a regular melée—"thrust–parry–thrust," hoarse shouts and cries as bayonet clashed on bayonet, and sixty prisoners were taken by the Middlesex.

An attempt was made to restore the Army Line, but the right flank of the Battalion was now in the air: a new line was begun at right angles to the Army Line and parallel with the St. Leger–Ervillers road, which enabled touch to be maintained with troops on both flanks.

Hot food, rations and ammunition were now issued, and the sixty German prisoners were made to carry the wounded back to the dressing stations.

20TH BATTALION.
24TH MARCH.

Reverting to the movements of the 20th Middlesex on the 24th March: soon after midnight 23rd/24th a Staff Captain from Brigade Headquarters arrived with orders to work in conjunction with the 14th H.L.I. and retake Mory: an order easy enough to give but impossible to carry out owing to the general situation. The C.O. then went off to confer with the O.C., H.L.I., but apparently the 20th Middlesex hung on all day to their positions south of Mory until, at about 5 p.m., the enemy launched a heavy attack against the 120th Brigade and the Corps on the right. The brigade on the right of the Middlesex was driven in and the 120th Brigade withdrew. The C.O. of the 20th Battalion then reported to 121st Brigade Headquarters that the situation was critical. The 120th Brigade, however, again advanced and reoccupied the trenches in the Army Line: the situation was then somewhat restored.

20TH
BATTALION.
24TH MARCH.

At 8.30 p.m. the 20th Middlesex received orders to gain touch with the East Surreys on the Western outskirts of Mory and dig in on a line west of the Mory-Favreuil road with the 120th Brigade on their right. This was done. The Battalion was then told it would be relieved by troops of the 127th Brigade, and Battalion Headquarters were ordered to Behagnies. But no relief arrived and as companies were digging in they were shelled by their own guns and forced (with battalions of the 120th Brigade) to withdraw to a sunken road north-east of Behagnies. Both flanks of the Middlesex were now in the air and the enemy, having developed a heavy attack on Ervillers, the Battalion was ordered back to a line east of the Arras-Bapaume road.* Arrived in this position they found their allotted trenches full of troops of the 42nd Division, and as it was now ascertained that the relief ordered would not take place, the Middlesex were placed in support just north-west of Behagnies.

Dawn broke on the 25th with every sign of further heavy fighting. In front of Ervillers the enemy's troops in large numbers were observed in every direction occupying the ridges east of the village.

25TH MARCH.

At 6 a.m. the 20th Middlesex moved to the spur just west of Behagnies. At about 2 p.m. that village was reported captured by the enemy and troops of the 42nd Division retired on Gomiecourt. But they were rallied and the trenches west of the former village were re-occupied and held all day despite the critical nature of the situation.

The 21st Middlesex hung on to their trenches until about 3 p.m. Reports then reached the C.O. of the loss of Behagnies and the advance of the enemy on Ervillers. In order, therefore, to prevent a turning movement from Gomiecourt (should the enemy occupy that place) the Battalion was ordered to take up a position west of Ervillers. Under heavy artillery fire and fighting practically all the way the 21st Battalion fell back to trenches south of Hamelincourt where they were in touch on the right

21ST
BATTALION.
25TH MARCH.

* The Arras-Bapaume line ran from the latter town in a north-westerly direction through Sapignies, Behagnies and Ervillers.

20TH AND 21ST BATTALIONS.
26TH MARCH.

with the East Surreys, East Yorks, Lincs, and troops of the 42nd Division. During the night further orders were received to retire to Bucquoy via Courcelles: this order the 21st Middlesex carried out without incident.

The 20th Middlesex also had moved during the night further westwards. Shortly after midnight the C.O. had been informed by the Battalion in front that the latter was withdrawing at 2 a.m. The O.C., Middlesex, then decided to begin his withdrawal at 1.30 a.m., but at 1.20 a.m. the enemy attacked "A" Company and drove them in: "B" Company was attacked almost simultaneously. Both companies re-formed at Battalion Headquarters, which were then near Bee Wood. Lewis-gun and rifle fire were then opened on the enemy who had begun to advance on Gomiecourt. Under cover of this fire the worn-out Middlesex withdrew in good order (flank and rearguards being maintained) in the direction of Logeast Wood. They formed up finally outside Ablainzeville and thence marched to Douchy les Ayette where they arrived at about 5 a.m. (26th) and went into billets*.

23RD BATTALION.

Meanwhile the 23rd Middlesex, of the 123rd Brigade, 41st Division, who, on the night of 23rd March, had bivouacked near the Aerodrome at Favreuil, had again been engaged with the enemy.

24TH MARCH.

At 11.30 a.m. on the 24th the 23rd Battalion took up positions in the reserve line near Favreuil and in rear of Hun Dump. Late in the afternoon the troops in the front line began to fall back and retired to the reserve line, where they were reorganised and put into the reserve line in the sector occupied by the Middlesex. At 9 p.m. a new line was taken up at the Monument (on the Bapaume–Sapignies road), where the Battalion, assisted by some Royal Engineers, dug in until dawn. No description of any fighting on the 24th is given in the Battalion Diary, but the casualty list tells its own story. The losses on that day were 13 other ranks killed, 57 wounded, 6 missing, 6 missing believed killed, 22 missing believed wounded.

25TH MARCH.

At 8 a.m. on the 25th the enemy opened heavy shell fire and his infantry attacked shortly afterwards. In massed formation

---

* The Battalion Diary of the 20th Middlesex makes no statement as to casualties suffered. The 21st Middlesex give their losses as 2 officers and 21 other ranks killed, 6 officers and 189 other ranks wounded, 6 other ranks wounded and missing, and 1 officer and 80 other ranks missing.

he advanced against our troops, who fell back across the Arras– 23RD
Bapaume road to the line held by the Middlesex. The latter 25TH MARCH.
held on doggedly to their position, and only when both flanks
had been uncovered by the retirement of troops on the right
and left did they withdraw by platoons and in an orderly manner,
though the Germans were actually in the trenches when Battalion
Headquarters began to move off. The next line taken up by the
23rd Battalion was behind Bihucourt, along the railway embankment; later, when another retirement became necessary, they
fell back to Achiet-le-Petit.

During the night the 41st Division was relieved and the
Middlesex, with other units, assembled at Gommecourt, taking
up some reserve trenches there. Their losses on the 25th were
again heavy; 13 other ranks had been killed, 61 wounded, 30
were missing, and 8 were missing believed either killed or wounded.

The Battalion's losses in officers were: The C.O. (Lieut.-
Colonel A. R. Haig-Brown) and 2/Lieuts. W. D. Tull and T. J.
Pitty killed; Capt. W. Hammond, Lieut. R. A. Green and
2/Lieut. G. Barton wounded, and Capt. B. T. Foss missing.

The 19th Middlesex (Pioneers of the 41st Division), who, it 19TH
will be remembered, were put into the line at Beugnatre on the BATTALION.
night of the 23rd March, were attacked by the enemy at about
6 p.m. on the 24th. The Pioneers were compelled to withdraw 24TH MARCH.
to Biefvillers, but not before they had inflicted heavy losses on
the enemy. The next morning they were again attacked by the
enemy, and, although the right flank of the Battalion was exposed,
the Pioneers hung on to their positions, inflicting heavy casualties
on the Germans, until they again had to fall back to Achiet-le
Petit, where they were ordered back to the reserve line at Fonque- 26TH MARCH.
villers on the 26th.

THE SOMME CROSSINGS.

The story now turns back to the morning of the 24th, to the 2ND AND 13TH
Somme south of Peronne, where the 2nd and 13th Battalions of BATTALIONS.
the Regiment were engaged in holding up the enemy's advance.

The night of the 23rd/24th March passed comparatively
quietly, but when dawn broke powerful attempts were made by
the Germans to force the crossings over the river.

The 13th Battalion, on the night of 23rd, had concentrated 13TH
at Licourt with two companies forward in close support of the BATTALION.
2nd Northamptons, who were holding the crossing. Early on 23RD MARCH.

13TH BATTALION.
24TH MARCH.

the 24th the Battalion received orders to withdraw and concentrate at Chaulnes. This move complete, the Middlesex went into bivouacs east of the town until 1 p.m., when orders were received to occupy defensive positions on the Puzeau–Punchy line, in support of the 7th Northamptons and Royal Sussex. Three companies were put into the front line, and one company with Battalion Headquarters at Puzeau. The night of 24th/25th passed quietly.

25TH MARCH.

At 7 a.m. on the 25th a counter-attack on the line Curchy–Dreslincourt, in co-operation with the French on the right, was ordered. The French counter-attack did not materialise, but the Northamptons and Sussex, supported by the 13th Middlesex, were heavily engaged with the enemy and had to fall back again to the positions occupied all night. The enemy followed up vigorously, and, supported by heavy artillery fire, drove back the two forward battalions. At about 6 p.m. "C" Company of the Middlesex was driven out of Puzeau, and the Battalion withdrew to a line crossing the eastern side of Punchy to the Punchy–Chaulnes road. Before daylight, however, on the 26th, another withdrawal to a more suitable position on the line Hallu–Chaulnes was made, without interference from the enemy. In the fighting on the 25th March Lieut. W. H. D. de Pass was reported missing and Lieut. W. R. T. Skinner wounded.

26TH MARCH.

2ND BATTALION.

North of the 13th Middlesex, the 2nd Battalion had remained throughout the 24th in the position taken up, *i.e.*, in the trenches and shell holes west of Villers-Carbonnel. On the night of the 24th/25th, however, the Battalion relieved the 2nd West Yorkshires in the defences of Happlincourt, Brie and Eterpigny Bridges over the Somme: the 2nd Devons were on the right of the 2nd Middlesex and the 7th D.L.I. on the left, holding Eterpigny Village.

24TH/25TH MARCH.

25TH MARCH.

On the 25th the 2nd Middlesex were heavily engaged.

The first attack was at Eterpigny, where, on the bridge, "C" Company had a post. This post was rushed at 7 a.m. and the garrison driven back on the supports. But 15 minutes later the post was re-established, only to be attacked again. The N.C.O. was killed and the remainder of the post withdrew. Once more the post was re-established; it was never seen again. At 7.30 a.m. a patrol was sent along the river bank and similarly disappeared.

By 8 a.m. it was apparent that the enemy had crossed the river, and 15 minutes later he attacked north and south of the

Eterpigny Bridge. On the left the 7th D.L.I. withdrew, with disastrous results to "C" Company of the Middlesex.

2ND BATTALION.
25TH MARCH.

"C" Company was now surrounded, but at once the order was given that there was to be no retirement and all ranks would hold out, "at all costs," to the last. And then ensued a desperate struggle. One gallant subaltern—2/Lieut. F. G. E. Mahany—with great courage and initiative, knowing that his company commander was in the village, fought his way through at the cost of all but three men of his platoon. Capt. A. M. Toye, commanding "C" Company, with six men, cut his way out of the village, and the little party, finding some 70 men of the 7th D.L.I., rallied them and even counter-attacked the enemy, and held on across the Eterpigny–Villers-Carbonnel road until the 2nd West Yorkshires came up and relieved the situation. Capt. Toye remained with the West Yorkshires until dark. For his conspicuous bravery and fine leadership on the 25th of March, he was subsequently awarded the Victoria Cross,* the official citation stating:—

"When the enemy captured the trench at a bridgehead, he three times re-established the post, which was eventually recaptured by fresh enemy attacks. After ascertaining that his three other posts were cut off, he fought his way through the enemy with one officer and six men of his company. Finding 70 men of the battalion on his left retiring, he collected them, counter-attacked, and took up a line which he maintained until reinforcements arrived. Without this action, the defence of the bridge must have been turned. In two subsequent operations, when in command of a composite company, he covered the retirement of his Battalion with skill and courage. Later, with a party of Battalion Headquarters he pressed through the enemy in the village, firing at them in the streets, thus covering the left flank of the battalion retirement. Finally, on a still later occasion, when in command of a mixed force of the brigade, he re-established, after hard fighting, a line that had been abandoned before his arrival. He was twice wounded within ten days, but remained at duty. His valour and skilful leading throughout this prolonged period of intense operations was most conspicuous."

In the action at Eterpigny the Battalion narrative proudly records that "all four platoons of 'C' Company obeyed the

* "London Gazette," d/7th May, 1918.

order to hold out at all costs without retirement. In all ten survivors escaped after they were surrounded."

Brie Bridge was next attacked.

Germans, moving quickly down the west bank of the river from Eterpigny, atacked the left post of " B " Company. Here also the same splendid discipline, the same heroic regard for the honour of the Regiment distinguished the fighting of the Die-Hards.

During several hours of heavy fighting the Company Commander sent his support platoon and a platoon of " D " Company to form a defensive flank between the railway and the river at the bottom of the valley.

Keeping under cover as much as possible, the Germans reached Brie Bridge and tried to carry the trenches at the bridge head. For an hour and a-half they made the most desperate efforts to cross, but each time were repulsed and driven back.

The simple narrative of the fighting in this part of the battlefield is given in full, for no paraphrase can add to what is really an epic :—

"The details of the fighting are obscure, as only the right platoon of ' B ' Company and the last support platoon of ' D ' Company got away. *The other six platoons of these two Companies perished at their post. As ordered by the Divisional Commander, there was no retirement. They held out at all costs.* The left platoon of ' A ' Company, which had been sent to reinforce ' B ' Company, has never been seen again."

May the splendid example set by these brave fellows, who were faithful unto death, be for ever an inspiration to all young soldiers to carry out their orders regardless of the cost.

The remainder of " A " Company were not seriously engaged during the day and withdrew, with the Devons, in the evening.

The right platoon of " B " was in the bridge defences with two Lewis guns, under 2/Lieut. W. J. Martin. For nearly two hours they kept the enemy at bay, exacting fearful toll of his troops. Capt. N. Wegg then posted them on the Amiens road near his Company Headquarters, overlooking the bridge. When the remnants of the Company were destroyed, 2/Lieut. Martin fell back upon " A " Company at Happlincourt and withdrew through the outskirts of Villers-Carbonnel with the left of the Devons.

The support platoon of "D" Company had been posted on a rise above the bridge, on the south side of the river, under cover. In anticipation of the afternoon attack the C.O. moved the platoon to a post north-west of the bridge. They finally fell back fighting, with Battalion Headquarters, when the order to retire was received from Brigade Headquarters.

2ND BATTALION. 25TH MARCH.

The story of that day of desperate and splendid fighting would not be complete without relating what happened to Battalion Headquarters.

The first news of the attack reached the C.O. (Lieut.-Colonel C. A. S. Page) at 9 a.m., from an officer of the 8th Division Machine-gun Battalion, who with two men had escaped after hand-to-hand fighting just south of Eterpigny; he reported that the latter place had fallen.

Battalion Headquarters, 2nd Middlesex, were then situated in an old trench about 200 to 300 yards north of the Villers-Carbonnel–Brie road and about 700 yards east of Villers-Carbonnel. Colonel Page at once formed a defensive flank in trench "A—A" with about fifty men of Battalion Headquarters, consisting of Scouts, Pioneers, Signallers and Runners. Major C. D. Drew with 2/Lieut. A. T. Goodman (Intelligence Officer) and 2/Lieut. D. W. Temple took command of the right portion of the trench.

A patrol of scouts was then taken out by Lieut. E. Frayne in order to gain touch with the enemy. At about 9.15 a.m. 2/Lieut. Cawdron, with five men, the only survivors of his platoon, came into Battalion Headquarters and confirmed the loss of Eterpigny.

Nothing happened until about 10.50 a.m., when the right flank of two companies of the 2nd West Yorkshires were seen moving down the Villers-Carbonnel–Eterpigny road. Knowing that the Germans were posted on the spur "B" with two machine guns, Major C. D. Drew saw that the West Yorkshires would be taken in flank. Immediately, on his own initiative, he led forward 20 details from Battalion Headquarters and counter-attacked the enemy, driving the Germans back up the valley and posting a Lewis gun and one Vickers guns to hold them off.

At 1.20 p.m. the little party was attacked by 60 Germans, but drove them off.

At 4.5 p.m. fresh German troops, in great force, advanced to the attack, and, seeing the futility of trying to hold them up, Major Drew fell back again to trench "A—A."

Meanwhile the Scout Platoon had almost been wiped out.

2ND BATTALION.
25TH MARCH.

Colonel Page, in order to protect Major Drew's right flank, had sent the Scout Platoon, under Lieut. E. Frayne, to take up position on Spur " D." The Platoon moved down trench " A—A " and then, in single file, down the valley " C." At about Point " C " they were surprised by a German machine gun at 200 yards' range and were nearly all killed or wounded. The remainder took what cover they could, but, being unable to move, were eventually captured. Lieut. Frayne was wounded and taken prisoner.*

The platoon sergeant—Sergt. W. Fox—was also taken prisoner, but, imbued with the Die-Hard spirit, knocked his guard down and escaped.†

At about 4.15 p.m. Colonel Page received final messages concerning " B " and " D " Companies: they were fighting to the last against overwhelming forces of fresh troops—a whole German division had been descending the slope east of the river all day without interference and had crossed at Eterpigny.

The little party at Battalion Headquarters now prepared to sell their lives dearly. Reinforced by two Vickers guns, the C.O., the Second-in-Command and the Adjutant, all taking a hand in the firing, engaged the enemy, who were now advancing over the crest at " B " and " D," and along a hedge on the sunken road near " C." The range was from 800 to 1,000 yards. Everyone shot well, and until dusk the Germans were prevented from crossing the high ground.

At about 5.20 p.m. a German aeroplane, flying low over the little party of Middlesex, called for barrage fire on the trench " A—A." German guns on the opposite crest of the valley then opened fire and, until after 7 p.m., fired ten rounds a minute on Colonel Page and his devoted comrades. Few casualties resulted from this fire and the men of Headquarters, showing an utter contempt for danger, continued sniping steadily through the barrage with the utmost coolness.

Then, at last, at 6.45 p.m., orders were received from Brigade Headquarters to retire. Colonel Page at once sent off an order to " A," " B " and " D " Companies to withdraw. The order had arrived too late. Three platoons each of " B " and " D " Companies and one platoon of " A " had already fallen at their posts or had been captured. " At all costs " they had carried out their orders to remain to the end and not withdraw.

---

* He died of wounds in German hands on 17.5.18.
† Three days later he was twice captured, but escaped on both occasions.

The runners with the messages came back and reported that the road at about " F " was in German hands. At about 7 p.m. the latter began to advance from the river on Villers-Carbonnel. They approached unseen to within 450 yards of Battalion Headquarters, but were there observed and stopped by fire. They then began to work forward into dead ground 200 yards in front of " A—A " trench, near the " *L* " of Pont les Brie.

2ND BATTALION.
25TH MARCH.

At 7.15 p.m. Colonel Page began the retirement of Battalion Headquarters. He first sent off Major C. D. Drew, the Adjutant (Capt. W. Evans), with half the party to a covering position at about " G." The remainder he sent back in batches upon the trench " A—G." All the while the gallant C.O. and two men—Privates Burgess (the C.O.'s servant) and Allen—both of " D " Company, fired " rapid " to cover the retirement. A Vickers gun also remained under Capt. Robertson, of the Machine-gun Corps. Finally, at 7.25 p.m., Colonel Page sent off the two men and, " after five last rounds rapid," followed them up the trench. Three minutes after the C.O. had left the trench the Germans occupied it ! The C.O. had himself fired over 200 rounds !

From 11 a.m. (when the Germans were first driven back by Major Drew) Battalion Headquarters, with only a platoon of " D " Company, had held the line " B, C, D, A—A " successfully until 7.25 p.m. In all, the Battalion maintained the defence of Brie Bridge from 7.0 in the morning until 7.0 at night against odds of six to one, for, judging by formations and frontages, three battalions of the German division which crossed at Eterpigny were employed against the Bridge.

The fine example set by the Commanding Officer of the 2nd Middlesex in this action will live long in the annals of the Regiment and amongst the imperishable deeds of the Great War.

The remnants of the 2nd Middlesex withdrew to Estrees through a rearguard of another Division.

In the gallant defence of the Somme crossings the Middlesex had lost four platoons of " C " Company, three of " B " Company, three of " D " Company, and one of " A " Company. " Eleven platoons," records the narrative, " in all perished in accordance with the order of no retirement and resistance at all costs."

2ND BATTALION. 25TH MARCH.

Twelve officers* and over 300 other ranks, killed, wounded or taken prisoner, were the losses of the Battalion, but as the narrative states :—

"Not once had an officer to reprimand a man. The fighting spirit was perfect and worthy of the traditions of the 77th. The 77th has never fought against such odds with such success except at Inkerman.

"*Thank God all ranks did their duty!*"

By the Amiens road the Middlesex returned to the defence of Estrees, where trenches on the outskirts of the village astride the road were occupied, but after an hour in this position another move was made to trenches just south of Deniecourt, on the road to Vermandovillers. In the latter position the Battalion was reorganised into four companies, each of 40 strong, lettered "W," "X," "Y" and "Z."

(III) THE BATTLE OF ROSIERES:

26th–27th March.

By the morning of the 26th the British troops south of the Somme were exhausted. Save for a mixed force of details, stragglers, schools personnel, tunnelling companies, Army troops, etc., there were no reserves. This mixed force,† therefore, was posted on the line Mezieres–Marcelcave–Hamel, and on the night of 25th Divisions were instructed that if the enemy seriously attacked in strength on the following morning they were to fall back, fighting rearguard actions, to the approximate line Le Quesnoy–Rosieres–Prayart.

Early on the 26th the enemy recommenced his attacks in strength south-westwards and westwards from Nesle: his intention now was to separate the French and British Armies and, by capturing Montdidier, interfere with the detraining arrangements made by the French, who were reinforcing the line.

About Hattencourt, in the neighbourhood of the St. Quentin–Amiens road, and at Herbecourt he also launched heavy attacks.

---

* Officers killed : Capts. H. N. Wegg and R. Launceton, 2/Lieuts. A. F. Liversedge, G. W. Ball and K. E. Stewart; wounded : Lieut. E. Frayne (*see* previous footnote), 2/Lieuts. W. Prior, A. T. Goodman, W. D. Bensted, A. E. Tillett (died of wounds, 25.3.18); missing : 2/Lieuts. A. Kirkham and J. C. Oliver.

† Carey's Force.

At about 7 a.m. the brigade on the right of the 13th Middlesex 13TH BATTALION. (of the 73rd Brigade, 24th Division), who on the night 25th/26th held a portion of the Hallu–Chaulnes line, was forced back and 26TH MARCH. the Battalion was ordered to withdraw fighting *via* Chilly and Meharicourt.

"D" Company, with details of Royal Engineers, under Major Prior, covered the retirement, which, in the difficult circumstances, was admirably carried out. But at Chilly the 72nd Brigade front was broken, the enemy attacked in flank, and the Middlesex were forced to form a defensive flank, under heavy artillery and machine-gun fire. The Germans were repulsed and the retirement on Meharicourt was then carried out. Eventually the Battalion spent the night at Warvillers.

At about 10 a.m. on 27th the Battalion moved forward to 27TH MARCH. support the Royal Sussex, "A" and "B" Companies in line at Artillery Dug-outs, "C" and "D" Companies and Headquarters Details in Warvillers Wood. "A" Company counterattacked the enemy successfully. The support companies moved up to Artillery Dug-outs at 2 p.m., but there seems to have been no more fighting throughout the remainder of the 27th, and during the night the 73rd Brigade was withdrawn to new positions covering Warvillers, the Middlesex holding from the Wood to Vrely.

Meanwhile the 2nd Middlesex had again been heavily engaged 2ND with the enemy. The Battalion, on reaching the road to Ver- BATTALION. mondovillers, south of Deniecourt, had taken up the following 26TH MARCH. positition (after the reorganisation previously mentioned): "W" Company on the right, "X" in the centre, "Y" on the left, and "Z" in support; the 2nd Devons were on the right and the 2nd West Yorkshires on the left.

They had received the order to fall back to a series of rearguard positions if attacked on the 26th. In preparation for this retirement "Z" Company was posted near Soyecourt.

At 10 a.m. the retirement began, the West Yorkshires moving off first, followed by "Y" Company, "X" Company hanging on in order to enable "W" to withdraw.

After the march had begun direction was changed to southwest, as a result of which "Y" Company was detached for some hours from the rest of the Battalion. The Battalion eventually occupied a position at Vermondovillers and then withdrew to

2ND BATTALION.
26TH MARCH.

Lihons. During the retirement " X " and " Z " Companies had some stiff fighting.

In front of Lihons the ridge was held by troops of the 24th Brigade (8th Division) and the Middlesex were directed on Rosieres, where they dug in between the Sucrerie and the road and railway crossing on the Meharicourt road; but the defences were merely shallow trenches and rifle pits.

At about 1 p.m. they were attacked by the enemy. On the left the Germans came close up to the trenches and were shot down, the Die-Hards successfully repelling the attack. During the evening, at about 6 p.m., the whole front was heavily attacked, but again the attackers were repulsed, leaving the ground covered with dead and wounded. In places the enemy got to within 300 yards of the Middlesex and then suffered appalling casualties. Capt. E. L. O. Baddeley was wounded during the attack.*

27TH MARCH.

The night of the 26th/27th was quiet, and apparently nothing happened until the afternoon of the 27th, when half of the reserve company, under 2/Lieut. J. L. Wenn, took part in a counter-attack under the C.O. of the 2nd West Yorkshires, west of Rosieres Station. Here 150 of the West Yorkshires, with a small number of 2nd Middlesex and some Royal Engineers, maintained a line north of the railway till further help arrived. The following paragraph from the official narrative will give some idea of the straits to which units were put to find fighting troops:

"During the afternoon Brigadier-General Grogan, with two battalions and a number of details, including the Pipe Band,† Drums, Tailors, Shoemakers and Storemen of the Battalion‡ made a most successful counter-attack and re-took Harbonnieres and Vauvillers. . . . The 23rd Brigade Guard of three N.C.Os. and six men of the Battalion fought very gallantly there."

Thus closed the Battle of Rosieres. At nightfall the line south of the Somme ran from Hamel (south of Sailly-le-Sec), thence south-east to between Harbonnieres and Vauvillers, Rosieres, Bouchoir to Boussicourt on the Avre River.

* "On this day, the 26th March, the Governments of France and Great Britain decided to place the supreme control of the operations of the French and British forces in France and Belgium in the hands of General Foch, who assumed control." This appointment was made imperative by the immediate danger of the separation of the French and British Armies.

† The story of how a Battalion of the Middlesex Regiment included a " pipe band " is interesting. These pipes originally belonged to the 16th Battalion. They were introduced by Col. J. Hamilton Hall. When the 16th Battalion was disbanded, the 2nd Battalion took over the pipe band.

‡ Of the 2nd Middlesex.

(IV) THE FIRST BATTLE OF ARRAS, 1918:
28th March.

Foiled in his attempt to reach Amiens and break through the British lines immediately north and south of the Somme, the enemy on the 28th March attacked in great force along the valley of the Scarpe at Arras, hoping thereby to gain greater freedom for the development of his offensive.

At 3 a.m. a bombardment of great violence, with gas and high-explosive shells, swept the British lines north and south of the river.

Between 7 and 8 a.m. the enemy, in massed formation, almost shoulder to shoulder, advanced to the attack. Immediately south of the Scarpe four hostile divisions were flung against the line with the intention of capturing Arras and the heights overlooking the town. North of the river three fresh German divisions, supported by two divisions already holding their front line, advanced against the line held by the 4th and 56th Divisions (between the Scarpe and Oppy) with the general line Vimy–Bailleul–St. Laurent–Blangy as their objective.

The weight of the enemy's attack, following the terrible bombardment to which his artillery had subjected our line, sufficed to carry him through our outpost lines, but our battle position (the Red Line) held and he could advance no further. Terrible execution was done on his troops that day: thousands were shot down as (gallantly enough) they advanced in six lines, trying to cut the barbed wire by hand. Yet, despite their great weight in numbers, they could not prevail, and the attack (save for the capture of the outpost line) ended in another and disastrous failure.

The 169th (right) and 168th (left) Brigades of the 56th Division held the front line at the time of the attack, the 167th Brigade being in Divisional Reserve. The 1/7th and 1/8th Battalions of the Middlesex Regiment were not, therefore, in the front line. But just before midnight the 1/7th took over the right of the line from Ditch Post to Bailleul East Post, the 1/8th remaining at Pont du Jour in support.

Considering their proximity to the front line, all day both Battalions had surprisingly few casualties, though the enemy's shell fire had swept the whole area of the front-line, support and communication trenches with the utmost fury.

[margin: 1/7TH AND 1/8TH BATTALIONS. 28TH MARCH.]

The German Offensives: Picardy 1918

1/7TH AND 1/8TH BATTALIONS. 28TH MARCH.

The 1/7th had 6 other ranks killed and 14 wounded; the 1/8th lost 2/Lieut. W. B. Green killed and 2/Lieut. H. J. Barker wounded and "died of wounds." Two killed and 7 wounded were the losses in other ranks.

On the 28th the 1/8th relieved the Queen's Westminsters in the front line (Red Line).

South of Arras on the 28th the enemy's repulse had been even more complete than east of the town. From the direction of Ablainzeville and at Bucquoy his attacks had been bloodily frustrated and he suffered enormous losses.

19TH AND 23RD BATTALIONS.

The 19th (Pioneers) and 23rd Battalions of the Regiment (of the 41st Division) were not, however, engaged with the enemy, the former being at Gommecourt in the reserve lines, and the 23rd in support west of Ablainzeville.

* * * * *

"With this day's battle" (28th March), records the Official Despatches, "which ended in complete defeat of the enemy on the whole front of his attack, the first stage of the enemy's offensive was checked, and eventually closed on the 5th April. During these days hostile pressure continued south of the Somme."

2ND BATTALION.

In the "hostile pressure" mentioned by the despatches the 2nd Middlesex were again involved in heavy fighting.

28TH MARCH.

It will be remembered that the 2nd Battalion on the night of 27th March was dug in in the neighbourhood of Rosieres. At 8 a.m. on the 28th the enemy made another strong attack on the line of the 8th Division. The Germans, however, never got within 300 yards of the Die-Hards, who kept them at bay and could easily have held on had not the flanking units been forced to fall back. A retirement was therefore ordered at 9 a.m. and began forthwith, under steady artillery fire and harassing fire from about 40 hostile aeroplanes which, like angry bees, buzzed in the air. Second-Lieut. H. Cawdron was wounded before leaving the trench and could not be removed.

The Battalion fell back to a trench line, strongly wired, east of Caix, though before taking possession of the trench the Middlesex lay out in front for an hour sniping the enemy as he advanced through Rosieres. At 6 p.m. the Adjutant (Capt. W. Evans) was wounded by a bullet from an aeroplane.

Meanwhile the French had retired from Caix. The enemy had been for about an hour held up in the wire in front of the

Middlesex, not daring to move owing to the deadly effect of their opponents' rifle fire. But the C.O., seeing that the position was no longer tenable (German white lights were going up from the northern outskirts of Caix), ordered a retirement. This was made by platoons covering one another. The acting Adjutant —Capt. A. M. Toye—who was sent through Caix with Battalion Headquarters, actually had a fight with the enemy in the streets of the village. After a series of exciting incidents the Battalion reached first Bihucourt and then Berteaucourt, where the Middlesex halted from 2 a.m. to 6 a.m. on the 29th and slept. The march was then resumed to Thézy and later to Jumel.

^{2ND} BATTALION.
28TH MARCH.

29TH MARCH.

On the 30th the march was resumed to Cottenchy, where the Battalion was reorganised into two companies—No. 1, of men fit to fight; No. 2, of those who needed a night's rest. Under the C.O., No. 1 marched to Castel, No. 2 remaining at Cottenchy. A third party (not previously mentioned in the records*), under Lieut. Birdwood, marched direct to Castel from Jumel.

30TH MARCH.

Castel is on the Avre, just north-west of Moreuil, and on reaching that place No. 1 Party dug in and held a bridge over the river. This position was held until 8 p.m. on the 31st, when the Middlesex were sent, under Capt. Toye, to reinforce the 2nd Devons in Moreuil Wood. The latter was only held by hand-to-hand fighting, but it *was* held and handed over to French troops at about midnight, 1st/2nd April. Second-Lieutenant P. H. E. Fairclough, with "A" Company's platoon, was cut off in the wood during a counter-attack and captured. No. 2 Company had in the meantime been moved up to Castel and there held the bridgehead.

31ST MARCH.

All that was left of the Battalion marched on the 2nd April to Dommartin, thence to Sains-en-Amienois, whence buses carried the worn-out officers and men to billets in Breilly.

Several of the C.O.'s remarks at the conclusion of this extraordinary story of endurance and tenacity of the 2nd Middlesex are worthy of note. Not a man had straggled on the march, not a man left the front line without orders. Every order was obeyed cheerfully and at once. Discipline was perfect in every sense: and Colonel Page's concluding remarks were: "The

* Apparently it numbered 50 other ranks, including the Drums, Shoemakers, Tailors and other details attached to the 2nd Devons.

fighting spirit was as high on the tenth day as on the first. *The pride of all ranks in the Regiment grew from day to day.*"

2ND BATTALION. 4TH APRIL.

The 2nd Middlesex were still in Breilly when the Battle of the Avre (4th April)* was fought.

13TH BATTALION.

Meanwhile the story turns back to the 13th Middlesex, who, on the night of 27th, were holding a line from Warvillers Wood to Vrely.

28TH MARCH.

At about 8 a.m. on the 28th the enemy again attacked, but was held until the 73rd Brigade was ordered to withdraw on Windmill Farm. More heavy casualties were suffered by the Battalion in falling back to this position. Later a further retirement took place to the Caix defences, and here the Battalion reorganised and held defensive positions until the troops were again ordered back to Villers, where until midnight the Brigade was concentrating. From Villers the Battalion marched with the Brigade back across the Avre to Castel.

There is little further to record of the 13th Battalion. Their losses during the operations which began on the 21st March were 9 officers and 153 other ranks, but, compared with the losses of other battalions, they were not heavy.

4TH APRIL.

On the 4th, when the Battle of the Avre was fought, the 13th Middlesex were in the Bois de Gentelles, in support of the 17th Infantry Brigade.

(VI) THE BATTLE OF THE ANCRE, 1918:
5th April.

On the 5th April the Germans attacked practically along the whole front from Dernancourt (south of Albert) to beyond Bucquoy, while again strong local attacks were made south of the Somme about Hangard. It is, however, with the enemy's attack in the neighbourhood of Rossignol Wood that the narrative deals, for, curiously enough, in this area his efforts were entirely disorganised by a local attack carried out at a somewhat earlier hour by troops of the 37th Division.

The 37th Division arrived in the Fonquevillers area at the end of March, and on the night of 1st/2nd April the 63rd Brigade relieved the 187th Brigade (62nd Division) in the Rossignol Wood sector in front of Gommecourt.

---

* The Battle of the Avre, 4th April, 1918, is one of the Battle Honours of the Middlesex Regiment.

The 4th Middlesex (Lieut.-Colonel H. A. O. Hanley) moved into support trenches west of Gommecourt. The attack on Rossignol Wood was carried out by the 8th Somersets and 8th Lincolnshire of the 63rd Brigade, the 4th Middlesex being in reserve, but with orders to move two companies up into the assembly trench (Cod Trench) after the attacking troops had gone forward. **4TH BATTALION.**

Zero hour for the attack was 5.30 a.m. on the 5th, at which hour both attacking battalions advanced. They succeeded in capturing the western edge of the Wood, but could not hold their gains. At nightfall there was very little change in the situation of the Brigade as it had existed before the attack. **5TH APRIL.**

The enemy, however, suffered very heavy casualties, for his troops were engaged in massing for a heavy attack when the British barrage fell on his trenches. The latter were packed full of troops, and the German losses were very heavy indeed. The 4th Middlesex Diary records that " all companies were eventually drawn into the line, but were not actually engaged."

The Battalion lost on the 5th April 3 officers killed or gassed* and 4 other ranks killed, 10 wounded and 12 missing.

The Actions of Villers-Bretonneux:

24th–25th April, 1918.

While the German attacks on the Lys were in progress local attacks had, meanwhile, taken place on both sides of the Somme, particularly in the neighbourhood of Hangard and about Aveluy Wood.

On the 24th April a more serious attack by four German divisions (in which for the first time British and German tanks came into conflict) was made on the Allied line between the Somme and the Avre valleys. At about 6.30 a.m., after a heavy bombardment lasting about three hours and again favoured by fog, the enemy advanced to assault the whole British line south of the Somme River. In the struggle which ensued the enemy's tanks broke through the line south-east of Villers-Bretonneux and, turning north and south, opened the way for his infantry.

The line east and south-east of the village was held at this period by the 8th Division.

After the heavy fighting which had concluded early in April,

* Killed, 2/Lieut. L. E. Moore; gassed, 2/Lieuts. J. E. Harrington and E. Elliott.

the 8th Division had moved back out of the line, the 23rd Brigade to the Ailly-sur-Somme area, where the 2nd Middlesex were billeted in Breilly. Several days were spent there before other moves (not of sufficient importance to detail) took place, the Battalion with other units of the Brigade finally reaching Saleux on the 13th. In this area training took place until once again the 8th Division was ordered into the front line.

The 23rd Brigade moved to Blangy–Trouville in Divisional Reserve on the 20th April, the 2nd Middlesex occupying a line west of Villers-Bretonneux. Major C. D. Drew commanded the Battalion in line, while Lieut.-Colonel C. A. S. Page remained with details at Camon.

On the night of 23rd/24th April the 23rd Brigade relieved the 24th Brigade in the right sub-sector of the 8th Divisional front, the 2nd West Yorks taking over the right and the 2nd Middlesex the left of the line. The trenches of the West Yorkshires curved round the eastern edges of Monument Wood as far north as the railway line, from which point the Middlesex continued the front to the Villers-Bretonneux–Lamottee road, just east of the cemetery.

"B" Company of the Middlesex was on the right, "A" in the centre and "D" on the left; "C" was in support; Battalion Headquarters were in the village.

The relief was uneventful. The early part of the night was quiet, though, owing to an expected enemy attack, the Divisional artillery carried out harassing and counter-preparation fire. Companies had been warned of the expected attack, and work on the defences continued, everyone being on the alert.

At 3.45 a.m. the enemy's guns opened an intense artillery and trench-mortar bombardment, and a lachrymatory-gas barrage was put down on the whole Divisional front. This barrage caused considerable casualties in the front line, as it continued for about two hours; it then lifted to the rear lines.

The Battalion "Report on Operations" consists of two portions, one up to the night of the 24th April, signed by Major Drew, and the other from the night, 24th/25th April, by the C.O. (Lieut.-Colonel Page). The former officer stated that, "owing to many officers and men of 'A' and 'C' Companies becoming casualties, the events in the centre of the line were not known, but from survivors of the flank companies ('B' and 'D'), the following appears to have happened":—

On the right (on " B " Company's front), immediately the enemy's barrage lifted, two hostile tanks approached the front line, firing their machine guns. Smoke shells, liberally used by the enemy, hid their approach so that they were not seen until they were about 30 yards in front of " B " Company. They then manœuvred into position from which they could enfilade our trench, causing further heavy casualties. The two tanks were followed by a third, and by infantry carrying *flammenwerfer*. Rifle and machine-gun fire could not stop the tanks, which passed over the front line. The third tank was heavily fired on from the support line, upon which it turned towards the latter and passed right over it, again causing many casualties.

The Commander of " B " Company (Capt. Brodie) ordered the remnants of the supporting platoon into the railway cutting, where they were secure from the German tanks, but the cutting was heavily shelled and the unfortunate survivors suffered further casualties. Captain Brodie, with seven men, the sole remnants of his Company, then made their way under heavy fire through the village to Battalion Headquarters.

In the meantime No. 15 Platoon, on the extreme left just south of the main Amiens-Warfusse road, had suffered heavily from the enemy's barrage. Owing to the smoke the Germans were not seen until they were only 20 yards to the right of the trench. Fire was at once opened, but, headed by eight men with *flammenwerfer*, the Germans turned towards the platoon. The *flammenwerfer* men were all shot down, but the enemy still surged forward. By this time the platoon had been reduced to one officer (2/Lieut. Martin) and five other ranks. But they pluckily faced the enemy. The 2nd Royal Berkshires (on the left of the Middlesex) swung back their right to form a defensive flank, and 2/Lieut. Martin and his men joined up with the Berkshires, remaining with them for two days.* Four hostile tanks and parties of the enemy were seen moving towards Villers-Bretonneux. Two parties of British prisoners being taken back under escort were also seen. The escorts of one party were shot down, but, in spite of whistles and signs, the prisoners ran south-east and again fell into the enemy's hands.

Between 6 a.m. and 6.30 a.m. Major Drew, who had collected some stragglers, went forward and entered the village, where he met Captain Brodie. The latter not only told Major Drew of

* He rejoined the Middlesex on 24th/25th April.

2ND BATTALION.
24TH APRIL.

the fate of "B" Company, but said that German tanks closely followed by large numbers of the enemy's infantry, were in the village. As communication had been cut between Battalion Headquarters and Companies, Captain Brodie was sent off to the left to gain what knowledge he could of the situation on that flank. Major Drew in the meantime moved his Headquarters back some three hundred yards to the west, in a valley, but on arrival there the enemy's barrage was falling heavily over the whole area and casualties were again heavy. Ordering Captain and Adjutant Toye to move up to the edge of the wood and reform as quickly as possible, the Major went off to reconnoitre the Cachy Switch, where he found some of the 2nd Devons. He then returned but found that, in his absence Captain Toye had been wounded and that the men had gone on, the barrage being equally heavy over the whole area.

Eventually the survivors of the Battalion under Major Drew were located in the Reserve Line, where they took up positions during the night 24th/25th.

During the night of 24th/25th Lieut.-Colonel Page, with four Officers from Details, arrived and relieved Major Drew.

25TH APRIL.

On the morning of the 25th a counter-attack was launched against the enemy. Brigade Headquarters had informed Colonel Page that his Battalion would advance with the 2nd Devons on the right and 2nd West Yorkshires in the centre, and clear all the enemy out of the wood and take up a line between the wood and the village. The three Battalions at this period numbered all told: Devons 6 officers and 300 other ranks; 2nd West Yorkshires—7 officers and 85 other ranks, and 2nd Middlesex 5 officers and 54 other ranks.

At about 2 a.m. all three Battalions had sent forward patrols to reconnoitre the enemy's position in the Bois d'Aquenne. At about 3.30 a.m. the three Battalions followed, moving forward along the Villers-Bretonneux road as far as the edge of the wood: they then deployed and pushed forward in skirmishing order.

The attack was entirely successful and the eastern edge of the wood was gained and consolidated, many Germans, six trench mortars and from twenty to thirty machine guns being captured.*

* The village itself was counter-attacked by a brigade of the 18th Division and two Australian brigades on the night 24th/25th, and by daybreak on the latter date had been practically surrounded; by the afternoon it was once more in our hands.

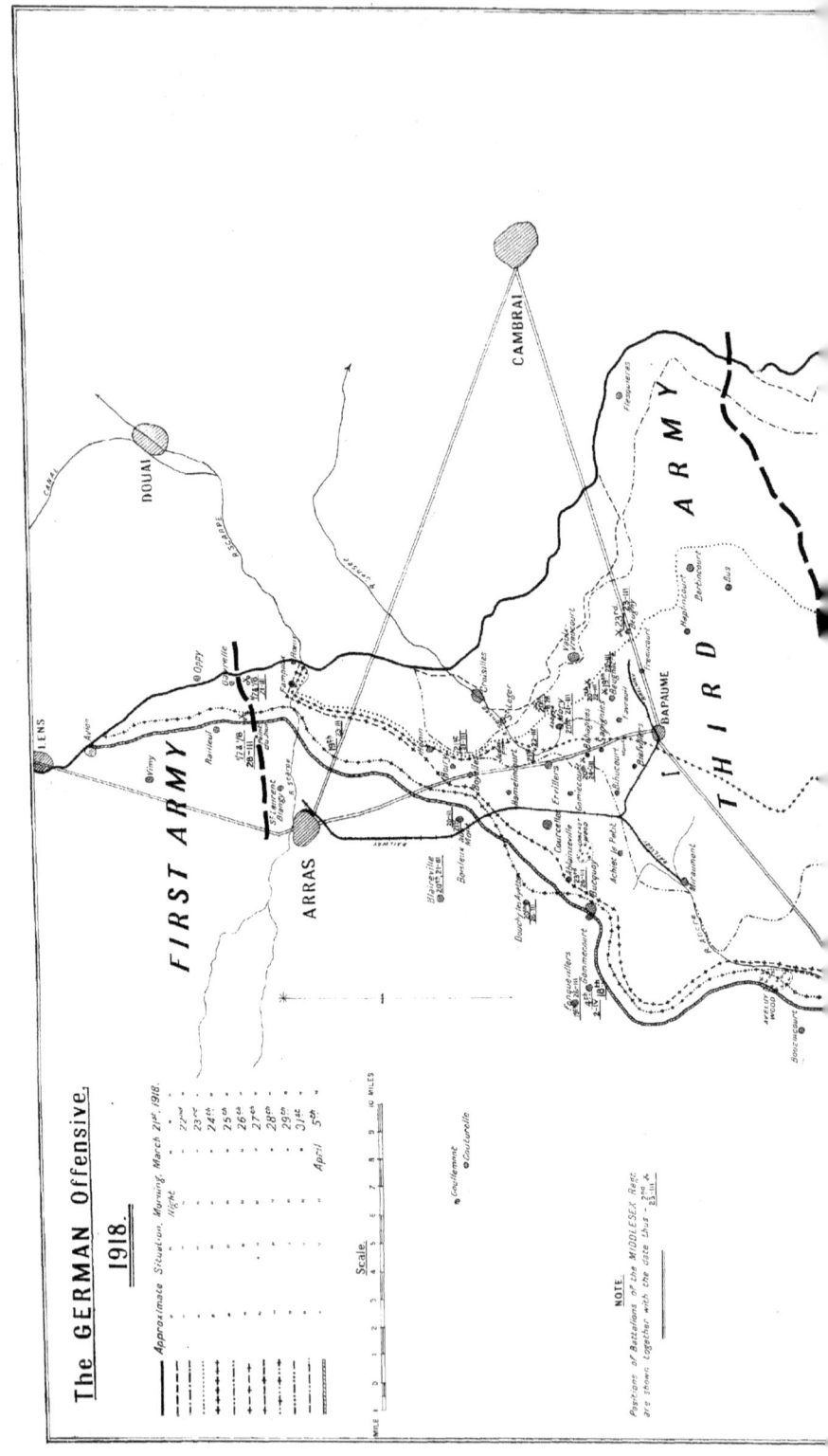

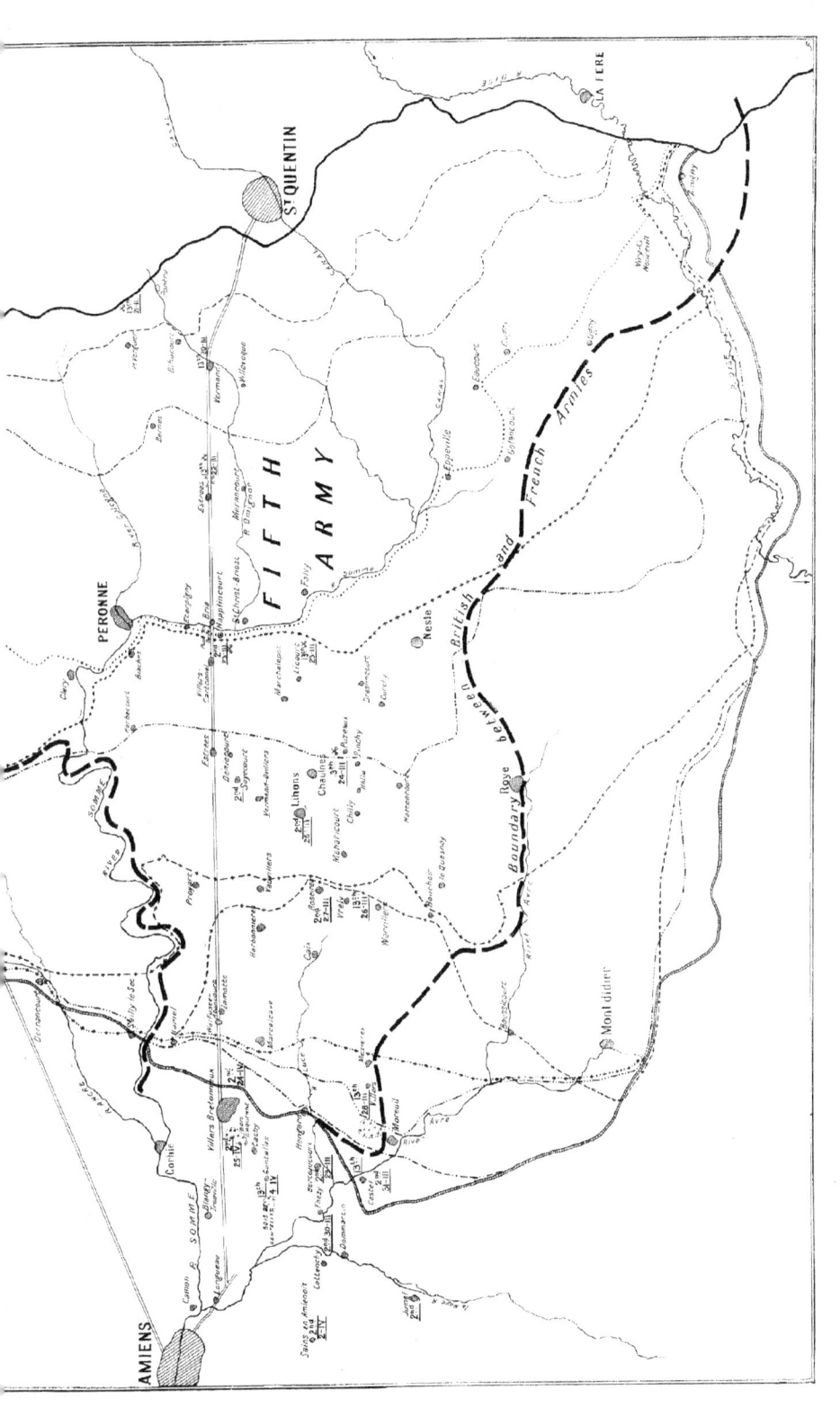

So far as the Middlesex were concerned Lieut.-Colonel Page stated that "the attack was made after four days in the line, after a bombardment of twenty-four hours, by the thirty-nine survivors of a battalion 585 strong. That is, after over 93 per cent. casualties. . . . During the night 25th/26th this party completed their trenches and erected 200 yards of double apron wire."

On the 26th 80 details and three officers arrived and two companies were formed, No. 1 consisting of " A ", " C " and Headquarters Companies, and No. 2 of " B " and " D " Companies.

During the night of 27th/28th April the Middlesex were relieved by a company of the 47th Australian Battalion, Colonel Page marching his sadly depleted battalion back to Billets in Blangy-Trouville.

The 2nd Middlesex lost in this action 13 officers* and 530 other ranks.

---

* Killed : Lieut. E. Cross. Wounded : Capt. and Adjt. A. M. Toye and Capt. R. H. Brodie. Missing : Lieut. J. H. F. Harvey and 2/Lieuts. F. D. Atken, C. P. Heppenstall, H. Howarth, F. W. Stafford, F. Pond, S. Slavitz, A. H. Palin, H. J. G. Morton and W. J. Francis.

CHAPTER XXXIV.

The German Offensives of 1918:

II. THE OFFENSIVE IN FLANDERS:
9th–29th April.

THE BATTLES OF THE LYS:
(I) THE BATTLE OF ESTAIRES:
9th–11th April.

THE enemy's advance on the Somme had been stopped, but only at great sacrifice. He had won a considerable area of ground and taken much war material and many prisoners from us: our reserves were greatly depleted. But he had not obtained his objectives. Readers of "My War Memories" will not fail to detect the tone of petulance and disappointment in General Ludendorff's book. With hopes of obtaining greater successes than he had had on the Somme, the German Chief of the General Staff turned his attention to the Lys front where our line was weakly held, for Sir Douglas Haig had been forced to withdraw no less than ten divisions from the northern part of his line in order to reinforce or replace his exhausted forces on the Somme.

A break through on the Lys front might well mean the realisation of the enemy's hopes which had been so markedly defeated at Arras.

On the night of the 7th April an unusually heavy and prolonged bombardment with gas shell was opened along practically the whole British Front from Lens to Armentières, and at about 4 a.m. on the 9th April the bombardment was recommenced with even greater intensity, high explosive being added to huge quantities of gas shell.

Between the La Bassée Canal and the Ypres–Comines Canal (opposite Aubers) the 2nd Portuguese Division held a Sector of the Allied line.

20TH AND 21ST BATTALIONS.

On the right of the Portuguese the 55th Division held the line from Givenchy: the 40th Division carried the line from the left of the Portuguese to Bois Grenier.

After their heavy fighting west of St. Leger, which had concluded on the 26th March, the 20th and 21st Middlesex of the 40th Division moved back out of the line for several days. But at the end of the month the Division was transferred to the Lys front, and on the 1st April the 121st Brigade took over the left sub-sector (Bois Grenier) of the new Divisional front, which extended just east of La Boutillerie to north-west of La Houssoie.

The 120th Brigade took over the right sub-sector of the Divisional front which extended from the right of the 121st Brigade to due east of Picantin, opposite a projection in the German lines named the Sugar Loaf; the 119th Brigade was in reserve. The 20th Middlesex, however, did not go into the front line but were in reserve at Fleurbaix and Canteen Farm.

On the 6th the 119th Brigade relieved the 120th Brigade, the 21st Middlesex being the Battalion in reserve.

On the night of 5th/6th April the 20th Middlesex relieved the 12th Suffolks in the right-sub sector of the Bois Grenier sector: Battalion Headquarters were at Wye Farm. On the following day Captain E. R. Samuel was sent back to the transport lines with "B" Company in order to train for a raid which the Battalion was going to make on the night of the 8th/9th.

This raid may be described as the prelude to the heavy fighting which took place on the 9th April and following days.

It was for the purpose of securing identifications, inflicting casualties on the enemy and the blowing up of any dug-outs found in the German lines.

9TH APRIL.

The raid was timed to begin at 4.55 a.m. on the 9th, but just after 4 a.m. the enemy's artillery bombardment began and the British guns immediately opened heavy counter-preparation fire, they continued firing after the raid began, with the result that the raiders could not enter the enemy's trenches. They, therefore, returned to their own lines.

A thick fog hung over the whole of the battle line, thus again favouring the enemy, for artillery observation was severely handicapped and even the machine gunners and infantry could not use their guns and rifles to advantage.

At 7 a.m. the enemy swarmed across No Man's Land and broke into the left brigade sector of the Portuguese Division. He then turned rapidly right and left, attacking the right of the 119th Brigade (40th Division) and the left Brigade of the Portuguese. The 119th Brigade appears to have been taken in flank badly, for soon the Germans had penetrated the Brigade support line. The 20th Middlesex, the right Battalion of the 121st Brigade then formed a defensive flank, but they also were overwhelmed, for the Battalion Diary states that: "Battalion Headquarters surrounded and posts attacked from rear. Commanding Officer, with part of Headquarters personnel, escaped and formed defensive flank in City Road. 'C' Company advanced from support position. Posts in City Road withdrawn to Shaftesbury Avenue together with 'A' Company, thus conforming to line being formed by support Company of 13th Yorkshire Regiment." That is all the Battalion Diary has to say of the operations on the 9th of April, but the Brigade Headquarters Diary reports that the 13th Yorkshires and 20th Middlesex were at 9 p.m. on the 9th placed under the command of the 34th Division.

20TH AND 21ST BATTALIONS.
9TH APRIL.

Meanwhile the 21st Middlesex, in 119th Brigade Reserve, who were between Laventie and Fleurbaix when the attack began, stood to at 4 a.m. and then moved up to battle positions. At 10 a.m. "C" and "D" Companies were ordered to occupy the machine-gun line, but the enemy was found to be in possession and the two Companies took up a line south-east of the Rue du Quesnes. Five minutes later the enemy was reported in the neighbourhood of Rouge de Bout and, advancing in a north-easterly direction on Sailly, Bac St. Maur and Fleurbaix. Battalion Headquarters were then withdrawn in short stages to a strong point in front of Sailly, having lost more than 50 per cent. personnel in casualties, including the adjutant and Second-in-Command. At this period, Details, moved up by Brigade Headquarters, arrived, but encountered the enemy across the Rouge de Bout–Sailly road. A line was then formed in front of Rue du Quesnoy. But at about 4 p.m., the enemy having entered Sailly, the remnants of the Battalion withdrew across the Lys and moved to the Steenwerck Switch: the bridge was then blown up by the Royal Engineers.

At 4.30 p.m. the Quartermaster, seeing the danger of his Store at Sailly falling into the hands of the enemy, set fire to it and withdrew across the river, posting two C.Q.M. Sergts. with Lewis guns on the north-eastern bank of the river to defend the bridge. Early in the evening the enemy was reported to be across the Lys

H

20TH AND 21ST BATTALIONS.
10TH APRIL.

in the neighbourhood of Bac St. Maur. The night of the 9th/10th passed without incident.

On the 10th the 20th Middlesex, under orders of the 103rd Brigade (34th Division), withdrew through Armentières, part of " A " Company joining the transport at Petit Sec Bois moved to Hazebrouck, the remainder of the Company with three officers joined the 29th Division. The C.O., with twenty-three other ranks, was with the 13th Yorkshires and 12th Suffolks at Nieppe.

At 3.45 a.m. the 21st Middlesex, who had spent the night of the 9th/10th in Steenwerck Switch, were heavily shelled by the enemy. They clung to their positions however until midday when, as the Switch was enfiladed with machine-gun fire, and the troops on the right had been withdrawn, they fell back to conform, and dug in in front of Petit Mortier. Although intermixed with the 12th Yorkshires and units of the 25th Division, the 21st Middlesex were in touch on the right with the 120th Brigade and on the left with the 121st Brigade.

On the night of the 11th/12th the 20th Middlesex at Nieppe were relieved and took up a position on the Bailleul–Nieppe road north of La Creche.

In the meantime, between 7 and 8 a.m. on the 11th, the 21st Middlesex with other troops fell back in stages and took up position in front of Le Verrier. During this withdrawal the C.O. (Lieut.-Colonel H. C. Metcalfe) was wounded, and Captain G. F. P. Worthington took over the remnants of the Battalion.

12TH APRIL.

Thus, so far as the 20th and 21st Middlesex are concerned, ended the Battle of Estaires. It is not possible to give details of the individual acts of gallantry, or of the fighting during the three days of the battle, as the confused nature of the reports make a coherent story impossible.

(II) THE BATTLE OF MESSINES, 1918:

10th–11th April.

1ST AND 18TH BATTALIONS.

10TH APRIL.

Although the 1st and 18th (Pioneers) Middlesex saw no fighting in this battle, both Battalions were in the area of operations. The 33rd Division was out of the line when the enemy attacked north of Bois Grenier on the 10th of April, but received orders to move forward. The 98th Brigade Group moved by rail to the Strazeele area on the 11th and at 5 p.m. was ordered to take up reserve positions behind the line Neuve Eglise–De Seule, and by midnight units were disposed in the Ravelsberg Camp area: the 1st Middlesex bivouacked north of the Ravelsberg road. 1ST AND 18TH BATTALIONS. 11TH APRIL.

The 18th Middlesex were at Meteren where they picqueted the southern and south-eastern exits of the town.

(III) THE BATTLE OF HAZEBROUCK:
12th–15th April.

At night on the 11th, the British line north of the La Bassée Canal ran from Givenchy through Festubert–Le Cason, Paradis, Merville, thence, bending back in a north-easterly direction west of Neuf Berquin, through Doulieu–Le Verrier to Steenwerck Station. From the latter place the line turned east, running round the eastern edges of Nieppe, then north to Petit Pont, round the lower slopes of Hill 63 to the western outskirts of Messines, eastern edge of Wytschaete to the old British front line on the Ypres–Comines Canal, east of Hollebeke.

Just before dawn on the 12th of April the enemy broke through about Pacaut and Riez du Vinage, but was stopped at the La Bassée Canal. At Merville also we were compelled to give ground.

North of Merville, at about 8 a.m., the enemy in great strength attacked on a front extending from south of the Estaires–Vieux Berquin road to the neighbourhood of Steenwerck.

The 31st Division, having come up into line, worn-out troops of the 40th Division were relieved, the 20th Middlesex (121st Brigade) marching back to the assembly ground at Strazeele, where they were joined by the 21st Battalion (119th Brigade). They then, with other troops, were ordered to dig a defensive position south-east of Strazeele. Neither Battalion took a further part in the actual fighting. 20TH AND 21ST BATTALIONS. 12TH APRIL.

(IV) THE BATTLE OF BAILLEUL:
13th–15th April.

At 2 a.m. (12th) the 98th Brigade was ordered to march to Dranoutre to come under the orders of the 19th Division. At 4 a.m. the Brigade marched from the Ravelsberg Camp area and

1st Battalion.
12th April.

reached its destination at about 7 a.m. where information was obtained that an enemy attack on Wulverghem was expected at any time. The Battalions of the 19th Division holding the line were weak and tired out and the 98th Brigade was in support. The 1st Middlesex were in the neighbourhood of Homburg Farm with the Argyll and Sutherland Highlanders and 4th King's at Daylight Corner. Shortly after midday fresh orders came to hand for the 98th Brigade to relieve other troops of the 33rd Division, as the enemy was reported to have broken through south-west of Meteren. So again the Brigade took the road, the Middlesex leading, and at 5 p.m. moved to St. Jans Cappel. On reaching the latter the Middlesex were ordered to hold Hills 40-45, south-east of Bailleul, while the Argyll and Sutherland Highlanders and 4th King's proceeded to the Asylum, Bailleul, in Divisional Reserve.

13th April.

At 11 a.m. on the 13th, the Middlesex received instructions from Brigade Headquarters that a British counter-attack on Neuve Eglise was to be expected, and that if it failed the line would probably be withdrawn to Crucifix Corner, in which event the Battalion would still be required to defend Mont de Lille and Hill 45. Later the Middlesex came under the orders of the 101st Brigade (34th Division), " C " Company being on Mont de Lille and " A " Company on Hill 45, " D " Company between, with " B " in reserve. Lieut. Ferguson was wounded during the day.

14th April.

During the morning of the 14th the positions of the Middlesex were modified; the Battalion, first under one Brigade and then under another, finally at 2.10 p.m. held positions on Hill 40, west of the Asylum. At 6.15 p.m., however, definite orders were received from the 74th Infantry Brigade that as the Steam Mill, south west of Bailleul, appeared to have fallen to the enemy, the Middlesex were to leave one Company to cover the roads on Hill 40 east of the Asylum, and the three remaining Companies were " to advance at once and counter-attack and restore the situation."

Leaving " D " Company at Hill 40, " A," " B " and " C " Companies moved off at 6.45 p.m. to the cross-roads near Appetit Farm where Battalion Headquarters were established and S.A.A. dumped. Companies then formed up in a field for the attack, " A " and " B " in front, " C " in support. At about 7.45 p.m. the advance began and pushed forward about one hundred yards north of the Bailleul–Meteren road, where they began to dig in.

Eventually the Battalion moved up to a position within two   1ST BATTALION.
hundred yards of the Steam Mill, the intention being to attack 14TH APRIL.
that place at dawn on the 15th, but before this could be done the
G.O.C., 74th Brigade, cancelled the order, the Battalion being
instructed to stand fast in its present position. On the 15th a 15TH APRIL.
patrol, sent forward to reconnoitre the Mill, found it empty and
later it was occupied by the 19th Brigade.

During the night of the 15th/16th the Battalion was withdrawn to the Meteren–Moulehouck line, the withdrawal being completed by 12.30 a.m. on the 16th of April.

Meanwhile the 18th Battalion had joined in the battle, for at 18TH
this period Pioneers, Cyclists, and every available man from BATTALION.
schools and reinforcement Companies had been rushed up into
action.

In a situation continually changing the Pioneers found themselves split up and attached to various units. At 8.30 p.m. on
the 12th, they were placed at the disposal of the 19th Infantry 12TH APRIL.
Brigade and the next morning at 7.30 a.m. " B " Company
reinforced the 1st Queen's : a little later " C " Company was
sent up to reinforce the XXIInd Corps Reinforcement Battalion.
At night half of another Company was sent to the Scottish Rifles
to fill a gap in the front line. No dispositions are given, but at the
end of the day the gallant pioneers had lost fifteen men killed and
forty wounded. On the 14th, as the enemy was reported massing
near Bailleul, three platoons were sent to picquet the Appetit
Farm–Meteren road. The farm was about two thousand yards
east of the village. During the day 2/Lieut. F. C. Wright and
2 other ranks were killed and 14 other ranks wounded.

The Battalion was relieved (with the exception of the three
platoons last mentioned) on the night of the 14th/15th, but on the
evening of the 15th they manned the Meteren–St. Jans Cappel 15TH APRIL.
switch line with the 5th Tank Battalion which held the front line
with Lewis guns : the Pioneers were disposed behind the Tanks.

(V) THE FIRST BATTLE OF KEMMEL :
17th–19th April.

During the 16th of April the enemy made a number of strong
local attacks on the Meteren–Wytschaete front, which were for
the most part repulsed, his losses being heavy. At Meteren and

18TH
BATTALION.
16TH APRIL.

Wytschaete, however, he succeeded in penetrating the line and, after confused fighting, established himself in both villages. Early in the morning the New Zealand Rifles withdrew through the switch line held by the 18th Middlesex and Tank Battalion and the right flank of the line fell back with them. The enemy then gained a footing in Meteren. The right Company of the Pioneers made a gallant attempt to check him, but was unsuccessful. The Battalion's losses on the 16th were 2 officers (2/Lieuts. H. C. Bradbury and H. P. Boreham) and 6 other ranks killed and 35 other ranks wounded. On the 17th the Pioneers were relieved and withdrew to Mont des Cats.

17TH APRIL.

1ST BATTALION.
16TH APRIL.

Meanwhile, dawn on the 16th found the 1st Middlesex about 1,600 yards due west of Schaeken where there was a small wood and a farm-house in which Battalion Headquarters had been established. Just before 10 a.m. the enemy was reported in Meteren and the troops on the right of the Die-Hards withdrawing, the G.O.C., 98th Brigade, then ordered Captain Welman (who was in command of " A " and " C " Companies) to counter-attack. At 1 p.m. this counter-attack was launched and, in spite of heavy machine-gun fire, succeeded in reaching the main road (presumably in Meteren itself). But the attacking Companies had suffered heavy casualties* and, as our guns were short shooting, Captain Welman ordered a withdrawal from the village. At 1.45 p.m., " B " and " D " Companies were sent up to reinforce " A " and " C " Companies. Between 4 and 5 p.m. some troops on the Meteren–Fletre road were seen to be falling back and again the line of the 1st Middlesex had to be re-adjusted; they then held a south-east to north-west line just north of Meteren with New Zealand troops on their left: their right flank, however, was in the air but refused.

During the evening three Battalions of French Chasseurs moved up to counter-attack Meteren, but an erroneous report reached them that the village was held by the British and the attack was cancelled. They nevertheless passed through the line held by the Middlesex and formed a front line north of Meteren.

17TH APRIL.

Early on the 17th of April the R.A.F. reported that the French troops were on their objective south of Meteren. This proved to be false, for Middlesex patrols, sent into the village to ascertain

---

* Three officers were wounded in this counter-attack: 2/Lieuts. G. W. Batley, A. V. Flowers and W. W. Lodge.

the truth of that statement, were fired on by the enemy, Lieut. 1ST BATTALION.
J. A. Adams being killed and 2/Lieut. T. D. Corke wounded. Up 17TH APRIL.
to 12 noon the Battalion also suffered some sixty other ranks
killed and wounded. During the afternoon and evening the
enemy's shell fire became less severe and finally ceased when darkness had fallen.

But just after midnight the enemy endeavoured to penetrate
the right flank of the Middlesex, where they joined up with the
4th King's but was frustrated.

The 18th passed without any incident of great importance. 18TH APRIL.
The enemy's shell fire was still heavy and there was at one period
considerable uncertainty as to the situation in front. But a
reconnaissance revealed the fact that French troops held the
front line east and north-east of Meteren and that the Middlesex
were in support positions. The Battalion at this period numbered
only sixteen officers and 399 other ranks. During the evening
Meteren was in flames and the sky was red from the glare of
burning houses. Two more officers of the Battalion had been
wounded during the day, *i.e.*, 2/Lieuts. A. G. Beaumont and
W. W. L. While.

Just before 1 a.m. on the 19th, two platoons of " B " Company 19TH APRIL.
were sent to relieve the 4th King's who had been reduced to a mere
skeleton. These platoons were placed under the orders of the
32nd Chasseurs. The day was fairly quiet.

During the night of the 19th/20th Australian troops arrived
and relieved the 98th Brigade and the French troops. The 1st
Middlesex then marched off by companies independently to
Boeschepe, the last of the Battalion arriving at that place at 5 a.m.
on the 20th. On the following day Lieut.-Colonel J. W. L. Elgee
proceeded to England and Lieut.-Colonel J. H. Hall arrived and
assumed command of the Battalion.

So tired and worn out were all ranks that instead of moving at
10 a.m. on the 20th, as was intended, Brigade Headquarters
ordered the move to take place on the 21st.

The operations between the 10th and 20th had cost the 1st
Middlesex 1 officer killed and 7 wounded, and in other ranks
35 killed and 102 wounded.

On the 21st the Die-Hards marched via Godewaersvelde 21st April.
and Cæstre to an aerodrome about one thousand yards northwest of Hondeghem where the men were accommodated in two
R.A.F. hangars and the officers in huts. But these billets were

H 4

1ST BATTALION. 22ND APRIL.
only temporary, for on the 22nd the Battalion again moved to an area south of Cassel, where several days were spent until, at the end of the month, orders were received to move to the Blaringhem area where the 33rd Division was to train and rest.

19TH BATTALION.
In the Battle of Béthune, 18th April, the Second Battle of Kemmel, 25th-26th April, and the Battle of the Scherpenburg, 29th April, no battalion of the Middlesex was engaged, directly, though the 19th Middlesex was in the area of the two last-named battles.

* * * * *

Meanwhile, in order to set free additional British troops for the Battles of the Lys, and in order to delay the execution of any plans the enemy might have for extending his attacks northwards, the gradual evacuation of the Passchendaele Ridge and of a good deal of ground east of Ypres was ordered. The first stages of the withdrawal were to be carried out on the night of the 12th/13th of April.

19TH AND 23RD BATTALIONS.
In this withdrawal the 23rd and 19th Middlesex of the 41st Division were concerned.

12TH/13TH APRIL.
The 23rd Middlesex had arrived at Hopoutre–Poperinghe on the 4th of April, whence they proceeded in motor buses to Eecke where several days were spent absorbing reinforcements and in training. On the 8th, however, they marched to Junction and Irish Camps. The next day they moved into the front line about two thousand yards north of Gravenstafel. On the night of the 12th/13th the Battalion was relieved (the front line becoming an outpost line) and withdrew to the main line of resistance (to Plum and Rat Keeps). On the night of the 14th/15th they again (less one company) fell back on the Wieltje–Potijze line where work was continued. The company left behind in the line carried out patrol work to Hill 35, during which 2/Lieut. J. M. Morrison was wounded. This same company raided the enemy on the 19th and captured Hill 35, but it was lost again in a counter-attack: 2/Lieut. R. E. Moorhouse and 2 other ranks were killed, 1 other rank was wounded and 7 were missing. On the 23rd Lieut.-Colonel B. A. Smith joined the Battalion and assumed command.

26TH/27TH APRIL.
The loss of Kemmel Hill again necessitated further withdrawal in the Ypres Salient, and on the night of the 26th/27th our troops withdrew to the general line Pilckem–Wieltje—western end of Zillebeke Lake—Voormezeele, the 23rd Middlesex to new positions near Machine-Gun Farm. Then ensued two or three weeks of *comparative quietude*.

CHAPTER XXXV.

The German Offensives of 1918.

III. IN CHAMPAGNE.

THE BATTLE OF THE AISNE, 1918:

27th May–6th June.

THE German offensives on the Somme and in the Lys Valley were over, but there was a prevailing opinion among the British General Staff that before the enemy resumed his main offensive on the Arras–Amiens–Montdidier front, the attack on the northern flank of the Allied line in Flanders would be followed by a similar attack on the southern flank. Such was the case, for at the end of May, the Germans launched a violent surprise attack on the Allied line on the Aisne front in which certain British divisions which had been sent there to rest were involved.

Marshal Foch, who had concentrated certain French divisions behind Amiens, had requested Sir Douglas Haig to replace them by sending British divisions to take their place on the Asine front, then a quiet part of the line. The British divisions sent were some of those which had gone through very heavy fighting on the Somme or Lys. They were the 8th, 21st, 25th and 50th Divisions, subsequently reinforced by the 19th Division. They formed the IXth Corps under Lieut.-General Sir A. Hamilton Gordon, and were to join the Sixth French Army. The despatches record that " the 8th Division (Major-General W. C. G. Heneker) had been involved south of the Somme in some of the heaviest fighting of the year and had behaved with distinguished gallantry. All these Divisions had but lately been filled up with young drafts and, despite their high spirits and gallant record, were in no condition to take part in major operations until they had had several weeks' rest."

The story of the 2nd Middlesex in the operations on the Somme is typical of the fighting prowess of the 8th Division which, though almost wiped out again and again, emerged with its spirit undimmed.

2ND BATTALION.

2ND BATTALION.
4TH MAY.

The 2nd Middlesex, with other units of the 23rd Brigade, arrived at Fere-en-Tardenois at 8.30 p.m. on the 4th May, and in a thunderstorm marched to billets at Dravegny, which village was not, however, reached until 5 a.m. on the 5th.

Training was carried out until the 10th when the Battalion began to move forward to the lines in a series of route-marches. On the 10th the Middlesex reached Breuil-sur-Vesle, on the 12th Ventelay. On the latter date, in very wet weather, the 23rd Brigade relieved the 217th Regiment of French Infantry in the left sub-sector of the 8th Divisional front, the right flank of which rested on the Aisne River, north-east of Berry-au-Bac, and the left north-east of La Ville and west of Juvincourt, the latter village being in the German lines.

The 2nd Middlesex, however, did not go into the front line, but were in reserve in Guyencourt. Here they stayed until the 20th, engaged in ordinary training. Their Diary records that Albuhera Day was spent in skill-at-arms competitions.

20TH MAY.

From the battle-scarred Somme battlefields the Division had come to a quiet and peaceful country. The weather was glorious, the Champagne country looking at its best. The depressing monotony of Flanders and the awful wreckage of the Picardy landscapes, with their blasted woods and ruined villages, had no counterpart in this fair country to which the tired and worn-out 8th Division had come. Only occasionally a shell would break the stillness of the perfect weather and the shell burst re-echo in the sleeping hills. And but for the front line trenches, dug in chalk, and the shell-holes and ground, honeycombed with dug-outs, one would hardly have known that the holocaust of war had passed that way. That such a quiet spot could exist along the Allied line seemed impossible.

27TH MAY.

On the 20th the Battalion moved up to the support line at Bois des Boches where they remained until the 27th, upon which date the Germans launched their great attack. For this quiet part of the line had been but a snare and a delusion. The Germans had fixed upon this peaceful part of the line on which to launch their great attack, just as we had selected the Cambrai front in November, 1917, where we knew battle-worn German divisions were resting.

On the 26th greatly increased movement behind the enemy's front line suggested an attack by the enemy. Two prisoners captured by the French on the previous night, had definitely stated that the enemy intended launching a great attack on the

27th May. At 6 p.m. all battle stations were occupied and the 2nd guns carried out a counter-preparation bombardment. But throughout the evening the enemy's artillery was silent.

The captured Germans had stated that the enemy's bombardment would open at 1 a.m. on the 27th and punctually at that hour there was a terrific roar. " Within a second a thousand guns roared out their iron hurricane. The night was rent with sheets of flame. The earth shuddered under the avalanche of missiles . . . leapt skyward in dust and tumult. Even above the din screamed the fierce crescendo of approaching shells, ear-splitting crashes as they burst . . . All the time the dull thud, thud, thud of detonations and drum fire. Inferno raged and whirled round the Bois des Buttes (23rd Brigade Headquarters). The dug-outs rocked . . . timbers started. . . . Men rushed for shelter, seizing kits, weapons, gas masks, message pads as they dived for safety. It was a descent into hell."

Such is the description of what that terrific bombardment was like by an officer present.*

The 25th Brigade was holding the right sub-sector of the divisional front, the 24th the centre and the 23rd the left, when the storm broke.

The 2nd Middlesex were in the battle zone in front of Ville au Bois, supporting the 2nd West Yorkshires who held the front line.

For three hours this savage bombardment went on and then, between 4 and 5 a.m., the enemy's infantry advanced to the attack. They broke through the line on either flank of the Division and gradually overwhelmed the troops of the 8th Division holding the front and support lines.

Of what happened to the 2nd Middlesex there is little record. The Battalion Diary has only the following entry: " Enemy bombardment commenced at 1 a.m. and continued till 5 a.m. (At) 4.35 a.m. a message received from O.C., ' B ' Company (Captain del Court) stating that all was well. 4.45 a.m. O.C. ' B ' Company reports to Battalion Headquarters that he has been overwhelmed by the enemy who are now close to Battalion Headquarters. C.O. sends Captain E. C. Lawson to Brigade Headquarters with message explaining the situation. As only Captain Lawson, 2/Lieut. J. J. Carter and twenty-one other ranks got out of the line it is impossible to record what became of the Company Commanders and other officers and men of the Battalion.

* Capt. Rogerson, 2nd West Yorks Regt., of the 23rd Brigade Staff.

2ND BATTALION.
27TH MAY.

Captain Lawson, 2/Lieut. Carter and twenty-one other ranks were detailed for guard on the three bridges crossing the Canal and Aisne, south of Pontavert, till they were prepared by the Royal Engineers for blowing up. This party then retired to Roucy and took up a defensive position till forced to retire on Montigny."

Fighting desperately, as they did on the Somme in March, the remnants of the Division fell back, contesting every bit of ground while there were men to hold on. On the 28th Major Drew rejoined the survivors of the 2nd Middlesex. On the 29th and 30th 2/Lieuts. Mahany and Polhill, with personnel of Lewis-gun and Gas School, rejoined with sixty other ranks and ten other ranks from Corps Signalling Schools. These officers and 2/Lieut. Carter and seventy other ranks were sent as details to the forward area, the drummers and pipers also going.

But on the night 29th/30th the 56th Brigade of the 19th Division had arrived to relieve the remnants of the 23rd Brigade, elements of the latter collecting at Nanteuil.

31ST MAY.

By the 31st of May the Allied line had been stabilized and on the 1st of June ran from north of Rheims, in a south-westerly direction through Coulommes, Bligny to Dormans, thence along the Aisne to Château Thierry, from which place it curved again in a north-westerly and northerly direction to west of Soissons. Thus the enemy had made a deep pocket in the French and British line. Again he had gained ground which was to be a danger to him.

As will be seen, practically the whole of the 2nd Battalion was lost in the Battle of the Aisne, and so great were the casualties that the 23rd Brigade was only able to form one composite company, consisting of 250 rifles, of which number there were only ninety-two other ranks belongong to the Middlesex.

2ND JUNE.

On the 2nd June this composite company moved to Etrechy, elements of the Brigade troops being still in the line. On the 9th a move was made to Broussy le Grand, and on the 12th the Brigade entrained at Fere-en-Champenoise with Lieut.-Colonel E. E. F. Baker (commanding 2nd Middlesex) in temporary command. Hangest was reached on the 15th where, on detrainment, all units marched to the Heucourt area, the Middlesex billeting in that village and in Croquison.

30TH JUNE.

By the end of June the 8th Division, with most of its units brought up to something near strength again, was in training in the Gamaches–St. Valery area, the 2nd Middlesex being billeted at Hebecourt.

CHAPTER XXXVI.

The Advance in Picardy.

THE SECOND BATTLES OF THE SOMME, 1918.

ON the 15th July the Germans made a heavy attack east and south-west of Rheims. They made progress at first and effected the passage of the Marne, but were then held by French, American and Italian troops. Three days later (on the 18th July) Marshal Foch launched his great counter-stroke on both sides of the salient, from Château Thierry and Soissons, which had been formed by the German advance. British troops took part in this attack* (two divisions on each side of the salient), and by the beginning of August the enemy had been forced back to practically an east to west line, from north of Rheims to the Aisne, just west of Soissons. The salient had disappeared. In none of these attacks, however, were Middlesex men engaged.

Just on three months had elapsed (between the close of the German offensive on the Lys and the beginning of August), and during that period the general situation along the British front was that of a state of active defence. The enemy was continually harassed and our artillery cost him grave losses.

At the end of July it was clear that the German Army had "shot its last bolt!" The enemy's ambitious attempt of the 15th July, followed by the brilliant allied counter-stroke of the 18th July, had completely changed the whole situation. The German soldiery, buoyed up with promises of success and an early termination of the War in their favour, were dispirited and had begun to lose faith in their commanders. The enemy had reached the greatest maximum of his strength—and it had not availed. On the other hand, the British Army was once more ready to take the offensive and the American Army was growing rapidly.

Towards the end of July the Allied Commander-in-Chief called a conference at which it was decided that a series of

* The XXIInd Corps, consisting of the 15th, 34th, 51st and 62nd Divisions.

offensives should be launched forthwith: the first with the object of disengaging Amiens and the freeing of the Paris-Amiens railway by an attack on the Albert–Montdidier front.

The first attack—the Battle of Amiens—launched on the 8th of August, was a staggering blow to the enemy,* and yielded immediate results in great captures.†

But in this attack no Battalion of the Middlesex Regiment was engaged.

Ten days were then spent in preparations for the next attack, *i.e.*, the Battle of Albert, 1918, which was launched on the 21st August on a front of about nine miles north of the Ancre from Miraumont to Moyenville.

(I) THE BATTLE OF ALBERT, 1918:

21st–23rd August.

In this battle, a limited attack, north of the Ancre, was to be launched by the Third Army against the line of the Albert–Arras railway on the morning of the 21st August: the 22nd was to be used to get troops and guns into position, and bring forward the left of the Fourth Army between the Somme and the Ancre: the principal attack was to be made on the 23rd by the Third Army and Divisions of the Fourth Army north of the Somme: the remainder of the latter, south of the Somme, were to push forward and cover the flank of the main operation. When the Third Army had forced the enemy to fall back from the Mercatel Spur, which would give us positions from which to attack Orange Hill and Monchy-le-Preux, the First Army (north of the Third) was to extend the front of the attack to the north. It was hoped to turn the western extremity of the Hindenburg Line and compel the enemy to undertake a further retreat.

At 4.45 a.m. on the 21st August, the 42nd, New Zealand and 37th Divisions (IVth Corps) and the 2nd and Guards Division (VIth Corps) attacked the enemy from north of the Ancre from Miraumont to Moyenville. This was the Third Army attack.

The 37th Division (63rd Brigade on the right and 111th Brigade on the left) was to capture and consolidate the high ground

---

* General Ludendorff described it as "The Black Day of the German Army."

† Nearly 22,000 prisoners and over 400 guns were taken by us and our front pushed forward 12 miles into the enemy's territory.

east of Bucquoy and Ablainzeville. The 4th Middlesex, on the right, and 8th Somerset Light Infantry, on the left, supported by the 13th Royal Fusiliers and 8th Lincolnshire respectively, were to attack from along the 63rd Brigade front.

4TH BATTALION. 21ST AUGUST.

There is little of outstanding interest to record between the end of April and the night before the attack of 21st August concerning the 4th Middlesex. On the night of 23rd/24th July the Battalion carried out a big raid on the enemy's trenches which was entirely successful, only one officer being wounded, *i.e.*, Captain S. Mirams. Twice before the night previous to the attack on 21st August (on the nights 10th/11th and 12th August) the enemy attempted to raid the Brigade front line, but suffered heavy losses and achieved nothing. Raids were very prevalent during the summer of 1918 : we made many big incursions into the enemy's trenches—it was a part of the " active defence " scheme.

The 4th Middlesex (Lieut.-Colonel W. B. Molony in command) were in their assembly positions one hour before zero (4.55 a.m.) on the 21st August. Three Companies (" B ", " C " and " D ") were formed up north and south-west of Bucquoy : " A " Company in reserve. The companies were formed up in two waves, the first to capture the objective and the second to pass through and form an outpost line.

Lieut. A. C. Mitchell was killed by an aeroplane bomb on the 31st May, whilst in hospital.

Fog covered the ground when at zero hour our barrage fell upon the enemy's positions in and about Bucquoy and, although there was slight loss of direction, our artillery fire was so accurate and effective that there was no great resistance from the enemy.

The Middlesex advanced splendidly and before 6 a.m. " B " Company reported the capture of the first objective on their front. Before 7 a.m. the Battalion had captured the whole front allotted to it. Troops of the 5th Division had passed through at 6.15 a.m. going towards the second objective in fine style.

Some stiff fighting with German strong points was encountered in Bucquoy before the Middlesex had captured their objective, but 117 prisoners, 7 machine guns and 8 trench mortars were taken. The Battalion then consolidated the line, though subjected to heavy shell fire.

On the 22nd the men were rested as much as possible during the day, but about 3 p.m. a warning order was received that the

22ND AUGUST.

240 *The Allied Advance* 1918

4TH BATTALION.

22ND/23RD AUGUST.

37th Division was to attack Achiet-le-Grand and Bihucourt on the afternoon of the 23rd : the 63rd Brigade was to be in support.

The Brigade moved to assembly positions north of Logeast Wood during the night 22nd/23rd where final preparations for the attack were made.

At 11 a.m. the next morning our barrage fell and the 63rd Brigade advanced in support, the 4th Middlesex on the right, 8th Lincolnshire on the left, 8th Somersets in reserve. Through the enemy's barrage the Battalion advanced until it neared Achiet-le-Grand, and finally consolidated a line about five hundred yards east of the Arras–Bapaume railway. About 5.30 p.m. orders were received to push on and get beyond Bihucourt, where two companies were to work round south of the village and one company north of it, all three connecting up in front. Companies advanced about five hundred yards but met heavy machine-gun fire. The Somersets then came forward and took up position between Bihucourt and Achiet-le-Grand and the Middlesex withdrew to their original positions where the night was spent in reorganising companies and in consolidating.

1/7TH AND 1/8TH BATTALIONS.

In the meantime the 1/7th and 1/8th Middlesex of the 56th Division had come up into line on the left of the Third Army front. The two Battalions reached support trenches near Blaireville at about midday on the 23rd and there received orders to attack the enemy on the following morning.

At the end of March the 1/7th (Major P. C. Kay, temporarily in command) and 1/8th (Lieut.-Colonel C. Pank) Middlesex were relieved by Canadians from the Arras front and moved back to rest billets in Villers-au-Bois.

For a little over four months the two Territorial Battalions were in and out of the line in the Arras area, and although the period was strenuous, even for trench warfare, there were only one or two incidents which call for mention.

Two raids in which the 1/7th took part are memorable. One on the night of the 24th April, by the enemy on the Battalion, resulted in fierce fighting in which the Middlesex lost 2/Lieut. S. A. Dore and five other ranks killed, and Captain Rose and twenty-nine other ranks wounded. The enemy's casualties could hardly have been less. But about five weeks later " The Great Raid " (as it was called) was carried out by the 1/7th on the enemy on the night of 28th May. This raid was an immense success and many of the enemy were killed, the 1/7th having only one man killed and twenty-three wounded. Little else of outstanding importance happened to the 1/7th Middlesex until the 56th Division was transferred to the VIth Corps on the 20th of August and ordered to move forward to the Bouvincourt area. *[margin: 1/7TH AND 1/8TH BATTALIONS. 20TH AUGUST.]*

The story of the 1/8th is very much the same as that of the 1/7th. On the 21st May the 1/8th raided the enemy successfully.*

Although the Battle of Albert, 1918, ends officially on the night of 23rd August, it will be obvious that the period of operations should be extended, for both the 4th Middlesex and the 1/7th and 1/8th Battalions were actively engaged with the enemy on the 24th.

We left the 4th Battalion on the night of 23rd August about five hundred yards east of the Arras–Bapaume railway, east of Achiet-le-Grand. Early on the morning of the 24th Captain F. F. Moorat was mortally wounded and died shortly afterwards. Orders had been received that the 63rd Brigade was to advance on Biefvillers with the New Zealanders, the 4th Middlesex supporting the 8th Lincolnshire on the left, and 8th Somersets attacking on the right. Biefvillers was occupied, but the village and valley west of it were under heavy shell fire and the Middlesex, though " dug-in " had a severe gruelling. That night orders were received by the 63rd Brigade to advance and attack the high ground on the Bapaume–Arras road, south of the Monument. The 4th Middlesex, with the 8th Lincolnshire in support, were to make the attack. These orders were cancelled, however, and fresh instructions for an attack on a two-battalion front arrived at about 1 a.m. on the 25th. Zero hour was to be 5 a.m. *[margin: 4TH BATTALION. 24TH AUGUST.]*

A heavy fog covered the ground when the attack began, but the 4th Middlesex, on the right, and 8th Lincolnshire, on the left, with the Somersets in support, moved off punctually at " Zero." *[margin: 25TH AUGUST.]*

There was a slight loss of direction, but companies were reorganised and the Quarries were attacked, from which the Middlesex took sixty prisoners. The records state that " during the attack there were many acts of individual heroism with the

---

* Officer casualties from the end of March to 20th August (inclusive) are as follows :—
1/7th Middlesex : Capt. A. E. Bowker (gassed 7th April), Capt. H. K. King (wounded 12.4.18), 2/Lieut. E. D. Beard (wounded 23.4.18), 2/Lieut. J. L. Sullivan (wounded 27.5.18), Lieut. W. S. Fielder and 2/Lieut. Owen (wounded 9.8.18) ; 1/8th Middlesex : 2/Lieut. H. R. Holland (missing 11.4.18), 2/Lieut. H. L. A. Oswald-Hicks (killed 12.4.18), 2/Lieut. J. M. Brodie (killed 16.5.18), 2/Lieut. G. E. Crow (wounded 23.5.18), Capt. W. H. Hale (died 8.6.18), Lieut. I. H. Greenwood (died of wounds 6.7.18).

4TH BATTALION.
25TH AUGUST.

result that the objective was captured at about 6.30 a.m." Eighty Germans, thirteen machine guns and a heavy trench mortar were taken. The Battalion then consolidated the captured position, though a heavy hostile barrage was falling. That evening the 4th Middlesex were relieved by a battalion of the 5th Division and moved back to Achiet-le-Petit.*

During these operations the 4th Middlesex suffered the following casualties : 2/Lieut. H. F. Backhouse and twenty-five other ranks killed ; Captain J. P Jamieson, Lieut. E. A. H. Fenn, 2/Lieuts, R. W. Seaby, J. H. Baird, F. H. Meacham, B. E. Goodwin, B. J. Hurding, H. E. Hodgkinson, W. A. Bloy and 213 other ranks wounded : twenty-five other ranks were missing.†

The 37th Division had cleared Favreuil late on the evening of the 25th August ; Sapignies, Behagnies and Mory had also fallen into our hands. Fighting desperately, the enemy clung tenaciously to his positions, but despite his gallantry could not withstand the onslaught of troops already inspired with the spirit of victory.

---

* The 4th Middlesex being in the area of the "Second Battle of Bapaume," 31st August–3rd September, are entitled to that battle honour, though they made no attack.

† The total for August was 11 officers killed and wounded and 299 other ranks killed, wounded or missing.

CHAPTER XXXVII.

The Advance in Flanders:

18th August–6th September.

WHILE the Advance in Picardy was in progress the Fifth and Second Armies in Flanders had also began to move and maintain ceaseless pressure on the enemy. 19TH, 20TH, 21ST AND 23RD BATTALIONS.

The heavy losses suffered by the enemy had, in July, forced him to shorten his line along the Flanders front, and as early as the 5th of August he had begun to effect local withdrawal on the southern flank of the Lys Salient. The development of the British and French offensive hastened the movement and on the 18th of August our patrols were able to make considerable advance opposite Merville. On the 19th Merville was taken and the British line advanced on the whole front from the Lawe River to the Plate Becque. In this advance the 20th Middlesex (43rd Brigade, 14th Division) and the 19th (Pioneers) and 23rd Middlesex of the 41st Division were concerned.

After the heavy fighting in April the 20th and 21st Middlesex were withdrawn from the line. Both Battalions had been through very heavy fighting and were considerably reduced in strength. On the 31st of May the former Battalion was reduced to Training Cadre and transferred to the 16th Division. On the 17th of June it was transferred to yet another division—the 14th—which embarked for England towards the end of the month to re-form. The 14th Division returned to France in July, the 20th Middlesex forming part of the 43rd Brigade. 21ST BATTALION. 20TH BATTALION.

The 21st Middlesex, however, had seen the last of their fighting days. The Battalion was reduced to Training Cadre strength on the 5th of May, and on the 3rd of June transferred to the 34th Division, to the 39th Division on the 17th of June, and, finally, to the 25th Division on the 29th. The latter Division had also been reduced to Cadre strength, and on the 30th of June left for England to be reconstructed. When, however, the Division 21ST BATTALION. 29TH JUNE.

21ST BATTALION.

returned to France in September the 21st Middlesex were left behind. The 21st was a fine Battalion and, as its record shows, put up many a splendid fight.

20TH BATTALION.
17TH AUGUST.

On the 17th of August the 20th Battalion arrived in the Proven area. On the 18th the Battalion moved to Siege Camp. On the following day the 43rd Brigade relieved the 148th Brigade in the front line in the Zillebeke area, the 20th Middlesex completing their relief at 12.30 a.m. on the 20th. Little, however, but active patrolling took place during this tour which ended on the 23rd/24th. On the night of the 28th/29th August an unfortunate shell caught " C " Company when employed on " working duties." One officer—2/Lieut. H. V. Smith—was killed, and three other ranks wounded.

The first intimation that the enemy was retiring was on the 21st when Brigade Headquarters wired that the enemy had evacuated the Kemmel area, and that he might therefore evacuate the Ypres front. The 20th Middlesex were then in the support line. They went into the front line on the 1st of September,

6TH SEPT.

but by the 6th were back in Orilla Camp in reserve.

About the middle of May the 41st Division again moved into trenches in the Ypres Salient, the 23rd Middlesex on the night

23RD BATTALION.

of the 17th/18th arriving on the north-eastern outskirts of the City. On the 21st/22nd they took over front-line trenches southeast of Potijze. There is nothing to record of this tour which was followed by a month out of the line in training. On the 1st of July the Battalion proceeded to the Kemmel front, moving into the forward trenches that night and relieving French troops. But here again, though movement of the enemy was reported, the Middlesex do not appear to have taken much part in pressing him

6TH SEPT.
19TH BATTALION.
6TH SEPT.

back. On the 6th of September the Battalion was out of the line, working on the defences at Ouderdom. The 6th of September also found the 19th Middlesex (Pioneers of the 41st Division) working on the roads east of Locre, Hallebast and Ouderdom.*

---

* There are no records of officer casualties up to this period in either Battalion.

CHAPTER XXXVIII.

The Breaking of the Hindenburg Line.
THE SECOND BATTLES OF ARRAS, 1918.
(I) THE BATTLE OF THE SCARPE, 1918:
26th–30th August.

THE two days fighting on the 24th and 25th of August in which the 1/7th and 1/8th Middlesex took part before the Battle of the Scarpe, 1918, began, must be looked upon in the light of operations designed to win positions before the defences covering the Hindenburg Line were attacked. As already stated, the two Battalions, with the 63rd Brigade, had reached Blaireville on 23rd August and during the evening of that date relieved the 1st London Regiment in the front line known as Boyelles Reserve Trench. {1/7TH AND 1/8TH BATTALIONS.} {23RD AUGUST.}

The orders to the 63rd Brigade were to attack the enemy on the morning of the 24th, the objective being the German trench known as Summit Trench. The 1/8th Middlesex were detailed to attack on the right, the 1/7th Middlesex in the centre and the 1st London Regiment on the left. {24TH AUGUST.}

The 1/7th Battalion completed the relief by 5 a.m. on the 24th, but during the operations lost R.S.M. W. Burt, who was killed close by Battalion Headquarters. He was a very gallant man, greatly respected by all ranks: he had served at the front ever since the Battalion landed in France.

At 7 a.m. the barrage fell and at once the advance began. This trench covered the village of Croisilles and was about 1,500 yards away. There was no hesitation as our screen of fire fell and swept the enemy's front line, and with " A " Company on the right, " B " on the left, " C " in support and " D " in reserve, the 1/8th Middlesex (Lieut.-Colonel C. H. Pank) advanced on Summit Trench. The latter was reached by 10 a.m. and consolidated, outposts being pushed forward The Battalion had

1/7TH AND 1/8TH BATTALIONS. 24TH AUGUST.

thus gained its objective at a loss of three officers killed (Captain C. J. Keeping and 2/Lieuts. G. E. Cousens and E. Child) and one (2/Lieut. W. J. Thorne) missing. The losses in other ranks were 51 killed or wounded.

On the left of the 1/8th, the 1/7th Battalion (Major P. C. Kay, commanding) similarly reached all its objectives. A small number of prisoners were captured while the Battalion lost about fifty all ranks, Lieut. H. Mummery being among the wounded.

Orders were received late in the afternoon to continue the attack at 7.30 p.m., the objective being Croisilles Reserve and the Hindenburg Line along the Brigade front.

But the enemy put up a very stout resistance: the powerful Hindenburg Line was still a big proposition to tackle and such a storm of machine-gun and rifle fire broke out as the attackers advanced that their progress was soon brought to a standstill. The result of the attack was that both Battalions were forced back to their original starting positions.

The 1/7th lost Lieut. G. E. Adamson and 2/Lieut. R. Cox killed and Captain Shipton wounded; about fifty prisoners and three machine guns had been taken during the day. The 1/8th had one officer—Captain R. F. M. Buller—killed, 2 officers (Lieut. H. F. Dampney and 2/Lieut. W. H. Fuller) wounded and 117 other ranks killed or wounded.

25TH AUGUST.

Throughout the 25th posts were established out in front of Summit Trench, and at about 4 p.m. orders came to hand that the Brigade would attack the enemy on the morning of the 26th at 3 a.m. Fooly Trench and Croisilles Reserve Trench being the objectives of the Brigade.

We were now drawing near the western end of the Hindenburg Line, and if we could turn it from the northern end the enemy would again be forced to retire. But the Germans also saw their danger and fought with desperate courage to frustrate the British intentions. At 3 a.m. on the 26th when the attackers advanced they were met by a perfect hail of machine-gun and rifle bullets, in the face of which it was impossible to advance. From the high ground north-west of Croisilles this fire was particularly deadly. The result was a failure. During the evening the 167th Brigade was relieved and moved back into Divisional Reserve between Boisleux St. Marc and Boisleux au Mont.

The 1/7th lost in this attack 2/Lieut. Pearson wounded and

Bullecourt Again

missing and 2/Lieut. Brewer wounded : 35 other ranks were also killed or wounded. [1/7TH AND 1/8TH BATTALIONS.]

The rest was of short duration, for on the 27th the 1/8th moved back to the line to the trenches in front of Croisilles. Early on the 28th the Battalion pushed out patrols, but they found the village still held by the enemy. Later, however, the Brigade reported that the enemy had vacated Croisilles, whereupon the 1/8th pushed forward platoons to work round north and south of the village. The day's operations cost the Battalion 1 officer (2/Lieut. W. A. Cousins) and 40 other ranks wounded. [27TH AUGUST.]

On this day also the 167th Brigade moved forward again, the 1/7th Middlesex to Boyelles Reserve. On the 29th the 168th and 169th Brigades drove the enemy from Bullecourt, but the latter Brigade had lost very heavily and the 1/7th were ordered to relieve the survivors. The relief was completed by 5.30 a.m. on the 30th August, Hornsey and Tottenham holding a line of posts in front. But hardly was the Battalion in position than the enemy counter-attacked all along the line : Bullecourt, Ecoust and Riencourt were lost, and the two forward Companies of the 1/7th Middlesex were forced back to the sunken road behind them. Here they stood firm and beat off a succession of determined attacks. On the left of the Battalion the 57th Division momentarily lost Fontaine but, supported by cross-fire from the Middlesex, re-took it almost at once.* [29TH AUGUST.]

At 10.45 p.m. verbal orders were received by the 1/7th to attack the enemy on the 31st—zero hour to be 5.15 a.m. [31ST AUGUST.]

Under a creeping barrage the 1/7th Battalion advanced on the left of the 168th Brigade, to which it was still attached. A fierce struggle now took place, but eventually Bullecourt fell into our hands again and the Middlesex captured the Factory northeast of the village. But they paid dearly for their success. Two more officers—Captain C. F. Challen† and Captain Limbrey were both severely wounded, and 79 other ranks were either killed or wounded. The Battalion had now been reduced to a fighting strength of 12 officers and 275 other ranks. The 1/8th remained in support throughout the operations.

That night the 1/7th were relieved and rejoined the 167th Brigade in Boyelles Reserve Trench.

* Here, again, from the operations described on the 31st August, it is obvious the official period of the Battle of the Scarpe, 1918, should be extended to that date.

† Died of wounds two days after the Armistice, 1918, i.e., on the 13th November.

4TH BATTALION.

The end of August saw our troops in a fine position. Their progress had brought them to within assaulting distance of the powerful trench system running from the Hindenburg Line at Quéant to the Lens defences about Drocourt (known as the Drocourt–Quéant Line): if we could break this line the whole of the enemy's organised position on a wide front southwards would be turned. Well indeed might the Germans show unmistakable signs of "nerves." The dramatic success of the Allied troops on various parts of his front and his huge losses in men and material were having a disastrous effect upon the German soldiery.

(II) THE BATTLES OF THE HINDENBURG LINE:

12th September–9th October.

On the morning of the 2nd of September the maze of trenches at the junction of the Drocourt–Quéant Line and the Hindenburg Line was stormed. This most gallant feat resulted in a precipitate retreat of the enemy along the whole front south of the point attacked. "Our troops," records the Official Despatches, "had pushed forward to a depth of over three miles along the Arras–Cambrai road and had reached the outskirts of Buissy. Cagnicourt, Villers-Lez-Cagnicourt and Dury were in our hands: 8,000 prisoners and many guns had been taken."

Black indeed was the German horizon!

In the Battle of Havrincourt, 12th September, and the Battle of Epéhy, 18th September, no battalion of the Middlesex Regiment took part, but if they saw none of the actual fighting they were, with their Brigade and Division, pushing on in rear of those who were engaged in breaking the resistance of the enemy.

On the 12th of September the IVth and VIth Corps of the Third Army attacked on a front of about five miles in the Havrincourt Sector, the 37th Division being amongst the divisions employed. Trescault was taken by the 37th Division and Havrincourt fell again to the 62nd Division. The 4th Middlesex had, however, withdrawn on the previous day to the ruins of Velu Château, as the 63rd Brigade was to be in reserve during the battle.

3RD SEPT.

Between the 20th August and the 3rd of September the 4th Middlesex made no move: they were engaged largely in salvage work. But on the latter date (the 37th Division having been ordered to relieve the 5th Division) the Battalion began to move forward at 3.30 p.m. via Achiet-le-Grand. At Favreuil tea was issued and the march afterwards continued via Beugny and Fremicourt, the Battalion eventually relieving the 14th Royal Warwicks of the 13th Brigade. The 63rd Brigade was now in support of the 112th Brigade, engaged in pursuing the enemy. The Somersets were on the right of the Brigade front and the Middlesex on the left. 4TH BATTALION. 3RD SEPT.

All along the British front there was intense enthusiasm: everyone knew the Bosche was hard put to it to hold up our advance. He did this by means of machine-gun posts in depth, that is when he had nothing but shell holes or woods to cling to. With great tenacity he was holding to his last system of organised defence—the Hindenburg Line—which, where it had not already been broken, was still a formidable obstacle. Yet no one doubted that "Jerry" was "on the run." Back across the old Somme battlefields, which had seen the ebb and flow of many a bloody contest, he was being chased for the last time.

On the 4th the Middlesex came in for a dose of "sneezing gas": on the 5th the 63rd Brigade relieved the left brigade of the New Zealanders in the line and during the night the enemy's shell fire was again heavy. On the 6th the Brigade began to advance through Havrincourt Wood with a view to clearing it of the enemy, in view of the forthcoming operations. Two companies of the Middlesex were attached to the 8th Lincolnshire and two to the 8th Somersets. 4TH SEPT.

Slowly the enemy was falling back but he was given no time to change his mind, the pursuit being vigorous. On the 7th the Middlesex, in moving up along Oxford Valley, were barraged by the enemy and had Lieut. Marshall and twelve other ranks casualties. By the 10th Havrincourt Wood had been cleared and a line handed over to the attacking brigades of the 37th Division, along the eastern and north-eastern edges of the Wood.

The general results of the attack on the 12th of September were that both Trescault and Havrincourt villages were taken and positions secured of considerable importance in forthcoming operations. 12TH SEPT.

At 7 a.m. on the 18th the Fourth and Third Armies, in heavy rain, attacked on a front of about seventeen miles from Holnon to 18TH SEPT.

4TH BATTALION.
18TH SEPT.

Gouzeaucourt and again broke into the enemy's lines to a depth of three miles. This advance was made through the deep, continuous and well-organised defences formed by the old British and German lines. Epéhy had also fallen into our hands.

The 37th Division was not in this attack—the Middlesex throughout the 18th were holding the eastern edge of Havrincourt Wood.

At the close of the Battle of Epéhy a conference took place between Sir Douglas Haig and Marshal Foch as to future operations. The decision arrived at was that four convergent and simultaneous offensives should be launched by the Allies (i) by the Americans west of the Meuse in the direction of Mezieres, (ii) by the French west of Argonne in close co-operation with the American attack and with the same general objectives, (iii) by the British on the St. Quentin–Cambrai front in the general direction of Maubeuge and (iv) by the Belgians and Allied forces in Flanders in the direction of Ghent.

"The results to be obtained from these different attacks depended in a particularly large degree upon the British attack in the centre. It was here that the enemy's defences were most highly organised. If these were broken, the threat directed at his vital system of lateral communication would of necessity react upon his defences elsewhere."

With troops who had been marching and fighting for weeks and were in need of rest, faced with the danger of reviving the declining moral of the German Army if he failed, Sir Douglas Haig nevertheless determined that the British attack was necessary and, moreover, that it was the essential part of the whole scheme.

The Official Despatches should be studied for a description of the Hindenburg Line at this period, with its powerful trench system. It was terribly strong both in natural and artificial defences.

(III) THE BATTLE OF THE CANAL DU NORD:

27th September–1st October.

The great battle known officially by the above title, but named by Sir Douglas Haig as the Battle of Cambrai and the Hindenburg Line, opened at 5.20 a.m. on the 27th of September. On the evening of the 26th September, between the neighbour-

hood of St. Quentin and the Scheldt, the Fourth, Third and First 4TH, 1/7TH
Armies (from right to left) held a line running from Salency AND 1/8TH
(west of St. Quentin) to Gricourt and Pontruet, thence east of BATTALIONS.
Villeret and Lempire to Villers-Guislain and Gouzeaucourt (both
the latter were in the German lines).

A very heavy bombardment was to be opened during the night
of 26th/27th along the fronts of all three Armies: this was to be
followed on the morning of the 27th by an attack by the Third 27TH SEPT.
and First Armies only, so as to deceive the enemy as to the main
front of attack.

The front of attack of the Third and First Armies was about
thirteen miles in extent, from Gouzeaucourt to the neighbourhood of Sauchy Lestree. This narrative, however, needs but a
brief comment on the general situation for both the 4th Middlesex
of the 37th Division, and the 1/7th and 1/8th of the 56th Division,
are entitled to the battle honour, these Battalions were in reserve,
the first-named in Third Army Reserve and the last in First Army
Reserve.

The results of the operations of the 27th and 28th of September
were that a wide break had been made in the Hindenburg Line—
the enemy's last stronghold. At the close of the first day of the
battle our troops had reached the line Beaucourt–Ribecourt–
Fontaine Notre Dame—east of Haynecourt–Epinoy–Oisy le
Verger. On the 28th, after the advance was continued, 28TH SEPT.
Gouzeaucourt, Marcoing, Noyelles sur l'Escaut, Fontaine Notre
Dame, Sailly and Palluel were taken.

(IV) THE BATTLE OF THE ST. QUENTIN CANAL:

29th September–2nd October.

At 5.50 a.m. on the 29th September the Fourth Army, supported by an intense artillery barrage, attacked on a front of
twelve miles between Holnon and Vendhuille. On the right of
the Fourth Army the First French Army continued the attack on
the St. Quentin Sector: on the left two corps of the Third Army
(Vth and IVth) had attacked at an earlier hour between Vendhuille
and Marcoing and had heavy fighting at Villers-Guislain, Gonnelieu
and the Welsh Ridge.

1ST AND 18TH BATTALIONS.

In the Vth Corps of the Third Army was the 33rd Division, containing the 1st Battalion (98th Brigade) and 18th (Pioneer) Battalion of the Middlesex Regiment.

After the heavy fighting on the Lys in April the 33rd Division was relieved and moved back to a rest area, the 98th Brigade marching to Blaringhem area on the 1st May, but the Brigade was only one day in this locality, for on the 2nd sudden orders were received to march to the Busseboom area, under orders of the 49th Division, until the arrival of 33rd Divisional Headquarters: the Brigade was also to be at the tactical disposal of the 19th Division in case the latter was seriously attacked. By the 3rd the 98th Brigade group was located in its new area, and at 12 noon on the 4th orders were received to relieve the 56th Brigade in the line from Ridge Wood (inclusive) to north-east of Elzenwalle: the 1st Middlesex (Lieut.-Colonel J. H. Hall) taking over the northern portion of the front line. Both on the 5th and 6th warnings were received of an intended hostile attack, but it did not materialise. Very early on the 8th, however, the enemy's guns began an intense bombardment of battery positions, back and forward areas; the French on the right were also heavily shelled. Two German prisoners, captured at 5.30 a.m., said the enemy was attacking at 7.30 a.m. with Dickebusch village and lake as their objectives. Our guns at once opened fire. At 7.45 no attack had developed along the 98th Brigade front, but ten minutes later British troops were seen falling back on the right, and at 9.15 a.m. German infantry were observed advancing along the general line Vierstraat to Hallebast cross-roads. Machine-gun and rifle fire was opened on them and they retired. The 2nd Argyll and Sutherland Highlanders, on the right of the 1st Middlesex, swung back their right flank. At 7 p.m. the 19th Infantry Brigade counter-attacked and restored the situation, driving the enemy out of all the positions he had occupied. On the 11th the 98th Brigade was relieved by French Troops and marched back to camp north of Abeele. The 1st Middlesex were near Watou and here the Battalion celebrated Albuhera Day, sending the Colonel of the Regiment (Lieut.-General H. Kent) the following message: "Albuhera: Heartiest greetings from all ranks 57th." A telegram of best wishes was also received from the 77th.

It was June before the Battalion moved back into the front line again, relieving the 16th K.R.R. on the southern side of the Ypres–Comines Canal, north of Voormezeele. On the night of

1ST MAY.

8TH MAY.

11TH MAY.

the 19th/20th the Battalion raided the enemy, the raiding party consisting of 2/Lieut. Jackson and 51 other ranks. But no identification was obtained though a stiff fight ensued. On the 14th of July the 1st Middlesex, in conjunction with the 2nd D.L.I., carried out a small operation " to retake G.H.Q.I. Line " which, apparently, had included Elzenwalle. This small affair was entirely successful and 41 Germans were taken prisoner, four machine guns also being captured. The remainder of the month was without incident. August found the Battalion still in the line in the Canal Sector. On the 4th of August the Middlesex moved back to Brandhoek. They went back again into the front line but on the 28th, being then out of the trenches, they entrained at St. Omer for the south : they had seen the last of the Ypres Salient. The train carried the Battalion via Aire, Berquette and St. Pol to Doullens, and at 2.15 a.m. on the 29th reached its destination. After detraining the Middlesex marched along the Doullens–Arras road to Pommera where they billeted. Fourteen days were spent in training and resting and then, on 15th of September, the 33rd Division, having joined the Vth Corps, movement orders arrived for the Middlesex to travel by bus to Les Bœufs.

[margin: 1st Battalion. 19th/20th June.]

The 16th was spent in fitting the Battalion for the line and trenches at Equancourt (into which the Middlesex were to move) were reconnoitred. On the 17th the Battalion marched to Equancourt, on the 18th was in position just east of Dessart Wood, and on the 19th took over support positions in the 98th Brigade Sector in front (west) of Villers-Guislain. Desultory fighting went on for two or three days and then on the night 23rd/24th September, the 1st Middlesex relieved the 2nd Argyll and Sutherland Highlanders on the right of the Brigade front, the former occupying a line south-east of Villers-Guislain. That night the 100th Brigade, on the right of the Middlesex, attacked the enemy in a northerly direction. The Middlesex were to assist in the attack by bombing southwards to near the left battalion of the 100th Brigade. They bombed a certain distance but found no sign of the battalion in question. On the night of 24th/25th September Villers-Guislain was subjected to two " gas projectile shoots " : a similar operation took place on the night 25th/26th. On the 26th the Battalion moved back to support positions west of Chapel Crossing. On the 28th Lieut. T. T. Soby was wounded in the head.

[margin: 16th Sept.]

[margin: 28th Sept.]

1ST BATTALION.

On the night of the 28th/29th the 1st Middlesex relieved the 5th Scottish Rifles in readiness for operations on the 29th.

The objectives allotted to the Battalion ran from Derby Post to the eastern end of Villers Hill : zero hour was 3.30 a.m.

The dispositions by companies were : "A" on the right, "D" in the centre, and "C" on the left : "B" Company was detailed to "mop up" the enemy's position.

29TH SEPT.

The attack was launched at 3.30 a.m. under an intense artillery barrage. At first all three of the attacking battalions of the 98th Brigade (1st Middlesex, 4th King's and 2nd Argyll and Sutherland Highlanders) reported progress. But later a check occurred. Villers-Guislain had been stormed and partially cleared of the enemy, but the latter began to filter back again into the village. The centre company of the Middlesex met with strong opposition at Gloster Road and "B" Company, after capturing 200 Germans, found itself surrounded and cut off. The C.O. of the Battalion reported the situation at 1 p.m. which showed but little progress and concluded with the statement that "remaining dispositions of 'C' and 'B' not known, 'C' believed to have gone forward to 'X.10.C.8.0.' (Villers Ridge), 'B' Company (three platoons) believed gone forward east along High Street, position obscure."

How the missing companies extricated themselves is unknown but they must have done so for the casualty list shows only 20 other ranks "missing."

30TH SEPT.

During the night of the 30th patrols observed that "the Bosche had gone back," and the line was therefore pushed forward to the Green Line, which ran on the Middlesex front from northwest to south-east just west of Honnecourt Wood, and from these positions patrols were sent out to the St. Quentin Canal to hold the crossings.

In the operations on the 29th of September the 1st Middlesex lost 4 officers (Lieuts. J. N. Beeman, D. W. Hay, J. C. B. Brown and E. S. Mathews) and 71 other ranks killed, 2 officers and 143 other ranks wounded, 1 officer and 16 other ranks "gassed" and 20 other ranks missing.

1ST OCTOBER.

On the 1st of October the Middlesex were holding the crossings of the St. Quentin Canal at Honnecourt. The village was clear of the enemy, but the troops holding the forward line were subjected to heavy sniping from some ruined houses on the canal. The canal could not be crossed as the footbridge had been destroyed and all approaches to it were swept by hostile machine-gun fire.

The Middlesex were relieved on the night of the 2nd of October 1ST BATTALION. and marched back to the neighbouthood of Vaucelette Farm in reserve.*

All along the front of the attack by the Third and Fourth Armies splendid progress had again been made, the enemy abandoning many villages which he found it impossible to hold in the face of our advance.

In the Battle of Beaurevoir, 3rd–5th October, the Middlesex were not engaged, and it was not until the Battle of Cambrai, 1918, began on the 8th of October that the Regiment again took part 8TH OCTOBER. in the operations.

(VI) THE BATTLE OF CAMBRAI, 1918: 8th–9th OCTOBER, AND THE PURSUIT TO THE SELLE RIVER.

In this Battle no less than six battalions of the Regiment took 1ST, 4TH, part, or are entitled to the Battle Honour as being in the immedi- 1/7TH, 1/8TH, ate area of the operations. They are the 1st and 18th Battalions BATTALIONS. (33rd Division), 4th (37th Division), 1/7th and 1/8th (56th Division) and 13th (24th Division).

On the evening of the 7th of October the front of the Fourth, Third and First British Armies from north of St. Quentin, at about Thorigny (where we joined up with the left of the First French Army), ran northwards through Montbrehain, Beaurevoir, thence crossing the road between Aubencheul and Villers-Outreux to Crevecœur, round the western outskirts of Cambrai and Abancourt, thence along the southern bank of the Sensée to Ecourt St. Quentin.

The great battle which was to open the next morning was the second and concluding phase of the British offensive in which the Fourth and Third Armies, with the right of the First Army, were to move forward with their left flank on the canal which runs from Cambrai to Mons, their right covered by the First French Army.

Having completed all arrangements the Third Army attacked at 4.30 a.m. and the First Army at 5.10 a.m. on the 8th of October:

* On the 4th of October Lieut.-Colonel J. H. Hall left the 1st Middlesex on appointment as Brigadier-General commanding the 197th Infantry Brigade. Major D. C. Owen assumed command of the Battalion.

4TH BATTALION.
8TH OCTOBER.

the front of attack extended from the right of the Fourth Army at Sequehart to the left of the Third Army just south of Cambrai. It is, however, with the attack of the Third and First Armies that this narrative deals, the 24th, 33rd and 37th Divisions belonging to the former Army and the 56th Division to the latter.

The 37th Division, to which had been allotted as a first objective that portion of the Masnieres–Beaurevoir line which lay on its front, and the sunken roads south of Lesdain, attacked with the 111th Brigade in front : the 112th Brigade was to capture the next objective, the high ground between Hurtebise Farm and Le Grand Pont : and to exploit success to east of Briseaux Wood. The 63rd Brigade was in reserve to be called upon at any moment.

Along the front generally our infantry and tanks quickly penetrated the enemy's front, for by this time he was fast wavering and his attacks were less stubborn.

It was, however, 6.30 a.m. on the 8th before the 63rd Brigade began to move forward, the Somersets and Lincolnshire taking up positions north-east of Gouzeaucourt and north of Gonnelieu respectively. The 4th Middlesex had, on the previous night, been attached to the 112th Brigade and had received orders to be at the Canal de l'Escaut at 2 a.m. on the 8th. In due course the Battalion reached its destination and, crossing the Canal, bivouacked in the neighbourhood of Vaucelles Copse. At 6.30 a.m. the Battalion moved on to the rendezvous at the western edge of Briseaux Wood. " C " and " D " Companies pushed forward as soon as the wood was cleared, but were held up by the machine-gun fire in front and from Guillemin Farm. The Battalion then fell back to the western edge of the wood where later they were joined by the Lincolnshire and Somersets, who took up positions north of the wood and south-west of Esnes, which during the day had been captured by the New Zealanders.

The Lincolnshire and Somersets carried out a night attack and reached the high ground east of the Esnes–Guillemin Farm road.*

Late that night orders stated that the 63rd Brigade was to carry on the advance of the 37th Division first to a line east of Haucourt. Zero hour on the 9th was to be at 5.30 a.m.

The Middlesex were in support of the Lincolnshire and Somersets when the advance began on the morning of the 9th of

---

* The losses of the 4th Middlesex on the 8th of October were 2 officers (2/Lieuts. H. E. Hodkinson and A. F. Stafford) wounded, and 41 other ranks killed or wounded.

October. But the enemy had again fallen back, on this occasion 4TH BATTALION. to Caudry, and there was little actual fighting to be done, for the 112th Brigade passed through the 63rd in pursuit of the enemy. 9TH OCTOBER. The 4th Middlesex that night billeted in Haucourt.

At midnight on the 9th the Middlesex were ordered to move to rendezvous at 3 a.m. (10th October) west of Ligny-en-Cambresis to support an attack on Caudry: the Lincolnshire and Somersets were to rendezvous also in the same neighbourhood, in order to go through the 112th Brigade and carry on the advance.

But there was no opposition when the 112th Brigade attacked, and the 4th Middlesex, passing through Caudry, formed up at Petit Caudry. The Lincolnshire and Somersets, passing through the 112th Brigade, went on to a line west of the Selle, the Middlesex following in support to Clermont Château. The Battalion Diary has the following interesting entry: "When the Battalion marched through Caudry they received a most enthusiastic welcome from some thousand civilians and were hailed as their deliverers from the enemy. The town was quite intact with the exception of one or two houses." But the Diary would have been more interesting if only some note had been added as to how many of the original 4th Middlesex of August, 1914, were serving with the Battalion during that dramatic period when once again, after four years, they were passing over the old field of the Battle of Le Cateau (26th August, 1914). For on the 10th October, 1918, 10TH OCTOBER. the Battalion passed over the very roads down which their comrades of 1914 had tramped, tired, thirsty and dusty, after a thirty-miles march to the little village of Audencourt, just west of Beaumont, where they billeted for the night 25th/26th August.

On the 11th the Middlesex moved forward to support the 11TH OCTOBER. Lincolnshire and Somersets who had pushed two platoons across the river. During the day there had been a certain amount of shell fire.

Orders had been received that the attack was to be continued on the morning of the 12th of October. The objective of the 63rd Brigade was the high ground east of the river and just east of the Neuvilly-Solesmes road. The Middlesex were to lead the attack of the Brigade at 5 a.m., with " A " Company on the right, " B " in the centre, and " D " Company on the left : " C " Company was to be in support to follow at a distance of 800 yards and " mop up " the railway line and help consolidate the main line of resistance.

I

**4TH BATTALION.
12TH OCTOBER.**

The barrage fell at zero with good effects on the right, but with poor results on the left. Heavy machine-gun fire from Bellevue and from the railway line in front encountered the advance and momentarily checked it, but the centre company, under 2/Lieut. H. M. Chaundy, gave the enemy " ten rounds rapid," which so demoralised him that he abandoned his machine guns and the advance continued. The railway line was thus gained by the centre and right companies and rifle fire opened on the retreating enemy. Sergeant Harris of " A " Company, having discovered that a German officer and his orderly were hiding in a tunnel under the railway, went in pursuit and killed both. The advance from the railway to the final objective (the high ground east of the railway) was then carried out without resistance.

The left company, however, suffering heavy casualties from machine-gun fire from Bellevue, was held up in its attack on that place. The German machine guns were stubborn and could not be put out of action. Only 2/Lieut. Bloy with a section, on the right of the company, succeeded in crossing the railway and took up position on the high ground left of " B " Company, but the remainder of the left company were forced to form a defensive flank.

The support company crossed the river through the enemy's barrage and sent a platoon to fill the gap between the centre and left companies: the other three platoons echeloned to the left to protect the flank from the north.

The enemy now discovered that the attack was not being pressed further, and began to dribble back in small parties to the high ground east of the Middlesex and then to push men down the railway from Bellevue where he opened fire on the Battalion then engaged in consolidating their positions. Orders were then received to withdraw to the line of the railway, but it was found impossible to hold the latter owing to the heavy enfilade fire the enemy had brought to bear upon it. The Middlesex were then withdrawn to the sunken road between the river and the railway where a line was organised. Patrols were pushed forward to the railway when the capture of Bellevue was reported, but the Battalion was relieved and moved back to Caudry.*

---

* The losses of the 4th Middlesex in this action were :—Killed : Capt. G. N. Viner, 2/Lieuts. W. J. Turner and R. E. McFadden and 19 other ranks. Wounded : Capt. A. J. Klaiber, Lieut. J. B. Bucknill, 2/Lieuts. J. P. Lindsay, J. L. Selfe and A. G. Andrews (died of wounds 14.10.18), and 95 other ranks : 15 other ranks were missing.

Meanwhile the 1st Middlesex (33rd Division) had been moving 1ST BATTALION. slowly forward in rear of the advanced troops. On the morning 9TH OCTOBER. of the 9th October the Battalion reached assembly positions west of Villers-Outreaux, as the 19th Infantry Brigade (the Advanced Guard of the Division) had passed through the outpost line of the 38th Division, the advance progressing well, Clary having been captured. At 9.30 that night a message reached the 1st Middlesex that " Bertry had been taken and some troops of the 19th Infantry Brigade are believed to be in Troisvilles, but latter not yet confirmed."

Bertry! Troisvilles! The 19th Infantry Brigade knew these two places well in 1914 in the Battle of Le Cateau: the 1st Middlesex then formed part of the Brigade, and it will be remembered how the Battalion with the 2nd Argyll and Sutherland Highlanders, in a gallant effort to cover the retirement of troops just west of Le Cateau, had a desperate fight with the enemy on the high ground north-east of Reumont.

And here again in 1918, just over four years after that fierce contest, they had come again to the scene of what was almost a titanic struggle : but on this occasion the Bosche was the fleeing enemy.

Late at night on the 9th of October the 98th Brigade was ordered to continue the advance at dawn next morning, the Argyll and Sutherland Highlanders on the right, 4th King's on the left, 1st Middlesex in support moving in rear of the King's men and protecting the left flank of the Brigade.

At 3 a.m. on the 10th, therefore, the Middlesex moving off 10TH OCTOBER. passed through Clary to a position east of Bertry, thence south of Troisvilles to the Inchy–Le Cateau road. From this position companies took up position just south of Rambourlieux Farm.

At 5 a.m. the Highlanders advanced under a heavy barrage to secure the high ground south-west of Forest to the cross-roads some two thousand yards west, the Middlesex being warned to be prepared to advance east and continue the defensive flank facing Montay, in touch with the 4th King's who were on the Le Cateau–Neuvilly railway on the left. During the day 2/Lieut. E. F. Johnson was wounded.

At 1.45 a.m., 11th October, the Middlesex were ordered to 11TH OCTOBER. form a defensive flank, with " A " and " B " Companies, against Neuvilly, under Captain Belsham : " C " and " D " Companies to " stand fast." At 9.10 a.m. the general situation was that a

<small>1ST BATTALION.</small> line was held just west of the Selle, with a small party of the Highlanders in a strong point on the eastern bank of the river*: the Middlesex were on a line north and south from north of Rambourlieux Farm to south of the Le Cateau–Inchy road.

<small>12TH OCTOBER.</small> Orders then came to hand that the 100th Brigade would pass through the 98th Brigade and attack the high ground east of the river. The attack took place at 5 a.m. on the 12th. This attack proceeded well at first, but both flanks were in the air and later the Middlesex were ordered forward to support the 100th Brigade. The 1st Battalion then dug in, in a ravine west of the Selle.

Subsequently the Middlesex were ordered to attack the enemy, capture first the crossings over the Selle on their front, and then a portion of the cross-roads north-east of the river. But, apparently, before the attack could take place the enemy had retired, for instead of attacking, the whole Brigade (98th) was reorganised, the Middlesex taking over a sector along the western bank of the Selle between Montay and Neuvilly with posts on the river, Battalion Headquarters being established in Rambourlieux Farm <small>13TH OCTOBER.</small> at 3.30 a.m. on the 13th of October. Thus the 1st Battalion had also reached the line of the Selle.†

<small>13TH BATTALION. 9TH OCTOBER.</small> The 24th Division (containing the 13th Middlesex, 73rd Brigade) had relieved the 63rd Division at Niergnies during the latter part of the 8th of October. On the morning of the 9th the Division, following close on the heels of the enemy, reached Awoignt, the 73rd Brigade occupying the village and taking up a line in advance of that place. The Brigade gained touch with the enemy at about midday, and found him occupying the line Cagnocles–Cauroir. The 13th Middlesex were in support during this advance.

---

* The 2nd Argyll and Sutherland Highlanders had made their attack with great gallantry and determination, having to wade and, even in places, swim across the river.

† Of the 18th Middlesex (the Pioneers of the 33rd Division) there is little of outstanding importance to record. Their work, as everyone knows who served in France and Flanders, was always strenuous, and during the stages of the Advance to Victory their devotion to duty, their splendid efforts in repairing the roads and communications were beyond all praise. Many a successful attack was in no small measure due to the fine way in which the gallant Pioneers had repaired the communications, which enabled guns and transport to move forward rapidly to the support of the fighting infantry.

Casualties amongst officers of the 18th Middlesex from the end of March, 1918, were: 2/Lieut. F. T. Smith, wounded 30.3.18; 2/Lieut. F. C. Wright, killed 14.4.18; 2/Lieuts. H. C. Bradbury and H. P. Boreham, killed 16.4.18; 2/Lieut. H. S. Barber, wounded 7.5.18; 2/Lieut. H. A. A. Howell, wounded 26.9.18.

On the 1st of April Lieut.-Colonel H. C. McNeille joined the Battalion and assumed command until the 2nd of October, when he broke his ankle and was evacuated to hospital on the 4th, Major C. P. Hinman assuming command.

The 13th Middlesex, after the heavy fighting south of the Somme in March, had moved on the 4th of April to the Bois de Gentelles, where the 73rd Brigade continued in support of the 17th Brigade. On the 5th they withdrew to Longeau where buses carried the Battalion to Saleux. On the 8th the Battalion reached Fressonville where nine days were spent in training. During this period (on the 14th) Lieut.-Colonel J. Greene was appointed to command the 10th Infantry Brigade (4th Division) and Major A. M. Hingley assumed command of the 13th Middlesex. _{13TH BATTALION.}

The 24th Division was transferred north to the Loos sector about the middle of April and the Middlesex arrived at Houdain on the 17th where a further period was spent in training before the Battalion marched to Bully Grenay on the 30th. On the following night (1st/2nd May) they went into the front line in the Hill 70 sector. On the 3rd Lieut. S. J. Squibb was wounded. On the 17th of June the Battalion made a very successful raid on the enemy: one officer—2/Lieut. G. J. Haynes—was killed. On the 19th of July 2/Lieut. H. G. Tickle was wounded "whilst making a very gallant attempt to secure identifications from the enemy." Another officer—2/Lieut. J. W. Pastfield—was killed on the 9th of September whilst walking round his posts on the outskirts of Lens.

July, August and September were quiet months in the line, for the enemy's attention was riveted further south where slowly he was being pressed back. It was not until the 1st of October that the 13th Middlesex were once again on the move. On that date they marched to Hersin and entrained for Montecourt, thence moving to Pommera where they billeted. They entrained at Pommera on the 6th for Hermies and marched to a point east of Mœuvres. On the 7th they marched to Graincourt, and on the 8th to the Rumilly area, from which place (as already stated) they, with other troops of the 73rd Brigade, pushed on to Niergnies where the 24th Division was relieving the 63rd.

The Middlesex spent the night of the 9th/10th October in the railway cutting in front of Awoignt. When dawn broke on the 10th it was found that the enemy had retired as far as Rieux, whither he was followed by the 9th Royal Sussex. But before reaching that place the Middlesex passed through the Sussex and pushed on until they met cyclists and cavalry who reported that the Germans were holding a line beyond Rieux and Avesnes. _{9TH/10TH OCTOBER.}

13TH BATTALION.
10TH OCTOBER.

The Battalion was then ordered to advance and succeeded in gaining the high ground north-east of Rieux, the objective allotted to it. This advance was not a bloodless affair, for it was made under heavy artillery and machine-gun fire, and at the close of the day the Battalion casualties had amounted to 6 officers and 100 other ranks, killed, wounded or missing.

"A," "C" and "D" Companies held the front line with "B" in close support, but the latter was subsequently pushed on into the forward line. This position was held during the night

11TH OCTOBER. of the 10th/11th. The next morning "B" Company, in the right centre, made a gallant attempt to extend the line along a sunken road, but met with considerable opposition: 2/Lieut. W. Earle was killed and Captain Clark wounded. During the morning, however, the line was established.

On this day also the C.O.—Lieut.-Colonel A. M. Hingley—was wounded by a machine-gun bullet while visiting the line, and Major R. S. Dove assumed command of the Battalion.

At about 6 a.m. the 17th Brigade passed through the line of the 73rd Brigade to continue the attack. The Middlesex were under heavy shell fire all night and during the following morning until they were withdrawn to billets in Rieux, where they remained

13TH OCTOBER. until the 13th when a move was made to Avesnes-Les-Aubert.

The 56th Division was on the northern fringe of the great battle which opened on the 8th of October, but there was therefore little actual fighting for the 1/7th and 1/8th Middlesex of the 167th Brigade.

1/7TH AND 1/8TH BATTALIONS.

The Brigade on the 1st of September was established in camp south of Boyelles, where cleaning-up, training, resting, etc., were carried on until the 8th when the Brigade Group moved by route march to relieve the 3rd Brigade in the Feuchy–St. Laurent Blagny area. In this position a few more days were spent until on the 13th the 167th Brigade relieved the 168th in the Estang–Lecluse sector, the 1/8th Middlesex and 1st Londons taking over the front line, and the 1/7th remaining in support. The 1/8th, beyond normal shelling, had "nothing to report" and were relieved on the night of 18th/19th. The 1/7th took over front-line trenches in the Recourt sector on the 17th, but there was "little doing" and the Battalion Diary reports that between 19th and 25th it was engaged in "holding front line, sending out patrols nightly and making a new main line of resistance."

The Battalion was relieved by the 1/8th on the following night

Palluel and Arleux

and, in view of the operations to be carried out by the Canadian Corps, 11th Division, and the 168th and 169th Brigades of the 56th Division, Colonel Pank advanced his headquarters. During the day patrols endeavoured to push out towards the Canal du Nord and also to Palluel, but little progress could be made owing to hostile machine-gun fire and snipers. Again at 4.30 a.m. on the 28th a patrol, consisting of a platoon, was sent out to reconnoitre Palluel. At 7.58 a report came to hand that the village had been occupied by the patrol which had captured eight prisoners and two machine guns.

1/7TH AND 1/8TH BATTALIONS.

Reinforcements, consisting of two platoons, were then sent out with instructions to proceed to Arleux, but no progress could be made as the enemy had machine-gun posts covering the approaches. Posts and supporting points were, however, established on all avenues of approach to Palluel. At 9 a.m. a patrol, moving on the Canal du Nord, reached the Canal, but then had to withdraw as our barrage was covering the advance of the 168th and 169th Brigades along the Canal from the south.

At 5.20 p.m., owing to a statement by a German prisoner that Arleux was only lightly held, Colonel Pank gave instructions for that place to be occupied. Under a barrage a patrol of one platoon, supported by another, advanced on Arleux and succeeded in occupying the southern portion of the village. A platoon was then sent forward in support, while another was sent off to Palluel.

But at about 3.30 p.m. on the 29th the Germans placed a heavy barrage of gas and high-explosive and machine-gun fire on Arleux, and the 1/8th were driven out and fell back on Palluel. That night they were relieved and moved back to reserve. The casualties of the Battalion from the 27th to 30th were 2 other ranks killed, 3 officers (2/Lieuts. G. E. Cross, H. J. P. Hull and H. J. Bowyer) and 61 other ranks wounded and 12 missing.

On the night of the 5th/6th of October the 167th Brigade relieved the 169th Brigade, the 1/7th Middlesex taking over the front line from the Queen's Westminsters, which consisted of a line of outposts from the Canal de la Sensée to the Canal du Nord. For several days active patrolling was carried out, the enemy being found continually on the alert. On the 12th, however, the Brigade ordered the 1/7th to seize the high ground east of Arleux, clear the village and Palluel and the eastern bank of the Canal du Nord. Preceded by strong patrols, the Battalion pushed forward immediately through Palluel and Arleux. Slight

12TH OCTOBER.

1/7TH AND 1/8TH BATTALIONS.

opposition from rifle and machine-gun fire was met with, but twenty prisoners were taken and the objective ordered by the Brigade reached, the Middlesex establishing a line of outposts along the Canal de la Sensée from the Glass Works to Point du Cartin. The 13th found the 1/7th Battalion still in possession of these posts, the enemy holding the opposite bank of the Canal, very much on the alert, as on the approach of patrols he immediately opened his rifle and machine-gun fire. The Battalion was relieved on this date and moved back, two companies to Hamel, and one each on the eastern and western sides of the Canal du Nord.

9TH OCTOBER.

The 1/8th did not move up to the front line until the night of the 9th of October, when they relieved the 4th Londons in the Palluel sector. They also carried out active patrolling and endeavoured to cross the Canal de la Sensée, without result.

CHAPTER XXXIX.

The Final Advance.

I. IN FLANDERS:

28th September–11th November.

THE BATTLES OF YPRES, 1918:

28th September–2nd October.

WHILE the Hindenburg Line was being stormed and broken the advance in Flanders proceeded apace. By the 6th of September the Lys Salient had disappeared and by that evening Kemmel Hill was once more in our hands and our troops had reached the general line Givenchy–Neuve Chapelle–Nieppe–Ploegsteert–Voormezeele.

At a conference at Cassel on the 9th of September details of operations to be carried out by the Allied Armies were discussed and decided. An attack was to be launched on the 28th of September by a certain number of divisions of the Second British Army (under General Plumer), some French divisions and the Belgian Army, the whole to be commanded by the King of the Belgians. The Second British Army was to attack on a front of about 4½ miles, south of the Ypres–Zonnebeke road, the 14th, 9th and 29th Divisions delivering the initial assault, supported later by the 41st and 36th Divisions: the Belgian Army, on the left of the British, was to continue the attack as far as Dixmude. There was to be no preliminary bombardment, but a barrage was to be placed on the enemy's trenches at zero, which had been fixed at 5.20 a.m.

Of the 14th Division the 43rd Brigade was to attack astride the Ypres–Comines Canal, with the 20th Middlesex on the right (south of the Canal), the 12th Suffolks on the left (north of the Canal), 10th H.L.I. in reserve. The 42nd Brigade was attacking on the right of the 43rd. This attack was a difficult operation for

20TH BATTALION.

20TH
BATTALION.
28TH SEPT.

the 43rd Brigade as it had to capture the Bluff, which had been turned by the enemy into an almost impregnable fortress, bristling with machine guns and trench mortars.

The Middlesex were to form up for the attack on Middlesex Road, and the two objectives allotted to the Battalion were (i) a farm on the southern Canal bank opposite the Bluff, thence the north-western and southern edges of Triangular Wood, (ii) in front of the Canal bank thence to and including White Château.

By 5 a.m. companies were in position in the assembly line, this operation having been carried out without noise or interference from the enemy, all helmets, brasses and bayonets having been dulled.

At 5.20 a.m. punctually the barrage fell and at once the attacking troops, moving forward in "worm" formation, advanced to the attack. The enemy was taken completely by surprise and although the Bluff (north of the Canal) proved a hard nut to crack at first, it was taken by an enveloping movement. South of the Canal the 20th Middlesex (Major W. W. Milne commanding) pushed on without much opposition, reached the White Château and finally occupied the exact position previously arranged for their final halting place, with the exception of the extreme right section which should have rested on the northern end of the Damstrasse. The latter was, however, in the possession of the enemy. A defensive flank was therefore formed which secured the right flank of the White Château.

In his report the Brigadier said: "I should like to draw attention to the fine fighting spirit of the men. Although looked down on before the fight as 'B' men of an inferior type to the 'A' men, they showed all the energy, keenness and fighting spirit of 'A' men, and although they may not be physically capable of undergoing the same hardship for a long duration, I feel the utmost confidence in them."

The 20th Middlesex lost in this attack 13 other ranks killed, 2 officers and 58 other ranks wounded, 6 other ranks missing. They captured 210 prisoners, one 3 in. and five 77 mm. guns and ten machine-guns.

The advance continued on the 29th but by about 2 p.m. the 20th Middlesex (of the 14th Division) were squeezed out of the line by the 41st and 34th Divisions whose inner flanks joined. The Battalion, therefore, was ordered to return to Dickebusch area and occupied Smythe Camp. On the 2nd of October the

Middlesex moved via Kruisstraat and Ypres to a field near Potijze where tents were pitched and huts erected. 20TH BATTALION. 2ND OCTOBER

The general result of the operations of the 28th of September was that we had pressed far beyond the farthest limits of the 1917 battles, and had captured Kortewilde, Zandwoorde, Kruissecke and Becelaere: the Belgians, on our left, had taken Zonnebeke, Poelcapelle and Schaap Baillie, and had cleared Houthulst Forest.

Ypres was freed at last from the enemy's shell fire: he had ruined the ancient city of the cloth-workers but could not capture it.

The advance began again early on the 29th and the 23rd Middlesex of the 123rd Brigade (41st Division) came into the battle-field. The Battalion passed through the 124th Brigade and pushed on, clearing Houthem Village. The advance from this point onwards for 2,000 yards was exeedingly rapid, prisoners being taken freely. There was, however, considerable machine-gun fire from the western side of the Comines Canal. After passing Houthem a platoon of the leading company under Sergeant Potts crossed the Canal to exploit success and returned with thirty-five prisoners and three machine-guns. Another platoon of the same company under 2/Lieut. Giffard collected some sixty prisoners. The leading company reached a point where they lined the road from the Canal towards Korentje, where three field guns and three machine-guns were captured: beyond this point, however, the Middlesex could not get, being held up by machine-gun fire from their front and from the western banks of the Canal. The enemy then tried to work round the left flank of the Battalion which appeared to be in the air, and at one period the situation was serious. But by skilful handling and the courage and resourcefulness of company commanders, who transferred troops to the threatened flank, the situation improved and finally, with artillery, was saved. The conduct of the company officers and men throughout the advance and subsequent defence and withdrawal was most praiseworthy. The Battalion had captured 110 prisoners, six machine-guns and four field guns. Casualties of the 23rd Middlesex were 5 officers and 130 other ranks, 25 of the latter being killed. 23RD BATTALION. 29TH SEPT.

The 122nd and 124th Brigades of the Division passed through the 123rd Brigade on the 30th of September and the Middlesex withdrew to billets ¾ mile south of Tenbrielen. At 9.35 p.m., however, the 123rd Brigade received orders to move on Gheluwe in support of the 123rd Infantry Brigade. 30TH SEPT.

23RD BATTALION. 1ST OCTOBER.

At about 10 a.m. on the 1st of October the Brigade moved towards Tenbrielen, the 23rd Middlesex to America Wood. At 3 p.m. the Brigade resumed the advance and at 4 pm. Colonel Smith (commanding 23rd Middlesex) received orders to deploy and attack in a south-easterly direction, the railway line running south-west from Menin being the objective. The march began ¼ mile south-west of Tenbrielen, but the movement was under the direct observation of the enemy at Wervicq, who at once opened fire with his heavy artillery. Although the road was congested by other troops the Middlesex arrived at America Corner. Here, however, the enemy's shell fire became very heavy and the Battalion deployed and changed direction south-east. The commander of the leading company was wounded, and the other two subalterns being in the rear of the Company, no one knew the plan of attack excepting the former officer. All the while the enemy's shell fire was terrific and it seemed as if there was going to be chaos when the C.S.M., with great promptitude and gallantry, rushed forward and took the two leading platoons in hand.

The attack did not succeed in reaching the objective allotted to it, but when darkness fell the 123rd Brigade held a line astride the Gheluwe–Wervicq road and about half-way between those two villages.

The 23rd Middlesex lost 10 other ranks killed and 5 officers, and 72 other ranks wounded. At 2.30 p.m. on the 2nd of October the Battalion, in co-operation with the 10th R.W. Kents, advanced and straightened out the line, which at 5.30 p.m. ran from 1,000 to 2,000 yards south of Gheluwe.

The official despatches thus describe the operations from the 29th of September to the 1st of October: "On the 29th of September our troops drove the German rearguards from Ploegsteert Wood and Messines and captured Terhand and Dadizeele. By the evening of the 1st of October they had cleared the left bank of the Lys from Comines southwards, while north of that town they were close up to Wervicq, Gheluwe and Ledeghem." The Belgians had passed the line Moorslede–Staden–Dixmude.

THE BATTLE OF COURTRAI:
14th–19th October.

At the close of the Battles of Ypres, 1918, it became necessary to re-establish adequate communication in the area of the old

Ypres Battles. The advance had been so rapid and to such an extent that our forward line was outdistancing the rear formations, the latter not being able to get forward until roads were repaired and bridges constructed, and all the necessary arrangements made for supplying a great army on the move. But by the end of the second week in October the restoration of the Allied systems of communication was sufficiently far advanced to permit of a resumption of the offensive. On the 14th, therefore, the enemy was again attacked on the whole front between the Lys River at Comines and Dixmude. The British sector in this attack occupied a front of about nine to ten miles from Comines to St. Pieter, on the Menin–Roulers road.

23RD BATTALION.

14TH OCTOBER.

The attack was launched at 5.35 a.m. on the 14th of October, but the 123rd Brigade was in reserve to the 122nd and 124th Brigades, which were attacking along the 41st Divisional front. The 123rd Brigade remained throughout the 14th concentrated just south of Artoyshoek (north-east of Gheluwe) and did not move forward until the 16th when the 23rd Middlesex, marching via Moorseele, relieved a battalion of the 36th Division in Heule, a small village just north of Courtrai, the 123rd Brigade having been ordered to take over the line held by the 108th Brigade (36th Division) east of Guilegheem, on the night 16th/17th October.

On the 17th the situation along the Brigade front was unchanged, though the artillery of both sides was active. Civilians, passing through the Brigade area, stated that the enemy had mined the roads leading towards the Lys and Courtrai. On the 18th the bank of the River and streets leading to it were kept by the enemy under continuous fire : the enemy bombing aeroplanes were also extremely active.

17TH OCTOBER.

At 11.35 a.m. the 35th Division reported the capture of all objectives. Units of the 123rd Brigade began, therefore, to push across the Lys. The Queen's got over first, two companies crossing at 12.30 p.m. Two companies of the 23rd Middlesex crossed the river at 2.35 p.m. and sent patrols through Courtrai which was found clear of the enemy. The British troops, as may be imagined, received a frantic welcome from the civilian population, who hailed the soldiers as their deliverers. At 11.50 p.m. the Middlesex reported that they had established a line along the railway (east of Courtrai), in touch with the 35th Division on the right and 11th Queen's on the left. The Battalion then billeted on the outskirts of Courtrai.

20TH BATTALION.
12TH OCTOBER.

Meanwhile the 20th Middlesex (in Brigade) had moved from Potijze to Wulverghem, arriving at that place by train on the 12th of October. On the 15th the Battalion moved by stages to Wervicq, in support, where the majority of the men were accommodated in "pill boxes" and were comparatively comfortable. On the 17th the Battalion received warning orders to move across the Lys in support of the two front-line battalions which had occupied Roncq. During the afternoon the Middlesex moved across the river and, the bridge being so narrow and unstable, the crossing took a long while. On the 18th the Battalion passed through the Suffolks to a line east of Mouscron via Roncq. The C.O. and Battalion Headquarters advanced through Tourcoing where they received a great many tokens expressing the joy of the inhabitants on being released from German rule. Some opposition was experienced at the latter stages of this march, but a line was established and held all night. At 6 a.m. the next morning

19TH OCTOBER. (19th) the final objective was reached and the Battalion received orders to occupy a line east of Petit Voisnage and Malcense, which was done without opposition from the enemy. Under verbal orders yet another move was made just after midday to a line between Croix Rouge and Dottignies. The line was established. This successful day had an unfortunate ending, for the Battalion Diary records "a bad night, plenty of rain, and rations lost."

* * * * *

23RD BATTALION.

The Battle of Courtrai ended on the night of the 19th of October according to the Report of the Battles Nomenclature Committee, but desultory fighting went on for some days following. For instance, before the next operation—The Action of Ooteghem, 25th October—took place, the 23rd Middlesex were engaged on the 22nd, 23rd and 24th of October.

The Battalion billeted on the eastern outskirts of Courtrai on the night of the 19th of October, but moved to fresh billets on the 21st, but began to move again on the 21st and by the night of

22ND OCTOBER. the 22nd had moved into position east of Knok. That evening orders came to hand to deploy on a road just east of Knok and advance on a two-company frontage at 11.30 p.m. The right of the Battalion was to be on the Canal, the objective the Hoske–Heestert road, some three thousand yards off. The attack was to begin at 2.30 a.m. on the 23rd in the hopes of surprising the enemy. At 11.30 p.m. the Middlesex moved off and arrived at a halting place five hundred yards in front of the road on which the Battalion had deployed. *23RD BATTALION.*

23RD OCTOBER. The 122nd Brigade had already, on two occasions, attacked at this spot without success. At 2.30 a.m., with the Royal West Kents on their left, the advance began and at once came under machine-gun fire, but the two forward companies of Middlesex pressed on and cleared the Bosche from two houses : one machine-gun was captured here. But shortly afterwards the right company was held up by a nest of machine-guns in front and could make no further progress : the left company was similarly held up from their left : the West Kents having failed to get on the left of the Middlesex was thus exposed. At 5 a.m., further advance being impossible, the left company withdrew to a line about three hundred yards in front of the 2.30 a.m. position : the right company also withdrew, making good the canal. In this position the remainder of the 23rd was spent.*

On the 24th at 2.30 a.m. the attack was resumed, with artillery support, the right company moving forward to the position reached the previous night. The left company followed on to within two hundred yards of Hoogmolen Hill, but eventually fell back to a line about one hundred yards in front of the line held the day previous. *24TH OCTOBER.*

THE ACTION OF OOTEGHEM:

25th October.

At 9 a.m. on the 25th the Battalion again attacked the enemy. This attack was in conjunction with the corps on the right and left, under a heavy artillery barrage. *23RD BATTALION.*

25TH OCTOBER. The final objective was about seven thousand yards eastwards.

With troops of the 34th Division on their right, the Queen's on their left, the Middlesex, still on a two-company frontage, advanced to the attack in excellent order and in close co-operation with the flanking battalions. The enemy had withdrawn most of his guns from the immediate front early in the morning and the ridge at Hoogmolen Hill was gained without difficulty. On going over the ridge, however, towards Keibergmolen the advance was hindered by our guns which were short shooting. Touch at

---

* By the morning of the 23rd of October the British held the general line of the Scheldt on the whole front from Valenciennes to the neighbourhood of Avelghem.

this period was lost with the Queen's who had met with considerable opposition. As the companies advanced down the hill at Hoske they were met by heavy machine-gun fire from the railway line on the right, and from houses in the village, but they pressed on most gallantly, and the two right companies, getting close to Hoske, cleared the enemy out. At 2 p.m. the railway close by Hoske had been crossed and, having reached the originally arranged halting place, the two rear companies passed through the leading companies and continued the advance until they came to Woffelstraat. But again heavy fire was opened and it was decided to consolidate a line west of the village, both flanks being made good. The next morning considerable sniping took place from Woffelstraat, but the village with 150 Germans was ultimately captured by the 10th Hants. The enemy then fell back across the Scheldt. After the Germans had withdrawn from Autryve they shelled the ground with gas shells and when the villagers came out into the open the enemy turned his machine-guns on them.

In the Action of Ooteghem the 23rd Middlesex lost 5 officers and 79 other ranks, 9 of the latter being killed.

On the 26th of October the 122nd Brigade again took over the front line and the 23rd Middlesex moved back to Courtrai and billeted there. On the 1st of November the Battalion moved to Sweveghem, and on the 5th to Kleinberg. The enemy by this date was falling back from the Scheldt, and on the night of the 8th the Middlesex were ordered to push on to Caster, which was reached at 3 a.m. on the 9th. The Battalion then went into billets, but later in the morning orders were received to attack at 1 p.m., the Middlesex being allotted a frontage of 1,000 yards. French troops on the left and the West Kents on the right of the Middlesex were also to attack the enemy.

The Middlesex crossed the river at Meersche and began the attack at 2 p.m. The objective, some 2,500 yards eastwards, was reached without opposition. At 6 p.m. a further advance of 1,000 yards was ordered, this also being carried out without incident. On the night of the 9th the Battalion was ordered to make yet another advance of 1,000 yards due east. This advance began at 9 a.m. on the 10th of November and no opposition was encountered until within three hundred yards of the objective. Outpost positions were therefore taken up for the night, touch being maintained with both flanks. The Bosche machine-guns withdrew during the night. On the morning of the 11th the

124th Brigade advanced through the 123rd, but at 11 a.m. operations ceased as the Armistice had been signed. 23RD BATTALION. 11TH Nov.

The 19th Middlesex (Pioneers of the 41st Division) were repairing the bridges on the Scheldt at Berchem when the Armistice came into force. 19TH BATTALION. 11TH Nov.

Meanwhile the 20th Middlesex (14th Division) had been pushing on towards the Escaut. We left the Battalion between Croix Rouge and Dottignies on the evening of the 19th of October. Later, orders were received to move on the 20th and take up two objectives, the first being a line about five hundred yards west of the Coyghem–Warcoing road, the second, the western banks of the River Escaut. 20TH BATTALION.

The Battalion marched at 8 a.m. on the 20th. After passing through Dottignies some slight opposition was experienced, mainly on the left flank from Coyghem and neighbourhood. The enemy also shelled Dottignies heavily, but the troops had passed through the village. At about 10 a.m. the first objective was reached. The final objective was reached at about 5 p.m. by the right company, but there was trouble on the left and the company on that flank had to swing round and pass through Espierres in order to get across the Grand Espierres. Thus the whole objective allotted to the 20th Middlesex had been reached, and at nightfall the Battalion consolidated the position. "A bad day," records the Battalion Diary again, "forward positions shelled, sniped, machine-gunned and trench-mortared and rear positions gas-shelled." 20TH OCTOBER.

On the 20th/21st patrols were pushed out but could not get across the Escaut. On this day "four prisoners drove into our left company in a car, having lost their way: belonged to administrative troops, doubt if they meant to lose their way!"

The same position was held until about 11.30 p.m. on the 21st when the Battalion marched back to the western edges of Dottignies. The 20th Middlesex had, as a matter of fact, seen their last fight. From Dottignies they moved to Luingne on the 24th, where they remained training until the 2nd of November. They then moved to Petit Audenarde until midnight on the 8th when they returned to Dottignies. On the 9th they again exchanged billets to Helchin, and on the 10th to Warcoing where, at 9.45 a.m. on the 11th, they received news that the Armistice had been signed and that hostilities were to cease at 11 a.m. 11TH Nov.

CHAPTER XL.

The Final Advance.
II. IN ARTOIS:

2nd October–11th November.

WHILE the Fourth and Third Armies, on the right flank of the First Army, had been rapidly advancing eastwards driving the enemy before them, the left flank of the latter, *i.e.*, the VIIIth Corps had remained almost stationary until towards the end of September. Indeed, by the 17th of October, the right corps of the First Army was between fifteen and twenty miles east of the left corps, producing a huge salient in the enemy's line from which he would have to retire, for there was by now no possibility of his enveloping his opponent's flanks.

Among the divisions forming the VIIIth Corps was the 8th which, after the disastrous Battle of the Aisne had, on the withdrawal of the British troops from Champagne, reached the Abbeville area for rest, refitting and training: the 23rd Brigade occupying Hautebut. On the 19th of July the 8th Division began to move to the First Army area, the 23rd Brigade to Mont St. Eloi. On the 20th the Brigade received orders to take over front-line trenches in the Acheville sector, east of the Vimy Ridge.

The 2nd Middlesex relieved the 1/4th Royal Scots in the La Targette area east of Vimy Village, but the line was comparatively quiet, and there is little to record for the remainder of July. In the beginning of August the Battalion held trenches in the Thelus area. On the 3rd 2/Lieut. F. Sharp was killed. On the 27th of August, as the result of a successful attack by the Canadian Corps on the right of the VIIIth Corps, who recaptured Monchy le Preux, the enemy evacuated the Arleux Loop opposite the 23rd Brigade front, and the latter immediately occupied the position. On the 28th of August 2/Lieut. P. C. Brooke was wounded: 2/Lieuts. Blake and Blackborow were gassed on the 31st.

2ND BATTALION.

28TH AUGUST.

2ND BATTALION

2ND SEPT.

The enemy appears to have used gas shells rather heavily against the 8th Division in September, for from the first day of that month the Diary of the 2nd Middlesex shows gas casualties. On the 2nd 2/Lieut. B. V. Vanstone was gassed; on the 4th 2/Lieut. J. J. Carter and 22 other ranks were similarly affected. On the 9th the Battalion was relieved and moved back to Hills Camp, but returned to the line in the Willerval sector on the 17th. On the 20th a successful raid was made on the enemy's trenches by a platoon of Middlesex, under 2/Lieut. D. Hazard. 2/Lieut. A. M. White was wounded on the 22nd.

26TH SEPT.

At midnight on the 26th of September the 8th and 20th Divisions attacked the enemy. The objectives of the 23rd Brigade were positions of Novia Scotia, Britannia and Brandy Trenches. Neither the brigade nor the battalion diaries contain an account of this attack, but apparently five platoons each from the 2nd Middlesex and 2nd Devons carried out the operation, which was highly successful. Britannia and Brandy Trenches were captured from the enemy and heavy casualties were inflicted on him: fourteen prisoners were taken. The Middlesex lost 2/Lieut. J. Green and 11 other ranks killed, and 2/Lieuts. H. C. Chinn and R. J. Badcock and about 38 other ranks wounded, 16 other ranks were missing. The records state that Lieut. A. C. Pearse rendered valuable services in laying the tape lines and assisting assaulting companies to their assembly positions. The records end with the following words: " By their magnificent fight the Battalion added yet more to the glorious traditions of the 77th."

7TH OCTOBER.

On the 7th of October the 8th Division again attacked the enemy holding the Fresnes–Rouvroy line, assisted by a heavy barrage of artillery and machine-gun fire. The 2nd Middlesex and 2nd West Yorkshires carried out the attack of the 23rd Brigade, with the 25th Brigade on the left.

Zero hour was at dawn (5 a.m.). The operations were again a complete success, Biache St. Vaast was captured and all objectives. At evening the Middlesex pushed out patrols to the western bank of the Canal west of Vitry. During the operations 2/Lieut. C. F. Blake and 4 other ranks were killed, Captain H. W. Hallet and 44 other ranks wounded, Captain W. Evans, Lieut. Hewlett and 2/Lieuts. L. H. S. Donn and J. E. Brawson were also wounded but remained " at duty."

By now the whole of the First Army was on the move, though

the enemy made desperate efforts to hold back the advance. On the 9th patrols endeavoured to penetrate into the northern portion of the Drocourt–Queant Line, but it was too strongly defended by outposts. Nevertheless the 23rd Brigade attacked positions north of Gloster Wood and on the north-western side of Vitry Marsh.

On the 11th of October orders were received from Divisional Headquarters to break the Drocourt–Queant Line* at dawn on the 11th inst.

Again the Die-Hards were in the front of the battle, for the 2nd Middlesex were on the right and the 2nd Devons on the left. Complete success again attended the operations and that portion of the line which lay between Fresnes and Brebieres road, inclusive, was taken and the position consolidated. "Objectives were taken with great dash," records the Brigade Diary, "and fourteen prisoners, including one officer, were captured." By noon the Middlesex had pushed forward sentry posts to the railway, but further advance was stopped owing to the Canadian Corps on the right being held up by the enemy from Mont Metier and Mont. St. George.

And now occurred what must have been almost unique in those days, the Brigadier himself personally led a platoon attack on the two points holding up the Canadians. He was accompanied by the C.O. of the Middlesex—Lieut.-Colonel E. F. Baker. The Battalion Diary relates this incident in the following words: "At 4 p.m. No. 15 Platoon, 'A' Company, led by Brigadier-General Grogan, V.C., and Lieut.-Colonel E. F. Baker, crossed the river and outflanked the garrison of those heights thus enabling the Canadian Corps to advance."

The operation of the 11th of October had been carried out with great dash, and before nightfall the 23rd Brigade had pushed on to the general line of the railway east of Brebieres.

On the 12th the 2nd West Yorkshires passed through the 2nd Middlesex and 2nd Devons and continued the advance as advanced guard, the enemy being pushed back to within four hundred yards of deviation of the Sensée, but it was impossible to cross the canal by daylight owing to machine-gun fire.

"By the evening of the 13th of October," records the Official

---

* This was the extreme northern portion of the line, the southern portion where it joined up with the Hindenburg Line had been broken on the 2nd and 3rd of September.

2ND BATTALION.
Despatch, "our troops had reached the western outskirts of Douai and were close up to the western banks of the Sensée Deviation and Haute Deule Canals, on the whole front from Apleux (south of Douai) to Vendil le Vieil."

14TH OCTOBER.
On the 14th of October* the 2nd Middlesex relieved the 2nd Devons in the front line, but no advance was made until the 16th when "D" and "C" Companies, having relieved "B" and "A" Companies in the outpost line, the first-named Company attacked and captured a German post out in front of the line.

The Capture of Douai:
17th October.

2ND BATTALION.
17TH OCTOBER.
Early on the 17th of October "D" Company of the 2nd Middlesex crossed the Scarpe Deviation and captured the towns of Courcelettes and Lambres. In the afternoon the Battalion advanced on Douai and Nos. 12 and 13 Platoons, again personally led by Brigadier-General Grogan and Lieut.-Colonel E. F. Baker (commanding 2nd Middlesex), entered Douai. They were the first British troops to enter the town after the German occupation. They then hoisted the Union Jack over the Town Hall amidst great enthusiasm, the civilian population receiving the troops with extraordinary welcome. A copy of a document describing this historic event was handed to each officer and man of the Battalion who entered Douai on this date, and later (on the 29th of October) Lieut.-Colonel Baker sent the Mayor a letter. The 2nd West Yorkshires then passed through the Middlesex, and the latter withdrew to Corbehem, south of the town.

18TH OCTOBER.
The 25th Brigade passed through the 23rd Brigade on the 18th of October, the latter becoming Divisional Reserve, gradually moving forward as the front line was pushed still further east. On the 20th the 2nd Middlesex marched to Frais Marais. The route lay through Douai and, on reaching the square, a short service was held to commemorate the entry of the Battalion into Douai on the 17th.

From this date onwards, to the morning of the 11th of November, there are, however, no records of the 2nd Middlesex coming to grips with the enemy again. The Battalion moved eastwards

---

* Lieut. H. Hazard was wounded on this date and died of his wounds on the 16th of October.

as follows: from Frais Marais to Marchiennes on the 23rd to 2ND BATTALION. Millon Fosse on the 25th, to La Croisette on the 26th where billets were obtained in the Château le Fontaine Bouillion, and to Tilloy on the 4th of November and to Escaupont on the 9th. From the latter village buses carried the Battalion to Thulin, south of the Mons Canal. The Middlesex were now in the historic area of the Battle of Mons, 1914. They "debussed" at Thulin at about 5.30 a.m. on the 10th of November and marched thence to Douvrain, which is north of the Condè–Mons Canal, and from four to five miles west of Ghlin. "B" Company was sent forward and occupied an outpost line at the latter village and they still held this position when the Canadians captured Mons early on the morning of the 11th of November.

There is an interesting note in the Battalion Diary which says: "Owner of the Château la Venière, north of Ghlin, stated that the 4th Battalion D.C.O. Middlesex Regiment, billeted there in 1914." There is, however, no confirmation of this in either the official or private diaries (including that of the then Adjutant of the 4th Middlesex) of August, 1914.

The Battalion Diary of the 2nd Middlesex for the 11th of 11TH Nov. November, 1918 records: "Armistice signed. Hostilities ceased at 11 a.m. Battalion moved to Ghlin. 'A' Company moved to Mazieres (Maisieres?) and took up outpost line. 'C' Company moved to Bruyere and took up outpost line."

Thus, without emotion, the 2nd Middlesex saw the close of the war, for no note of triumph nor expressions of joy are written in the Battalion Diary.

In the meanwhile, further south, the Advance in Picardy had been proceeding rapidly.

CHAPTER XLI.

The Final Advance.
III. IN PICARDY:
17th October–11th November.

THE BATTLE OF THE SELLE:
17th–25th October.

THE enemy was now hurrying eastwards with all speed, though covering his withdrawal mainly by means of rearguards formed of machine-gun companies, placed in depth, and his artillery. We had reached the line of the Selle River, but our communications, owing to the rapid advance, were naturally somewhat dislocated. By the 17th, however, they had improved on the Le Cateau front, and it was possible to resume operations for the forcing of the Selle positions and attainment of the general line Sambre et Oise Canal–Western edge of the Forest of Mormal–Valenciennes. This advance would bring the important railway junction of Aulnoye (where the main line from Mezieres and Hirson linked up with the main line to Maubeuge, Charleroi and Germany) within the effective range of the British guns.

Operations were then planned to begin on the 17th of October by an attack by the Fourth Army on a front of about ten miles from Le Cateau southwards: the First French Army was to operate west of the Sambre et Oise Canal.

The assault was launched at 5.30 a.m. on the 17th. During the first two days the enemy's resistance was obstinate, but both British and American troops made good progress, and by the evening of the 19th the Germans were driven across the Sambre et Oise Canal at practically all points south of Catillon where the line followed the valley of the Richemont, east and north of Le Cateau. On the 20th the Third and First Armies attacked on the line of the Selle north of Le Cateau, and again the enemy's resistance was strong, nevertheless he could not stay the advance:

1ST BATTALION. the high ground north of the Selle was captured and our patrols reached the River Harpies. North of Haspres the First Army made progress on both sides of the Scheldt Canal and occupied Denain.

The capture of the Selle positions was followed almost immediately by operations for the attainment of a general line running from the Sambre Canal along the outskirts of the Forest of Mormal to the neighbourhood of Valenciennes.

The original front of attack stretched from east of Mazinghien to Maison Bleue, north-east of Haussy—a distance of some fourteen miles.

The Fourth, Third and First Armies took part in the attack which opened at 1.20 a.m. on the 23rd of October. The Third Army attacked with the Vth, IVth, VIth, and XVIIth Corps, the 33rd and 21st Divisions carrying out the attack of the former Corps. Of the 33rd Division the 98th Brigade was attacking on the right and the 19th Brigade on the left.

In the attack of the 98th Brigade the 1st Middlesex were to lead the assault by capturing the village of Forest, enveloping it on both sides. " C " Company was to be on the right, " A " on the left, " B " Company to " mop up " Forest, and " D " in support. The 4th King's were then to pass through the Middlesex and capture the second and third objectives; this was the second phase. In the third phase the 2nd Argyll and Sutherland Highlanders were to advance through the 4th King's and capture the fourth objective, the 1st Middlesex meanwhile moving up to support the Highlanders. The 100th Brigade was then to advance through the 98th and capture the final objective near Englefontaine.

Zero hour for the attack of the Middlesex had been fixed for 2 a.m.

23RD OCTOBER. The advance began punctually on time, but nothing was heard until 2.45 a.m. when a message was received by Battalion Headquarters from Captain Tate, commanding " B " Company. This said : " On outskirts of Forest. Everything going splendidly. Enemy retiring. Very few casualties." An hour later " A " Company was in Forest, having suffered rather heavy casualties : the remaining companies had already passed the village and had captured their objectives to time. " B " Company estimated that 200 prisoners had been captured in Forest.

At about 6 a.m. the 4th King's passed through the Middlesex, and by 12.45 p.m. had captured their objective, the 19th Infantry 1ST BATTALION. Brigade, on the left of the 98th, having been similarly successful. 23RD OCTOBER. Thus the three companies of 1st Middlesex, who were to have gone forward to support the King's, were not required, and the Battalion was able to move forward to support the 2nd Argyll and Sutherland Highlanders. The general result of the day's fighting was that an advance had been made to about two hundred yards west of the fourth objective.

At 4 a.m. on the 24th the advance was continued. The 2nd 24TH OCTOBER. Argyll and Sutherland Highlanders on the right, and 1st Middlesex on the left, formed up on a general line about two hundred yards west of Farm du Bois de Bousies–Paul Jacques road, continuing to the north. The 4th King's were in support. Very heavy machine-gun fire met the gallant Die-Hards as they advanced and many were shot down. The Battalion was now getting very weak in numbers and this, combined with exposed flanks, made progress very difficult. At 6.5 a.m. Captain Broad reported that the enemy's machine-gun fire was extremely heavy, but he believed that, although he could not get touch, some of the Battalion were ahead of him, though the enemy also was in front. At 7.25 a.m. he reported that he had " D " Company with " C " Company—totalling only fifty men. At 8 a.m. " C " Company had reached the cross-roads east of Wagnonville, with the Highlanders on the right and " B " Company on the left : the enemy were about two hundred yards in front. A bridge across the stream, which ran across the Roman road just south of the cross-roads, had been destroyed.

The situation, however, changed at about 9.15 a.m. when the 19th Brigade was seen advancing on the left, but by now the 98th Brigade had suffered such serious losses that the 100th Brigade took up the advance and passed through the former : the Middlesex then took shelter on the cross-roads with the 2nd Argyll and Sutherland Highlanders on their right.

In a sunken road the Battalion reorganised. Gallant Battalion. After weeks of hard fighting and marching, such fighting indeed as had never been seen before, because knowing that the enemy was " on the run," every officer and man put forth all his strength. Very little sleep, very little rest, marching, fighting, fighting, marching—it seemed never ending and now here was the Battalion so pitifully weak that it could only muster ninety other ranks, with Captain Tate in command. During the two days'

1ST BATTALION. fighting Captain F. Broad, Lieut. A. C. T. Kroenig and 2/Lieut. R. E. Holland had been killed ; Lieut. A. A. T. Harris had been so severely wounded that he died on the 24th. Lieut. F. J. Smith had also been wounded, while 2/Lieut. C. E. Cade was missing.

On the 25th the 100th Brigade was ordered to capture Engle-
25TH OCTOBER. fontaine during the night of the 25th/26th October.

The 1st Middlesex were not, however, in this attack, for the Battalion was still reorganising and on this day was formed into one company. It is indeed of historic importance to record this reorganisation, for the Battalion had no Lieut.-Colonel, no Major, and no Captain, and was commanded by a subaltern. The entry in the Battalion Diary states that : " The Battalion was reorganised as a company under the following officers—Lieut. Tatham (commanding), Lieut. Dobbs and 2/Lieut. Jarvis. The strength of the company was as follows : ' A ' Company, 1 officer and 30 men ; ' B ' Company, 2 officers and 30 men ; ' C ' Company, 1 officer and 42 men, and ' D ' Company, 2 officers and 40 men."

(The Battle of the Selle officially ends on the night of the 25th of October, but it will be seen that fighting continued on the 26th.)

26TH OCTOBER. At 1 a.m. on the 26th the 4th King's made an enveloping attack on Englefontaine from the south, whilst the 1st Queen's made a similar attack from the north, the 1st Middlesex meanwhile establishing themselves south-east of Brasserie. The attack was successful, but the right flank was not secure, and the Die Hards had to occupy a line of posts south-east of Englefontaine, linking up with the 18th Division on the right.

That night the 38th Division took over the line of the 33rd Division, but the Middlesex were only partially relieved, the remainder withdrawing without relief. The Battalion then moved back to Montay and there went into billets.

It was through Montay that the original 1st Battalion marched into Le Cateau on the night of the 25th of August, 1914, where, tired and worn out (they had marched nineteen miles that day), the Die-Hards, with other units of the 19th Brigade, bivouacked in the square and goods station.

18TH BATTALION. The Diaries of the 18th Middlesex tell a wonderful story of work carried out during the advance. On the 23rd they received
23RD OCTOBER. orders to move forward at 5.10 a.m. to regain the Montay–Forest-Croix road " as far forward as the situation permitted." Everyone knows what that meant : that the gallant Pioneers would push on—far into the danger zone—for they were of that stuff. They

realised how much the advance depended on them and they worked hour after hour often under heavy shell fire. Again on the 24th and 25th their labours were required on the main roads. On the latter date two officers—Lieut. B. L. Fish and 2/Lieut. A. Poynton—with 10 other ranks were wounded: 5 other ranks were killed. And every day until the advance to Victory was over (and even beyond that) their Diaries still tell the same tale of work willingly and faithfully carried out.

18TH BATTALION.
25TH OCTOBER.

The 4th Middlesex, though in the area of the battle, took no part in the operations. The Battalion remained at Caudry until the 23rd of October, but on that day marched to Viesly, as the 37th Division had relieved the 5th Division in the front line. On the 21st Lieut.-Colonel W. B. Molony left the Battalion to proceed to England on a six-month tour of duty. All ranks were sorry to lose Colonel Molony, whose tireless energy and good leadership during the advance were largely responsible for the Battalion's fine record. He was succeeded by Major P. Grove-White. On the 24th the Middlesex made another move—to Beaurain via Briastre, but their stay in this village was only for a few hours, for during the evening they relieved troops of the 111th Brigade in support on the eastern and south-eastern outskirts of Neuville.

4TH BATTALION.
23RD OCTOBER.

The 63rd Brigade relieved the 112th Brigade in the front line on the 27th, the Middlesex again in support moving to Salesches.

27TH OCTOBER.

The Battle of the Selle had yielded further splendid results. At the close of the operations the western outskirts of the Forêt de Mormal had been reached, we were within a mile of Le Quesnoy, and Ruesnes and Maing had been captured. During the 26th, 27th and 28th Englefontaine had fallen and our line was established well to the north and east of the Le Quesnoy-Valenciennes railway, from the outskirts of Le Quesnoy past Sepmeries and Artres to Famars.

By the end of October the succession of heavy blows dealt by the British forces had had a disastrous effect—both moral and material—upon the enemy. His enormous losses in guns, machine-guns and ammunition could not be replaced, his troops were practically exhausted, and he had no reserves to replace the vast numbers captured by the Allies. No less than 20,000 prisoners and over 400 guns had been captured in the Battle of the Selle and the enemy had been utterly beaten. The capitulation of Turkey and Bulgaria and the imminent collapse of Austria, had made Germany's military situation impossible. But if her Armies were allowed to withdraw undisturbed to shorter lines there was a danger that the struggle might last through another winter. This had to be prevented at all costs and the British Army was, therefore, to attack a vital centre which would anticipate the enemy's withdrawal and force an immediate conclusion of hostilities.

Accordingly orders were issued that the XVIIth Corps of the Third Army and the XXIInd and Canadian Corps of the First Army were to attack on a front of about six miles south of Valenciennes (roughly from Vendignies to the southern edge of the Forest of Raimes).

THE BATTLE OF VALENCIENNES:

1st–2nd November.

Only one Battalion—the 13th, of the Middlesex Regiment was in the area of this Battle, the 24th Division forming part of the XVIIth Corps.

The 13th Battalion between the 13th of October and the 1st of November was out of the battle area, but on the later date moved from Haussy to Bermerain, billeting for the night in the village. On the following afternoon the Battalion relieved other units in the front line, first moving to the high ground in rear of Maraisches, and then after dark taking over a line from the 2/5th Gloucesters in front of the village, from near Pont des Vaux to the River Rhonelle, one company continuing the line south of the river in touch on the right with the Guards Division. These positions were held until the afternoon of the 3rd of November when, patrols having reported that the enemy had again fallen back, the line was advanced and at dusk was established between Jenlain and Villers-Pol.

Valenciennes had been captured by the Canadians who had made progress beyond that town.

THE BATTLE OF THE SAMBRE:

4th November.

The moment had now arrived for the decisive blow. This was launched by the Fourth, Third and First Armies (in that order from right to left) on the 4th of November, the front of attack extending from the Sambre River, north of Oisy, to Valenciennes—a front of about thirty miles. 1ST, 4TH, 1/7TH, 1/8TH, 13TH AND 18TH BATTALIONS.

Six battalions of the Regiment were in this final attack, either in the front line, in support, or in reserve: they were the 1st, 4th, 1/7th, 1/8th, 13th and 18th Middlesex.

This attack was a difficult operation, for along the southern area of attack the Sambre had to be crossed: in the centre lay the great Forêt de Mormal, and north was the fortified town of Le Quesnoy: the enemy, therefore, had great facilities for defence. But to troops, confident of victory and assured of their own superiority, these obstacles were not likely to stay the advance.

At dawn on the 4th, after an intense bombardment of the enemy's positions, our troops advanced to the attack. On the right the Fourth Army (with the First French Army on its right), after stiff fighting crossed the Sambre and captured La Folie and Landrecies, and at nightfall its left had advanced to about the centre of the Forêt de Mormal. In the centre of the attack the Third Army pressed forward on the right of the Fourth and similarly reached the centre of the Forest, capturing Le Quesnoy, with its left pushed well forward towards the Grand Honelle River.

The 111th and 112th Brigades of the 37th Division attacked due east from just south of Le Quesnoy, but the 63rd Brigade was in reserve and the 4th Middlesex did no actual fighting. At 11.20 a.m. the Battalion concentrated on the south-eastern outskirts of Ghissignies and remained in that position until about 3.15 p.m., moving at that hour to an area north-east of Louvignies.* The Battalion had just settled down with rations issued when orders were received to return to Ghissignies. On the 5th the Middlesex withdrew to Neuville. In the latter village Lieut.-Colonel W. G. Chapman met the Battalion and took over command from Major Grove-White. 4TH BATTALION. 5TH Nov.

The fighting days of the 4th Middlesex were over,† for they remained in Neuville until the morning of the 11th when at 8.10 the Battalion took the road to Caudry, and it was while on the line of march that news was received of the signing of the 11TH Nov.

---

* Near Ghissignies, *not* Louvignies near Bavai.
† This was true not only of the Great War, but in the history of the Battalion, for after the War was over the 4th Middlesex were subsequently disbanded: a great loss to the British Army.

4TH BATTALION.
11TH Nov.

Armistice at 11 a.m. The Battalion Diary records that the men "cheered wildly."

By 2 p.m. the Battalion was settled in billets in Caudry.

The 33rd Division was one of the reserve divisions of the Third Army when the attack began on the 4th of November, but received orders to continue the attack on the 5th.

1ST BATTALION.
4TH Nov.

At 11.30 a.m. on the 4th the 1st Middlesex paraded and marched to Englefontaine where orders were received respecting the attack to be made at 9.30 a.m. the next morning. The Battalion billeted in Englefontaine for the night, but at 4.15 a.m. fresh orders arrived advancing the hour of the attack and the Battalion was immediately paraded and marched with the rest of the Brigade to Carrefour de la Tourelle (in the Forêt de Mormal) which was reached at 12.30 p.m. Here Lewis-gun limbers, etc., were unloaded and the Battalion, in artillery formation, advanced through the Forest. No Germans were, however, encountered and the Middlesex reached Berlaimont at 4 p.m. where the 98th Brigade had been ordered to rendezvous.

At 5 p.m. the Die-Hards were ordered to attempt the crossing of the Sambre "with the local materials available." "B" Company carried out this work and about midnight, with "A" and "D" Companies, crossed the river in the face of opposition from the enemy's machine-guns. "C" Company remained on the near side covering the crossings, but at 2 p.m. on the 6th with Battalion Headquarters, crossed the river and the whole Battalion was assembled in the area of the Aulnoye station, the men resting for the remainder of the day. At 6 a.m. on the 7th the Brigade paraded and advanced along the road to Pot de Vin. The head of the column, however, met with opposition from machine-gun fire and was temporarily held up. The Middlesex then turned off the main road and endeavoured to work round Pot de Vin from the south. The movement progressed though under shell fire, one shell killing Lieut. W. L. Hudspith and 2 other ranks and wounding 2/Lieut. E. F. Johnson who had rejoined the Battalion from hospital only that morning, and who died of his wounds on the 10th of November.

The Battalion eventually reached its objective, a series of posts behind the Maubeuge–Avesnes road, by dusk. The enemy's machine-gunners were still putting up a vigorous fight and, what with heavy rain and darkness, further progress was impossible.

At 8 p.m. orders were received that the 98th Brigade would be 1ST BATTALION.
relieved by units of the 38th Division.

The 1st Middlesex withdrew at 4 a.m. on the 8th, after relief, 8TH Nov.
to Aulnoye station area, marching thence at 10 a.m. to Sassegnies
where the remainder of the day was spent in resting.

For the 1st Battalion also the War had ended, for three days
were spent at Sassegnies, resting and re-fitting, and it was there
that news came through that Germany had signed the Armistice
at 11 a.m. on the 11th of November. 11TH Nov.

Their own division not being in the front line of attack on the
4th of November, the 18th Middlesex (Pioneers) of the 33rd 18TH
Division, were attached to the 38th Division and were employed BATTALION.
in filling in craters which the enemy had blown all along the roads,
and in bridging the river at Berlaimont. The Pioneers were at 11TH Nov.
Croisil Inn when the Armistice came into force.

The 24th Division, also belonging to the Third Army, attacked
from just north of the Rhonelle River, the 13th Middlesex (73rd 13TH
Brigade) holding a portion of the line Jenlain–Villers-Pol. At BATTALION.
6.30 a.m. on the 4th the remaining battalions of the 73rd Brigade 4TH Nov.
passed through the Middlesex and drove the enemy over the
Aunelle River. The Middlesex then concentrated near Le Coron
and, during the afternoon, advanced through Wargnies-le-Grand
a line being established east of that village. Again the enemy's
machine-gunners had put up considerable opposition, Captain
H. R. Mallett being amongst the casualties suffered by the
Battalion.

Early on the 5th the line was further advanced, but the 17th
Brigade came up and moving through the 73rd Brigade the latter
withdrew to billets, the 13th Middlesex finding accommodation
in Wargnies-le-Petit where they remained until the 7th of November. On the latter date they moved to Bavai (place of immortal
memories to the original British Expeditionary Force) and billeted
during the night of the 7th/8th of November. The following
night the Battalion billeted in Le Louvion.

On the morning of the 9th the 13th Battalion moved out to 9TH Nov.
what proved its last contact with the enemy. The advance was
by way of La Berlière and Les Bas Vent where the Middlesex
who had been in support up to this point, went into the front
line with the 7th Northants on the right and 9th Royal Sussex on
the left. The line was now advanced to about one thousand
yards east of the Mons–Maubeuge road, but little opposition was

K

experienced: the enemy's fire was feeble and battalions had little trouble in getting forward. At 4 p.m. the Middlesex received orders to return to Les Bas Vent and billet there. On the 10th the Battalion moved to and billeted in La Berliere. On this day Major H. H. Hebden assumed command of the Battalion. The next morning the Middlesex again changed billets, on this occasion to Le Louvion, and it is possible that they were on the march thither when the Armistice was signed: no reference to that great event appears in their Diary.

The 1/7th and 1/8th Middlesex had arrived in the Denain area on the 31st of October, the former at Le Moulin and the latter at Douchy. Neither Battalion took part in the earlier stages of the Battle of the Sambre, for they did not move up to the front line until the night of the 6th/7th, the 167th Brigade being the Reserve Brigade of the 56th Division. On the night of the 6th of November the Brigade, however, relieved the 169th Brigade in the forward area, the 1/7th and 1/8th Middlesex moving up in front of Angreau—1/8th on the right, 1/7th on the left.

The situation at this stage was that the 168th and 169th Brigades had crossed the Grand Honelle during the 6th, but in a heavy counter-attack the 169th had been driven back again. The 167th, therefore, relieved the latter with the object of carrying on the attack.

The attack was to take place at 9 a.m. on the 7th of November, the first objective being a line just east of Onnezies, the second objective the main road west of Montignies, the third objective a line three hundred yards east of Montignies.

Under a very heavy barrage the attack began at the hour stated. By now the Germans were practically demoralised and beaten, but there were still a few of the enemy who stuck to their guns and were able to temporarily hold up the advance. The 1/8th* captured their first objective but were then brought to a standstill by heavy machine-gun fire from the Bois de Daubois: the 1/7th carried the first and second objectives and were held up just short of the third objective.

On the 8th the attack was continued, the 1/8th capturing all their objectives and pushing their line beyond the fourth objective. Ferlibray was captured. The 1/7th, on the left, again repeated

---

* Their losses on the 7th of November were 2 other ranks killed, Lieut. E. W. Hazeldene and 13 other ranks wounded.

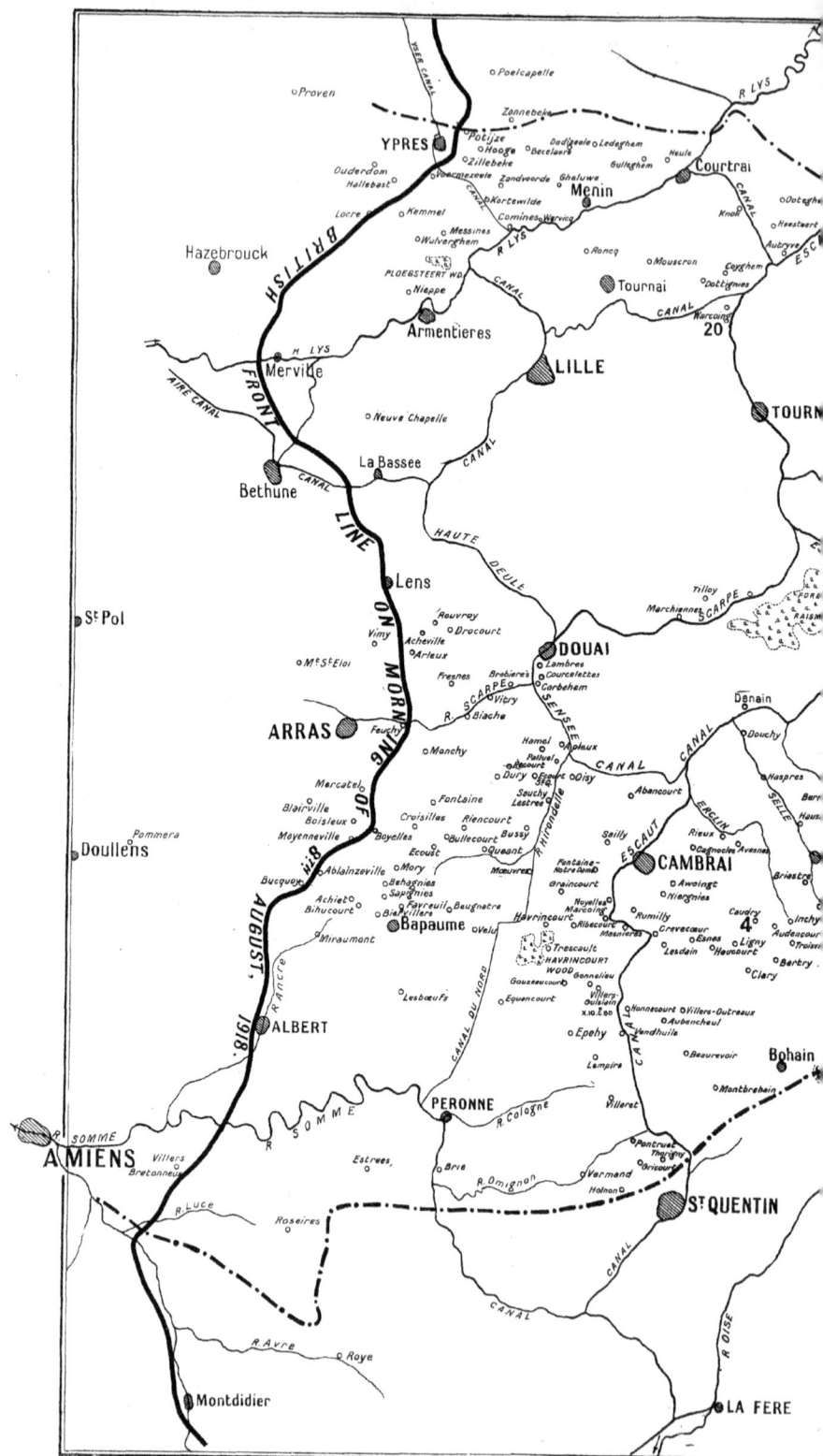

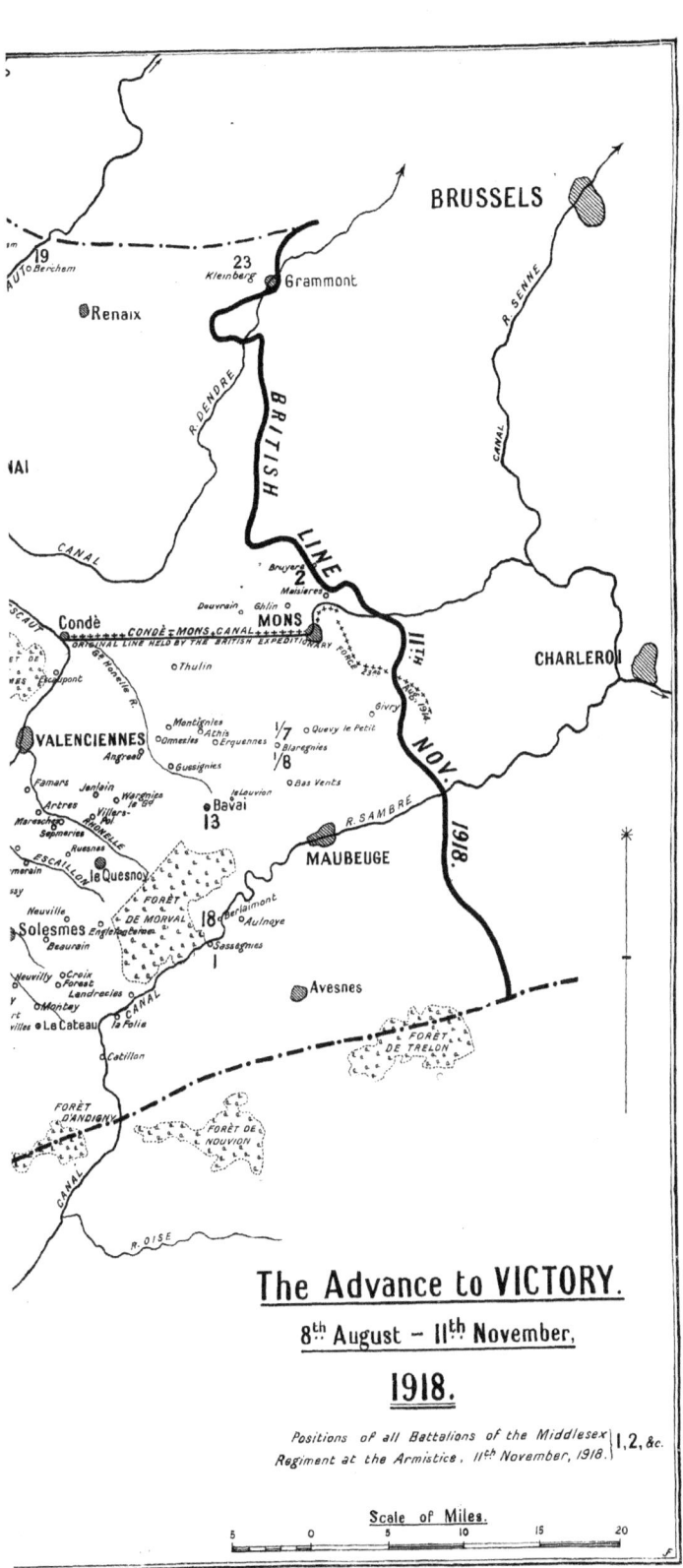

their successful advance of the 7th and took all three objectives, including Athis. During the afternoon they reached their final objective—a ridge one thousand yards east of Erquennes. Again on the 9th both Battalions took all their objectives. The 1/8th reached and consolidated a line two hundred yards east of the Mons–Maubeuge road—the final objective. The 1/7th reached a line along the railway east of Le Dessous and pushed a patrol into Quevy le Petit. But during the afternoon both Battalions were relieved and the 1/8th withdrew to billets in Blaregnies and the 1/7th to Le Dessous. 1/7TH AND 1/8TH BATTALIONS.

The enemy was now in full retreat and incapable of offering a resistance to the advance of the victorious British troops.

The Territorial Battalions of the Regiment in France had fought their last battle with the enemy.

There is little more to be told. On the 11th of November at 9.30 a.m. the following order was circulated by Army Headquarters: 11TH Nov.

" Hostilities will cease at 11 a.m. on November 11th. Troops will stand fast on the line reached at that hour, which will be reported by wire to G.H.Q. Defensive precautions will be maintained. There will be no intercourse of any description with the enemy until receipt of instructions from G.H.Q. Further instructions will follow."

CHAPTER XLII.

The Eastern Theatre of the War:
THE NEAR EAST—ITALY AND SALONIKA.

I. ITALY AND SALONIKA.

THE absorbing interest of the great battles along the Western Front tend to draw attention from the operations in the Near East and eastern theatres of the war, but it must not be forgotten that while in France and Flanders vital events were taking place, British troops in Italy, Salonika, Palestine and Mesopotamia were also engaged in fighting the common enemy in accordance with the general plans of the Allied Powers: and if their struggles with the foe were less frequent than in the main theatre of the war, the hard conditions under which they lived and fought were often far more difficult and trying owing to the insidious attacks of deadly disease and treacherous climates, than in France and Flanders.

1917.

ITALY.

Neither the 19th Middlesex (Pioneers) nor the 23rd Middlesex (123rd Brigade) of the 41st Division, after withdrawal from the Battle of the Menin Road Ridge (20th–25th September) were again engaged in the Battles of Ypres, 1917. Early in October the Division moved to the Belgian coast and took over a sector in the Nieuport area, the 23rd Middlesex relieving the 20th Durham Light Infantry at Nieuport Bains at 12 midnight, 11th October. Active patrol work was at once begun, patrols swimming the canal on the night of 12th and reconnoitring some two hundred yards of the enemy's ground without discovering any Germans. Trench mortars and *minnenwerfer* were frequently used by the enemy in this sector, but were gradually silenced by the Divisional Artillery. This tour, the last spent by the Battalion before the Division left for Italy, ended on 15th when the Middlesex marched back to camp at La Panne. At the latter

19TH AND 23RD BATTALIONS.

11TH OCTOBER.

19TH AND 23RD BATTALIONS.
4TH NOV.

place training was carried out until 4th November when a move was made to Teteghem. On 13th the Battalion paraded at 8.40 a.m. and marched to the Wormhoudt district and on 15th entrained at Esquelbecq station for Italy.

Four days in the train brought the Middlesex to Cannes where breakfasts were eaten and at 1 p.m. that date (19th) the Italian frontier was crossed. Two days later (at 2 a.m. on 21st) Vigasio was reached where detraining took place immediately. Nine days of marching through strange and picturesque country was now before the Middlesex, during which they billeted in and passed through Della Scalla Isola, Opiano, Ronaldo, Nanto, Piazzola, Massanzago, Istrana and Selva, moving from the latter place to Giavera, their final destination, on 30th November.

30TH NOV.

At Giavera the Battalion was placed in reserve while the Queen's, D.L.I. and West Kents took over the line held by the 53rd and 54th Italian Regiments on the Piave River, the 41st Division having been put into the line to relieve the 1st Italian Division from Nervesa to C. Serena, 123rd Brigade on the right, 122nd Brigade on the left. But it was not until the night of 16th December that the Middlesex moved into the front line on the Montello, the 123rd Brigade having been ordered to relieve the 122nd Brigade in that sector. A heavy fall of snow and the shelling of "D" Company by 60 mm. guns (during which two other ranks were wounded, the first casualties in Italy) are the first incidents recorded of that tour which ended on the 24th when the Battalion was relieved and moved back to reserve billets. The Battalion Diary ends the year with a note that on New Year's Eve the bells of St. Angeli were rung.

Of the Pioneers (19th Battalion) there is little to record with the exception that they were employed on the Nervesa defences as soon as the Division took over the line from the Italians.

SALONIKA.

The early days of the campaign in Salonika are not very interesting. The assistance which the Allies did their best to extend to the Serbs was too late and was insufficient to prevent the overrunning of Serbia, first by the Austro-German Army, and later by Bulgarian troops, for Bulgaria had declared war on Serbia in October, 1915, which declaration was followed immediately by declarations of war on Bulgaria by Great Britain and France.

The 10th, 22nd and 26th British Divisions were already at Salonika when the 28th Division from France landed in November and December and, as already stated, the 3rd Middlesex of the 85th Brigade of the latter Division, were engaged in digging a new line of defences north-east of Salonika when the year closed.

January, February and March of 1916 were uneventful; days, weeks and months were spent in digging and the practice manning of trenches. One day a week was given up to battalion training and another to brigade training. The weather was bitterly cold and, though shelter was of the poorest description, there was as yet a marked absence of sickness amongst the troops. As a slight variation from digging the 85th Brigade carried out a tactical scheme early in April, which entailed three or four days of marching, i.e. to Rumanli, Hapazali, Guvesnes, then back to Rumanli.

The general situation in May was roughly as follows: the greater part of the British forces were concentrated within the prepared line of Salonika, extending from Stavros in the east to the neighbourhood of the Galiko River on the west, though a mixed force had been pushed forward north of Kukus to support the French who were watching the right bank of the Vardar and the northern frontier of Greece.

But early in June the occupation of advance positions along the right bank of the River Struma and its tributary the Butkova from Lake Tahinos to Lozista Village was begun and the 28th Division started to move forward first in a northerly and then in a north-easterly direction. On 5th June the Middlesex handed in all tents, stores, kits, etc., and the Battalion Transport joined. The next day the 85th Brigade Group marched to Ambarkoj, the first stage. On the 7th the march was continued to two miles north-west of Sarigol, west of Kukus, but on the 8th orders were received to move at once to Guvezne which was reached (via Ambarkoj).

The march took place in a terrific heat, the sun was overpowering, and many men were overcome. Others suffered greatly from blistered feet, for before the march began many men had been issued with new boots; no materials for boot-mending were obtainable and whenever a man's boots were worn through a new pair had to be issued. To make matters worse the roads were poor. On the 11th the Brigade Group continued the march

3RD BATTALION.
13TH JUNE.

along the Salonika–Seres road, until on 13th the Brigade reached Orljak, a small village just west of the Struma, the Middlesex arriving at about 9.30 p.m.

On 14th the relief of troops of the 10th Division began. The Middlesex marched at 4 a.m. from their bivouacks at Orljak and took over defence positions from the Irish Rifles as follows : " B " Company Kopriva Bridge, with Battalion Headquarters and " D " Company at Kopriva in support : " A " Company took over the ford over the Struma about one and a-half miles south-east of Kopriva, " C " Company a ford about one and a-half miles northwest of Kopriva, with two platoons forming a detached post on a ford another one and a-half miles further up the river. By the end of June the 28th Division was established on its new front (85th Brigade on the right and 84th on the left) from Orljak to the junction of the Cavdalar–Bursuk road and the River Struma (85th Brigade), and from the left of the 85th Brigade to the neighbourhood of Kranmah (84th Brigade) in touch with the right of the 57th French Division. Each sub-sector was held with two battalions in the line and two in reserve.

Between Lakes Butkova and Tahinos the Struma ran through a fairly flat valley. North of the river there were wide stretches of country with scarcely a rise until the lower slopes of the hills beyond Savjak and Demirhissar were reached. North of these two places the country was wild and rugged, rising in places to between 1,000–2,000 feet. South of the river, however, there was only a narrow stretch of land before the hills were reached, though between Orljak and Kranman the highest point was only some nine hundred feet above the sea level. Between the river and the foot of the hills there ran what was described as an " important track " : it was the only kind of road between Orljak, Kopriva and Lozista. In the valley north of the Struma were many villages of which Barakli Dzuma, Ormanli, Haznatar, Barakli, Elisan and Kumli were probably best known to the 3rd Middlesex. Just where the enemy's front line was there are no records to denote, but apparently his trenches were not very close to the northern banks of the Struma, for after the Battalion relieved the Irish Rifles there is nothing to record but " situation normal,"

16TH JULY.

and indeed, until the Battalion was relieved on 16th July and moved back first to Gumusdfre and then to Hamzali there is no mention of contact with the enemy. But since taking over the Kopriva defences disease had ravaged the Middlesex and by the

9th July no less than nine officers and 229 other ranks had been sent to hospital suffering from pyrexia (fever)*. On the 7th August the strength of the Battalion was only 20 officers and 301 other ranks.

3RD BATTALION.
7TH AUGUST.

The Middlesex sent a composite company of four officers and 104 other ranks to occupy the ground between Hills 920 and 285 on 20th August.

In a special order of the day issued by the G.O.C., Salonika Army, on 30th August, it was announced that Roumania had declared war on Austria-Hungary and that " one of the most important aims of military policy adopted in this theatre of operations has been effected."

It was well worth while telling the troops that for the constant fight against climatic conditions and disease as well as the hard life led by all ranks seemed at last to have some purpose.

At the beginning of September the line held by the 85th Brigade stretched from Hill 920 to Hill 285—about three miles—divided into three sections. During the month several drafts joined the Middlesex from England, as well as many officers and men returned to duty from hospital, and by the end of the month the strength of the Battalion had risen to 24 officers and 870 other ranks.

The intense heat of the summer had given way to cooler weather when, at the end of September and early in October the Action of the Karajakoi's, including the capture of Jenikoj† took place, but in this offensive the Middlesex were not involved. On the 13th, however, they sent a patrol (one officer and twenty other ranks) across the Butkovo to reconnoitre Bursuk, which was found unoccupied. On the 21st the Battalion set out for Gumus Dere, via Paprat and Hamzali: the move was completed by nightfall on 23rd. By the capture of Jenikoj the British line had been pushed forward to the line Agu Mah–Homondos–Elisan–Ormanli, and on 26th the Middlesex sent two companies across the river to work on the defences at the two latter villages.

On the 30th the Battalion moved to Kopriva Bridge where, with two companies of East Surreys, the Buffs and the M.-G. com-

30TH OCTOBER.

---

* With the appendices to the 28th Divisional G.S. Diary there is a document which states that, on account of the health of the troops, as many as possible were to be withdrawn from the Struma Valley, and the river looked upon as a line of observation only and not as a line of resistance.

† Official dates: 30th September–4th October, 1916.

3RD BATTALION.
31ST OCTOBER.

pany, they formed the Divisional Reserve in the attack to take place on the 31st October on Barakli Dzuma.

The enemy's defence line ran along the foothills on the opposite side of the valley. He also occupied the large village of Barakli Dzuma and a line of trenches across the low ground from Savjak to Butkova Lake. In the operations planned for the 31st October the capture of Barakli Dzuma and the advancement of the British line were the objectives. Heavy rain had fallen, water pouring down from the hills on both sides of the valley and the river was considerably swollen. The villages of Elisan, Cavdarmah, Ormanli and Haznatar had therefore been occupied as a preliminary measure, within which bridges were thrown across the Struma.

There are no records of the 3rd Middlesex having taken an active part in the attack of 31st October, which was entirely successful, 350 prisoners being taken, with the exception of " D " Company which at 10 a.m. was sent across the river to Cavdamar as a carrying party, returning at 7 p.m. and rejoining the Battalion which all day long had remained in Divisional Reserve at Kopriva Bridge.

2ND Nov.

On the 2nd November, however, the Middlesex received orders to move on 3rd to Barakli Dzuma and take over " B " sector from the King's Own. By the 4th the Battalion held a portion of the line of the defences of the village with three companies, one company bring in Brigade Reserve at Ormanli.

Patrol work was in the direction of Barakli* and Ernikoj and touch with the enemy maintained. On the 6th 2/Lieut. Hollinghurt and Sergeant Coleman were wounded by rifle fire—the first casualties recorded in the Battalion Diary. On 11th Sergeant Dawes was wounded, also on patrol. On the 15th the artillery bombarded Ernikoj and Spatova and on the 16th an attack was made on Barakli by the Suffolks, " A " Company of the Middlesex taking up a position north of the Barakli Dzuma–Barakli road, one thousand yards from and facing the northern exits of the latter, and acting as a covering party whilst the Suffolks attacked from the south. The village was taken and occupied by the 85th Brigade.

The winter season had now set in and frequent rains rendered the valley of the Struma wet and heavy. Soon snow appeared on the hills north of the valley. Transport and communication

---

* There were two villages, one Barakli Dzuma and the other Barakli.

became more difficult, indeed, sudden rises in the river rendered 3RD
communication precarious so that the construction of bridges BATTALION.
had to be begun.

Throughout November and December patrol work continued
and these excursions occasioned frequent encounters with the
enemy. On 7th December, during a patrol towards Ernikoj, 7TH DEC.
2/Lieut. Taite was wounded and brought in later by 2/Lieut.
Burn. Fine patrol work on the night of 16th/17th brought
congratulations from the Corps and Divisional Commanders.
The year closed with the Battalion at a strength of 44 officers and
1,079 other ranks. Lieut.-Colonel W. Miller commanded the
Battalion.

From the standpoint of engagements with the enemy of 1917.
primary importance, the year 1917 was destined for the 3rd
Middlesex to be even less active than that of 1916 : there were no
actions even of the nature of the " Affair of Barakli Juma'a."
Nevertheless there was constant patrol work along the whole
front, for no opportunity was lost of pushing forward or gaining
ground whenever possible. Summed up in a few words, therefore,
the Middlesex throughout the year 1917 were chiefly engaged in
patrolling the country in front of their sector when in the front
line, in marching to other sectors, or in training when relieved
from their more arduous work of keeping a vigilant watch upon
the enemy.

The month of January was a fair example of work in the front 3RD JANUARY.
line : on the 3rd a patrol went out under 2/Lieut. Hewitt to
search the ground in a north-westerly direction and returned with
a " nil " report. The same officer took out another patrol on
the night of 5th but was fired on and wounded. On 8th a platoon
under 2/Lieut. Harmsworth attacked an enemy trench and cleared
it, the officer and five other ranks being wounded*. On 26th the
Battalion began to change places with the 2nd East Surreys at
Haznatar (west of Barakli Juma'a). In February malaria again
claimed many victims, two officers and 76 other ranks being
evacuated to hospital. The 2nd March saw the Battalion taking 2ND MARCH.
part in a demonstration along the whole front. Haznatar was
flooded on the 9th of the month, the average depth of the water
in the village being two feet : the Struma had begun to overflow
her banks. Training in Ormanli was begun during March, but

* 2/Lieut. Harmsworth died of wounds on 9th January.

3RD BATTALION.	towards the end of the month the Battalion moved north-west to the Lozista area, Battalion Headquarters being established in the village, companies moving to Big Tree Well, Osborne Spur, Hill east of Lozista and Kureni: a standing patrol, furnished alternately by "C" and "D" Companies for four days at a time, was established at Butkova. Three more officers and 90 other ranks went down with malaria during March.
8TH APRIL.	On 8th April 2/Lieut. Dean and one other rank went out on patrol from Butkova in a north-easterly direction. An hour after a sentry in the village heard firing from the direction taken by the patrol. The latter did not return and some hours later an officer and 21 other ranks were sent out to search the country, but returned with no news of Lieut. Dean or the man who had gone
12TH JUNE.	out with him. On the 12th 2/Lieut. Lightfoot with 21 other ranks went out from Butkova in the direction of Dzaferli and returned with three Bulgar prisoners. The 12th June saw the Battalion on the road to Bashanli, thence via Rajanovo and Elesti, to Vaisili where training began. Malaria was again responsible for five officers and 198 other ranks being evacuated to hospital.
27TH AUGUST.	In July the Middlesex again moved back into the front line, on this occasion to Mahmudli (via Baisili) where they were attached to the 83rd Brigade, relieving the 2nd Yorks and Lancs, and 2nd Welch in the trenches on 17th and 18th. Dova Tepe and Kara Orman were posts held by the Battalion. Patrol work in this sector was chiefly carried out in the Todorova area. The 3rd Middlesex were relieved by the 10th Devons and moved to Mahmudli on 27th August where training until 6th September occupied the Battalion. On the latter date an advanced party left camp, followed by the Battalion, for Sirt Dere, via Kurkut: the Battalion was moving back to its old sector at Orljak Bridge. On 7th and 8th Morova and Lahana (respectively) were reached, and on 9th after reaching the 64 kilo stone on the Lahana road "C" Company and two platoons of "B" Company went forward on 10th and took over the defences of the Orljak Bridge, the remainder of the Battalion marching to XVIth Corps Headquarters. Within the next four days the Middlesex were established in the Orljak Bridge defences.
7TH NOV.	A raid on Prosenik carried out by The Buffs on 7th November, during which the 3rd Middlesex (in support) marched to Nevoljen and entered Topolova, and a raid on Kalendra carried out by "B" and "C" Companies from Orljak and "A" and "D" Companies

from Nevoljen on 7th December, are the only incidents of note during the last two months of the year, and New Year's Eve found the Battalion still holding the Orljak Bridge defences with a strength of 28 officers and 956 other ranks.

Another Battalion of the Regiment, the 26th (Pioneers), commanded by Lieut.-Colonel H. W. Blakeney, destined for the east, had left Flixton Camp, Bungay, on the 11th of August, 1916, and, after embarkation at Devonport, arrived at Salonika on the 24th. But after getting ashore and going into bivouacs, the Battalion re-embarked for Stavros on the 28th where they arrived next day. On disembarking at Kara Tasi the Pioneers marched to Ano Krusoves where they formed camp near 80th Brigade Headquarters of the 27th Division, to which they had been posted.

Road making and the clearing of ground for an aerodrome occupied the Battalion for some days, but on the 10th of September during a demonstration against the enemy, the Battalion was held in reserve. By the 23rd of the month the Pioneers had completed their work on the aerodrome and companies took turns in going into the line for instruction in trench warfare. Early in October they moved to new billets in Kopaci, which was also a new area of work. This entailed a march of from some twenty to thirty miles. The Battalion set out on the 10th and reached Kopaci on the 14th, but the next day received orders to march on to Mahmudli where they camped in the neighbourhood of the village.

The somewhat monotonous round of work as Pioneers was relieved towards the end of October when the 26th Middlesex were ordered to take part in a demonstration against the enemy. On the 29th the Battalion first moved up to the right bank of the Struma, near Gun Bridge, and there came under the orders of the 81st Brigade. Early next morning they left bivouacs and marched to Bala where they took over the trenches and posts of the 1st Royal Scots. The demonstration took place on the 31st of October* the 26th Middlesex operating with the 1st Argyll and Sutherland Highlanders against the enemy. It appears, however, to have been a bloodless affair, for there are no records of casualties having been suffered. The Pioneers were relieved at 5.30 p.m. and marched back to bivouacs in the neighbourhood of the Struma. On the 1st of November they returned to camp at Mahmudli. There is, however, little else to record of interest

---

* It was to assist troops further north who were attacking Barakli Juma's.

26TH BATTALION.
1917.

31ST DEC.

3RD BATTALION.
1ST JANUARY.

15TH MARCH.

6TH APRIL.

for the remainder of the year, and on New Year's Eve the Battalion was still in the Mahmudli area.

The year 1917, so far as the 26th Middlesex were concerned, was one of hard work and little of the excitements of battle. The Battalion saw nothing of the operations at Doiran in April and May. From the " strength return " in the records there does not appear to have been much sickness among the Pioneers, nor are any casualties recorded. The keeping of diaries was always an irksome business, and the Pioneers day after day record nothing but " ditto-ditto " or " same as for ———." Weeks and months are passed over thus and but little information as to their life in the battle area is available. The end of 1917 found them in the neighbourhood of Dimitric where 27th Divisional Headquarters were established.

The 3rd Middlesex (Lieut.-Colonel Miller, commanding) began the year 1918 with a strength of 28 officers and 959 other ranks. They were in the Orljak area. At an inspection on the 31st of January by the Commander-in-Chief, the Battalion was congratulated on its excellent appearance and " turn out," and on the following day the Corps and Brigade Commanders also sent their congratulations. During the third week in March a change took place in the location of the Battalion, for the 85th Brigade (28th Division) had been ordered to take over the sector held by the 79th Brigade (26th Division) in the Butkova Valley. The Middlesex were among the first troops to move and on the 15th took the road from Orljak to Lahana. On the 16th, 17th, 18th and 19th they marched to Miroua, Kurkut, Alexia and Indzekli respectively, remaining billeted in the latter village until the 21st when they relieved the 10th Devons in the left sub-sector of the Dova Tepe sector, just south of the Butkova River and the railway.

Two platoons of " D " Company made a demonstration on the 6th of April against Akindzali Wood. They reached a position three hundred yards south of the wood and opened fire. The enemy replied with heavy rifle and machine-gun fire and later put down an artillery barrage. The Middlesex lost in this affair 11 other ranks wounded (1 died of wounds later) and Captain F. Defries and 2 other ranks missing: the officer was later reported killed.

The sector held by the Middlesex formed a salient of which Dova Tepe was the northern apex. The Butkova River and the railway ran side by side round the salient. Dova Tepe was about eight miles north of Indzekli, and north-west of the latter village, in between that place and the Butkova, was Popovo, with Karadzali and Babovo a mile or two north. Across the Butkova, opposite the left face of the salient, were the villages of Bulamac, Frozili, Calki and Karali. Patrols were constantly reconnoitring these villages. On the 26th of April Karali was well reconnoitred, for a raid was to take place on the village. The raiding party, consisting of one platoon, left No. 21 Work on the 30th—two platoons to form a covering party, while the remaining two platoons followed north of Karali. The latter then swept through the village. Two Bulgars were killed and others wounded. Casualties in the Middlesex were 1 officer and 2 other ranks slightly wounded. The patrol then withdrew. *3RD BATTALION.* *26TH APRIL.*

In May the "summer line" was sited and dug, and this work occupied the troops for the remainder of the month, the main line being occupied on the 2nd of June. Patrols were now very active along the whole front, Todorova and Hodza Bridge being visited almost every other night by strong parties of fifty other ranks and an officer. There was, however, very little to report, and week after week passed without incident of sufficient importance to mention. Equally bare of exciting details was August. Even in September, when the Second Battle of Doiran took place, the narrative, from the regimental point of view, is not very interesting, for the 3rd Middlesex were not in the front of the battle, the 85th Brigade supporting the Greeks who attacked the Bulgars on the 18th of September. *18TH SEPT.*

THE BATTLE OF DOIRAN, 1918.
18th–19th September.

The Battle of Doiran, 1918, which opened on the morning of the 18th of September, had been preceded by operations on the 14th, during which the enemy's line from Sokoi to Vetrenik was attacked. This attack was successful and at 6 a.m. on the former date a Greek Division, with the 27th and 26th British Divisions, attacked the Bulgarian lines between Lake Doiran and the Vardar, the 27th Division operating west of the river. This was the main attack. Simultaneously with the main attack a subsidiary and surprise attack was launched around the eastern and northern sides of the lake against the Bulgarian trenches on the slopes of

3RD BATTALION. 18TH SEPT.

the Beles range. The attacking troops in the subsidiary attack were the Cretan Division, supported by the 84th and 85th Brigades of the 28th Division and the artillery of the latter.

At nightfall on the 18th the position was roughly : the Cretan Division held the enemy outpost line—Long Wood–Akindzali–Kudzakoria Wood : the 84th Brigade from the Wood—1331/1945 –Cakli Station Bluff : 85th Brigade in reserve.

West of Doiran Town, Teton Hill and Petit Couronne had also been captured.

As already stated the 3rd Middlesex, as part of the 85th Brigade, were in support to the Greeks who were attacking the range of hills north of the Butkova. Just before midnight (18th) orders were received for the Battalion to take up a defensive position from a point four hundred yards south-east of Kodza Koria to a point four hundred yards north of Akindzali, to cover the withdrawal of the Greek Division. By 4 a.m. on the 19th the Middlesex had taken up positions, all four companies in line with Battalion Headquarters in Karali. At 11 p.m. that night, however, they withdrew to the line Akindzali–Karali–Patol Tree, in order to join up with the 84th Brigade on the right. Three companies held the line, the fourth taking over Bulamac with Battalion Headquarters, as reserve.

20TH SEPT.

On the 20th Akindzali and Karali were intermittently shelled, but it was the last " flicker of the flame," for the Bulgarians were already beaten. Events along the Western Front, where the Germans were being forced back to their frontier, suffering enormous losses, and the victorious progress of the Allies had taken the heart out of the Bulgarian resistance. Turkey was beaten, the Austro-Hungarian army was falling back before the Italians, and in every theatre the Central Powers had as good as lost the War.

22ND SEPT.

On the 22nd, the 3rd Middlesex, being then at Surlovo, information came to hand that the Bulgarians were falling back along the whole line and the pursuit of the enemy was ordered. The 83rd Brigade of the 28th Division was ordered to take up an outpost line from Kara Oglular–Speckled Hill, Hill 230 and Lake Doiran. The 85th Brigade was ordered to follow, the Middlesex to form the advanced guard of the Brigade. The Battalion set out on the 23rd to march to Doiran, but owing to the ravages of influenza, was formed into two companies. On the 24th they reached the neighbourhood of Cerniste (west of Doiran), on the

25th Dzuma Boraji, on the 26th a camp 1,000 yards north of Boluntili : by the 27th they had reached camp near the crest of Beles on the Boluntili–Bjansko track, and on the 28th Dzuma Obasi. In the latter place they remained for several days. The Battalion was now very weak and could only muster 18 officers and 239 other ranks. The strenuous marching, carried out since the 18th of the month, the hard conditions of the advance and sufferings of the men from influenza, had resulted in no less than five officers and 442 other ranks being evacuated to hospital since the 16th. 3RD BATTALION. 27TH SEPT.

By the 30th of September the Bulgarian Government had asked for, and had been granted an Armistice, and on that date hostilities were suspended.

On the 1st of October the 3rd Middlesex were reorganised into two companies of four platoons each, two Lewis guns to each platoon. Training then began. Several days also were spent in salvage work. Rain fell heavily on the 9th and the next day, to everyone's relief, orders were received to get ready to move. The Battalion left Dzumasi Obasi on the 11th and marched to Sobrezir. This march was followed by others to Hazanli, Hirsova, Janes, Sarigol, Ambarkoj and Guvesne : the latter place was reached on the 22nd and the Middlesex went into billets. During these marches reinforcements joined and on the 31st of the month the strength of the Battalion had been brought up to 15 officers and 580 other ranks. 1ST OCTOBER.

A fortnight was spent at Guvesne, then on the 6th of November the 3rd Middlesex returned to Lembet, where they awaited embarkation orders. On the very day that the Armistice was signed in France (11th November) the Battalion embarked aboard H.M.T. "Katoumba" and on the following day sailed from Salonika for Constantinople. 6TH NOVEMBER.

Meanwhile the 26th Middlesex (Pioneers), attached to the 27th Division, spent the first six months of the year 1918 at work in the Divisional area, Divisional Headquarters being then at Dimitic. But early in July the Division moved to the XIIth Corps area, west of the Vardar. 26TH BATTALION.

The transport and personnel of the 26th Battalion left for the new area near Dreveno on the 1st of the month, and were joined on the 11th by the remainder of the Battalion which, on detraining at Gumendze Station, moved off to camp five miles north. In this area the Middlesex spent the ensuing weeks hard at work round Mayadag. There is little of outstanding importance in the Battalion Diaries, but one item may be mentioned: on the 14th of August the Pioneers sent £50 back to England for St. Dunstan's Home, proceeds of the sale of refreshments of the Regimental Revue Party. It is the one human touch in those brief records of hard work and seemingly little rest.

On the 1st of September the Roche Noir Salient, north of Barakli Mah and Alcak Mah, was attacked by the 27th Division and captured. The 26th Middlesex furnished parties of men as stretcher bearers for this operation and were also engaged in digging a communication trench between Roche Noir and Meunier after the former had been captured.

On the 18th of September the Battle of Doiran, 1918, opened. The Pioneers were by this time reduced to a strength of 740 other ranks: disease and casualties during the past few weeks had begun to thin the Battalion out. When the Battle began the Middlesex provided guards for Gumendje and Bohemitza bridges.

Doiran and the Bulgar trenches west of the town having fallen into the hands of the Allies, the 27th Division on the western bank of the River Vardar began the pursuit of the enemy in a northerly direction. On the 23rd the Pioneers, less those men who were unfit for marching left in the old camp area, concentrated at L'Eperon under orders of the Division. The next day they marched to Artillery Berg and on the 25th to Pardovica. At the latter place they remained one day, then on the 27th began three days' hard marching. They reached and camped at Mravanca that night, moved to Cestovo on the 28th, and to Izlis on the 29th, in which place they billeted until the 18th of October. Their strength on reaching Izlis was 31 officers and 560 other ranks: malaria and hard marching was responsible for many men having to be evacuated to hospital.

The 26th Battalion came under orders of the 82nd Infantry Brigade on the 18th of October and marched to Strumica, from which place they turned eastwards, and by the 21st had reached the Livunovo–Petric area. On the 22nd "A" and "B" Companies with transport moved to Rupel for work on the railway, halting one night at Marinopolje. For four days the Battalion remained thus split up but on the 26th the move was continued to Starcovo, on the 27th to two kilos north-east of Gumendza, on the 28th to Kriva Livada, on the 29th to Krupnik where the Pioneers rested, and greatly they needed it, for they had already

lost twelve men who died from malaria and pneumonia, and their 26TH
strength was now 27 officers and 432 other ranks. They continued BATTALION.
the march to Karaszukoj on the 31st. Several more days on the
road and at last the Battalion, on the 10th of November, marched 10TH Nov.
into familiar surroundings at Orljak where they rested throughout
the whole of the 10th.

There is little need to follow in detail the movements of the
26th Battalion, for the War was over, but when the 27th Division
moved to Constantinople the Pioneers moved also, arriving on
the 28th of December. They did not land, however, but went
on to Baytoum where they landed on the 31st.

Thus, so far as the Middlesex Regiment was concerned, ended 31ST DEC.
the campaign in Salonika. If the troops in that theatre of the
War saw but a small amount of fighting, they nevertheless lived
under extraordinarily hard conditions and their struggle against
disease was a noteworthy feature of the operations.

CHAPTER XLIII.

The Eastern Theatre of War:
II. PALESTINE.

STILL further east, the 2/10th Middlesex in 1917 saw much hard fighting, carried out under climatic and other difficulties, during the Invasion of Palestine.   2/10TH BATTALION.

At the beginning of 1917 the Battalion was at Mazar holding the defences of that place for, after the Battle of Rumani in August, 1916, the British line had been gradually pushed forward until, when the New Year dawned, El Arish had been reached. South-east of the latter place a small action with the Turks had been fought at El Magdhaba* on 23rd December which ended in the capture of that place by the Desert Column, and on 9th January a brilliant little affair at Rafah† resulted in the capture of 1,600 prisoners and much war material. In neither of these affairs were the Middlesex engaged, the first month of the year being spent in training and field firing when released from their duties of holding defensive posts.   23RD DEC., 1916.

In February, however, they began to move forward and on the 1st marched to Maaden, on the 2nd to Bardawil, and on the 3rd to El Arish where the Battalion formed the Brigade Reserve. The 53rd Division then was engaged in relieving the 42nd Division which had been ordered to France.   1917.

THE FIRST BATTLE OF GAZA.
26th–27th March.

By the 5th February " pipe head," that is to say, the head of the water supply (beyond which the general line could not be advanced) had reached El Arish and the construction of the railway ahead of that place had begun. It was the 22nd before another advance was possible, mounted troops pushing on to Sheikh Zowaiid, while the infantry of the Division began to move   5TH FEB.

---

* The Affair of Magdhaba, 23rd December, 1916.
† The Action of Rafah, 9th January, 1917.

2/10TH BATTALION.
23RD FEB.

forward, the 2/10th Middlesex marching to El Burg: on the 23rd the Battalion reached Sheikh Zowaiid, occupying an outpost line until the close of the month. On the 1st March the Middlesex marched to Long View, forming reserve for the Brigade outpost line, but it was 21st before the Battalion began the march to Rafah, thence to Khan Yunis on 24th, and finally to Deir el Belah (eight miles south-west of Gaza) on 25th where a halt was called for from three to four hours. From Deir el Belah the Battalion moved forward to take part in the First Battle of Gaza, 26th-27th March.

Deir el Belah (a picturesque village of farms and olive groves, with some ruins and a shrine) was the only wooded area between the gardens of the towns of Gaza and Khan Yunis. Between the village and Gaza the great Wadi Ghazze ran in a north-westerly to south-easterly direction—a formidable crossing before the advance on the town. All approaches to the latter were covered by cactus hedges which, particularly on the southern side, presented great difficulties. They were of such a height and thickness as to be destructible only by high explosives or prolonged work: as natural obstacles they were stronger than any the Turks could have constructed. The hostile trenches south of Gaza were only approachable up bare slopes. Practically until close to the city there was no cover for an attacking force.

The three objectives of the British were (i) to gain the line of the Wadi Ghazze in order to cover the advance of the railway, (ii) to prevent the enemy withdrawing unmolested from Gaza, (iii) the capture of the city with its garrison by a *coup de main*. The attack was to be carried out by the Desert Column (two mounted divisions and the 53rd Division), the 52nd and 54th Divisions and two brigades (one a camel brigade and the other the 229th Brigade of the newly formed 74th Division).

The enemy's main body (estimated at between two and three divisions) was in the Tel el Nejile–Huj area, south of the Wadi el Hesi, covered by detachments about Gaza, Sheria–Hereira and Beersheba. The scheme of the attack was for infantry, supported by artillery, to assault Gaza from the south while mounted troops enveloped the town from the east and north.

It is almost impossible for those who were not on the battle-field to appreciate the great difficulties experienced in supplying water for both infantry and cavalry. The latter especially, operating in hostile country, without an adequate supply could not "carry on" unless they were fortunate in finding wells or 2/10TH BATTALION. could carry sufficient water with them. It is well to point this out.

Of the 53rd Division the 158th Brigade (on the right) was to attack Ali el Muntar, and the 160th Brigade (on the left) the Labyrinth. Both Brigades were to begin crossing the Wadi Ghazze at 3.30 a.m. on 26th: the former was then to advance to a covered position behind the Mansura Ridge, the latter to the neighbourhood of El Sheluf: the 159th Brigade was in reserve with orders to follow the 158th Brigade across the Wadi and remain on the right bank until further orders.

Artillery ammunition was limited, but it was to be used chiefly in bombarding the "Labyrinth," a group of trenches enclosed by cactus hedges (natural defences already referred to), due south of Gaza.

The 54th Division, on the right of the 53rd, was to cover the rear of the latter, whilst on the left Money's Detachment, operating along the coast, was to divert the enemy's attention.

The 160th Brigade left Deir el Belah at 1 a.m. on 26th and by 26TH MARCH. 3.45 a.m. had crossed the Wadi Ghazze. The advance on El Sheluf was then begun, the Sussex (the leading Battalion of the Brigade) reporting that they had occupied the prominence known as the El Sire Ridge at 5.10 a.m. Orders were then issued to push on to the El Sheluf Ridge. With the Middlesex in close support, the Sussex reported their position on the latter ridge at 7.55, the 2/10th reaching the ridge and halting there at 8.45 a.m.

The advance had, hitherto, been carried out in a dense mist which from dawn had covered the whole of the battlefield. At about 8.15 a.m., however, it cleared. Nevertheless the advance of the cavalry on the extreme right had been seriously delayed by the mist, though eventually they succeeded in enveloping Gaza from the north and east.

At 11.30 a.m. orders were issued from 160th Brigade Headquarters for the Sussex (on the right) to attack Ali el Muntar, and the 2/10th Middlesex (on the left) "The Labyrinth."

Scouts reported that both objectives were strongly held and Brigade Headquarters asked for artillery support. The time was now about 12.22 p.m.

From the very brief account of the Battle contained in the Diary of the 2/10th Middlesex, it is not possible to give more than

2/10TH BATTALION. 26TH MARCH.

a brief outline of the attack: neither do the diaries of other units (including that of Brigade Headquarters) lend much assistance.

The 2/10th advanced to the attack of "The Labyrinth" at 11.50 a.m. and at 1.30 p.m. they reported "Labyrinth cleared and a position seized on a grass ridge facing town at about eight hundred yards distance, with left resting in cultivated and broken ground."

The next entry is at 5 p.m. and records that the battalion line was reinforced by two companies of the 2/4th Queen's. But the intervening period had been spent in hard fighting. Progress must have been terribly difficult for in the Brigade Diary it is stated that four belts of barbed wire entanglements were up in front of the Middlesex: they had to negotiate the cactus hedges as well. At about 3.30 p.m. the 2/10th had asked for reinforcements and more ammunition. At 7 p.m. the O.C., Middlesex, reported that unless reinforced his position would be untenable, but he was ordered to consolidate the position won. The impossible nature of the country is shown by the fact that water and S.A.A. had to be carried up by hand, over a distance of $1\frac{1}{4}$ miles.

Just before midnight 160th Brigade Headquarters received orders to withdraw to a line running from Green Hill to El Sheluf, and by 4.30 a.m. the Brigade had fallen back as directed, the Middlesex holding the front line with the Queen's and Sussex in reserve.

Apparently "The Labyrinth," that amazingly difficult position to capture, had to be abandoned—a bitter pill indeed for those who had striven most gallantly throughout the 26th first to capture and then to hold it.

But the reason was that, although the infantry attack as a whole was a success and Gaza had been enveloped as planned, the enemy had been able to rush reinforcements up and force the cavalry to fall back while the town had been reinforced, and the British infantry who had pressed up to the outskirts found themselves unable to hold the positions gained.

Eventually the whole line was withdrawn to the western banks of the Wadi Ghazze, for although the Turk's counter-attacks on the 53rd and 54th Divisions were repulsed, to hold the positions won permanently was deemed impossible. The 160th Brigade fell back to Sheikh Reschid, reaching that place at about 1.30 a.m. on 28th March, the 2/10th Middlesex (the left unit of the Brigade) taking up an outpost line at that place.

28TH MARCH.

The Battalion had suffered heavy casualties through the operations: 4 officers had been killed* and 5 wounded, whilst in other ranks the losses were 14 killed, 108 wounded, and 26 missing.

2/10TH BATTALION.

THE SECOND BATTLE OF GAZA.
17th–19th April.

The conditions confronting the British in the Second Battle of Gaza were entirely different from those which obtained during the First Battle. At the time of the latter Gaza was merely a point in the Turkish outpost line, but in the Second Battle the attacking forces were opposed to a definite system of strongly organised defences, running from the sea coast, through the town, and thence along the Beersheba road to Abu Hureira—a distance of twelve miles.

Time was necessary in order to prepare for the next attack. The interval, spent by the British in bringing up stores and troops, guns and ammunition, as well as making reconnaissances and sending out patrols, was also spent by the enemy in throwing up new works and generally perfecting his line of defences. His strength was now estimated at about thirty-five battalions and one hundred guns.

The first step on the British side was to extend the railway, which by early April had reached Deir el Belah, five miles from the Wadi Ghazze. Reservoirs were then constructed and the water supply improved considerably. The weather was reasonably cool and the health of the troops good.

The operations were to consist of two phases: in the first the three infantry divisions which were to make the attack, *i.e.*, 54th, 52nd and 53rd in that order from right to left, were to cross the Wadi Ghazze and take up positions extending from the Sheikh Abbas Ridge through Mansura to Kurd Hill (54th and 52nd Divisions), thence in a north-westerly direction to the coast (53rd Division): mounted troops were to cover the right of the 54th Division by demonstrating towards Abu Hureira.

The 53rd Division was to cross the Wadi west of the Rafah—

---

* No names of officers killed are given either in the Battalion or Brigade Diaries. "Officers Killed in the War" gives two officers killed—Capt. R. O. C. Watson and 2/Lieut. G. E. Quibell—possibly in Palestine.

Gaza road and push forward an outpost line from Red House through Tell-el-Ujul to Money Hill and also occupy the coast between Marine Hill and Cheshire Clump.

2/10TH BATTALION.

16TH/17TH APRIL.

The crossing of the Wadi Ghazze and the capture of the outpost line took place on the night 16th/17th April and was effected with only slight opposition in the centre of the line. On the morning of the 17th April (at 7.30 a.m.) the 54th and 52nd Divisions held the line Sheikh Abbas Ridge, Mansura to Kurd Hill, while the 53rd Division had occupied the line allotted to it with the 4th Queen's on Brown Hill. On the night of 17th the latter Division pushed forward an outpost line running from the enemy's side of Softly Hill to the sea, just north of Marine View: the 160th Brigade was on the right and the 158th on the left: touch with the 52nd Division was maintained at Kurd Hill.

Throughout the 18th the British artillery on land, and naval guns at sea bombarded the Turkish positions, and final preparations for the main attack were made.

The main attack was to take place from Sheikh Abbas and Mansura: the 53rd Division, on the left, after securing Sampson Ridge, was to push on and occupy the Turkish trenches west of Gaza, but not enter the town.

18TH APRIL.

On the night of 18th the attacking troops moved to their assembly positions, the 160th Brigade at 8 p.m. being disposed as follows: 2/4th Queen's, Red House; 2/4th West Kents and 2/10th Middlesex, Money Hill, 1/4th Sussex, Garden Post.

19TH APRIL.

The artillery bombardment was to begin at 5.30 a.m. on 19th and the infantry attack at 7.30 a.m.

The attack of the 53rd Division, however, began fifteen minutes before the attacks of the 54th and 52nd Divisions in order to attract the enemy's attention to that flank.

The 2/10th Middlesex began their advance at 7.15 a.m., their objective being the right redoubt on Sampson's Ridge. The attack, however, progressed slowly owing to heavy machine-gun fire from the wooded area east of the ridge. At 11.15 a.m. the Battalion was reinforced on the right flank by the 1/4th Sussex. It is disappointing, however, that no details exist of the bayonet charge which took place at 1 p.m. resulting not only in the capture of the ridge, but also of two Turkish officers and forty-three other ranks. Fifteen minutes later the Middlesex began consolidating the new position, a gap on their right being filled by the 1st Herefords. On the left of the 160th Brigade the 159th Brigade

Gaza not Captured

had little difficulty in pushing forward to just north of Sheikh Ajlin. On the right of the 53rd Division the 54th and 52nd Divisions had made progress towards the Beersheba road, Middlesex Hill and Blazed Hill, then back to Heart Hill. But Gaza was not captured, the enemy's resistance was too formidable, while the British artillery could not give sufficient support owing to lack of ammunition, and without adequate artillery support no infantry could have done more against the powerful hostile defences (natural and artificial) held by troops of no mean fighting quality. [2/10TH BATTALION. 19TH APRIL.]

The final line consolidated ran from the Sheikh Abbas Ridge in a north-westerly direction to Lees Hill, Heart Hill, crossing Sampson's Ridge and the western side of Bunker's Hill to the sea just north of Sheikh Ajlin.

At 3.45 a.m. on 20th April the 2/10th Middlesex were relieved and moved back to the sea shore north of the Wadi Ghazze. [20TH APRIL.]

The Battalion's losses on the 19th/20th were 2 officers killed and 7 wounded, and in other ranks 27 killed, 8 died of wounds, 6 missing and 132 wounded.

The Second Battle of Gaza was followed by a period of about six months of comparative inactivity. From Gaza to Beersheba, a distance of about thirty miles, the Turks were busy strengthening their defences: the British did the same, for before another attack on the town could take place a vast amount of preparation was necessary. Moreover, the hot weather was at hand and the principal efforts of the opposing forces would be to fight disease and leave the fighting with one another to cooler weather.

In both Battles of Gaza the 2/10th had had hard luck. Very gallantly in the first attack they had stormed the Labyrinth, and in the second action had taken Sampson's Ridge with the bayonet —all to no purpose. But they had done their best and had done it well, too.

After the second failure to take Gaza trench warfare once more set in. Between May and October several moves in the line and in reserve took place, also one or two items of special interest.

Lieut.-Colonel V. L. N. Pearson, commanding 2/10th Middlesex, was appointed to command the 160th Brigade and Major A. P. Hohler assumed command of the Battalion.

In August there were several small brushes with the enemy. On the 11th a patrol of one officer and twenty other ranks, reconnoitring Sugar Loaf Hill, stumbled on a listening post of three Turks and killed them. Two days later, a raiding party, consisting [11TH AUGUST.]

2/10TH BATTALION. of three officers and three platoons, raided Sugar Loaf and met a Turkish raiding party. A sharp fight ensued which resulted in the rout of the Turks, who left one officer and one man in the hands of the Middlesex: two dead Turks were also taken in and buried. On 15th a party of two officers and two platoons rushed Sugar Loaf with the bayonet and captured it. Two desperate attempts by the enemy to recapture the hill were driven off by Lewis-gun fire, thirty-eight dead Turks being counted.

25TH AUGUST. Towards the end of the month (on the 25th August) the Battalion was withdrawn to Deir el Belah for intensive training, which lasted until the 24th October. On the latter date, however, the 2/10th left Deir el Belah and, marching in a south-easterly direction, reached Esh Shellal where the Battalion took up an outpost line on the right of the 53rd Division, on the Wadi Hanafish, in touch with the 74th Division on the left.

THE THIRD BATTLE OF GAZA.
27th October–7th November.
THE CAPTURE OF BEERSHEBA.

Although the third and final Battle of Gaza began on 31st October, the capture of Beersheba being the first phase of the operations, two events place the opening of the Battle four days earlier—on the 27th. The bombardment of the Gaza defences began on the latter date, and also the Turks attacked a line of outposts near El Girheir, held by Yeomanry who were engaged in covering railway construction. The gallant resistance made by the Yeomanry enabled the 53rd Division to come up in time and the Turks withdrew, having suffered heavy losses.

In the scheme of operations about to begin Sir E. H. Allenby (who had taken over command of the Egyptian Expeditionary Force in June) intended launching his principal attack against the left flank of the main Turkish position, *i.e.*, Abu Hereira–Tell el Sheria. A necessary preliminary to this attack, however, was the capture of Beersheba in order to secure the water supplies at that place and give room for the deployment of the attacking forces on the high ground north and north-west of Beersheba, from which direction Abu Hereira and Tell el Sheria were to be attacked. Success here might well force the enemy to fall back from the rest of his fortified positions, including Gaza, with its formidable defences.

The enemy's right at Gaza was to be attacked with a view to 2/10TH
keeping him uncertain as to where the main attack was to fall.   BATTALION.
In the attack on Beersheba two Divisions (60th and 74th) were 31ST OCTOBER.
to assault the hostile works between the Khalasa road and the
Wadi Saba, masking the works north of the Wadi with the Imperial
Camel Corps and infantry : troops of the 53rd Division, further
north, were to cover the left of the Camel Corps. Mounted
troops were to take up a line opposite the southern defences of
Beersheba.

The attack was entirely successful, the town being captured
at about 7 p.m. by a fine charge carried out by Australian mounted
troops. The 2/10th Middlesex, however, took no part in the
actual attack, and it was not until next day (1st November) that 1ST Nov.
they moved off at 5 a.m. from Hill 765 (east of the Wadi Hanifish)
to the town where they remained halted until 5 p.m. The
Battalion then moved out and took up a position about one mile
south of El Muweileh. The 53rd Division then occupied a line
from Towal abu Jerwal (six miles north of Beersheba) to El
Muweileh (about four miles north-east of Abu Irgeig) where,
with the Imperial Camel Corps, the 53rd Division was to secure
the flank of the attack on Sheria.

On the 2nd November the 2/10th Middlesex again moved
forward, taking up an outpost line vaguely described as from X.5
to V.32 (north-west of Tuweiyil abu Jerwal), where they were in
touch with the 1/4th Royal Sussex on the right and 159th Brigade
on the left. This line they retrenched for, although the Turks
had lost Beersheba, they evidently intended disputing further
advances north. In spite of fairly accurate shell fire the Middlesex
dug themselves in, one officer (who died of wounds next day and
whose name is not given) and seventeen other ranks being wounded.
The Battalion was relieved that night by troops of the 74th
Division, but remained in and around El Muweileh.

The 53rd Division had, however, received orders to attack the 3RD Nov.
line Ain Kohleh–Tell Khuneilfeh on 3rd. At dawn, therefore,
on that date the Middlesex marched via Towal abu Jerwal to a
position about 1,500 yards south-east of Ain Kohleh, on the left
of the 2/4th Royal West Kents. The advance was difficult : the
enemy was found holding Ain Kohleh and Khuweilfeh with considerable and increasing forces. Rifle and machine-gun fire
caused the Middlesex to lose one other rank killed and two officers
and six other ranks wounded.

2/10TH
BATTALION.
4TH NOV.

Increasingly heavy hostile rifle and machine-gun fire broke out on the 4th November. During the day the Middlesex obtained touch on the left with the 159th Brigade, a trench-mortar battery of the latter doing good work against the enemy. On the night of 4th/5th a company of the Middlesex was lent to the 2/4th West Kents to assist them in an attack, but rejoined the Battalion during the evening of the 5th. Four other ranks were killed on the 4th and sixteen wounded, while on the 5th the casualties were two other ranks killed and two wounded.

At 9 a.m. on 6th two companies were sent off to the 158th Brigade about two or three thousand yards south-east of Tell Khuweilfeh: the remainder of the Battalion followed at 1.30 p.m. At 4.30 p.m. a company was moved up to support the 1/7th Royal Welsh Fusiliers on the Tell owing to a heavy counter-attack. This attack was beaten back by the guns. Finally, the whole Battalion was moved forward to relieve the R.W. Fusiliers on the ridge east of the Tell.

The operations of 6th November had resulted in the capture of the Tell el Khuweilfeh and, although we were at one time driven off it again, it was recaptured, together with another hill which much improved the situation, in a fine counter-attack. The official despatches, referring to this day's fighting, stated that "the stubborn fighting of the 53rd (Welsh) Division, Imperial Camel Corps, and part of the mounted troops during November 2nd to 6th drew in and exhausted the Turkish reserves and paved the way for the success of the attack on Sheria." Seven hundred prisoners and nine guns were taken by the 53rd Division.

The night of 6th/7th was characterised by patrol activity around the Tell, but no serious attack was made. The Middlesex lost on 6th two other ranks killed, two officers and ten other ranks wounded.

7TH NOV.

On the 7th several attempts by the enemy to advance were beaten off with rifle and Lewis-gun fire and rifle grenades, while at one period a bayonet charge forced him to retire rapidly and, in falling back, he had to pass through our barrage which took heavy toll of his troops. In the evening a general retirement by the Turks began, followed by machine-gun and artillery fire. Only a few snipers were left behind but these were adequately dealt with. Casualties on the 7th were three other ranks killed and twenty wounded.

On this day Gaza fell and the British troops in that sector of

the line by nightfall had reached a line well to the north and north- 2/10TH
east of the town, while in the centre the line had been pushed BATTALION.
forward to about a mile north of Tell el Sheria.

On the 9th the Middlesex rejoined the 160th Brigade and 9TH Nov.
were placed in reserve. Apparently the Battalion made no move
until 13th when it occupied the high ground from Dahariyeh to
Burs el Beiyara,* returning to bivouacs at nightfall : the operation
was repeated on the 14th.

By the 14th the Desert Mounted Corps, the 57th and 75th 14TH Nov.
Divisions and Australian mounted troops had reached an outpost
line south-west of Ramleh, north-west of Jerusalem, but in these
operations the 53rd Division was not engaged. The 2/10th
Middlesex remained in the same bivouacs until the end of
November. Their total losses during the month were one officer
died of wounds, 13 other ranks killed, four officers and 71
other ranks wounded.

THE CAPTURE OF JERUSALEM.
7th–9th December.

Until the 3rd December the 53rd Division and XXth Corps
Cavalry (the whole known as Mott's Detachment) remained in
the Khuweilfeh area, but on that date began to move in a north-
easterly direction along the Beersheba–Jerusalem road.

The 2/10th Middlesex, during the night 3rd/4th marched to
Dilbeh, thence to bivouacs one mile south of Hebron. Here they
remained until the 6th. On the latter date, however, the 160th
Brigade marched through Hebron towards Bethlehem, the
Middlesex taking up an outpost position from Hill 170 to Beit
Fejja.

On the 7th the advance was continued three miles north along 7TH DEC.
the Bethlehem road, until the enemy was found holding the high
ground in front. In a thick mist the Queen's and Middlesex
advanced to clear the Turks off the hill, but the enemy evacuated
it without meeting the attack. That night the 2/10th bivouacked
with outposts pushed out on the high ground.

Although for nearly a month the 53rd Division had not been
engaged with the enemy, it was nevertheless playing its part in

* The action of El Mughar was fought on this day, but the 2/10th Middlesex were
not engaged, though they were granted the Battle Honour.

2/10TH BATTALION.

driving back the enemy. Its duty, that of flank guard, may have seemed uninteresting and, indeed, the diaries between the 7th November and the 7th December make but dry reading. All the attacks were being made north-west of the Division where the Turks were being driven from position to position until by 6 p.m. on 7th they had lost Jaffa and Ramleh and the 60th and 74th Divisions were within striking distance of the Holy City.

With the exception of the 158th Brigade, which was south of El Dhaheriye, the 159th and 160th Brigades and the Corps Cavalry had reached the Bilbeh area, roughly ten miles south-west of Jerusalem.

Delayed by the weather and the strength of the enemy's resistance, the 53rd Division was not able to get into position to attack the high ground west and south-west of Beit Jala until 9 a.m. on 8th, the main attack from the west of Jerusalem having begun at dawn. That day, towards dusk, British troops were reported to have passed Lifta and to be in sight of the City. A sudden panic thereupon fell upon the Turks west and south-west of Jerusalem. "At 17.00 (5 p.m.) civilians were surprised to see a Turkish transport column galloping furiously citywards along the Jaffa road. In passing they alarmed all units within sight or hearing, and the wearied infantry arose and fled, bootless and without rifles, never pausing to think or fight. Some were flogged back by their officers and were compelled to pick up their arms: others staggered on through the mud, augmenting the confusion of the retreat."* That is a picture of the last Turkish resistance before Jerusalem.

8TH DEC.

The 53rd Division had cleared the high ground at Beit Jala and some Corps Cavalry, moving right across the front of the Division, cut the enemy's line of retreat by getting astride the Jerusalem road where it turns east from the valley of Jehosophat. At night the Turks made no counter-attacks and, without hope of being able to hold their positions, retired to a line north and north-east of the City.

After four centuries the Holy City had at last been wrested from the Turks—the "Day of deliverance had come!"

9TH DEC.

The City was surrendered officially on the 9th December, but the 2/10th Middlesex saw nothing of that historic happening. They had marched to and bivouacked at Beit Jala on that day.

* "A Brief Record of the Advance of the Egyptian Expeditionary Force."

Just at that period all the discomforts of the campaign were theirs but none of the excitements or the honours of battle. On the 11th they marched from Beit Jala to Mar Elias, taking up an outpost position in and around Sur Bahir.

2/10TH BATTALION.
9TH DEC.

Although the troops of the 160th Brigade were engaged with the enemy on the 17th the 2/10th Middlesex made no move from their bivouacs north of Mar Elias. On the 19th they sent a company to hold Kh. Deir Ibn Obeid, the remainder of the Battalion marching back to Brigade reserve.

On the 21st December, however, the Battalion took part in an attack on Ras es Zamby, and greatly distinguished itself.

21ST DEC.

At 5 a.m. three companies of the Queen's, supported by two brigades of R.F.A., a section of " Heavies " and machine guns, moved forward to advance the outpost line of the Brigade: two companies of the 2/10th Middlesex (under the command of the O.C., Queen's) were in reserve.

The objectives were (i) Ras es Zamby, (ii) a strong artery known as The Wall joining the first objective to (iii) White Hill.

The leading company of the Queen's was to capture Zamby and clear the ground on the forward slopes for about one hundred yards: the second company was to follow the first to Zamby and make good The Wall, then continue its advance and seize White Hill; the third company was to follow the second to The Wall and remain there in support. The Middlesex were to remain at the assembly position (given as J.4.d.central) in reserve.

The leading company of the Queen's, after moving forward, found a small hill (Cheshire Hill) between them and Zamby, occupied by a Turkish post. The latter was beaten off, but counterattacked and was again dispersed, this time by grenades. But beyond this point the Queen's were unable to advance, for violent machine-gun fire from Ras el Sufa and their right flank swept the terrain. The advance being held up, the artillery were asked to place a twenty-minutes concentration on Zamby and The Wall.

The Middlesex were then ordered to advance through the Queen's and seize Zamby. Under cover of the artillery barrage " D " Company of the Middlesex crept forward and assaulted Zamby immediately the guns lifted: the assault was successful. The Queen's followed the Middlesex and made good the ground in advance of Zamby, the second company of the Middlesex (" A ") and a company of the Queen's pressing forward parallel with The Wall seized White Hill.

Consolidation of the ground won now proceeded and, though heavy counter-attacks were launched by the Turks, they were repulsed. At about 7.30 p.m. "A" and "D" Companies of the Middlesex were withdrawn and the positions were held by the Queen's, reinforced by one company of the 2/10th which had not been engaged during the day.

"I wish to make special mention," said the Brigadier in his report to Divisional Headquarters, "of the gallant conduct of the company of Middlesex (under Captain McIvor) which, although in reserve, advanced without hesitation across a fire-swept zone and captured Zamby. If it had not been for this company's fine spirit the operations might have resulted in failure."

The 2/10th had six other ranks killed and two officers and 23 other ranks wounded.

The smallness of the losses of the Middlesex does not give any idea of the fighting, for the Queen's losses were nine officers and over one hundred other ranks.

But Zamby and White Hill were not done with yet.

Both on the 24th and 26th December Brigade Headquarters had received warnings that the Turks intended launching strong counter-attacks against the British line, but it was not until 5.45 a.m. on the 27th that the attack materialised. At that hour the 2/4th Queen's at Zamby, The Wall and White Hill were heavily attacked under cover of a heavy hostile bombardment.

The ground on the forward slopes included several wadis which afforded the enemy covered approaches. Since the occupation of Zamby and White Hill the enemy, from Sufa and positions on either flank, had kept the two places under a persistent and heavy fire. The consequence was, that the Queen's had been unable to construct adequate defences giving a good field of fire and were forced to hold the crest and reverse slopes.

When the Turks attacked the guns had opened fire, but in spite of prompt and strong artillery support, the Queen's had to beat off with bombs several close attacks by the enemy.

At 11.30 a.m. the Middlesex (less the company still at Deir Obeid) moved out to support the Queen's. At 12.10 p.m. the latter, having been compelled to withdraw from Zamby and White Hill, two companies of the Middlesex attacked the former place and retook it. Leaving three platoons to garrison Zamby the two companies of 2/10th then started out to re-occupy White Hill. On the way they met an enemy counter-attack at Zamby and were therefore engaged in beating the Turks off instead of going on to re-occupy White Hill. The position of the Battalion was now one company (less two platoons) in reserve at Flunders Post; one platoon holding Flunders Post; one platoon holding Cheshire Hill; two companies at Zamby. At 10.15 p.m. that night the Battalion (less one company) was relieved and took over outposts from the 1/4th Royal Sussex, *i.e.*, one company at Jub er Rum, one company at Sussex Hill, one company at Sur Bahir. The three companies during the day had suffered nine other ranks killed, one officer and 74 other ranks wounded.

2/10TH BATTALION.
27TH DEC.

Meanwhile the detached company at Deir Obeid had been in action: at 7.25 a.m. Turkish cavalry, strength about seven hundred, were reported approaching from Muntar. Our mounted patrols withdrew and at 9.15 a.m. an enemy battery opened fire on Obeid from the direction of Mar Saba. Under cover of the guns and his dismounted cavalry he worked up to within one hundred yards of the Monastery which the Middlesex were holding. The Turks were, however, stopped by Lewis-gun and machine-gun fire. All day long fire was exchanged between the Middlesex and the enemy, and at 6 p.m. the latter brought up two field guns and tried to breach the Monastery walls from the eastern end. The attempt was unsuccessful. At 7 p.m. a British battery from Abu Dis opened fire and eased the situation considerably.

The defence put up by the Middlesex was excellent, for they were practically surrounded but held on grimly to their positions, defeating every attempt of the Turks to capture the place.

At 5.30 a.m. on 28th the enemy battery again opened fire, but had only fired four rounds when the divisional artillery silenced him.

28TH DEC.

At 10 a.m. the 1/4th Sussex relieved the detachment of 2/10th Middlesex, the latter having suffered two other ranks killed and thirteen wounded.

The operations in which the Middlesex were engaged between the 26th and 30th December were part of the fighting officially known as the " Defence of Jerusalem."

Palestine, 1918:
Operations in and beyond the Jordan Valley.

As a result of the operations up to the end of 1917 the Egyptian Expeditionary Force had driven the Turks out of all Philistia and

2/10TH BATTALION.
1ST JANUARY.

almost all Judæa, and when New Year's Day, 1918, dawned, held a line running from about five miles east of Jerusalem in a northerly direction for some seven or eight miles when it turned back, first westwards and then north-westwards to the coast at about El Haram. The line east of Jerusalem was held by the 53rd Division, to which the 2/10th Middlesex (Major W. C. Oodling, commanding) belonged, but their Brigade, the 160th, had been relieved on the 1st of January and on that date the Battalion marched from Bethphage to Bireh in Divisional Reserve. Heavy rain fell during the greater part of the day and the Battalion reached billets wet through. Ten days were spent out of the line, but on the 11th the 160th Brigade again relieved the 159th east of Jerusalem, the Middlesex relieving the 1/4th Cheshires from Don Post to Ryall's Post.

18TH JANUARY.

A small operation by the 160th Brigade took place on the 18th of January, whereby the line was advanced to Sheikh Abdullah. The 2/4th West Kents made the attack, two platoons of "D" Company of the 2/10th Middlesex lending assistance. At the close of the operation the Middlesex moved back into Brigade Reserve. At the end of January the Battalion was again in Divisional Reserve at Bireh.

THE CAPTURE OF JERICHO.

19th–21st February.

The first two weeks of February were uneventful, but during the third week operations were undertaken against Jericho.

19TH FEB.

In operation orders issued by the 160th Brigade on the 19th it was stated that the 60th Division was to carry out an attack against Jericho with the object of driving the Turks east of the Jordan and inflicting on him as much loss as possible. That Division was to advance to the general line El Muntar–Arak Ibrahim, and capture Ras el Tawil. On the same day the 53rd Division was to advance to the high ground between Wadi el Ain and the Taiyibeh–Jericho road, occupying Rummon, in order to be in a position to keep the road under fire : the 160th Brigade had been allotted the latter task. The 1/4th Royal Sussex Regiment, 2/4th Royal West Kents and 2/10th Middlesex were to carry out the task allotted to the 160th Brigade.

On the night 18th/19th of February the Sussex were to bivouac in the Wadi Kanabis, about 2,500 yards south-west of Rummon, 2/10TH BATTALION. having previously sent one platoon to take up position at the Wadi Junction in front. The West Kents were to advance their line at 7 p.m. to a line running from Kefr Nata through Kh. Idris to the Wadi Asa. At 8 p.m. the 2/10th Middlesex were to concentrate at Deir Diwan, the Queen's taking over the lines of the former Battalions at 5 a.m. on the 19th.

The objective of the Sussex in the attack was the high ground west of Rummon. The 2/10th Middlesex were to capture the high ground south of the village and the village itself : this attack was to be made from the south, the Battalion having secured the crossing over the Wadi Asa, about 2,500 yards south of Rummon.

The 2/10th set out from Deir Diwan at 10 p.m. and secured the crossing without opposition.

The attack began at 5.30 a.m. on the 19th. "C" Company 19TH FEB. of the 2/10th Middlesex launched the attack of that Battalion but was at first held up by about one hundred Turks with one machine gun. Two platoons of "D" Company were then sent up as reinforcements, and by 8.45 a.m. the village had been taken. The Sussex had secured their objective without opposition.

The losses of the 2/10th in this affair were nine other ranks killed, one other rank died of wounds, one officer (name not given) and nine other ranks wounded.

Throughout the afternoon of the 19th Rummon was heavily shelled, but no casualties were suffered.

The night of the 19th/20th was quiet. Strong patrols pushed out found no signs of the enemy. The 20th was without incident except for the rain which fell in torrents at intervals. The same positions were held as on the previous night. The Wadi Asa was reconnoitred and reported almost impassable for troops. No crossings were found. During the day all units were busy road making, for only tracks existed and these were quite inadequate.

On the 21st Jericho was occupied by Australian and London troops.

Bad weather prevailed throughout the 22nd and 23rd and rain and hail fell. At night a patrol succeeded in crossing the Wadi Asa and found a group of Turkish trenches and sangars which had been evacuated by the enemy. On the 24th the Middlesex 24TH FEB. advanced their line to the high ground north-east of the Wadi Asa without opposition. Similarly the next day an officer's patrol from the Battalion reached Kubbet Rummamaneh and found unoccupied trenches into which the Battalion moved. On the 26th the 159th Brigade took over the line and the 2/10th marched back to Burz Beitin.

The 160th Brigade Diary has the following note at the end of February: "During the past month the climatic conditions have tried the troops highly. Successive days of soaking rain entailed hardship, especially when holding the line. The health of the men has stood the strain well. Rations have, as usual, been excellent. A few cases of 'trench foot' have occurred, but the small number of such cases shows the careful attention given in this regard by unit commanders."

Jericho having been captured a slow and methodical advance began eastwards towards the River Jordan.

For the first eight days of March the 2/10th Middlesex remained at Burz Beitin employed on road making. The Brigade formed a temporary pioneer battalion with troops from all units, Captain J. C. Downie of the Middlesex being in command.

ACTIONS OF TEL ASUR.

8th–12th March.

On the 9th of March the Battalion marched out of Beitin to a position described as "N.9" in the Diary which, as near as the poor maps will point, seems to have been about one thousand yards west of Kusr Hajleh and 1,500 yards east of Kh. Kere Ana. At dusk two companies were detached to fill a gap between the 60th and 74th Divisions then engaged in attacking the Turks. The Battalion (less two companies) marched by night to Tel Asur arriving at 4.55 a.m. on the 10th, when they drove off the enemy who was then attacking: one other rank was killed and one officer and four other ranks were wounded in this affair. On the night of the 10th the Sussex passed through the Middlesex and occupied advanced posts, the latter Battalion on the afternoon of the 11th relieving the Sussex: these posts were north of the Wady el Kelt.

An attack was ordered on Kh. Amurien and the high ground north-east of the line held by the 160th Brigade. The West Kents were to carry out the operation, "C" Company of the Middlesex being attached to them for the capture of Kh. Amurien which was to be occupied by 4 a.m. on the 12th. The West Kents occupied their objective with but little opposition, but the

Middlesex, having to advance over unreconnoitred ground, and to an objective not pointed out to them on the ground, were unsuccessful. They advanced up the slopes against considerable opposition with few casualties until within a short distance from the top, but at this point heavy fire from machine guns and rifles was opened by the enemy both from Kh. Amurien and a low feature some five hundred yards south-east of it. Bombs were also thrown in large numbers from the Turkish defences in Kh. Amurien. In the face of such opposition " C " Company of the Middlesex had to withdraw, having suffered the loss of one officer and fifteen other ranks wounded and two officers and twenty other ranks missing.* _{2/10TH BATTALION. 12TH MARCH.}

On the 13th the 160th Brigade was relieved and moved back to reserve and on the 15th marched to Jerusalem. Only two days' rest were allowed the Brigade, for on the 17th all units marched to Talat ed Dumm. At 4.30 p.m. on the 18th the march forward was resumed via Jericho, the Brigade bivouacking that night in the Wady Nueimen. The following day at 6 p.m. all units marched to the Wadi Auja to relieve the 181st Brigade (64th Division), the 2/10th Middlesex taking over the right of the line, with their right company at the junction of the Wadis Obeideh and Auja, with small posts on the north side of the latter. _{19TH MARCH.}

PASSAGE OF THE JORDAN.

21st–23rd March.

On the 21st of March one platoon of the 2/10th Middlesex with two machine guns made a feint at crossing the Auja ford over the Jordan. No mention of this is made in the Battalion Diary, indeed, there are no entries in the records between the 19th and 26th of March. Nor are there any further details in the diaries of the higher formations. _{21ST MARCH.}

The general situation on the morning of the 21st of March (according to the map), issued with the official despatches, is as follows : one battalion of the 180th Brigade (60th Division) held the river crossing at Ain el Saraba ; the 177th (with the 180th Brigade in rear) was opposite El Ghoraniyeh ; the 160th Brigade (as already described) held the line at the junction of the Wadis Obeideh and Auja.

* No names of officer casualties are given in the Diary of the 2/10th Middlesex.

L 4

2/10TH BATTALION.
21ST MARCH.

It was at this period that a raid by "Shea's Group" (consisting of the 60th Division, the Anzac Mounted Division and artillery) was ordered on the enemy's line of communication in Gilead. Reconnaissances had shown that the Jordan at this period of the year was unfordable at every available point and that it was only possible to throw bridges across at Makhadet, Hajlah and Ghoraniyeh. It was decided to throw troops across at Hajlah and Ghoraniyeh while feints were made at Auja and some other points along the front while the 180th Brigade forced the passage in between.

This was the reason for the feint crossing made by the 2/10th Middlesex.

At 8 p.m. on the 23rd the Battalion advanced from Wadi Auja (leaving one company at the junction of the Wadis Auja and Mellahah) and took up a line some six thousand yards north with the right on the Wadi Mellahah.

28TH MARCH.

On the 28th at about 4 p.m. the enemy pushed forward strong reconnoitring patrols towards the one company of Middlesex in posts east of the Wadi Mellahah, east of the junction of the Wadis Obeideh and Auja. They were driven off by rifle, machine-gun and artillery fire and suffered casualties estimated at about thirty. On the 29th and 30th the Battalion has the following entries: "Enemy advanced cavalry screen against our front to within 1,200 yards: withdrew at dusk without attacking. Also same on 30th March."

Meanwhile the Jordan had been crossed by Shea's Force and by the end of the month Es Salt had been occupied and Amman was being attacked. But the Middlesex, as shown, did not cross the river.

The Brigade Diary again sums up the happenings for the month thus: "During the past month the troops have been engaged in road making of an arduous nature, continually advancing the line by night and some stiff fighting in minor operations. The weather has been bad, both cold winds and heavy rain combining to try the physique of the men. On the whole the health of the Brigade has been good."

In order to persuade the enemy that the ultimate advance of the Egyptian Expeditionary Force would be by way of Es Salt and Amman, everything was done to compel him to keep the whole of his Fourth Army east of the Jordan. A second raid was launched on the 29th of April with this intention, but large enemy reinforcements forced back the right of the Egyptian

29TH APRIL.

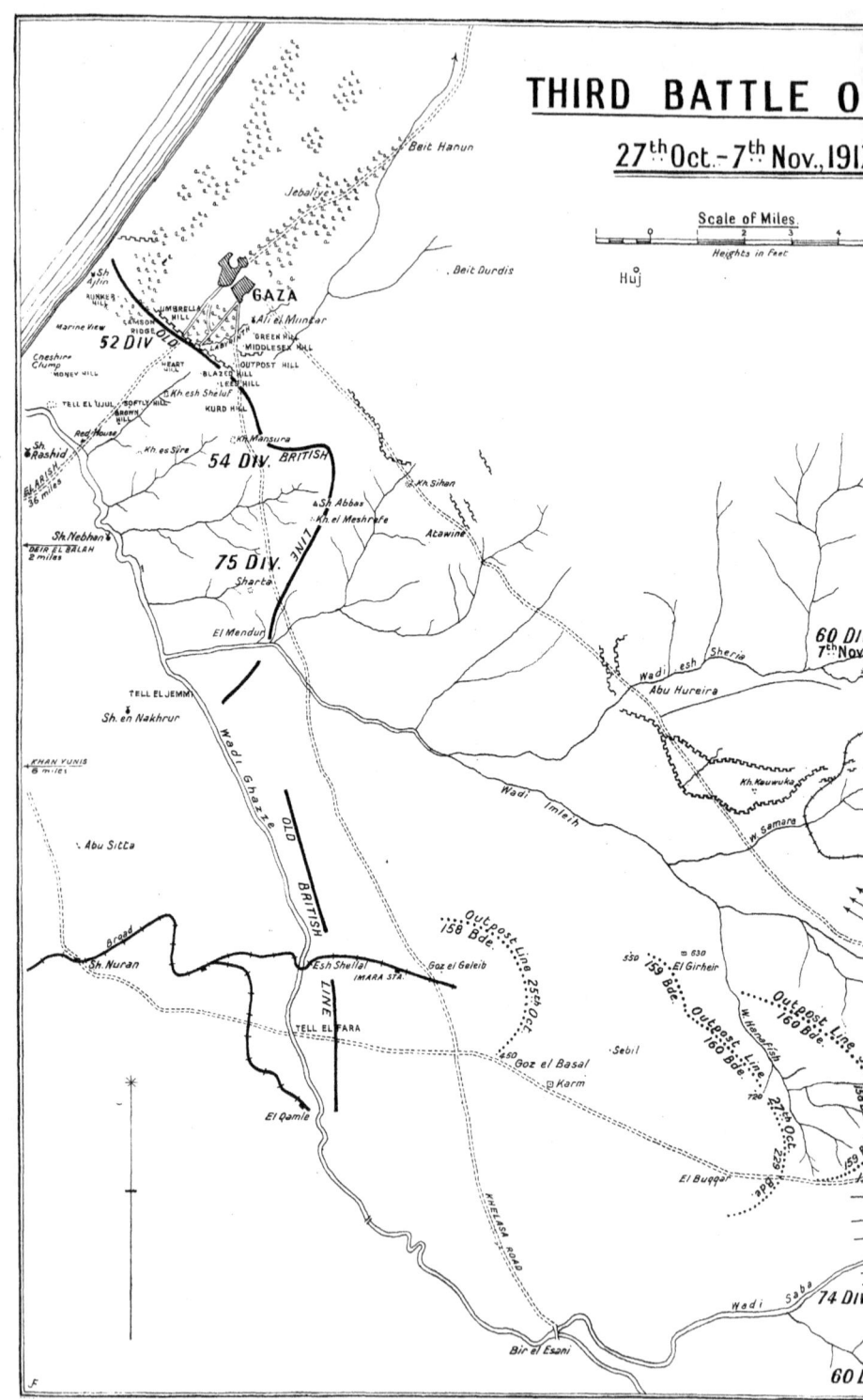

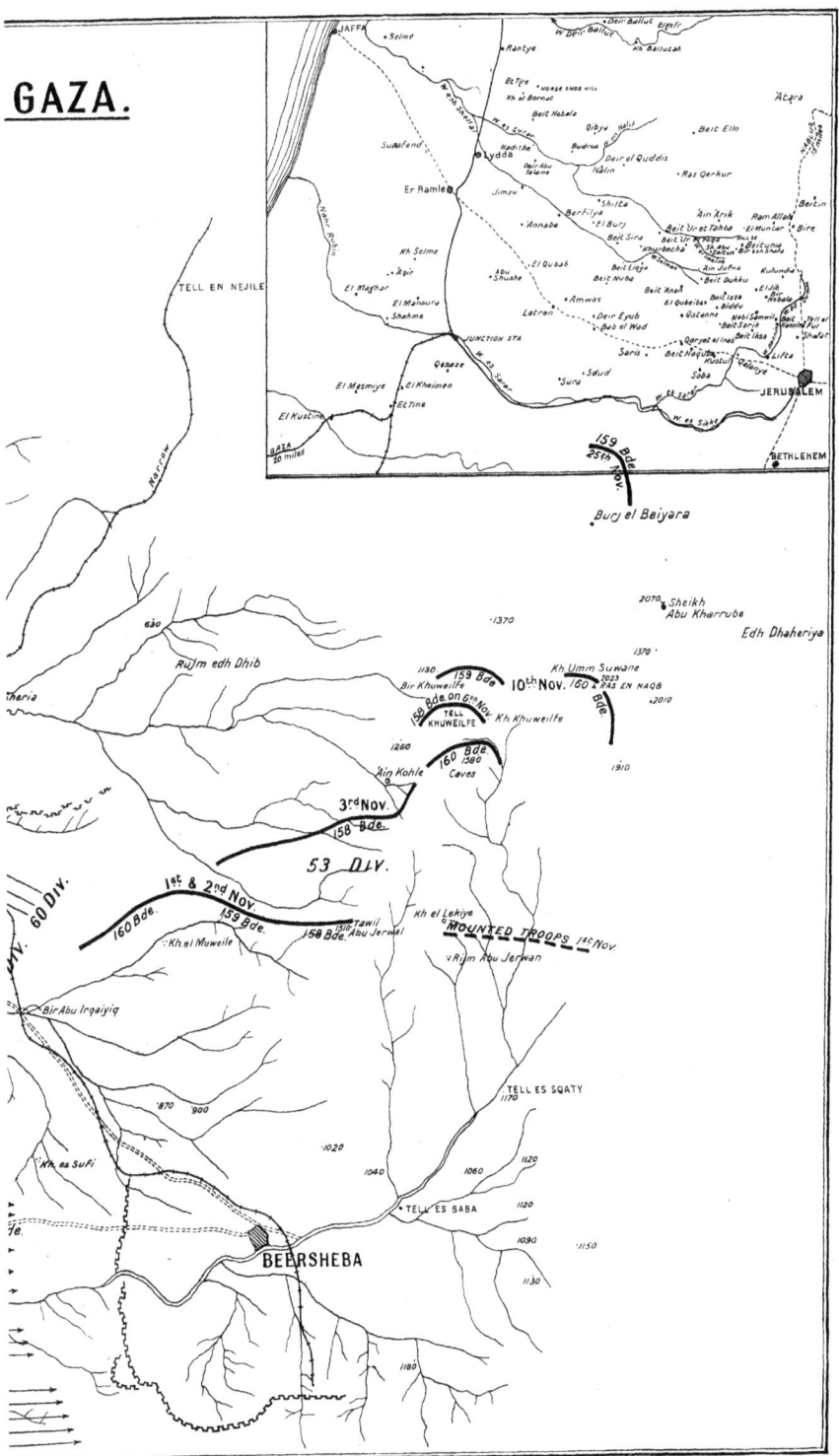

Expeditionary Force and by the 29th of the month a north and south line was held some six miles east of the river.   2/10TH BATTALION.

In this fighting, however, the 2/10th Middlesex took no actual part. They had a small affair with the Turks on the 27th of April. They had taken over a bivouac area from the West Kents west of the Jordan and south-west of El Ghoraniyeh on the 22nd with a post and Lewis-gun team pushed forward to Round Hill which overlooked the river. There were still some Turks on the hill, but on the 22nd the Middlesex cleared them off, one officer and four other ranks being wounded during the action. On the 1st of May another brush with the enemy took place. " C " Company was then holding Ide Hill and at about 9 p.m. one hundred Turks attacked but were driven off both by the Middlesex and the artillery.   29TH MARCH.

Two Companies, " A " and " B " raided the enemy's position on Fife Knoll on the night of the 22nd/23rd of May at 8.45 p.m. The Knoll was rushed but the enemy fled to his main sangars on a ridge to the north. Several Turks were killed and the raiders lost one other rank missing and six wounded.

On the 28th the Battalion was relieved and moved back into Divisional Reserve.

On the 7th of June the Middlesex relieved the 1/5th Welsh on the line Beachy Head–Sinjil Ridge astride the Nablus Road. This sector was in the new brigade area facing north, the 160th Brigade having as their boundary the Tel Asur area. On this date also Lieut.-Colonel Hohler left to command the 160th Brigade and Major C. Jarrett assumed command of the 2/10th Middlesex.

June was unproductive of any incident of importance. Casualties were light, and work was carried out in tactical wiring, strengthening the defences, etc. The Battalion was relieved by the 1/6th Royal Welsh Fusiliers on the 7th of July and moved back to Dar Jerir in Divisional Reserve, moving thence on the 18th to the Ramallah area where the remainder of the month was spent.

August, however, saw the end of the services of the 2/10th Middlesex in the War, for they were disbanded on the 20th without going back again into the front line. It was hard lines, for they had gone through all the hardships of the advance against Gaza and Jerusalem and had acquitted themselves well and with distinction. Their lot, however, was not uncommon, for many fine battalions were disbanded to fill the ranks of other units badly in need of reinforcements.   20TH AUGUST.

CHAPTER XLIV.

India and Mesopotamia.

THE story turns now to the 1/9 (Territorial) Battalion of the Regiment.

The period at Sittingbourne until the Battalion entrained for India on the morning of the 29th of October 1914 calls for no special mention. As with most other Territorial battalions at that period, the time was completely occupied with intensive training outside the town. Drafts of recruits of very fine physique poured in during the first weeks, and very soon the Battalion was 1,200 strong, all volunteers for foreign service. In common with the rest of the Brigade, the Battalion volunteered for service overseas as soon as it was called upon to do so. The small minority who, not grasping the fact that this was going to be a fight for our existence as a nation, considered the claims of family first, were speedily replaced by overseas volunteers from the depot at Pound Lane, where Major Dixon, who had rejoined from the Reserve, was doing yeoman service in training and equipping the eager recruits. In time the commanding officer was authorised to return to the depot all home-service men, and when the orders for India came he had in all some 1,400 foreign-service men from whom to pick the 805, the strength at which the infantry units for India were to embark. The 30 officers were as easily found as the men an overflowing "waiting list" being one of time's revenges on the young men who "had no time for soldiering" before the War.

On October the 29th the Battalion said good-bye to Sittingbourne, and by nightfall had embarked with their comrades of the Middlesex Infantry Brigade on one or other of the ten transports lying at Southampton to carry the Home Counties Division to India. The right-half Battalion and Headquarters were shipped in the "Dilwara" and the left half with the second-in-command in the "Dongola." The left half scored, as their "trooper" was nearly double the tonnage of the right half's, and each half shared their ship with another battalion.

1/9TH AND 1/10TH BATTALIONS.

The 1/10th Battalion had a still bigger ship—the " Royal George " —entirely to themselves, whilst the unfortunate N.C.Os. and men of the 9th right-half Battalion were cooped up 'tween decks of an old transport meant to accommodate 1,000, the actual number of troops in her being 1,300. Very heavy weather was met with during the first few days, and the misery and discomfort of the overcrowded troop decks of the " Dilwara " had to be seen —and smelt—to be appreciated. Then her steering gear got smashed up by the heavy seas, her coal bunkers were alight, and finally H.M.S. " Bacchante," the escorting cruiser, ordered her to break away and make for " Gib," where she staggered in, much to the relief of all concerned, on the evening of November 3rd. Refitting, etc., at " Gib " was completed by the 8th of November, on which day the " Dilwara " sailed to pick up the convoy at Suez. The five days at Gibraltar had been made very cheery ones for the 1/9th by the hospitality of its old comrades of the 1/7th and 1/8th Battalions, who nearly killed them with kindness. On November the 16th the " Dilwara " rejoined the convoy at Suez.

Meanwhile Turkey had come into the War, the " Emden " had been cleared off the high seas by H.M.A.S. " Sydney," and the way was once more clear for the big convoys, one of which, with the Wessex Territorial Division aboard, had just safely reached Bombay. The Home Counties Division passed most of them and exchanged news ; the biggest convoy—52 ships from Australia—was met at Aden, where the 1/9th had the pleasure of congratulating the " Sydney " on her victory. Altogether the voyage out was a liberal education in " Empire and what it means," for the young Cockney Territorial soldier, and when the Division landed at Bombay on December 2nd all ranks had probably imbibed more of the atmosphere of Empire than in all the previous years of their lives. Orders were awaiting the 1/9th to proceed to Dinapore (Bihar and Orissa—the old western Bengal), detaching three companies to Dumdum, near Calcutta, where the small-arms factory means a garrison always. " E," " F," and " H " Companies were detailed for this under Major Montgomerie. The Battalion entrained at Bombay on the 3rd of December, arriving at Dinapore on the evening of the 6th, less the three companies, which arrived at Dumdum on the morning of the 7th. It should have been noted that all regular adjutants had been withdrawn from the Division half an hour before sailing from Southampton. Lieut. D. B. Somervell was appointed to the adjutancy of the 1/9th, when Capt. Heap was transferred to the 3rd Battalion on October the 29th.

1/9TH BATTALION.

The Battalion now settled down to the ordinary routine of a British Regiment of the Line in India, with the addition of more intensive training. It is a recognised part of the duty of a garrison of an Indian station to have a movable column ready to march at a moment's notice, and the O.C. Station at Dinapore was responsible not only for the safety of that place, but for the capital of the Province of Bihar and Orissa, the town of Bankipore. Here were Government House and all the machinery for running a big Indian province. Adjoining Bankipore is the town of Patna, with a large population wholly Indian and mainly Mussulmans of a fanatical order. These two towns are some eight miles from Dinapore, and in case of trouble prompt action by the garrison of the latter place would be essential. At the time of the arrival of the 1/9th Middlesex this consisted of that Battalion, less three (afterwards four) companies, the 2nd Devon Battery, R.F.A. (T.), and the depot companies of the 89th Punjabis; from these units the movable column was made up, plus details of the S. and T. Corps. There was also a local defence scheme in case action further afield should be necessary, including protection of the big bridge over the Sone River some 30 miles to the westward, and of the railway, etc., but these details were the concern of O.C., Dinapore, who, during the 14 months the Battalion was stationed there, happened by seniority to be their own Commanding Officer. As far as the Battalion was concerned, its main work consisted in strenuous preparations for service in the field, which during the first three months meant preparing for the Kitchener Test.

On the 15th of December, 1914, Brigadier-General A. Money, G.O.C., Presidency Brigade (Calcutta), afterwards Major-General Sir Arhur Money, Chief of Staff to Sir Stanley Maude in Mesopotamia, inspected the Middlesex and the detachment, and reported most favourably on the Battalion. By his orders the Battalion at the beginning of February was redistributed, the change being necessitated by the need for a garrison at Barrackpore (some 15 miles from Calcutta), where the regular British units, excepting the R.F.A., which was now found by a Devon battery, had not been replaced. The garrison of Barrackpore was responsible for the Ishipur small-arms factory, as that of

15TH DEC.

Dumdum was for the small-arms ammunition factory at that place and the gun factory at Cossipur on the Hoogly River. Finding guards for these factories was strenuous work in hot weather, especially from Dumdum, where malaria was terribly rife, and also a disease new to British troops, known as Kala Hazar, or "Black Sickness," from which the 1/9th unfortunately lost several men, as it did also at Dumdum from malaria.

The result of the redistribution was that the Battalion was from February posted as follows :—

At Dinapore.—Headquarters and "A," "B" and "C" and "G" Companies (in May, when the four-company system was adopted, these became "A" and "B" Companies, scouts and machine gunners).

At Dumdum.—"E" and "H" Companies (in May, "D" Company and signallers).

At Barrackpore.—"D" and "F" Companies (in May, "C" Company).

In February, Major Montgomerie was transferred to the staff of the 8th Division at Lucknow, and command of Dumdum devolved on Capt. Bartholomew. The Barrackpore garrison was commanded by Capt. Stratton.

Early in March the headquarter companies at Dinapore marched to camp at Anandpur, on the Sone River, 10 miles from the Station, and carried out intensive company and battalion training, culminating in the Kitchener Test. Field firing was the chief feature of this training, and as all who have soldiered in India know this work can be carried out under ideal conditions. Through O.C. Station, the police are informed as to dates and areas required, the villages are cleared by them, and no one is allowed within a certain cordon. Targets are set up in accordance with the schemes and tactical features of the ground, and the practice carried out resembles the real thing as nearly as possible when there is no "opposite number."

The test was carried out under the eyes of the Brigade Commander during three strenuous days, ending with a night march back to barracks and a fight with the 89th Punjabis, the defenders of the station. It is gratifying to record that the Battalion received an excellent "chit" from the G.O.C. and was reported for active service anywhere.

It was now nearing the end of March, the hot weather had set in, and hard work in the open was no longer possible for white troops; in fact, the last week in camp had been sufficiently trying for all ranks, so that the Battalion was glad to settle down to hot weather conditions. A good deal might be written here as to what these were like in a small station when the methods of a hundred years ago still prevailed; it is better perhaps to draw the veil over the various types of disease that tested the *morale* of the troops during the next six months. It can be stated, however, that " the men were splendid," their keenness on games and the care of the R.A.M.C. officers and their constant teachings as to hygiene, temperance, etc., kept the death roll, at any rate, light, though the hospital was full up all the time. [1/9TH BATTALION.]

The Battalion was entitled to send three parties from each of its stations to the hills during the hot weather, so that by the end of the season practically all ranks had been off the plains for a certain time at least, and by a stroke of luck the hill station for the 8th Division in 1915 was Darjeeling, in the north-eastern Himalayas, under the shadow of Kinchenjunga and the eternal snows.

On the 11th of May the Battalion sent its first draft to Force " D " (Mesopotamia), Lieut. Fisher and 30 other ranks going out as reinforcements to the 2nd Norfolks. They were followed in August by another 20 ranks, and during the year Lieuts. Toovey and Hickling were sent out in response to an order for subaltern officers to be despatched independently. It might be mentioned here that before the Battalion itself left India for Mesopotamia at the end of 1917, Capts. Bartholomew and L. Mellersh Jackson, and Lieuts. Lamont, Frankau, Thompson and Williamson were sent out at different times. All these officers lived to tell the tale with the exception of Lieut. Hickling, who was killed outside Amarah in the Spring of 1916; in him the 1/9th lost a gallant and promising young officer. Of the 50 other ranks some 30 got back, the others perished at Kut or in captivity. [11TH MAY.]

Albuhera Day, May 16th, is always kept with great enthusiasm wherever the Die-Hards find themselves. This year the 1/9th and 1/10th Battalions' hill parties were concentrated at Darjeeling, and both there and at Dinapore, Dumdum and Barrackpore by the 1/9th, and Fort William (Calcutta) by the 1/10th, the day was fittingly celebrated and a cable was sent to the 57th (1st Battalion) in France. This routine was observed by the 1/9th throughout the War, except that in 1918 the festive side was of necessity omitted, though the remembrance—per cable—was not. [1/10TH BATTALION. 1ST BATTALION.]

India — 1915-1916

1/9TH BATTALION.

The tedium of the hot weather at Dinapur was mildly relieved in August, when some hundred German missionaries and their families were interned there. They were repatriated in the late autumn, being useless to their country from a military point of view, though quite the contrary whilst left at large to spread propaganda amongst the natives of Bihar and Orissa.

In December, 1915, the 1/9th Middlesex were ordered to prepare to move 1,500 miles north to Rawalpindi, the Aldershot of India, a change eagerly welcomed by all ranks as giving some chance of seeing service on the frontier and getting into a healthier climate.

21ST JANUARY.

On January the 21st, 1916, the 2/4th Somersets having taken over Dinapore and the two Calcutta Stations, the Battalion entrained for Rawalpindi after 14 months' service in their first stations, and arrived at Rawalpindi on the 24th, very cold, but already much invigorated by the snap in the air. The Battalion marched into a rest camp close to the railway, being played in by the bands of the 6th East Surrey and 1st Yorkshire Regiments. The Brigade Commander, General Watson, welcomed them by handing the C.O. his orders to mobilize at once for Force " D " (Mesopotamia). To say that the Battalion was delirious with joy may be an exaggeration, but it was something near the truth. At last, at last " it " had come.

The mobilization was completed, and for ten days the moving-off orders were awaited, when, alas for dreams of glory they arrived in form of a cancellation of previous orders. So that was *that*, and gloomily, silently, the 1/9th settled down to garrison duty once more. It says much for its discipline that there was no half-heartedness about the way the Battalion worked, but it was a bitter pill, more especially as the 1/9th alone had passed more than 4,000 recruits through its depot since August, 1914.

On January, the 31st, the Battalion was inspected by the Brigadier, and on February, the 5th, by the G.O.C., 2nd (Rawalpindi) Division (Major-General Sir G. Kitson) and favourably reported on. Company training and field firing were now in full swing. For the latter the country around Rawalpindi is particularly well adapted, being to the northwards a tumble of wild and rocky ridges, a great contrast to the rolling, cultivated plains of Bihar, and some very useful work was put in. It bore fruit in the first phase of the Kitchener Test, carried out on February the 23rd under the eyes of the Brigade Commander.

A 15-mile march ended in an attack on a series of positions occupied by the targets disposed along the rocky ridges, which were carried and made good in succession. The casualties amongst the chatties (earthenware pots) proved that the musketry of the Battalion had improved out of all knowledge since 1914. The remainder of the test was, unfortunately, not carried out, owing to orders coming in for the Battalion to move by route march to Nowshera, in the North-West Frontier Province, to join a brigade temporarily formed there for mountain-warfare training. The Battalion moved out of Rawalpindi in the early morning of March the 8th, and marched into camp at Nowshera at midday, March the 14th, after 94 miles of hot and dusty marching. The route was on the Grand Trunk Road throughout and crossed the Indus at Akbar's Fort of Attock, thence by the banks of the Cabul river, on which Nowshera lies. This was the first of many treks carried out by the 1/9th, where the two-wheeled A.T. cart and country bullock wagon of the south gave place to the mule and camel, and the vigorous training in loading and off-loading and animal management carried out by the transport section, under the energetic Transport Officer—Lieut. Frankau—earned for the Battalion a fine reputation. The mountain-warfare training at Nowshera ended on April the 13th, and included some of the most strenuous work the Battalion had yet encountered, but all ranks were by now well acclimatized and as fit as the proverbial fiddle.

On the 14th of April the unit moved to the hills by route march, reaching their stations, Ghora Dhaka and Khanspur (15 miles north of Murree) on the 17th. Ghora Dhaka is 7,700 feet above seal-level and Khanspur 7,000 feet. " A " Company and Headquarters were at Ghora Dhaka, " B," " C " and " D " Companies below at Khanspur, where was the only piece of level ground, just large enough for a football ground and ceremonial parade ground. To get to the rifle ranges was almost an expert piece of mountaineering, but Table " B," etc., were successfully accomplished within the first two months. Mountain-warfare, training, musketry and " regimental exercises without troops," filled up most of the working days, with, of course, daily close-order drill, handling of arms and the early morning physical training. Football and khud (cliff) climbing in the afternoon, dances and concert-party shows in the evenings, made up the social side of the men's lives ; one hill station is pretty much like another.

1/9TH BATTALION.
9TH JUNE.

On June the 9th the new G.O.C., 2nd Division—Major-General Bunbury—inspected the stations, and on June the 16th the Battalion held a memorial service for Lord Kitchener on the Khanspur parade ground.

The strength of the Battalion had been steadily sapped since its arrival in the north by the withdrawal of skilled men of all and every kind of trade, and the want of a reinforcing draft was becoming serious. It was then with feelings of relief that the news of an early draft was received, and its arrival on June the 12th was something of an event. But unfortunately the people at home had failed to realise that physically unfit men are worse than useless in India, and some 50 per cent. of this draft of 200 men came under that category; in fact, some of these unfortunates went into hospital on arrival at Rawalpindi and stayed there until they could be re-shipped home. This draft formed part of the 1,000 men despatched from Karachi for the journey across the Scinde Desert in June in a train packed on the cold-weather scale and made up of ancient corrugated-iron-roofed cold-weather carriages. Twenty men died of heat stroke on that passage, of whom three were men of the 1/9th, and 132 were left in various hospitals *en route*, including 27 of the 1/9th draft.

However, the survivors who managed to keep clear of hospital soon shook down, and there was some good stuff amongst them, but a letter home perhaps accounted for a very different lot, physically, when the next draft arrived early in 1917.

Early in June the units scattered over the Galis stations—that is, along the road and " pipe lines " between Murree and Abbottabad, 60 miles to the north, had been transferred from the Abbottabad Brigade and formed into the new Galis Brigade, commanded by Brigadier-General C. C. Luard, lately commanding the 1st Durham Light Infantry, who had superintended the training of the composite Brigade in mountain-warfare at Nowshera. The result of having the Brigade Commander within touch—Headquarters were at Changla Gali three miles from Ghora Dhaka—was to speed up and co-ordinate the training during the season in the hills, and the Battalion owed much to General Luard, whose keen interest they will always remember.

27TH JULY.

On July the 27th the Battalion had once more to part with one of its limbs, one company being ordered to garrison Fort Attock, which guards the big bridge over the Indus, the only link between the Punjab and the North-West Frontier Province.

"D" Company (Capt. Bartholomew) was selected for this duty, and remained at Attock until it rejoined at Hasan Abdal in October, much stricken by malaria, which was rife at the Fort.

1/9TH BATTALION.

A senior officers' course held by the Brigadier at Changla gave "B" Company some hard work on top of Mokshpuri (some 10,000 feet high), where they dug a trench system for the benefit of the officers undergoing the course (including the C.O. and second-in-command of the 1/9th).

On October the 19th the hill season came to an end, and, proceeding downhill by route march, the Battalion reach Rawalpindi once more on the 23rd, and marched into camp on the golf links. Here it lay, furnishing many guards and fatigues for the Rawalpindi garrison, until November the 8th, when it entrained for winter quarters under canvas at Hasan Abdal, on the Grand Trunk Road some 30 miles north-west of Rawalpindi. The garrison at Hasan Abdal comprised five battalions of Nepalese infantry and the 1/9th Middlesex, and the whole formed the Galis Brigade, under Brigadier-General Luard.

19TH OCTOBER.

"D" Company rejoined from Attock, when the Battalion moved into camp at Hasan Abdal, and by the time the reunited unit had settled down to company training it had to be up and on the move again, this time to Serai Kala, eight miles towards Rawalpindi on the never-to-be-forgotten Grand Trunk Road. It moved there on November the 18th, and until it marched into camp at Hasan once more on December the 19th was hard at work as a unit of Jhelum Brigade (Brigadier-General Peterson). The Brigade comprised the 1st Duke of Wellington's 1/6th East Surreys, 1/9th Middlesex and the Prasupatti Prasad Regiment (Nepalese). The Brigade carried out much strenuous work, half civilised and half mountain-warfare. From the 12th to the 19th of December the Brigade took part in the 2nd (Rawalpindi) Divisional manœuvres against a flagged enemy, marched many dusty miles, and bivouacked in a different place each night (when it was not carrying out a night march). No one wept when Christmas brought a "Europe" (stand off) day or two back in camp at Hasan Abdal. During manœuvres the Commander-in-Chief had come up from Delhi and had seen the Division at work on a field day. The Brigade at Hasan Abdal lost General Luard, who was replaced just before Christmas by Brigadier-General Dyer, and the Battalion was under his cheery command until it moved to join the 43rd Brigade, 16th (Indian) Division (Major-

12TH DECEMBER.

General W. Cross Barrett) at Burhan. This move took place on February the 4th, 1917, and was not much appreciated, as it meant another dose of manœuvres, an absolute dust-heap of a camp, and a break in the continuity of training. (It will be observed that there had been no opportunity given to the unit for steady *company* training since it left Rawalpindi in March, 1916.)

1/9TH BATTALION.
4TH FEBRUARY.

The 43rd Brigade comprised the 1/5th Somersets, 1/9th Middlesex, 2/2nd Gurkhas, and the Mahindra Dal Regiment (Nepalese), and was commanded from February the 4th to 24th by the O.C., 1/9th Middlesex. From that date until the 16th Division dispersed to hot-weather stations, the Brigade Commander was Colonel E. Money, 1st Gurkhas.

" B " Company had been detached and sent to Abottabad to finish its musketry course when the Battalion moved to Burhan, and rejoined just before manœuvres. These lasted from February the 27th to March the 8th, and were carried out in wild and difficult country some 25 miles south-west of Burhan—more dust for the 1/9th and still more on its return to Burhan, where dust storms were the rule rather than the exception.

14TH MARCH.
7TH RESERVE BATTALION.

On March the 14th a very fine draft of 198 men arrived from the 7th Reserve Battalion at Tunbridge Wells, and made a welcome addition to the depleted Battalion, and on March the 25th, with a sigh of relief, it shook the dust of Burhan from its jaded feet and entrained for Ambala. This station, a fine and important one in the Punjab, with a big garrison, was reached on the 27th : the Battalion was quartered in the British Cavalry Lines. Brigadier-General Hendley was in command at Ambala, and during its eight months under him the Battalion learnt to appreciate his fine soldierly qualities. Other British units at Ambala were the 1/7th Hants and some batteries of R.F.A.

10TH APRIL.

On April the 10th " C " and " D " Companies (less two officers and 70 other ranks " C " Company detached to Sabathu, Simla Hills), with the Band and Headquarters, moved by route march to Solon, 5,000 feet up the hills on the Simla main road, marching in on April the 15th.

This commenced the third hot weather for the Battalion, and this history having rather gone into details concerning the previous two, and also the previous three cold weathers, it is proposed to continue the narrative in the form of a more or less concise diary (work and play being more or less the same year in

and year out, according to the seasons), until the Battalion moved 1/9TH BATTALION.
to Mesopotamia.

9TH MAY.
May the 9th, 1917 : A draft of 29 other ranks from the Essex Regiment arrived Solon.

July the 20th : The half-battalions changed over, Headquarters remaining at Solon, the C.O. making frequent visits of inspection to Ambala.

In July, command of the half-battalion there devolved on Capt. Stratton, Major Hewett being appointed to command at Kasauli, the hill station for the Ambala Brigade. Major Beach had been filling a staff appointment since the summer of 1916, also Capts. Bartholomew and Tupper and various junior officers had been detached from the Battalion, which, on the other hand, had been reinforced by young officers from home.

During the six months in the hills the usual visitations of inspecting generals had taken place, including the Inspector-General of Infantry, Northern Army, Brigadier-General G. Christian, who reported in very flattering terms on the training of the Battalion. On October the 6th Headquarters and the half-battalion in the hills moved down to Ambala, entraining at Kalka—two days' march—and arriving Ambala late at night on the 7th.

Once again the Battalion settled down for winter training, but not for long, for on the 10th of October the ever-awaited orders for active service arrived at last. The Battalion was to form the British unit in the 53rd Brigade, 18th (newly formed) Indian Division for Mesopotamia. Mobilization started at once, all detached officers were applied for and came in with few exceptions. The adjutancy of the Battalion had now been taken over from Capt. Somervell by Capt. E. Scott, who held the appointment until the cadre came home in August, 1919.

1/10TH BATTALION.
On November the 5th two drafts arrived, 100 men from the 1/10th Middlesex at Lucknow and 200 from the 1/25th London Regiment at Jullundur.

10TH NOVEMBER.
On the 10th the Brigade Commander inspected the Battalion and wished them luck on service, and at last on the 14th of November the 1/9th marched out of barracks for service in the field. Malaria had knocked out some 200 men during the last few weeks, but fortunately the newly arrived drafts enabled the Battalion to keep up to strength, and it paraded for the last time at Ambala, strength 29 officers 939 other ranks.

1/9TH BATTALION.

During its three years in India the Battalion had three times been reported on as " up to the standard of a pre-war British unit in India," and no Territorial battalion of infantry could ask for higher praise than that. It was now up to it to " make good " on its Indian reputation.

The Battalion, leaving in two troops trains by half-battalion, and played to the station by its good comrades of Ambala, the 1/7th Hants, reached Karachi on the morning of November the 16th and marched into rest camp, where it lay for three days. All ranks much appreciated seeing the sea once more, and especially the glorious bathing.

MESOPOTAMIA.

19TH NOVEMBER.

On the 19th of November the 1/9th Middlesex (Lieut.-Colonel J. L. Blumfeld, commanding) embarked at Karachi aboard H.T. " Egra " and put out to sea. The voyage was uneventful, and on the morning of the 23rd the troops disembarked at Magill, an outlying area of Basra.

The Battalion at once marched to the rest camp at Makina, also on the outskirts of Basra, on the edge of the desert. The Brigade Commander (Brigadier-General C. A. F. Sanders) had already arrived with his staff and had proceeded up river, leaving the 1/9th, the first unit of the 53rd Brigade, to await orders. The Middlesex spent the time in route marching and in training. They had brought their band with them (instruments in packing cases as " regimental baggage ")—the only British unit to do so. The band played at several hospitals in Basra, and later it was heard far north of Baghdad, where it relieved many a monotonous hour when (as an officer of the Battalion puts it) " bully beef and chlorinated ' Eau de Tigris ' seemed to fill the horizon as well as the inner man."

2ND DECEMBER.

Their stay at Basra, however, soon came to an end, for on the 2nd of December (exactly three years since they had disembarked at Bombay) the 1/9th Middlesex embarked on a paddle steamer (" P " Boat) and two barges, lashed one each side, and steamed up the Tigris as far as Qurnah.

Qurnah is the reputed " Garden of Eden " : of the " garden " there is now nothing to be seen but the usual date palms along the riverbank, and after spending an uncomfortable night in crowded huts, the Battalion entrained early on the morning of the 3rd for

Amarah, where camp had to be pitched in darkness, as it was late 1/9TH BATTALION. before the Middlesex marched in. A site for the Divisional camp had been selected some miles up stream on the left bank of the Tigris, and on the 5th of December " A " Company (Major 5TH DECEMBER. Beach) was detached for the purpose of covering working parties, also to assist in laying out the camp.

It was here that the Pathan of the North-West Frontier of India, compared with the Arab, was proved to be a mere infant at the game of rifle thieving. Orders had been issued that every man was to sleep with one arm through the sling of his rifle, the butt under his armpit, and muzzle under his knee—not a comfortable companion for the night. These orders were strictly carried out, yet on the night of the 6th/7th four N.C.Os. were robbed of their rifles. Later, at Amarah, although the sling (according to fresh orders) was wound round the wrist by one end, another man had his rifle stolen, the thief having cut the sling. The same night an officer's long tin uniform trunk was stolen from his tent, though the perimeter of the camp was patrolled by double sentries without intermission. Without doubt the Arab was an expert thief.

At this period the weather, hitherto hot and dusty, changed suddenly for the worse; icy winds set in and a cold rain fell, turning the desert (which is not sand, but alluvium) into a vast sea of liquid mud.

On the 13th of December the Battalion embarked on a big paddle steamer for Kut, *en route* to Baghdad. After two days of intense cold Kut was reached, and the Middlesex went ashore to a rest camp for two days. Entraining at Kut on the night of the 17th the Battalion arrived at Hinaidi (rail head for Baghdad) on the 18th and went into a rest camp where they were joined by their old comrades the 1/89th Punjabis, the second unit of the 53rd Brigade to arrive. On the 23rd both Battalions marched eight miles, through Baghdad across the Tigris by the north bridge (a bridge of boats), to Iron Bridge on the right bank. Within the next four days the Brigade was concentrated at Iron Bridge, the other infantry battalions being the 1/3rd and 1/7th Gurkha Rifles.

On the 5th of January, 1918, the Divisional area extended 5TH JANUARY. from the Tigris, six miles south of Akab* south-westwards through Feluja (on the Euphrates, west of Baghdad), thence

* Akab is about fifty miles due north of Baghdad.

1/9TH BATTALION.

south to Abu Sukhair. This area included the Euphrates from Feluja to Abu Sukhair. Divisional Headquarters were at Baghdad. The concentration of the whole Division was, however, a slow process and, pending the arrival of the 53rd Brigade transport, the Euphrates' portion of the Divisional area was taken over by the 52nd Brigade of the 17th Indian Division.

The remainder of December, 1917, and the whole of January, 1918, was spent by the 1/9th Middlesex in fatigue duties and in training. On the 1st of February, however, orders were received for the 53rd Brigade to move to the Hilla–Kifl–Kufa–Abu Sukhair area.

1ST FEBRUARY.

The move began on the 7th of February, the Middlesex marching out of camp at a strength of 24 officers and 787 other ranks. The first stage was to Mahmudmah, a distance of 18 miles. The Battalion Diary records that a few men fell out, otherwise all ranks were very fit. On the 8th, the Brigade marched to Khan Haswan, 14½ miles; on the 9th to Khan Mahawih, 14 miles; on the 10th to Hilla, 13 miles, where "A" and "D" Companies joined the 1st Echelon for detachment duty at Kufa. These companies, therefore, went on and camped for the night on the southern side of Hilla, ready for resuming the march on the following day. "B" and "C" Companies with Battalion Headquarters, were at Camp Hilla, 1¼ miles north of the town.

The Detachment crossed from the left to the right bank of the Shatt-el-Hindie on the 12th, and marched on Kifl, thence on the 13th to Kufa, occupying Tramway Post. But the camp was two miles from the river, which meant that the better part of the 14th was spent in watering animals and drawing water. During the remainder of the month the camp was therefore re-arranged. At Kufa certain supplies were obtained locally, *i.e.*, chickens at a rupee each, fish at five annas a pound, eggs at one anna each, dates four annas a pound, and milk at three annas a pint. Training and the improvement of camp occupied the Detachment until the 21st of the month.

In the meantime, "B" and "C" Companies and Battalion Headquarters at Hilla were similarly engaged in fatigue duties and in training. The 1/9th Middlesex were now split up as follows: 14 officers and 410 other ranks at Hilla, 8 officers and 350 other ranks at Kufa, 2 officers and 92 other ranks still at Iron Bridge.

On the 22nd of February the Detachment (less two platoons) formed part of the Post Movable Column and marched to Najaf. There is, however, mothing to record of this incident.

<small>1/9TH BATTALION. 22ND FEBRUARY.</small>

On the 2nd of March, Lieut.-Colonel J. L. Blumfeld left the Battalion for Baghdad, and command was assumed by Major W. P. Hewett. On the 5th, orders were received for the formation of the Hilla Movable Column, for which the 1/9th Middlesex were ordered to find 200 rifles.*

A small party of from six to eight Arabs raided the Middlesex camp at Hilla on the night of the 8th of March, at about 1.15 a.m. They succeeded in getting away with four kit bags and one rifle, cutting the sling by which it was attached to the owner without waking him. The thieves were seen by the sentries and fired on and presumably one of them was hit, as a scream was heard, and in the morning a pool of blood was found about a quarter of a mile from the camp, in the direction in which the Arabs fled. The night was very dark and overcast. On the 8th, the Detachment at Kufa was recalled by Brigade Headquarters. On the 9th, "A" Company moved to Kifl, followed on the 10th by "D" Company, and on the 11th both companies proceeded to Hilla, the Battalion being once more reunited. The two companies had had a hard march of twenty-two miles, rain falling almost all the way to Hilla. Only six men fell out, suffering from sore feet.

If the Middlesex saw no fighting at this period the conditions under which they lived were no sinecure. The Battalion Diary for the 16th of March records: "Rain throughout night of 15th/16th, with break about midnight; also high wind from south. Two tents blown down and camp a mixture of mud and water. Spent day re-casting drainage system. Sharp rainstorm in the afternoon." Late on the following day a platoon had to be sent out to assist a Pack Wireless Column, stuck on the Musaiyib road.

<small>16TH MARCH.</small>

Two days later, a wave of excitement swept over the camp. Early in the morning Brigade Headquarters had received a wire from Kufa stating that Captain Marshall, the Political Officer at Najaf, had been murdered just outside the walls of the city. The 53rd Brigade at this time was distributed as

---

*This Column consisted of D Squadron 10th Lancers, one section 207th Machine-Gun Company (200 rifles), 1/9th Middlesex, one company (200 rifles), 1/7th Gurkha Rifles, and one section 37th Combined Field Ambulance.

1/9TH BATTALION.
18TH MARCH.

follows: At Hilla, 53rd Brigade Headquarters, 1/9th Middlesex, "D" Squadron 10th Lancers, and 207th Machine-gun Company (less two Sections). Other units of the Brigade were at Kala Aba Siya, Kufa, Abu Sukhair and Musaiyib.

The Movable Column set out from Hilla for Najaf at 11.30 a.m. Two companies of Middlesex ("A" and "C"), commanded by Major W. P. Hewett, accompanied the Column, as the 1/7th Gurkhas and one section of the 207th Machine-gun Company were on their way to Feluja. Major G. Beach assumed command of "B" and "D" Companies at Hilla. On the 19th these two companies also left for Kufa to take part in the operations.

THE BLOCKADE OF NAJAF

Najaf is the Holy City of the Shiite Mohammedans, held in great reverence by the Arabs. At the time the Political Officer was murdered, reactionaries, styling themselves the "Committee of Rebellion," though in the minority, terrorised the remaining inhabitants of Najaf. Owing to the holy shrine being in the middle of the city, which was surrounded by a very high bastioned wall, it was deemed inadvisable to shell the place, or even to attempt to take it by direct assault. A blockade of the city was therefore ordered until all those implicated in the murder of Captain Marshall were given up. The blockade was to be carried out by the 53rd Brigade by means of a cordon of military posts joined up by barbed wire round the city.

Najaf was irregular in shape—six-sided—the principal gate, Kufa Gate, being on the south-western side. Outside the gate were a number of buildings through which tram lines ran to Blockade Camp, some 2,000 yards away. Immediately east of the tram shed was Attiyah's Khan (or Marshall's Serai). North of that place was a little house named Somerset House, and north again of the latter, a large Arab graveyard. In the south-eastern corner of the city walls was the Hawaish Gate, beyond which was the Hawaish Mound. North of Kufa Gate were the Turkish Barracks and Misraq Bastion.

22ND MARCH.

On the 22nd, "A" and "C" Companies of the 1/9th Middlesex reached Blockade Post, some 1,300 yards east of Najaf, where with other units of the Brigade they took part in establishing a cordon from south to north-west around the city. Nine picquets (numbered from the left) with Blockade Post as headquarters, were formed, Nos. 1, 5, 6, 7, 8, 9 by the Middlesex, 1/9TH BATTALION. and 2, 3 and 4 by the Punjabis. One platoon was allotted to 22ND MARCH. each post with Lewis guns or machine guns. During the morning there was a good deal of sniping from the city walls and from the graveyard, the rebels finding excellent cover on the high walls and in the bastions, but it was not until afternoon that the first casualty occurred, one man being wounded.

At about 2.30 p.m. on the 23rd, " B " and " D " Companies, under Major Beach, arrived, and a little later relieved a composite platoon from the other companies in No. 10 Post (a new picquet beyond the cliff and the Bahr el Najaf), and also the Punjabis in Attiyah's Khan.

The relief was effected without difficulty. During the evening picquets improved their posts, though it was not easy work. The soil was hard but friable, dissolving into sand and dust, so that revetting became necessary. The Arab snipers were less active, but No. 8 Picquet reported that they had shot two of the enemy, one being killed and the other rescued by his friends. On the 24th the cordon was gradually extended round the western outskirts of Najaf.

On the 25th the enemy's snipers were again busy; they had taken up position on the big mound outside the Bab el Saghir and in a white house opposite No. 12 Picquet. The officer in charge of the post (Lieut. Melville) reported that one N.C.O. of " D " Company (Corporal James) was killed by a sniper. The next day No. 12 Picquet had its revenge, killing two Arabs.

Apart from the usual work on the posts and general strengthening of the blockade line, the only incidents of interest on the 27th were first the capture of an Arab who was trying to get into the city, and the killing of another Arab who, with a small party of the enemy, managed to get through near M. 8. They were fired on and one was killed. Several more days passed, each very much resembling the other, until the 2nd of April, when the Somersets began to relieve part of the Middlesex. A rest khan had been established at Kufa, where troops from the blockade line might get a wash for themselves and their clothes and two complete nights in bed. On relief, therefore, the Middlesex moved back to rest.

On the 4th it was decided to attack the two mounds at 4TH APRIL. Hawaish Gate, held by the insurgents. The loyal Arabs in the city were, however, first given the opportunity of taking the

1/9TH BATTALION.

7TH APRIL.

mounds and handing them over to us in order to prevent the bombardment which would have to be carried out if we attacked them. But the insurgents in the city in Najaf were too strong for the remainder of the Arabs and orders were therefore issued to attack the mounds on the 7th of April. The Gurkhas were to assault the mounds, Nos. 10 and 12 Platoons of the 1/9th Middlesex (under Lieut. E. W. Thompson) forming the reserve; the latter were to take up position south of the mounds.

At 6.10 a.m. on the 7th, the howitzers opened fire on the two mounds, and at 7.30 the Gurkhas (in two parties) left their "jumping-off" place and advanced towards their objectives. There was little or no opposition and in less than an hour the two Hawaish mounds were taken and the position consolidated: a post was established at the Hawaish Gate. On the 8th, after a conference, the C.O. of the Middlesex obtained leave to occupy the mound north-west of the city, known as Sanger Hill, on the night of the 9th/10th of April.

The approaches to the hill were reconnoitred on the 9th and found to be good. At 4.45 a.m. on the 10th, No. 11 Platoon, under Lieut. Thompson, rushed the hill and carried it practically without opposition. The platoon was established on the crest of the hill by 4.54 a.m. and began at once to dig itself in. The position was, however, only about 150 yards from the White House (in the hands of the insurgents), from which snipers could harass No. 11 Platoon. The guns were therefore ordered to shell the house and during the shelling No. 11 Platoon withdrew while the howitzers knocked holes in the building and generally made it untenable. The platoon, with some sappers and miners, then returned to Sanger Hill and continued consolidating it. Later in the day, a bastion (Amara Bastion) in the city wall, which was only some thirty yards away but which overlooked the rear of the position on Sanger Hill, was occupied without opposition. On the 11th, Thompson's Tower (about 200 yards south of Amara Bastion), on the city wall, was occupied.

Piece by piece the city wall was being occupied and the cordon was getting ever closer round the insurgents. On the 12th, Middlesex Bastion (450 yards east of Amara Bastion) was occupied by No. 16 Platoon, under Lieut. A. F. H. Melville, without opposition. An attempt to knock a hole in a bastion proved too long a process, for after three hours' work little progress

had been made. The assaulting party was therefore withdrawn 1/9TH BATTALION.
and sent through the street inside the city wall without a shot
being fired at them. The bastion was found untenable and a
house close by was occupied.

The weather at this period was changeable. Thunder-
storms were frequent, and at times heavy rain fell. Some days
were hot and fine, but the nights were apparently cold, for in
one place in the Battalion Diary of the Middlesex, it is stated
that " two blankets quite acceptable." The health of the
Battalion was good, though one or two cases of exhaustion were
reported. The work was hard and fairly constant, for although
there was practically no fighting, the blockade line was being
continually pushed forward in places, which necessitated the
digging of fresh trenches and posts.

The blockade was, however, doing its work admirably. The
insurgents were becoming less truculent and there were signs of
an early collapse of the rebellion. On the 20th, the Political 20TH APRIL.
Officer (Capt. Balfour) entered the city to confer with the loyal
Arabs. Then on the 24th five prisoners of importance (three of
them prescribed persons, including Kadaim Subbi) were taken.
On the 28th, at 8.30 a.m., Captain Balfour again entered the
city. On this occasion he was escorted by a platoon of " A "
Company, under Captain J. H. Hewlett and 2/Lieut. Cross.
The platoon was organised into two bombing parties, each con-
sisting of six men. A composite company, consisting of three
platoons of " D " Company and one platoon of " C " Company,
under Captain Tupper, waited in reserve at Hawaish Gate.
The Political Officer left the city at 9.45 a.m. without incident.

On this date the Battalion Diary records that the hot weather
had apparently set in, the inevitable sign being the flies, which
had become troublesome. " They are bad," reports the diary,
" in spite of spraying and ' Tanglefoot '." " However," the
diarist says, with commendable optimism, " in a week or so we
ought to get them within bounds." As if anything could reduce
the extraordinary malevolence and persistence of the Mesopotamian fly !

On the 30th the end of the blockade appeared imminent, for 30TH APRIL.
Abdul Karim, the last of the important insurgents, was captured.
Sentries were ordered to be reduced to one every two hundred
yards, which would lighten duties considerably, though they were
still very heavy.

1/9TH BATTALION.
2ND MAY.

Late on the 2nd of May, orders for raising the blockade at 12 noon on the 4th, and the consequent movement of troops, were issued by Brigade Headquarters. In anticipation of these orders the Middlesex had already begun to take down the barbed wire. This task was continued and finished on the 3rd, only two barriers remaining in the city. The latter were lifted at 12 noon on the 4th, and half-an-hour later the first party of inhabitants from the city, consisting of one man, a boy and a donkey issued from the gates.

"Thus ended the blockade," records the Battalion Diary of the 1/9th Middlesex, "after six weeks' very strenuous work for the blockading party."

The C.O. of the Middlesex (Lieut.-Colonel W. P. Hewett) then assumed command of Najaf.

So far as the rebellion was concerned, the final act took place on the 30th of May, when 11 Arabs, who had been tried and found guilty of participating in the murder of the Political Officer, were hanged.

Meanwhile, the 1/9th Middlesex, less the garrisons of Hawaish Mounds, Thompson's Tower, Amara Bastion and Buraq Bastion, went into billets at Tramway Terminus. On the 7th, regular routine was again started, but into the life of the Battalion during the remainder of its stay in the Najaf area it is not necessary to go. Only one incident may be mentioned. On the 16th of May, Albuhera Day was kept with all due ceremony. Even in the Mesopotamian desert it was not forgotten. The Battalion had a holiday. An inter-platoon relay race round the city walls took place in the early morning. Surely such a race as had never before happened in this somewhat remote part of the world. In the evening the 1/9th Middlesex played the 1/4th Somerset at football, but lost.

17TH MAY.

By the 17th of May the defences of Najaf were practically completed, and two days later the Middlesex received orders to move to Kufa on the 20th, *en route* for Akab.

At 5.45 a.m. on the 20th, the Battalion set out from Najaf, and at about 8 a.m. reached the left bank of the river at Kufa and went into camp. Later in the day orders were issued to continue the march to Kala Abbasiye on the 21st, Culvert Camp on the 22nd, Hilla on the 23rd and Khan Mahawil on the 24th. These moves were duly carried out, the men marching well. At the latter place the Middlesex entrained for Balad, reaching that station at 8.15 p.m. where, after detrainment, the Battalion bivouacked. At 5.15 a.m. on the 25th the march to Akab began, 1/9TH BATTALION. that place being reached at 8.45 a.m. The Battalion had then to cross the Tigris before reaching camp. Only one small river 25TH MAY. steamer was available and it was between 3 p.m. and 4 p.m. before the crossing was finished. The camp was on the bluffs, 1½ miles from the left bank of the river, and no one was sorry to turn in that night, for the whole move from Kufa had been very trying.

On the 29th of May, the 1/9th Middlesex were ordered to relieve the 1/3rd Gurkhas in the right sector of the Adhaim bridgehead defences. The relief was carried out on the 30th.

During June, July, August and September the heat prevented active operations, and there is nothing to record concerning the 1/9th Middlesex. The Battalion remained at Akab, the 18th Indian Division being then in the Samarra area with detachments at Tikrit, Daur, Qantarat and Akab, the 53rd Brigade being located in the latter area.

On the 30th September, 1918, the Turkish forces on the 30TH SEPTEMBER. Mesopotamian front held the following positions: Ana, Fat-ha, Kirkuk and Sulaimaniya, with outposts pushed forward to Alus, Shuraimiya, Tauk, Chemchemal and Halebja. The British line ran roughly from Khaniquin to Qara Tepe, thence to Kifri, Tuz Khurmatli, Tikrit and Sahiliya.

Early in October preparations were put in hand for an advance up the Tigris by the 1st Corps (17th Division situated in the Tikrit area and 18th Division in the Samarra area), and two cavalry brigades, with the line of the Lesser Zab* as the first objective. A small column from the IIIrd Corps was to advance on the line Tauq–Kirkuk–Alton Kopri and prevent the Turks in that area moving down the Lesser Zab.

On the 29th of September, Lieut-Colonel W. P. Hewett left for leave in England. The following day an epidemic, known as "Bombay Fever,"† broke out in the Battalion, 1 officer, 37 British other ranks, and 8 Indian other ranks being affected. On the 1st of October, 52 British other ranks were down with 1ST OCOTBER. the "fever"; on the 2nd, 4 officers and 46 other ranks; on the 3rd, 2 more officers and 72 other ranks. For a week or more, fresh cases occurred and the Battalion strength suffered greatly so that training was impeded, and by the 5th had almost entirely ceased.

* Sometimes referred to as the "Lower Zab."
† Influenza.

1/9TH BATTALION.
6TH OCTOBER.

Meanwhile, warning had been received of impending operations, and on the 6th all N.C.Os. and men were employed in clearing camp in preparation for the move.*

On the 8th of October, the 18th Division began to concentrate at Tikrit, the 54th Brigade with attached troops marching to that place from Samarra. On the 10th, the 1/9th Middlesex, with other troops of the 53rd Brigade, set out on the march from Akab to Tikrit. The first stage of the march was to a camp at Beled Station, where the Battalion spent the remainder of the 10th. On the march 65 men fell out—all of whom had had influenza. On the 11th, the march was continued to Istabulat, 82 other ranks falling out from the same cause; on the 12th, Samarra was reached, less men falling out. On the 13th the Middlesex arrived at Camp Qantarat ar Risasi. The next day, to everyone's relief, the 53rd Brigade Column reached Tikrit, where for two or three days everything was done to enable the men to regain their strength in view of the forthcoming operations.

The Advance on Mosul.

ACTION OF FAT HA GORGE,
23rd–24th October.

By the 18th of October the concentration of the 18th Division at Tikrit was complete, the three Infantry Brigades (53rd, 54th and 55th) with divisional troops being on the left bank of the Tigris: the 17th Division was on the right bank. Two crossings over the Jabal Hamrin (the Ain Nukhaila and Darb-al-Khail Passes) had been reconnoitred and occupied, and forward dumps at Jift Post had been formed.

At this period the bulk of the Turkish forces (about 9,000 rifles and 59 guns) was located on the Tigris, holding a position of great natural strength astride the Fat Ha Gorge. The Tigris, with roads on both banks, ran through this gorge, which was flanked on the east by the north-western end of the Jabal Hamrin and on the west by the north-western end of the Jabal Makhul.†

---

* The total number affected by influenza was 11 officers and 288 other ranks.

† The Jabal Hamrin and Jabal Makhul were two rugged ranges of hills rising to 1,500 and 1,600 feet respectively.

The Turkish trenches covered the entrance to the gorge and extended up and over the Jabal Hamrin and Jabal Makhul.

Opposite the junction of the Lesser Zab with the Tigris the Turks had constructed a second strong position astride the Jabal Khanuka and Jabal Makhul, as well as trenches to defend the line of the Lesser Zab and a bridge at El Humr which gave them free movement between both banks of the Tigris.

An attack on the Fat Ha Gorge having been ordered, the 17th and 18th Divisions took up positions on the right and left banks respectively.

The 1/9th Middlesex (forming part of Column B, 3rd Echelon, 53rd Brigade) marched from Tikrit with the 1/3rd Gurkhas, the L.T.M.B. and 37th C.F.A. at 10 p.m. on the 20th, but it was 12.30 a.m. on the 22nd before they arrived at Jift (left bank), where the 53rd Brigade was to assemble. That march was extremely trying. The roads were very dusty, the men still suffering from the effects of influenza, and the majority had bad feet.

The 53rd Brigade as a whole then continued the march from Jift, and at 6.30 p.m. (25th) arrived at Umm al Lilah. By the morning of the 23rd both the 17th and 18th Divisions had completed their preliminary moves and were in touch with the enemy on the right and left banks of the Tigris. A force under Brigadier-General Lewin had also reached Taza Khurmatli, 12 miles south-east of Kirkuk.

Orders were to attack early on the 24th. During the afternoon of the 23rd Nightingale's Force moved along the crest of the Jabal Hamrin against the left of the Turkish positions, whilst mounted troops moved round the north of those hills. This action was so successful that during the night of the 23rd/24th the Turks abandoned the Fat Ha passes before daylight on the 24th.

The Middlesex, with the 207th Machine Gun Company and L.T.M.B., had left Umm al Lilah and had taken up their assembly line from which they were to attack the enemy, when, at 9 p.m., information was received that the Turks had evacuated the Fat Ha positions and both banks of the river. All units were then ordered to stand fast for further orders. These came to hand during the night, and at 8.30 a.m. on the 24th the 53rd Brigade marched to Tel ad Dhahab. This was a march of 16½ miles, 6 of which were through the gorge, the Middlesex doing that

M

distance without a halt in order to allow troops in rear to follow up rapidly. At 11.30 a.m., when 2½ miles north of Fat Ha, the 1/9th Middlesex halted to water animals. On reaching their destination " B " Company found outposts to cover the Brigade front, " D " and " A " Companies taking over later. The Brigade then closed in under the outpost line for the night.

North of the Jabal Hamrin, British cavalry had, after a 45-mile march through waterless country, reached the Lesser Zab some 20 miles above its confluence with the Tigris, and found the Turks holding the right bank in strength. In spite of opposition a crossing was forced over a deep ford near Uthmaniya.

Thus the action of Fat Ha Gorge, so far as the 1/9th Middlesex was concerned, was a bloodless affair.

ACTIONS ON THE LESSER ZAB.

25th October.

The official despatches state that : " On the 25th the 7th Cavalry Brigade and the leading (53rd) Infantry Brigade of the 18th Division forced a crossing over the Lesser Zab, near its confluence with the Tigris, in face of considerable opposition with heavy shell fire."

At 8 p.m. on the 24th the 53rd Brigade had been ordered to make a reconnaissance of the Lesser Zab for the purpose of throwing a bridge across the river and for forming a bridgehead. The 1/9th Middlesex (less " D " Company) were to march with the main body, " D " Company was to form the rearguard.

The Brigade set out from Tel ad Dhahab at 5 a.m. on the 25th, and, after covering two miles, the animals were watered. On resuming the march, and about three miles from the Tel, the advanced guard of the Brigade came under artillery fire from the right bank of the Tigris. Verbal orders were then issued to attack the enemy. The advanced guard was reinforced, the 1/3rd Gurkha Rifles being echeloned 500 yards to right and 300 yards to rear of the leading Battalion, *i.e.*, the 1/7th Gurkhas. Two Companies (" C " and " B ") of the 1/9th Middlesex, under Capt. J. N. Lamont, were echeloned 500 yards to left and 300 yards in rear of the 1/7th Gurkhas, the two remaining companies being kept in reserve to follow 1,000 yards in rear. A platoon, under Lieut. K. Wright, was detailed as left flank guard,

600 yards out to the Tigris. With instructions to take special care of his left flank, Capt. Lamont led with " C " Company, " B " followed at a distance of 100 yards.

After an advance of about 1,500 yards hostile shells began bursting ahead, and both companies shook out into artillery formation. Shells began to fall closer to the Battalion. A check of five minutes then occurred, and two sections of the 207th Machine Gun Company debouched from a deep depression: they were following up the 1/7th Gurkhas. Next, several shells dropped among the two companies of Middlesex, but did no harm. As the confluence of the Tigris and Zab was reached, shrapnel began to burst on the Middlesex, and machine-gun and rifle bullets, fired at extreme range, wounded four men slightly. The men, however, showed no concern at the fire, but pressed on.

After an advance of three hours the leading platoon came upon one company of the 1/7th Gurkhas with two sections of the 207th Machine Gun Company. Capt. Lamont, therefore, went over to the C.O. of the Gurkhas, who, with three companies of his Battalion, was in a depression to the left of the Middlesex. The latter officer said he was going to cross the Zab 1,000 yards further up, and arranged with Capt. Lamont to follow up in the depression on the left.

Capt. Lamont then sent back a runner to Brigade Headquarters, informing the G.O.C. of his position. The Brigadier arrived soon after and ordered the two companies of Middlesex to move through some thick crops in the direction of the corner of a cliff on the far side of the river. The Staff Captain, with seven Lewis gun sections, had already been sent there to fire on any Turks leaving the high ground and escaping to the left. The two companies moved through the cultivation in single file and when they came to the edge the Lewis gunners found two guns ready to fire. Orders were then given to dig in, while three strong picquets of one platoon each, from " C " Company, pushed forward close to the river bank. " B " Company was in reserve close to the edge of the cultivation. At about 1.30 p.m. the mules were unloaded and pakals* filled.

At 4.15 p.m., Capt. Lamont was ordered to cross the river by the ford, with his two companies. Picquets were recalled, and were in by 5 p.m., when the crossing began at once and was

* A pakal is a skin used in the East for carrying water.

1/9TH BATTALION.
25TH OCTOBER.

completed in darkness. No Turks were seen, neither had any been seen throughout the day.

Meanwhile, "A" and "D" Companies, with Battalion Headquarters, followed with Brigade Headquarters, in reserve. They also came under long-range shell fire from the right bank of the Tigris. The First Line Transport during the advance also came in for fairly heavy shelling, and, but for the skill and devotion of the Transport Officer (Lieut. F. D. Duirs), must have suffered heavy casualties. At about 2 p.m. the G.O.C. gave permission for all ranks to eat half of their emergency rations. At approximately the same time the Turks were seen leaving the high ground on the right bank of the river, and (as already stated) the Lewis Gun Section was sent up to reinforce the two companies of Middlesex on the left bank of the Tigris. The advanced guard, having reached and crossed the Lesser Zab about two miles from the confluence of the two rivers, a crossing was established, "D" Company of the Middlesex remaining on the left bank to guard it and to assist ration carts, due to arrive during the evening.

That night each unit of the 53rd Brigade found its own picquets, the Brigade closing in on the high ground on the right bank of the river. The 1/3rd Gurkhas were on the right, 1/9th Middlesex in the centre, and 1/7th Gurkhas on the left. "A" Company (Capt. J. H. Hewlett) found picquets for the Middlesex. The other three companies then indulged in the luxury of a well-earned rest. All ranks had behaved admirably throughout the day. With very little food or water they had advanced about 11 miles over rough, open country, mostly under fire, the actual attack being over about 5 miles of ground. The strength of the Battalion was 536.

At midnight, 25th October, the line of the 18th Division ran from Zarariya to Shumait, thence along the right bank of the Tigris to a point about two miles from the Tigris junction. The latter position was held by the 53rd Brigade; the artillery were south of the Lesser Zab and opposite Mushak; the 54th Brigade was bivouacked near the guns. Divisional Headquarters were at Tel ad Dhahab and the 55th Brigade was at Fat Ha. The 51st Brigade of the 17th Division, on the right bank of the Tigris, had pushed on through the Fat Ha Gorge along the Jabal Makhul and held a point about one mile south of Mushak, also the southern portion of the crest of the Jabal. Divisional Headquarters were at Qala Jabbar.

The Turkish positions extended from Balalij along the crest 1/9TH BATTALION. of the Jabal Makhul to southwards of Ain Dibs, thence to the Tigris below Mushak. They were strongly dug in on a position of great natural strength and had posted machine gunners and riflemen on the precipitous heights, razor-backed spurs, steep slopes, and above the winding ravines, from which they could hamper the attack.

Expectations were rife that the Turks would evacuate these positions. The 18th Division was therefore ordered to be ready to move at dawn on the 26th and to send patrols with machine guns to prevent the enemy repairing the Humr bridge, and that, if the enemy had not retired when the Division started, the bridge was to be watched.

THE BATTLE OF SHARQAT.

26th–30th October.*

Soon after 6 a.m. on the 26th the 17th Division, on the right 26TH OCTOBER. bank of the Tigris, began to advance, but was almost immediately checked by the Turks in front of Mushak. By 10.40 a.m. little or no progress had been made.

On the left bank the G.O.C., 18th Division, had ordered a column, consisting of a cavalry brigade and artillery, to push on up the Tigris at 6 a.m., the 53rd Brigade to follow as soon as relieved by the 54th Brigade. But by 6 a.m. a pontoon bridge that was being constructed over the Lesser Zab was not completed, and as the ration convoys could not get across before dark the forward movement of the cavalry and artillery column was cancelled, and only the cavalry were ordered to advance towards Sharqat in order to give support to the 17th Division and prevent the enemy escaping to the left bank of the Tigris. The cavalry went out as ordered, but as men and horses had consumed their rations and could not maintain themselves, they had to retire at dusk.

Throughout the 26th the 53rd Brigade remained on the right bank of the Lesser Zab, pushing patrols well forward. The 1/9th Middlesex made no advance. The 54th Brigade reached the Lesser Zab during the day and formed the reserve, the 55th

* The Battles Nomenclature Committee date the Battle as from the 28th of October; it will be observed from the above description that it began on the 26th. The official area of the battle is the Tigris above the Fat Ha Gorge.

M 3

1/9TH BATTALION.
26TH OCTOBER.

Brigade remaining at Fat Ha. Only one move of real importance was made by the 11th Cavalry Brigade on the 26th: that Brigade crossed the Tigris north of Sharqat and established itself facing south on the Hawaish nullah line, thus cutting off the Turks from Mosul.

During the night of the 26th/27th the enemy beat a precipitate retreat, and as it was essential to lend the Cavalry Brigade a helping hand, the 53rd Brigade closed its outposts and prepared to move forward.

27TH OCTOBER.

Between 10 and 11 a.m. on the 27th the 53rd Brigade moved north along the left bank of the Tigris, the Middlesex marching with the main body, less "D" Company as rearguard. At about 3 p.m. the Brigade arrived at Sakhir An Nami Rocks (nine miles), where the men had breakfast and the animals were watered. Here the G.O.C. explained the situation to unit commanders. The 17th Division was pushing up the right bank of the Tigris; the 11th Cavalry Brigade had crossed the Tigris and had formed a line across the Turkish lines of communication, the cavalry having their headquarters at Hawaish; the 54th Brigade was following up the 53rd, the right flank of the latter being protected by the 7th Cavalry Brigade; the guns were coming up on the Brigade right.

Three thousand Turks were reported facing south, four miles south of Sharqat, while 500 cavalry with two guns were opposing the 11th Cavalry Brigade, various small bodies of Turks being between.

Verbal orders were then issued by the Brigadier to march at once to assist the 11th Cavalry Brigade, the plan being to extend the line of the mounted troops from their left flank, on the left bank of the Tigris, facing south in crescent shape, to prevent any attempt by the enemy to cross to the left bank. The 1/3rd Gurkhas were to be in touch with the Cavalry Brigade, the 1/9th Middlesex in the centre, and the 1/7th Gurkhas on the left; "D" Company of the Middlesex to be in Brigade Reserve. At 4.30 p.m. the Brigade moved and marched north-west until short of Sharqat, then due north, for one hour, finally to some mounds on the left bank of the river, some 1,200 yards due east of Hawaish. It was 5 a.m. on the 28th before these positions were reached. The distance covered was 30 miles. Few men fell out, though a great many were suffering from very bad feet, shortage of food and overwork. But the Diary of the 1/9th

Middlesex records that: "The Battalion proved itself fully equal to the task imposed upon it. Owing to the lateness, 'D' Company, relieved from R.G. duty, L. Zab, it had to march for three hours, with only two halts of five minutes each, to catch up Brigade. It arrived in good condition, which reflects great credit on its commander, Capt. A. F. H. Melville, and all ranks of the Company."

1/9TH BATTALION. 28TH OCTOBER.

Fifteen minutes after the infantry of the Brigade had reached their dispositions (according to orders already mentioned) they began to dig in; the Turks were across the river and it was almost certain that at daylight they would be observed by the enemy and subjected to heavy fire.

As dawn broke the Middlesex moved away from the river in artillery formation and were ordered to lie down in all available cover.

Immediately after this movement had taken place the enemy's guns opened fire. It was then found that the position selected by the Brigade was exceptionally bad, for the mounds acted as targets for the Turkish gunners. As daylight increased the shelling became heavier, and at about 8.15 a.m. Capt. J. H. Hewett was severely wounded by shrapnel and was evacuated to the A.D.S. The Brigadier then ordered two companies ("A" and "D" were chosen) of the Middlesex to dig in facing south on a front of 800 yards, with their right 520 yards from Brigade Headquarters, to cover any movement of the enemy from the direction of Sudairat should he cross the river; "B" and "C" Companies were in reserve. But by 10 a.m. the enemy's fire had slackened and he only fired when there was any sign of movement. The Battalion Medical Officer (Capt. J. Campbell), owing to the enemy's fire, had had to move his Aid Post no less than four times. By 2 p.m. only periodic bursts were fired by the Turks.

At 4 p.m. three companies of the Middlesex were ordered to march to Qabr Gazi, a distance of about three miles, and dig themselves in along the river front, where they were to fire on any enemy seen coming down the river or attempting to cross to the left bank. Carrying tools, and suffering badly from their sore feet, the three companies ("B," "C" and "D") moved off. Before marching, water, for the want of which the troops had been thirsting all day, was issued, pakals having been brought up. During the first 1½ miles of the advance and 800 yards from setting out, Turkish guns firing in enfilade from the right

1/9TH BATTALION.
28TH OCTOBER.

bank of the Tigris, shelled the three companies, but the 18th Divisional Artillery silenced them after 15 minutes. No sooner had Qabr Gazi been reached than again the Turks shelled the companies heavily for 20 minutes, but by 5.30 p.m. the men were digging in, some occupying natural formations in the ground.

During the evening the Brigadier sent a verbal message of thanks and congratulations to the C.O., Middlesex (Major F. C. L. Stretton), thanking the Battalion for the manner in which the task assigned to it had been carried out, and the Diary has these words: " All ranks are grateful at being able to prove themselves worthy of the Regiment." It was always like that —" The Regiment "—the first thought, in every battalion of the Middlesex. In the Mesopotamian desert *esprit de corps* was every bit as keen as it was in France and Flanders.

On the night of the 28th of October the situation of the Turkish forces was precarious. The 17th Division had advanced to within about two miles of Sharqat, along the right bank of the Tigris and the Jabal Makhul, and was still engaged in pursuing the enemy towards the 11th Cavalry Brigade, which still held the Hawaish position. On the left bank of the river the 53rd Brigade prevented Turks crossing and escaping eastwards, while westwards of the enemy the Light Armoured Motor Brigade kept him from heading off in that direction.

At 2 a.m. on the 29th " C " Company of the Middlesex moved to Tel al Aqr, and " A " Company relieved the 1/3rd Gurkhas. At 10 a.m. the C.O. was informed by telephone from Brigade Headquarters that there were no enemy opposite the Middlesex, as the advance of the 17th Division had been very satisfactory. The C.O. was ordered to let the men have breakfast and companies were then to retire " at leisure " to Brigade Headquarters. But at about 12.30 p.m. orders were received to re-occupy the positions in front of Qabr Gazi, which was done. By 1 p.m. the Battalion was in position.

Throughout the 29th the Turks had been pressed relentlessly and were all but surrounded, though offering a stiff resistance. The attack was ordered to be continued on the 30th. At dawn on the latter date the enemy was held to his ground by the 17th Division on his southern flank, the cavalry north, and the 18th Division east.

At 6.30 a.m. the 18th Division was disposed for attack as follows: On the right bank of the Tigris the 7th and 11th

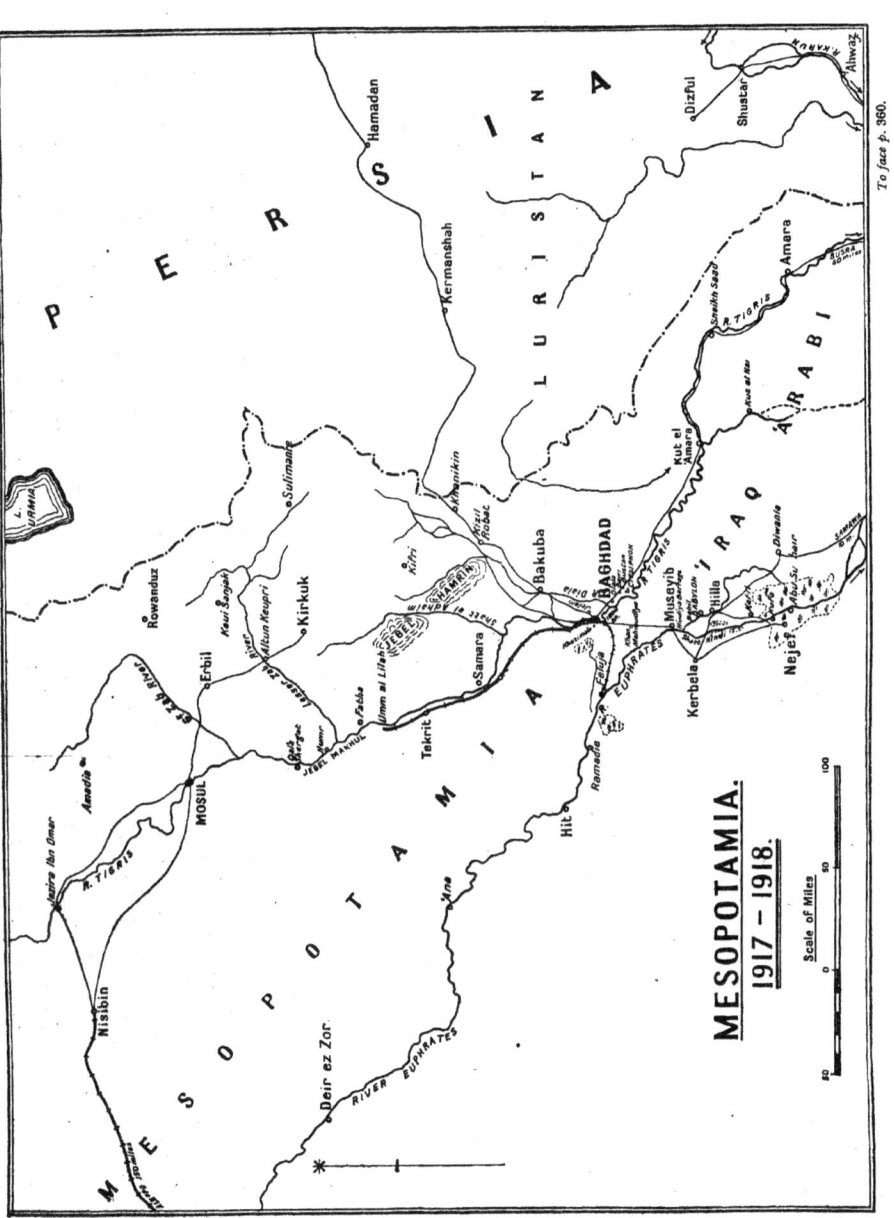

Cavalry Brigades, with two brigades of Field Artillery and Machine Gun Companies. On the left bank, to support this attack, the 1/9th Middlesex with artillery and machine guns, while two battalions with machine guns were in reserve opposite Sharqat. 1/9TH BATTALION.

The troops had already deployed when a white flag went up, and shortly afterwards information was received that the whole Turkish force had surrendered. From 8,000 to 9,000 prisoners, including the Turkish commander, were taken. Two batteries of artillery also surrendered, 30 guns having been destroyed by the enemy.

At 4 p.m. the 1/9th Middlesex moved to bivouacs 800 yards west of Qabr Gazi.

In the affair of Qaiyara and in the Occupation of Mosul on the 3rd of November the 1/9th Middlesex took no part. On the 31st they set out on a long march of 17 miles back to the right bank of the Lesser Zab.

On the 31st of October Turkey, having previously asked for it, signed an Armistice, and hostilities were ordered to cease as from that date. 31ST OCTOBER.

CHAPTER XLV.

Siberia: and the Murmansk Adventure.

FRANCE and Flanders, Italy, Salonika, the Gallipoli Peninsula, Egypt (Western and Eastern), Palestine and Mesopotamia, were not the only theatres of war in which the Middlesex fought, for during the summer of 1918 the 25th (Garrison) Battalion saw service in Siberia and "No. 1 Company" in 1919 was engaged in Northern Russia in a fruitless endeavour to help the "White Russians."*

25TH BATTALION AND NO. 1 COMPANY.

SIBERIA, 1918.

The 25th (Garrison) Battalion† was raised by Colonel John Ward, M.P., who took it out to India for guard duties. Later the Battalion was transferred to Hong Kong, and it was there that in July, 1918, orders were received to proceed to Vladivostok.

1918.

25TH BATTALION.

The Battalion embarked on the "Ping Suie" at the end of July, and on the 3rd of August disembarked at Vladivostok and marched off to barracks, 4½ miles away.

3RD AUGUST.

The British Expeditionary Force had, according to Colonel Ward, been ordered to Siberia to assist the orderly elements of Russian Society to reorganise themselves under a national government and to resurrect and reconstruct the Russian front. Under German directions the Soviets had released their German and Austrian prisoners of war (of which there were many thousands), armed and organised them into formidable armies, and set them to the work of terrorising the Russian people and destroying the country.

A mixed force of Cossacks and Czech troops (numbering some three thousand, indifferently armed) was already operating on the Oussurie front, and these the War Office ordered Colonel Ward to join: half of his Battalion was to be despatched immediately

---

* "White" Russians were soldiers of the old regime as opposed to the "Red" or Soviet troops.
† This Battalion consisted of " B.1 " men.

to the front. At 9 p.m. on the 5th of August a detachment of 18 officers and 503 other ranks, with Colonel Ward in command, left the barracks and marched to the station in full marching order, each man carrying 120 rounds of ammunition. Entrainment took place immediately, and just after midnight the Middlesex left Vladivostok. Soon after 6 o'clock on the 6th of August they reached Nikolsk, where the Battalion was hospitably received : thence the journey was continued until they reached Slagena, a fairly large town before Kraevesk. The Middlesex then went into quarters at Spascoe, which Colonel Ward decided to make his forward base. On the 7th, with the Czech commander, he visited Kraevesk and examined the line right up to the outposts, eventually deciding to send forward 243 men with four machine guns to take up position on the right flank. The enemy's centre was at Shmakovka, but only that day he had been observed moving about 180 men with three machine guns towards Uspenkie, a small town situated on the extreme right front of the Middlesex. This advance threatened the right flank of the British and Czech positions, and unless countered would result in a withdrawal to a point further south. Colonel Ward, therefore, took up a position at Kamarovka, the pivot of the whole defensive position. The right flank of the force rested upon Uspenkie and was guarded by Ateman Kalmakov's force of about 400 Cossacks, two machine guns and four small mortar guns.

On the night of the 9th/10th of August, 273 officers, N.C.Os. and men, including the Machine-Gun Section and Signallers, arrived at the front at Oussuri, and with his company commanders and the Czech commander, the C.O. of the Middlesex rode to Kamarovka and arranged the positions his men were to occupy. On returning to Kraevesk, Colonel Ward made final arrangements for the troops to take up positions early on the 11th of August. At 11 p.m., however, guns suddenly began firing, and a telephone message was received at Headquarters that Ateman Kalmakov was being attacked by hostile artillery and infantry, and that the Cossack commander wanted the company of Czechs, guarding the crossing at the north, to be moved up to the Olgovka road to cover his retreat. This was done.

At 11.45, Bolshevik troops were reported attacking the Cossack outpost at Stepanovka, and Colonel Ward advised the Czech commander to send half a company along the Runovka to assist the company already stationed there, with orders to "resist to the last" what appeared to be a serious attempt to turn the whole flank of the defensive positions.

<small>25TH BATTALION.</small>

At midnight (10th/11th August), 6 officers and 180 men of the Middlesex, with a section of the Mobile Machine-Gun Section of 43 men with four machine guns, were moved to positions behind Kamarovka to guard the passages over the river leading to Olgovka and Runovka and await events. The Czechs and Cossacks, however, beat off this opposition and the Middlesex were not engaged.

On the 11th, Colonel Ward received intimation from the British Military Representative of the War Office in Siberia to retire back to Efgenefka, and was already loading baggage when a telegram arrived from the O.C. French troops, who had arrived to take over command of the Ossouri front, arranging an interview at Kraevesk station. The French troop train had already arrived at the latter station *en route* for the front.

<small>11TH AUGUST.</small>

Colonel Ward's narrative of events has the following statement, which is interesting: "I rode over and had a lengthy interview with him upon the whole situation. Information had been brought in that the enemy's forces were much larger than had been hitherto thought possible. However strong our positions, the fact that our total forces on this immediate front did not amount to 3,000 men, as opposed to an enemy force of about 20,000, was unsatisfactory, and Major Pichon (commanding French troops) asked me to remain with my detachment at the front until the French battalion had taken up its position in the line."

The position was indeed serious, and the inequality in numbers more than dangerous, but the Japanese, as soon as they heard the British and French had landed at Vladivostok, arranged to send a division (the 12th), while the Americans also, not to be outdone, despatched a "strong force."

Meanwhile the Middlesex, Czechs and the Cossacks were hard put to it, for the Bolsheviks were pressing.

The conditions under which the Middlesex lived were anything but comfortable. No tents had been provided, and officers and men had to house themselves in bivouacs formed of branches of trees covered with marsh grass. Siberian plague was prevalent and all water had to be boiled. The 11th and 12th were characterised by intermittent shell fire. On the 13th, Colonel Ward was warned to be on the watch, as enemy forces, estimated at

<small>13TH AUGUST.</small>

25TH BATTALION. 13TH AUGUST.

about seven battalions with cavalry, were manœuvring in front. On the 13th there was an encounter between the opposing armoured trains. At night heavy rain fell and the bivouacs very quickly became a hopeless bog, with from six inches to a foot of water. Swarms of mosquitoes helped to make the night thoroughly miserable.

On the 14th, the enemy was observed still endeavouring to work down the right flank. At 5 a.m. on the 15th heavy hostile shell fire drove the Cossacks' outposts out of their positions at Olgovka, and they were compelled to retreat from their main position. The C.O. of the Middlesex was therefore asked to move up in the direction of Runovka and cover the retreat of the Czech infantry which had gone to the assistance of the Cossacks. At 5 p.m. the Middlesex took up position behind Runovka across the road and began to dig in : by daylight on the 16th a fairly strong line had been dug across the marshy ground.

On the 16th the situation appeared not only serious, but critical. The enemy continued to push his way forward on the right and had advanced his artillery to the right rear of the main defences, having driven in all troops on the river Oussurie. But a Naval 12-pdr., with a well-trained gun crew, came from H.M.S. "Suffolk," and the second shot caught a patrol of about twenty of the enemy and nearly wiped it out, which had the effect of damping the ardour of the main body. A hostile landing on the shores of Lake Khanka, opposite Spascoe, was then reported, and the Middlesex at the base in that town were ordered to assist the local Czechs in stopping or delaying this movement. This was satisfactorily carried out.

17TH AUGUST.

At 4.30 a.m. on the 17th the enemy began another bombardment along the whole front and along the right flank to right rear. For three hours they searched the road behind the Middlesex, but there were no casualties. Two Czech field guns took up position on Colonel Ward's right and did good work in keeping down the enemy's fire. The French commander then informed Colonel Ward that he had asked the Japanese at Nikolsk for one battery of artillery and a squadron of cavalry for scouting. The reply is interesting : "*The Japanese commander stated that no help could be expected from him,*" to which the C.O. of the Middlesex appended the following comment : "If this is a correct statement of the Japanese attitude, I see no alternative but retirement."

It *was* correct, as will be seen later.

An attempt to cross the river south of Runovka on the 18th ended in disaster for the enemy, who left many dead on both banks owing to the excellent marksmanship of the Cossack machine gunners. A suggestion by the French commander that the Middlesex and French troops should retire and take up a new position at Syvagino was promptly negatived by the C.O. of the former. Later, two more 12-pdr. guns from the "Suffolk" arrived, and the French commander said he would now hold on until the arrival of Japanese troops. The Naval guns forced the enemy to retire 2,000 yards to a line of safety.

25TH BATTALION. 18TH AUGUST.

The climax came on the 20th of August. At 4 a.m. heavy gun-fire broke out along the whole right flank; the solitary field gun with the Middlesex opened fire and set alight an enemy observation tower. Then at 7 a.m. came a report that under cover of the darkness the Bolsheviks had crept into the Cossack positions at Antonovko, captured the artillery and machine guns, and had become masters of the positions. Ateman Kalmiakov rallied his Cossacks and gallantly tried to retake the position, but failed, and was retiring towards Kraevesk. The French commander at once suggested a withdrawal, and, seeing the hopelessness of the situation, with no chance of assistance, Colonel Ward concurred. Preparations had begun for the withdrawal when the French commander asked the C.O., Middlesex, to reoccupy his position at Runovka, as Japanese troops were moving up to the flanks from Syvagino. By 9.30 a.m. the Middlesex had reoccupied their original positions.

20TH AUGUST.

But the assistance of Japanese troops was a myth, and at 11 a.m. the French commander again proposed that the whole line should retire from along the river Oussurie and entrain at Kraevesk for withdrawal to Syvagino.

The withdrawal was made and the troops entrained for Syvagino, where on arrival Colonel Ward was informed by a War Office message dated August 18th that the Middlesex were under the command of the Japanese forces.

The Japanese commander at Syvagino was Colonel Inagaka, who appointed Colonel Ward to the command of the reserves at that place, consisting of one battalion of Czech troops, one detached company of Czechs, one company of Japanese infantry, one company of 25th Middlesex, and about 600 Cossack cavalry under Ateman Kalmakov. The Machine-Gun Section of

25TH BATTALION.

Middlesex (four Maxims and fifty men), with the Naval detachment of four 12-pdrs. on two armoured trains, with 22 naval ratings under Captain Bath, R.M.L.I., had taken up positions in the front line at Dukhovskaya, about four miles north of Syvagino, under the command of Major Pichon (French Commandant), who commanded the left wing of the Allied front. This was on the 21st of August.

22ND AUGUST.

Of the 22nd there is nothing to record, but the stage was set for the first pitched battle with the Bolsheviks.

THE BATTLE OF DUKHOVSKAYA.

23rd–24th August, 1918.

23RD AUGUST.

The following is Colonel Ward's narrative of the operations, which began on the 23rd :—

"August 23rd. During the night Major Pichon ordered Lieut. King, M.G.O., to take two machine guns to a post some 200 yards in front of the line to guard the armoured train observation post on the left, and the Czech left front. About 10 a.m. the enemy had worked his way forward to within about 200 yards of the observation and machine-gun posts, and Petty Officer Moffat, R.N., suggested a withdrawal within the lines. A few minutes later Major Pichon ordered a withdrawal. Directly the enemy observed this movement they rushed the posts, and only the great coolness of the Machine-Gun Officer, Lieut. King, and Petty Officer Moffat saved this little party. Part of one machine gun and some material was lost owing to the impossibility of rapid retirement with this comparatively heavy type of machine gun. It was unfortunate that a gun should be lost; but no fault attaches to anyone for the occurrence. The new position stretches from the railway at Dukhovskaya to the right for a distance of about 10 miles. The left wing, resting on the railway, is composed of two armoured trains with four 12-pdr. guns, manned by a detachment from H.M.S. 'Suffolk' under the command of Captain Bath, R.M.L.I., with one company of Czech infantry on the left and machine-gun sections of the Middlesex Regiment of 50 men and four Maxim guns, under Lieut. T. C. King, on the right of the railway. The grouping of the Allies following on the right and one Czech battalion, one French battalion, all under the command of Major Pichon. From the centre to the right flank the whole position is held by Japanese troops, both infantry and artillery. The reserves are in Syvagino under my command. They include 200 men of the 25th Middlesex, one company French infantry, one company Japanese infantry, and 600 Cossack cavalry.   *25TH BATTALION. 23RD AUGUST.*

"Later. 8.30 p.m. Artillery fire broke out along the whole line, under cover of which the enemy made a determined attack upon the centre, which was repulsed with the loss of two machine guns."*

"At 1.45 a.m." (on the 24th of August), Colonel Ward states, "as commander of the reserves, I received from the Japanese Headquarters the following orders :—

"'1. All the enemy attacks were driven back to-day. We gain two machine guns and five captures.

2. The Allied troops will attack the enemy, inflicting upon them an annihilating disaster to-morrow, the 24th August.

3. The Japanese troops will attack the enemy, starting [from] the present line at 3 o'clock, the 24th, morning.

4. The reserves, British, French, Kalmakov's Force and a few Japanese companies will be under the command of Japanese Colonel Inagaki, will arrive at the north-western side of Dukhovskaya at 2 o'clock to-morrow morning.

(Signed) S.OI.
Lieut.-General,
Commanding 12th Division.'"

Colonel Ward says: "One observation about the 'order,' the distance from Syvagino to Dukhovskaya is four miles. The order was delivered at my Headquarters 15 minutes before the time for rendezvous, four miles distance. I conveyed the order to the French, the Czech, Japanese and Cossack detachments under my command. The French and Czech troops prepared to move rather slowly. The Japanese and Cossacks made no effort to mobilize, the British were ready, and by 2.10 a.m. (exactly 25 minutes after the order was received) marched out of Syvagino to the rendezvous.

"By a rapid night march we arrived near the north-west end of the town of Dukhovskaya at 3.45 a.m., one hour and forty-

* The *enemy* lost the machine guns.

25TH BATTALION.
23RD AUGUST.

five minutes behind time. Colonel Inagaki could not be found, nor had the other detachments arrived.

"The battle opened instantly and numerous heavy shells ploughed up the ground around us. Having no one to direct me, I was left to act on my own initiative. The Japanese infantry were advancing in extended order about a quarter of a mile on the left of the railway, and in similar order about 200 yards on the right of the railway, leaving a gap along the railway itself. I decided to place my detachment in this gap and make the advance a complete line. Five enemy armoured trains were on the line at intervals right ahead. Enemy troops occupied the wood in front and the slopes on the left flank. The artillery on the armoured trains shelled and machine-gunned the advance, but their fire was unsteady, the shrapnel bursting too high and the shells churning up the ground behind the advancing troops. A few shots from our artillery broke the line behind the two most advanced enemy trains, making their retreat impossible. The machine-gun and artillery fire from these trains caused many casualties among the Japanese troops on either flank, but the volume of rifle fire from our direction rendered the enemy guns facing us from the front train quite harmless, until a shell set the train on fire, which destroyed the whole of its personnel.

"The gunners in the second train, finding it impossible to man the guns on their unsheltered platforms, retired to the trucks and fired point blank at the troops on either side, until despatched by rifle and bayonet. Seeing their trains destroyed, a party of the enemy on our extreme left raised a white flag, but as another party still further towards our left rear continued to fire, the Japanese cavalry charged the positions and cleared both parties. There were no prisoners taken. I continued to advance along the railway and took an armed enemy prisoner, whom I disarmed and placed under a British guard and returned to the rear. The advance continued until the wood sheltering the station at Kraevesk, eight miles from the start, was reached. The Japanese troops swarmed on to the wooded hill on the left, but as this was my previous headquarters, I knew that a small curved cutting would afford me good shelter for my advance. I proceeded round this curve and discovered an armoured train standing in the station 400 yards distant. An enemy officer was standing beside the engine, at whom I fired. A $2\frac{1}{4}$-inch gun answered my shot, but missed its mark, and the struggle for the station began.

Our advance had carried us so far ahead of the artillery that it was now a fight—armoured train versus rifle. The train opened fire with its artillery and machine guns at short range, causing many casualties among the Japanese on my right and rear, which caused them to retire behind the hill. Sheltered by the cutting, my small advanced party held on and peppered the train with rifle fire with such good effect that the train slowly retreated out of the station, but again came to a standstill about 600 yards distance. Keeping a log storehouse in line with the train, my party advanced and sheltered behind the store and again opened fire. The Japanese now advanced and occupied the station, and ordered the advance to stop, pending the arrival of the artillery. I ordered a rally of my detachment.

"The Battle of Dukhovskaya put an end to the Oussurie operations, for it was a decisive defeat of the enemy. He was, indeed, entirely demoralised and did not make another stand east of Lake Baikal."

It is not possible, however, in a regimental history to continue the narrative of subsequent events, which frequently took the form of political action, in which the presence of British troops lent great assistance.

From the Oussurie front the 25th Middlesex, with the Allied forces, pushed north and then east along the line of the Siberian Railway by Lake Baikal, Irkutsh and Omsk until, in 1919, the Battalion returned to England. Of his Battalion Colonel Ward said : " One and all behaved like Englishmen—the highest eulogy that can be passed upon the conduct of men."

25TH BATTALION. 23RD AUGUST.

MURMANSK.

Although No. 1 Special Company of the Middlesex Regiment did not land at Murmansk until the 19th of April, 1919, that port had been occupied by the Allies in the Spring of 1918.

The operations in Northern Russia were, in conjunction with those in Siberia, planned especially with the idea of forming an eastern front which would force the Germans to keep troops there instead of despatching them to France and Flanders ; also it was necessary to hold Murmansk in order to prevent the Germans using it as a submarine base, for it was the one Russian port open all the year round, *i.e.*, was not frozen up, as Archangel was.

No. 1 COMPANY. 19TH APRIL, 1919.

No. 1 Company.	The two ports Murmansk and Archangel were both occupied by the North Russian Expeditionary Force when the story of No. 1 Company begins.
3rd April.	On the 3rd of April, 1919, a War Office telegram was received at Mill Hill, ordering the formation of No. 1 Special Company Middlesex for immediate service overseas with the North Russian Expeditionary Force. The N.C.Os. and men were to be picked from regular soldiers who were forming the nuclei of the 2nd and 4th Battalions then stationed at the Depot.

The Company was almost exclusively formed of N.C.Os. and men who had seen long service on the western and other fronts. This Company of volunteers of the Regiment was commanded by Major C. D. Drew.

On the 9th the Company entrained at Tilbury Docks aboard the "Porto."*

The voyage was uneventful, and on the 16th the vessel entered the Kola inlet and dropped anchor off Murmansk. The Company disembarked on the 19th and marched to the Marine Barracks, where officers and men were accommodated.

Working parties and guard duties occupied the Company for several days, and then on the 30th No. 1 Platoon was sent off south as escort to a trainload of undesirables, who were deported to the enemy's lines. On this day also the Company received orders to be prepared to move to Kem. Less No. 4 Platoon, which remained at Murmansk for similar duties as carried out by No. 1 Platoon, the Middlesex left for Kem on the 2nd of May, arriving on the 4th, but they were ordered to continue their journey to No. 19 Siding (on the railway between Lakes Vigozero and Segozero).

5th May. The Company arrived at No. 19 Siding on the 5th and detrained. A camping ground was cleared and tents pitched. On the 6th at 2 p.m. a telephone message from the 237th Infantry Brigade called for 100 men to proceed to Maselga at once, as the enemy was believed to be preparing a counter-attack. Nos. 2 and 3 Platoons left by train at 4 p.m. and proceeded to railhead some 15 miles south of Urosozero, thence by march route along the railway to Maselga. No counter-attack materialised, and the Company occupied outposts or patrolled the line.

* The "Porto" was formerly the "Prinz Heinrich," the German ship which carried the German Crown Prince on his Colonial tour. She had been seized by the Portuguese and loaned to Great Britain.

On the 14th of May, however, winter kit was handed in and preparations made for an advance beyond No. 13 Siding, beyond which the K.R.R.C. Company had forced the enemy.

At 7.15 a.m. on the 15th the Company, in fighting order, left by train for No. 13 Siding to support the Rifles. The latter were to attack and drive the enemy towards No. 12 Siding. Nos. 1 and 4 Platoons had by now rejoined the Company.

On arrival at No. 13 Siding the Middlesex pushed down along the railway and had a sharp fight with the enemy, finally driving him back. On the 16th the advance was continued and No. 12 Siding occupied. Here the railway had been damaged, and further advance was inadvisable until the rails had been repaired.

Another brush with the enemy took place on the 19th. The Rifles—the advanced force—had made an unsuccessful attack and had been practically cut off. The Company marched to their assistance and relieved them.

It was intended to attack the enemy on the 20th of May, but he was found to be evacuating his positions, and patrols from No. 1 Company, pushed down the railway, reached No. 11 Siding without opposition. That night the Middlesex were accommodated in a village half a mile north-west of No. 11 Siding, and No. 3 Platoon was sent off to capture Lumbushi. This was quickly done, 10 prisoners being captured.

On the 21st, in co-operation with the Serbs and Italians (both of whom had representative forces in North Russia), the town of Medvyejya Gora was captured and the Company spent the night on outpost duty on the hills east of the town.

No other operations took place during May, and it was the 12th of June before the next attack took place. On this occasion No. 10 Siding was subjected to a night attack, and by the morning of the 13th the operation had been successful. The Company then took over outpost duties until the 15th, when a move back to Medvyejya Gora took place.

Gradually the line was being extended, and on the 6th of July the Company entrained to No. 9 Siding, marching on detrainment to Kapaselga village. Here the Middlesex took over outposts from the Russians.* " The relief," records the Diary, " was not a very orthodox one. Most of the sentries were asleep, and picquets simply disappeared when we arrived, and no attempt to hand over orders was made."

* These Russians were anti-Bolshevists.

No. 1 Company.
26th July.

The K.R.R.C. Company was also at Kapaselga, and from time to time relieved the Middlesex. Until the 26th of July the Company remained in the locality, patrolling, wiring trenches and doing garrison work generally. On that date they entrained and returned to Medvyejya Gora.*

On the 1st of August the Company returned to Kapaselga, taking over the outpost line from the Olonetz Regiment. Patrol work occupied most of the night hours. No. 8 Siding, Mogilniki and Lake Lijomozero were all visited, but the records state " no enemy encountered."

Nos. 1 and 2 Platoons were despatched to Mogilniki and Mayozero on the 8th, as on the previous day the enemy were reported in occupation. Both places were entered by the Middlesex and held, no enemy being seen. The platoons returned to Kapaselga at night.

13th August.

On the 13th the Bolshevists attacked the posts, but were easily beaten off, leaving one officer dead on the ground.

The last action in which the Company took part was fought on the 17th of August. The account is given in full as an instance of the character of the fighting in which the Middlesex had been concerned :—

17th August.

" Company entrained (at Kapaselga) and left School House at 8 a.m. Detrained at railhead two bridges north of Siding 8. Major Lang, Marines, and one battalion were attached to Company. We attacked along railway line, two platoons on each side. No. 1 Platoon with No. 3 in support on the right, No. 2 with No. 4 in support on the left. Four enemy were seen and fired at in No. 8 Siding and retired on to their main position, where the enemy replied with heavy rifle and machine-gun fire. Firing was more accurate than usual for the ' Bols,' and a good many bullets struck the ground between front and support positions. His position was shelled and Company attacked. His position had been hastily evacuated, and dixies of hot water and burnt pancakes were found ; also a large amount of ammunition, several rifles and barbed wire. Company advanced again ; progress had to coincide with attack of Karelian Company on

---

* In Major-General Sir C. Maynard's book on the Murmansk operations he mentions a heavy attack on Tivdiya by 800 " Reds," most of whom were Finns. " The garrison," he states, " commanded by Capt. Cursons, of the Middlesex Regiment, and consisting almost entirely of the Olonetz Regiment, put up a great fight and finally beat off their assailants with considerable loss."

post road. Patrols were sent to post road to keep touch. No. 1 Company advanced to Siding 7A, approximately 5 versts south of No. 8 Siding. The enemy blew up bridges as we advanced. On reaching Siding 7A an outpost position was taken up. No. 4 Platoon on right (responsible for railway), No. 3 Platoon on left. No. 2 Platoon returned to No. 8 Siding as escort to guns. No enemy were seen during night. A large fire was observed well in rear of enemy line, which may have been a forest fire. Heavy firing was heard from Vakshozero direction. A patrol was sent to Karelians at junction of post road and track from Siding 7A. Our casualties were nil." _{No. 1 Company. 17th August.}

The Company returned to Kapaselga on the 18th, but three hours later left for Medvyejya Gora. On the 20th the Middlesex entrained for Kem, where the Company took over duties of a varied nature.

Nothing more of interest happened until, finally, on the 20th of September, the Company arrived at Murmansk. On the 11th of October H.M.T. "Menominee" left Murmansk for England with No. 1 Company aboard and arrived at Tilbury on the 17th, but lay off in the river until the following day. On the 18th the Company disembarked and entrained for Clipstone Camp, Notts, where it was attached to the 3rd Battalion of the Regiment. _{18th October.}

Thus ended the Murmansk adventure so far as No. 1 Company was concerned. It was not a very strenuous affair so far as fighting was concerned, but it is an interesting incident in the history of the Regiment.

Conclusion.

It is unnecessary to follow in close detail the numerous battalions of the Middlesex Regiment from the moment the Germans laid down their arms—a beaten and broken enemy—to their return to England and demobilization. But history demands a brief reference to their subsequent movements after the Armistice.

The 1st Middlesex from Sassegnies marched to Sarbarras on the 12th of November to Vendegies on the 15th, and Caullery on the 16th, where billets were occupied until the 10th of December. Then came a series of moves which eventually brought the Battalion to Avesnes until the end of 1918.*

The 2nd Middlesex, who had moved to Ghlin after 11 a.m. on the 11th of November, marched to Mazieres on the 12th, thence on the 17th to Taitignies, where they remained until the 17th of December. They were at Ath when the New Year was ushered in, and their records state that: "The majority of the Battalion stayed up to see the Old Year out."

The 3rd Middlesex, having sailed from Salonika on the 17th of November, reached Constantinople, where they were still garrisoned at the fall of the year.

In Caudry the 4th Middlesex stayed until the 1st of December, when they marched to Haussy, and on the 2nd to Villers-Pol. On the 14th a series of moves began which brought the Battalion to Beves; here the remainder of the year passed quietly.

The 1/7th Middlesex moved from Harveng to Bougnies on the 12th of November, thence on the 26th to Quevy le Grand, where they were billeted until the 28th of December. The Battalion then moved to Mons for the remainder of the year. The 1/8th Middlesex, whose Headquarters were at Château de Warelles on the 11th of November, moved to Quevy le Petit on the 15th, and, with the 1/7th Battalion, marched into Mons on the 28th of December.

The 1/9th Middlesex from the Lesser Zab finally arrived at

---

* The records do not go beyond 1918, but several battalions of the Middlesex Regiment eventually served on the Rhine as part of the Army of Occupation; others returned to England in 1919 and were disbanded.

Sharqat on the 23rd of November, where the remainder of the year was spent. The 13th Middlesex remained at Le Louvion until the 17th of November, when, by route-march stages via Warnies le Grand, Rouvignies, Auberchicourt and Lecelles, the Battalion reached La Glanfries on the 26th and remained there throughout December until the New Year dawned. The 18th Middlesex (Pioneers), who were at Berlaimont when the Armistice was signed, remained in that village until the 16th, then by route march they moved to Malincourt, which place they reached on the 19th and were billeted until the 11th of December. A series of moves then took them to Fricamps, and by the end of the month they were at Havrincourt. The 19th Middlesex (Pioneers) at Berchem, bridging, on the 11th of November, continued their work for two or three days, then they also took the road, and at the end of 1918 were at Bas Oha. From Warcoing the 20th Middlesex marched to Tourcoing on the 13th of November and stayed there until the end of the year. This Battalion's Diary closes with the words : " A merry New Year all round." They deserved it ! From Kleinberg the 23rd Middlesex moved via Hoogstraat, Grammont and Thollenbeek to Ghoy, where they arrived on the 21st. On the 13th of December they again set out by route march for Latinne and saw the New Year in in that village. The 26th Middlesex (Pioneers) have already been mentioned as being at Batoum when 1918 ended.

Thus, so far as the records show. Into all the details of the Regiment's activities as part of the Army of Occupation in Germany, or in working on the old battlefields of France and Flanders, or the duties of other battalions which were further afield, in other parts of the War area, it is not proposed to go :

" By the long road they trod with so much faith and with such devoted and self-sacrificing bravery,"* they had arrived at Victory.

From Albuhera, 1811, to the Somme Battles of 1918 was a far cry, yet the spirit of the Regiment remained the same, always the same. The now-famous death cry of Colonel Inglis at Albuhera —" Die hard, 57th, die hard ! "—was echoed at Ypres in 1915 by that gallant young subaltern who encouraged his men with words which have a sacred place in the hearts of all members of the Regiment—" Let us die like men, like Die-Hards ! " ; and yet again on the Somme in 1918, when almost surrounded, the

* From the Official Despatches.

C.O. of a battalion of the Middlesex, which had fought its way out only after a fierce and bloody struggle, wrote in his narrative of the operations the words: "Thank God! the Regiment did its duty."

In that spirit the Die-Hards fought, in that spirit they died. But those who gave their gallant and brave lives are not forgotten. The blood-red poppies of the Flanders fields bloom and wither away, but in the spring they bloom again, and yet again—the eternal promise of the Almighty. So in men's hearts the memory of dead comrades who have gone before never dies, but springs afresh each year:

> "They shall not grow old, as we who are left grow old,
> Age shall not weary them, nor the years condemn.
> At the going down of the sun and in the morning,
> We shall remember them."

INDEX.

Battalion:
1st: 3, 13-16, 55-58, 119, 124-131, 171, 172, 177, 178, 226-232, 252-258, 259, 260, 282-284, 287-290, 335, 377
2nd: 3, 13, 16, 17, 24, 93-96, 103, 104, 109, 116, 117, 172, 173, 178-180, 193, 194, 203-212, 214-216, 218-221, 233-236, 275-279, 377
3rd 3, 295-305, 377
4th: 3, 29, 44, 45, 49-53, 60-64, 105-107, 119, 122, 131, 132, 134, 135, 142, 143, 173, 180, 183, 217, 239-242, 248-251, 255-258, 285, 287, 288, 377
1/7th: 3, 29-33, 39-44, 46-51, 68, 71-73, 109, 110, 112, 114, 115, 146, 147, 149, 154, 155, 159, 161, 167, 169, 174, 180, 181, 183, 191, 213, 214, 240, 241, 245-247, 251, 255, 262-264, 287, 290, 291, 332, 377
1/8th: 3, 29-33, 39-41, 47, 49-51, 62, 68, 71-74, 109, 110, 112, 113-115, 146, 147, 149, 154, 155, 159, 161, 166, 167, 169, 174, 180, 181, 183, 191, 213, 214, 240, 241, 245-247, 251, 255, 262-264, 287, 290, 291, 332, 377
2/7th 3
X 7th Res. Bn. 34
2/8th 3
1/9th 3, 331-361, 377
1/10th 3, 332, 335, 341
2/10th 3, 309-329
3/10th: 3, 132, 133, 135-139, 142, 176, 177, 181-183
11th: 3, 29, 33, 34, 37-39, 49, 53, 62, 63, 68, 74-77, 146, 148-151, 154, 159, 160, 161-163, 167, 169, 174, 181, 182, 183
12th: 3, 6-11, 13, 25, 68-70, 93, 104, 105, 117, 143, 174, 181, 182, 184
13th: 3, 29, 34-36, 45, 53-55, 80, 87-89, 93, 94, 96, 97, 101-103, 146, 174, 175, 184, 191-193, 203, 204, 211, 216, 255, 260-262, 286, 287, 289, 290, 378

Battalion—*contd*.
16th: 3, 17-19, 53, 58, 59, 109-112, 119, 122, 123, 131, 132, 139-142, 146, 148, 149, 151-155, 159, 160, 161, 163, 164, 167, 170, 175, 181, 182, 184, 185
17th: 3, 5, 7, 10, 11, 13, 24, 25, 53, 61, 62, 64-68, 146, 161, 162, 165, 166, 168-170, 175, 176, 181, 182, 185, 186
18th: 3, 13, 16, 56, 119, 131, 172, 178, 226, 227, 230, 252, 255, 284, 285, 287, 289, 378
19th: 3, 80, 81, 83, 90, 93, 94, 98, 101, 119, 122, 191, 198, 199, 203, 214, 232, 243, 244, 273, 293, 294, 378
20th: 3, 13, 19-23, 146, 156-160, 170, 176, 187, 188, 194-196, 200-202, 224-227, 243, 244, 265-267, 270, 273, 378
21st: 3, 13, 19-23, 146, 156-160, 170, 176, 187, 188, 194-202, 224-227, 243, 244
23rd: 3, 80-87, 89, 90, 93, 94, 98-101, 119-122, 191, 198, 202, 203, 214, 232, 243, 244, 267-273, 293, 294, 378
25th 363-371
26th .. 3, 301, 302, 305-307, 378
No. 1 Company .. 371-375

Officers:
Baker, Lieut.-Col. E. E. F. 236, 277, 278
Beach, Major G. 341, 343, 346, 347
Beevor, Lieut.-Col. M. .. 181
Bendall, Lieut.-Col. F. W. D. 30, 109, 114
Bicknell, Lieut.-Col. F. .. 29
Blakeney, Lieut.-Col. H. W. .. 301
Blumfeld, Lieut.-Col. J. L. 342, 345
Bridgman, Lieut.-Col. G. A. .. 63
Cade, Major A. G. 172
Cautley, Lieut.-Col. C. H. 132, 135, 183
Chapman, Lieut.-Col. W. G. .. 287

INDEX—continued.

Officers—contd. Page
Dawson, Major A. C. 29, 45 ;
Lieut.-Col. A. C. 60
Dawson, Lieut.-Col. L. H. .. 94
Dixon, Major 331
Dove, Major R. S. 262
Drew, Major C. D. 173, 207,
  208, 209, 218, 219, 220, 340
Dunlop, Lieut.-Col. F. P. 19, 21, 157
Elgee, Lieut.-Col. J. W. L. 15,
  16, 124, 172, 231
Emery, Major 31, 32
Fenwick, Lieut.-Col. H. T. .. 5
Finch, Lieut.-Col. H. W. E. .. 16
Forbes-Robertson, Major J.
  123 ; Lieut.-Col. J. 151, 163, 164, 184
Frend, Major S. R. 94
Greene, Lieut.-Col. J. .. 45, 261
Grogan, v.c., Brig.-Gen. G. W.
  St. G... .. 212, 277, 278
Grove-White, Major P. 285, 287
Haig-Brown, Lieut.-Col. A. R.
  83, 94, 203
Hamilton Hall, Lieut.-Col. J.
  17, 103, 116, 173, 212, 231, 252, 255
Hanley, Major H. A. O., 16,
  124, 125, 127, 128 ; Lieut.-
  Col. H. A. O. .. 173, 217
Harrison, Major G. L. .. 174
Hebden, Major H. H... .. 290
Hewett, Major W. P., 341,
  345 ; Lieut.-Col. .. 350, 351
Hill, Major F. R. 152
Hingley, Major A. M., 191,
  261 ; Lieut.-Col. A. M. .. 262
Hohler, Major A. P., 315 ;
  Lieut.-Col. 329
Hull, Major-General C. P. A... 29
Inglis, Colonel 346
Ingpen, Lieut.-Col. P. L. 30,
  32, 39, 109, 113, 114, 115, 147
Irons, Lieut.-Col. A. 94
Isaacson, Major P. de St. Q. .. 115
Johnston, Lieut.-Col. W. H. H.
  6, 69, 117
Johnson, Major F. S. B., 21 ;
  Lieut.-Col. F. S. B. .. 156
Jowett, Major C. 329
Kay, Major P. C., 115 ; Lieut.-
  Col. P. C. .. 147, 167, 174
  181, 240, 246
Kelly, Lieut.-Col. G. C. 64, 161
Kent, Lieut.-Gen. H. 252
King, Lieut.-Col. E. J. 40, 42,
  43, 47, 48, 72, 114, 147

Officers—contd. Page
King, Major S. 31
McNeille, Lieut.-Col. H. C. .. 260
McReady-Diarmid, v.c., Capt.
  A. M. C. .. 146, 165, 168, 169
Metcalfe, Lieut.-Col. H. C. .. 226
Miller, Lieut.-Col. .. 299, 302
Milne, Major W. W. 266
Molony, Lieut.-Col. W. B. 239, 285
Montgomerie, Major 334
Morris, Lieut.-Col. F. G. G. .. 123
Morris, Major C. H. 156
O'Neill, Major 133
Oodling, Major W. C. 324
O'Reilly, Major T. W. 58 ;
  Lieut.-Col. T. W. 123
Owen, Major D. C. 255
Page, Major C. A. S 173 ;
  Lieut.-Col. C. A. S. .. 193,
  207, 208, 209, 215, 218, 220, 221
Pank, Major C. H., 115 ; Lieut.-
  Col. C. H. 147, 166, 174, 240, 263
Pargiter, Lieut.-Col. 33
Pearson, Lieut.-Col. V. L. N... 315
Pereira, Maj.-Gen. Sir C. E. .. 5
Podmore, Major H. 174
Prior, Major 211
Samuel, Lieut.-Col. W. H. 19, 156
Smith, Lieut.-Col. B. A. 232, 268
Stafford, Lieut.-Col. R. S. H.
  161, 165
Storr, Lieut.-Col. H. .. 15, 172
Stretton, Major F. C. L. .. 360
Thompson, Lieut.-Col. B. A. .. 17
Toye, v.c., Capt. A. M. .. 205
Ward, M.P., Colonel John 331,
  332, 333, 334, 335, 336, 337, 339
Webb-Bowen, Lieut.-Col. W. I.
  29, 44, 45
Wollocombe, Major T. S., 33 ;
  Lieut.-Col. T. S. 37, 63,
  149, 162, 174, 183

Operations :

Aisne, 1918, The Battle of the 233
Albert, 1918, The Battle of .. 238
Ancre, 1918, The Battle of the 216
Arleux, The Battle of .. 63
Arras, 1917, The Battles of .. 27
Arras, 1918, The First Battle of 213
Arras, 1918, The Second Battles
  of 245
Bailleul, The Battle of .. 227
Bapaume, The First Battle of . 199
Battles of the Somme, 1918,
  The First ,, ,, .. 191

INDEX—continued.

Operations—contd. | Page

- Bourlon Wood, The Capture of .. 156
- Broodseinde, The Battle of .. 134
- Cambrai, 1917, The Battle of .. 145
- Cambrai, 1918, The Battle of .. 255
- Canal du Nord, The Battle of .. 250
- Courtrai, The Battle of .. 268
- Doiran, 1918, The Battle of .. 303
- Douai, The Capture of .. 278
- Dukhovskaya, The Battle of .. 368
- Estaires, The Battle of .. 223
- Eve of the German Offensive, 1918 177
- Fat Ha Gorge, Action of .. 353
- Flanders Offensive, The 79, 91
- ,, The Advance in .. 242
- Final Advance : Flanders .. 264
- ,, ,, Artois .. 275
- ,, ,, Picardy .. 281
- Gaza, The First Battle of .. 309
- ,, The Second Battle of .. 313
- ,, The Third Battle of .. 316
- German Counter-attacks at Cambrai, 1917 160
- German Offensives of 1918: Picardy 189
- German Offensives of 1918: Flanders 223
- German Offensives of 1918: Champagne 233
- Hazebrouck, The Battle of .. 227
- Hindenburg Line, The British Advance to the 1
- Hindenburg Line, The German Retreat to the 12
- Hindenburg Line, The Breaking of the.. 245
- Hindenburg Line, Battles of the 248
- India 331
- Italy 293
- Jericho, The Capture of .. 324
- Jerusalem, The Capture of .. 319
- Jordan Valley, Operations beyond the 323
- Jordan, The Passage of the .. 327
- Kemmel, The First Battle of.. 229
- Langemarck, 1917, The Battle of 108
- Lys, The Battles of the .. 223
- Menin Road Ridge, The Battle of the.. 118

Operations—contd. | Page

- Mesopotamia 342
- Messines, 1917, The Battle of . 79
- ,, 1918, The Battle of 226
- Miraumont, The Actions of .. 2
- Mosul, The Advance on .. 352
- Murmansk 371
- Najaf, The Blockade of .. 346
- Ooteghem, The Action of .. 271
- Palestine 309
- Passchendaele, The First Battle of 142
- Passchendaele, The Second Battle of 143
- Picardy, The Advance in .. 237
- Pilkem Ridge, The Battle of.. 97
- Poelcapelle, The Battle of .. 139
- Polygon Wood, The Battle of.. 131
- Rœux, The Capture of .. 74
- Rosieres, The Battle of .. 210
- Salonika 294
- Sambre, The Battle of the .. 286
- St. Quentin, The Battle of .. 191
- St. Quentin Canal, The Battle of the.. 251
- Selle River, The Pursuit to the 255
- Selle, The Battle of the .. 281
- Scarpe, 1917, The First Battle of the.. 36
- Scarpe, 1917, The Second Battle of the 53
- Scarpe, 1917, The Third Battle of the.. 68
- Scarpe, 1918, The Battle of the 245
- Sharqat, The Battle of .. 357
- Siberia 364
- Somme Crossings, Actions of the 199, 203
- Somme, 1918, The Second Battles of the 237
- Tank Attack at Cambrai, 1917 149
- Tel Asur, Actions of 326
- Valenciennes, The Battle of .. 286
- Villers-Bretonneux, The Actions of 217
- Vimy, The Battle of 36
- Winter in the Trenches, The Last 171
- Ypres, 1917, The Battles of .. 91
- ,, 1918, The Battle of .. 265
- Zab, Actions on the Lesser .. 354

HARRISON AND SONS, LTD., Printers, St. Martin's Lane, W.C.2.

www.ingramcontent.com/pod-product-compliance
Lightning Source LLC
Chambersburg PA
CBHW070306230426
43664CB00015B/2652